Churchill's Ministry of Ungentlemanly Warfare

Also by Giles Milton

Churchill's Ministry of Ungentlemanly Warfare

The Mavericks Who Plotted Hitler's Defeat

GILES MILTON

Picador | New York

The Library of Congress Cataloging-in-Publication Data is available upon request.

ISBN 978-1-250-11902-5 (hardcover)
ISBN 978-1-250-11904-9 (e-book)

Our books may be purchased in bulk for promotional, educational, or business use. Please contact your local bookseller or the Macmillan Corporate and Premium Sales Department at 1-800-221-7945, extension 5442, or by e-mail at MacmillanSpecialMarkets@macmillan.com.

Originally published in Great Britain as *The Ministry of Ungentlemanly Warfare* by John Murray (Publishers), an Hachette UK Company

10 9 8 7 6 5 4 3 2

For Simon,
ever the gentleman

Clive, my dear fellow, this is not a gentleman's war. This is a life and death struggle. You are fighting for your very existence against the most devilish idea ever created by a human brain – Nazism. And if you lose there won't be a return match next year, perhaps not even for a hundred years!

The Life and Death of Colonel Blimp
Michael Powell and Emeric Pressburger

Contents

CONTENTS

Prologue

THE WORLD WAS going mad in the spring of 1939, or that's how it seemed to Joan Bright. A jaunty twenty-nine-year-old with swept-up hair and a button-down dress, she had travelled to London in search of secretarial work, having just turned down a job in Germany as governess to the children of Rudolf Hess, the Deputy Führer of the Third Reich.

When she mentioned her need for employment to an old friend, he gave her a strange piece of advice. He said he could get her work if she 'went to St James's Park Underground Station at 11 a.m. on a certain day, wearing a pink carnation'. He added that a lady would be waiting for her and would whisk her away for an interview.

Joan only half believed what her friend had said. Indeed as the day approached, she felt convinced that he was playing a practical joke. But she went to the rendezvous at the appointed time and, sure enough, there was the mystery woman. She offered a whispered introduction and pointed towards a red brick Edwardian mansion block in the distance, indicating that this was the building in which the job interview would take place.

Joan was led on a roundabout route to the building, passing through the maze of alleys and backstreets that lie between Broadway and St James's. Her dizzy imagination went into overdrive. She convinced herself that the woman had chosen the route quite deliberately 'in order to reach it unobserved'.[1] She still knew nothing about the job for which she was being interviewed, but had high hopes of acquitting herself well. She had previously worked at Chatham House, where her efficiency and discretion had left a deep impression on her colleagues.

Only as she was led up to the fourth floor of the residential mansion block did she realize that this was to be no ordinary job interview. She was ushered into an office that overlooked Caxton Street and introduced to a military officer by the name of Chidson, 'short, ginger and very precise'.[2] He gave a cursory introduction and then slid a sheet of paper across the desk and told her to sign it. She was too nervous to ask what it was. She simply scribbled her name at the bottom and handed it back to the colonel. As she did so, she noticed that she had just signed the Official Secrets Act.

Colonel Chidson took the paper, fixed his steely eye on Joan and asked if she knew why she had been brought to Caxton Street. When she shook her head, he told her that she was being interviewed for a job so secret that she would be tortured if she were ever to be captured by the Germans.

Joan was completely lost for words. She had been expecting to be tested on her typing skills, her shorthand and her ability to make a good strong cup of tea. In the silence that followed, Chidson got up from his seat, beckoned her over to the window and pointed towards a shadowy figure standing on the corner of Caxton Street and Broadway.

'He has been there all morning, watching,' he said. 'When you leave here, don't let him see you; turn left and keep going.'[3]

Joan had not yet been offered a job, at least not formally, and yet the manner in which the colonel was speaking suggested that she had already been accepted. He asked her to be seated and once again reiterated that 'very dreadful things' would happen to her if she were to be caught by the Germans. This time, he was rather more specific. 'You will get needles up your toenails.'[4]

Half of her wanted to treat the whole thing as a grand hoot, one to recount to her flatmate, Clodagh Alleyn, later that evening. Yet Colonel Chidson remained cold and unsmiling throughout the interview, which Joan took as a sign that he was in deadly earnest. She also knew that in the newspapers and on the wireless the talk was of nothing but war.

Just a few weeks earlier, on 15 March, Hitler had scored his latest coup by marching his storm-troopers into Bohemia and Moravia. In doing so, he completed his annexation of what had previously been Czechoslovakia. The German soldiers met with so little resist-ance that a jubilant Hitler was able to travel to Prague on the following day and proclaim a new addition to the Third Reich. Henceforth, Bohemia and Moravia were to be a German protect-orate, firmly under the rule of Berlin. Although Britain's Prime Minister, Neville Chamberlain, insisted that Hitler's annexation was not an act of aggression, there were many in the country who felt that his policy of appeasement had passed its sell-by date.

Joan was among those who felt a deep sense of unease, worried that Britain was being dragged into a conflict for which it was woefully ill-prepared. But when she weighed up everything that she'd been told by Colonel Chidson, the prospect of full-time employment and a generous salary overrode all her fears about the future. Besides, she was young, unattached and fancy-free. And a strange job in a strange office might just add to the gaiety of life. She convinced herself that it was all 'good clean fun' and thanked the colonel for what she assumed to be the offer of employment. She promised to show up for work punctually on the following morning.

Although she would have never admitted it to Colonel Chidson, she was rather excited to be joining an office 'in which fact and fiction played so smoothly together'.[5] Yet she couldn't help but quicken her pace as she emerged from the building into Caxton Street, and she studiously avoided catching the eye of the mysterious man who was still standing on the street corner.

Joan would have to wait another twenty-four hours before learning what her new occupation entailed. In the intervening time, she could do little more than ponder over the strange situation in which she found herself. She felt torn between happiness at having a job and a vague sense of unease at what that job might involve. It was as if someone were leading her into a bizarre twilight world in which all the cherished norms had been subverted.

Joan Bright was not alone in finding her world turned upside down in the spring of 1939. Sixty miles to the north of London, in Bedford, a caravan enthusiast named Cecil Clarke was tinkering in the work-shop behind his house at 171 Tavistock Street when his wife summoned him to the telephone. There was someone who wanted to speak to him.

Clarke took the receiver and found himself having a conversation that was as strange as it was unexpected. The person at the other end was not calling about caravans, that much was clear. Nor was he enquiring about the new anti-rolling suspension system that Clarke had recently invented. Clarke tried to probe the caller for more information, but the man declined to reveal why he was calling and was, by his own admission, 'very guarded'[6] when Cecil asked as to his identity. All he would say was that the two of them had met a couple of years earlier, and that he would be paying a visit to Tavistock Street on the following day.

Cecil Clarke hung up the phone, still puzzling over the caller's identity and utterly perplexed as to what he might want. But in common with Joan Bright, he had a vague sense that his life was about to take an altogether more exciting twist.

In that, he was correct. The visit on the following day was to change his life.

I

The Third Man

ECIL CLARKE VIEWED his caravan with the sort of affection that most men reserve for their wives. He polished it, tinkered with it and buffed up its cream paintwork with generous quantities of Richfield Auto Wax.

More than fourteen feet in height, it stood taller than a London double-decker and its low-slung chassis was a revolutionary piece of engineering. But the real joy of Cecil's creation was its luxurious interior. It came with lavatory, bedrooms and an en suite bathroom. It had hot and cold running water and its own home-built generating plant. It also had a well-stocked bar. Little wonder that Cecil referred to it as his 'Pullman of the road'.[1]

He had built it in his workshop behind the family home in Bedford. At weekends he would hook it to the family charabanc and take it on road trials, hurtling through the local country lanes while his wife Dorothy clutched the dashboard and their two sons, John and David, made mischief in the back.

The young lads yelped with delight when their father announced that he was taking the family off to north Wales. There were a few tense moments as they bid their farewells to Bedford: Cecil had added a new bedroom on the caravan's first floor and the vehicle was now so tall that he had to stop at every bridge and check that they had the necessary clearance.

Once they were out on the open road, obstacles such as bridges were quickly forgotten. He got 'rather blasé' and simply 'charged at every bridge he came to – fortunately without any real damage'. The fact that young John and David were larking about on the roof of the caravan, 'getting a fine view of the countryside',[2] did not seem to bother him one jot.

Cecil 'Nobby' Clarke had set up his company, LoLode (the Low Loading Trailer Company) in the late 1930s, with himself as principal designer and Mrs Clarke as company secretary. All LoLode's caravans came equipped with a unique suspension system that promised passengers a smoother ride than any other caravan on the road. It was a promise in which Clarke took considerable pride, for he was the designer, the engineer, the architect and the mechanic.

Clarke was portly and bespectacled, a lumbering gentle giant with heavy bones and a mechanic's hands. Half boffin, half buffoon, he had more than a touch of the Professor Branestawm about him. An enthusiastic smoker and fervent patriot, he was viewed by his neighbours with affection tinged with humour: 'the embodiment of an ideal,' thought one, 'always in his own way striving after the betterment of society.'[3] In Cecil's case, the 'betterment of society' meant building more comfortable caravans. Those Bedford neighbours would smile knowingly to one another as they watched 'Nobby' buffing the paintwork of his beloved vehicles, unaware that he had the hands of a magician and the brains of a genius.

Caravans were not the only thing that quickened his pulse. As a young volunteer in the First World War, he had got himself attached to a pioneer battalion that specialized in explosives. He acquired an early taste 'for making loud bangs'[4] and won himself a Military Cross for his part in helping to blow the Allies to victory in the Battle of Vittorio Veneto. Although he had made the transition back to civilian life with greater ease than many of his comrades-in-arms, there was a part of him that continued to harbour dreams of making loud bangs.

In the summer of 1937, Clarke had submitted a LoLode advertisement for inclusion in his favourite magazine, *Caravan and Trailer*. Describing his vehicle as a 'three berth living van of the most advanced design',[5] it even had a servants' quarters at the rear.

The editor of *Caravan and Trailer* was a man named Stuart Macrae, an aviation engineer by training who had fallen into the world of journalism by accident rather than design. He was intrigued by the pictures of Clarke's outlandish creation and decided to pay a visit to Bedford, taking the day off work in order to meet him.

His first impression was one of disappointment. Clarke was 'a very large man with rather hesitant speech, who at first struck me as being amiable but not outstandingly bright'. He was soon forced to revise his opinion. Clarke had an expanding brain that functioned like an accordion. He sucked in ideas, mixed them together and then expelled them as something altogether more melodious. Where most people saw problems, he saw only solutions.

Clarke opened up the yard behind the house in order to show Macrae 'his latest brain child'. It was huge, far bigger than it looked in the pictures, and 'streamlined into the bargain'. Macrae was stunned: he felt as if he were looking at 'something from the future'.[6]

Clarke proposed a spin round the Bedfordshire countryside, with himself at the wheel and his guest in the caravan. Macrae made himself comfortable on the Dunlopillo cushions and got happily sloshed on the various bottles in the well-stocked bar. 'And as there were no breathalizers in those days' – nor any stigma attached to drink-driving – he was able to drive back to London without fear of being caught by the police.

When he was back at work the following morning, somewhat sore of head, he wrote a fulsome article about Clarke's extraordinary prototype. And there the story might have ended, for Stuart Macrae quit his job at *Caravan and Trailer* soon afterwards and took up a position as editor of *Armchair Science*.

But one morning in the spring of 1939, Macrae's secretary answered the phone to a most mysterious caller. 'There's a Geoffrey Somebody on the phone,' she called across the office: he was calling on a matter of some urgency. Macrae took the call and found himself speaking to someone called not Geoffrey, but Millis Jefferis.

Jefferis said that he was keen to find out more about one of the items featured in the latest issue of *Armchair Science*. 'You have an article about a new and exceptionally powerful magnet. I want full information about this magnet right away, please.'

Macrae was taken aback by the caller's gruff manner and asked to know more. 'Well it's a bit awkward,' admitted Jefferis. 'I'm not at liberty at present to tell you what this is about.' He suggested that they meet for lunch and talk it over in private.

Forty-eight hours later, Macrae found himself in the Art Theatre Club, seated opposite one of the most extraordinary individuals he had ever met. Millis Jefferis had 'a leathery looking face, a barrel-like torso and arms that reached nearly to the floor'. To Macrae's discerning eyes, 'he looked like a gorilla'. But when the gorilla opened his mouth, 'it was at once obvious that he had a brain like lightning'.

Jefferis explained that he worked for a highly secret branch of the War Office, one that specialized in intelligence and research. With international tensions on the rise, he had been tasked with devising unconventional weaponry that might be needed in the near future.

His interest in magnets stemmed from a revolutionary underwater mine that he was trying to develop. Its explosive charge was coated in magnets and equipped with a time-delay detonator. The idea was that it 'would stick to the side of a ship when placed there by a diver, and go bang in due course and sink the said ship'.[7]

The need for such a weapon was real and urgent. Less than six months earlier, in the winter of 1938, Hitler had launched his Plan Z, the immediate and dramatic strengthening of the German Kriegsmarine. The plan envisaged the construction of 8 aircraft carriers, 26 battleships and more than 40 cruisers, as well as 250 U-boats. Britain was in no position to compete in such a naval arms race and was faced with having to find a more creative way to redress the balance. Senior figures in the War Office and Admiralty decided that sinking German ships would be more cost-effective than building British ones.

But Jefferis faced an insurmountable problem. He was unable to find magnets that would function underwater and was also too busy to build a reliable time-delay detonator. Without one, he knew that his half-built magnetic mine wouldn't work.

After a well-lubricated lunch finished off with goblets of brandy, Macrae rashly offered to take over the project. One of his previous jobs had been designing bomb-dropping mechanisms for low-flying aircraft. He was more than willing to tackle this new challenge. Jefferis was surprised by Macrae's offer, but glad to accept. He said that 'he had a private bag of gold from which he could at least pay my expenses'.[8]

It was only later in the day, when the mists of brandy had cleared, that Macrae began to regret his decision. He didn't have a clue how to build a magnetic mine and nor did he have a workshop in which to experiment. As he pondered how best to proceed, he was suddenly reminded of Cecil Clarke, his prototype caravan and his Bedford garage. He called LoLode and, without revealing who he was or why he was calling, arranged for a meeting. The following morning, he pitched up at 171 Tavistock Street with a bagful of magnets and a cry for help.

Stuart Macrae's visit to Cecil Clarke's Bedfordshire workshop came at an ominous moment in international relations. A few days after Hitler had marched his storm-troopers into Bohemia and Moravia, he ordered them into the Baltic port of Memel, in Lithuania. Memel was a German-speaking enclave that had been detached from Germany after the First World War. Hitler had repeatedly denied having any designs on the port, but in the wake of his Prague triumph he demanded Memel's capitulation. Lithuania's Foreign Minister was faced with acceding to the Führer's demands or risking a full-scale military invasion. He had little option but to agree.

'A large, blazing swastika announces to the traveller that the administration of Memel has changed hands.' So wrote an English journalist who got the scoop of his life by happening to be in the port when the storm-troopers marched in. 'In village windows, candles flicker and a Brownshirt parade continued till a late hour.'

Hitler arrived in triumph the following morning and welcomed Memel's overwhelmingly German population into the Fatherland. Ominously, he declared that the Third Reich was 'determined to master and shape its own destiny, even if that did not suit another world'.[9]

The Prime Minister, Neville Chamberlain, continued to chase after a peaceful solution, even after the illegal annexation of Memel. 'I am no more a man of war today than I was in September,' he said in reference to the previous year's Munich Agreement that had handed the Sudetenland to Hitler.[10] But not everyone agreed with his policy of appeasement, and some were starting to prepare themselves for more direct action. Among them were Stuart Macrae and Cecil Clarke.

Clarke was delighted to renew his acquaintance with Macrae, for the two men had got along famously when they had first met. This time around, Macrae was invited into the Clarke family home and offered a snack. 'Sweeping a number of children out of the living room,' he later wrote, 'which also had to serve as an office, he filled me up with bread and jam and some awful buns and then got down to business.'

Clarke showed characteristic enthusiasm from the outset, informing Macrae that lethal weapons could be constructed from the simplest pieces of equipment. Macrae was nevertheless surprised to find that their first port of call was Woolworths on Bedford High Street. Here, they bought some large tin bowls. Next, they visited a local hardware store and bought some high-powered magnets. And then they took everything back to Tavistock Street, where Clarke created 'an experimental department by sweeping a load of rubbish and more children off a bench'.

Clarke took to the task in hand with undisguised relish. He commissioned a local tinsmith to make a grooved metal ring that could be screwed on to the Woolworths' bowl. When this was done, he poured bitumen into the ring and used it to secure the magnets. His idea was to fill the bowl with blasting gelatine and then screw on a makeshift watertight lid.

The key factor was to make the mine light enough to stick to the side of a ship. 'Eventually after using up all the porridge in the house in place of high explosive for filling, juggling about with weights and dimensions, and flooding Nobby [Clarke's] bathroom on several occasions, we got this right.'

It was one thing to design a weapon, quite another to make it work. Clarke and Macrae took themselves off to Bedford Public Baths and, after explaining to the janitor that they were conducting vital military research, obtained permission to use the main swimming pool once it was closed to the public.

They propped a large steel plate in the deep end and then strapped the welded Woolworths' bowl to Clarke's ample stomach. 'Looking as if he were suffering from advanced pregnancy, he would swim to and fro removing the device from his belt, turning it over and plonking it on the target plate with great skill.' It worked perfectly.

The mine stuck to the metal plate each time and remained securely in position.

There was just one thing missing. A bomb could not explode without a detonator, and the detonator for this particular weapon needed to be absolutely reliable. If it exploded too early, it risked killing the underwater swimmer.

Clarke set about designing a spring-loaded striker that was held in a cocked position by a soluble pellet. When the pellet dissolved in the water, the striker would hit the detonator and the bomb would explode. But finding a suitable pellet proved difficult. The two men tried all manner of devices but none of them worked in a satisfactory fashion. Pellets made of powder dissolved too quickly. Pellets that were too compact didn't dissolve at all.

In the end, it was Clarke's children who inadvertently provided the solution. As Cecil swept them off his workbench for the umpteenth time, he upset their bag of aniseed balls and dozens of sweets rolled across the floor. Macrae popped one into his mouth and began playing with it on his tongue. As he did so, he was struck by how it shrank in size with absolute regularity. It was exactly what was needed. Clarke rigged up his strikers to the children's aniseed balls while young John Clarke looked on crossly. Each spring-loaded striker was placed in 'a big glass Woolworth's tumbler' and put through a series of tests until Clarke had worked out the exact time it took for the sweet to dissolve.[11]

'Right, that's 35 minutes,' he would shout across the living room.[12] Sure enough, the aniseed ball would slowly dissolve over the course of half an hour until the striker was suddenly released. There was no explosive charge, so the damage was confined to the glass, which invariably shattered and fell to the floor in pieces. Mrs Clarke spent her afternoon sweeping up fragments of broken glass.

The men were delighted that their idea had worked. 'The next day the children of Bedford had to go without their aniseed balls,' recalled Macrae. 'For not wishing to be held up for supplies, we toured the town and bought the lot.'

The last remaining problem was to find a suitable means of storing their magnetic mine. It was essential that the aniseed ball be protected from damp, otherwise the mine risked exploding while in storage.

Their solution was once again homespun but inventive: they pulled a condom over the striking mechanism and found that it formed a perfect damp-proof sleeve, expanding neatly over the various bumps and creases.

Thus it was that two middle-aged gentlemen found themselves walking around Bedford, going from chemist to chemist, buying up their entire stocks of condoms, 'and earning ourselves an undeserved reputation for being sexual athletes'.[13] Macrae neglected to record whether, nine months later, Bedford experienced any short-term spike in its birth rate.

Just a few weeks after his introductory luncheon at the Art Theatre Club, Macrae was able to show Millis Jefferis the prototype magnetic mine that had been given the provisional name of limpet. Jefferis immediately recognized Cecil Clarke's weapon as a work of technical wizardry. For a little less than £6 (including labour), he had produced an explosive device that was lightweight, easy to use and devastatingly effective, one that had the potential to be a game-changer in time of war. For if a single diver equipped with a single limpet mine could destroy a single ship, then it stood to reason that a team of divers could destroy a fleet of ships. And that made it a very significant weapon indeed.

It was also extremely versatile. Its magnetic surface meant that it could be used to blow up turbines, generators, trains – anything, indeed, that was made of metal. It was the perfect weapon for sabotage, small, silent, deadly, and with a touch of dark mischief that particularly appealed to Jefferis.

Cecil Clarke returned to his caravans in Bedford, unaware of the fact that unknown men in clandestine offices were already planning his initiation into a world so secret that even most ministers in Whitehall knew nothing of its existence.

It was the very same world into which Joan Bright found herself entering on a seemingly unremarkable spring day in 1939.

Joan Bright turned up at Caxton Street for her first day of work knowing only that she was being employed by an organization so secret that she risked torture if captured by the Nazis. She assumed matters would become clearer once she was installed in the office:

instead, the mystery only deepened. The building was almost deserted when she reported for duty and there was not even Colonel Chidson to greet her. She was escorted to the fourth floor and told to wait for the rest of the staff to arrive.

'I sat at my new desk and took stock of my surroundings,' she later wrote. There was an Imperial typewriter, a small pile of documents and the stale smell of cigarette smoke that pervaded everything. The carpets, curtains and even the woodwork stank of old cigarettes.[14]

Joan cast her eye over the books on the shelves and was surprised to find that they contained none of the usual volumes kept in government offices. Instead, there were works by Trotsky, well-thumbed pamphlets about Sinn Fein and a number of books about the Arab rebellion, including Lawrence's *Revolt in the Desert*. Increasingly mystified, she began to wonder what sort of place she had joined.

Her boss swept into the office shortly afterwards, arriving with his briefcase, his homburg and his affectations. Lawrence Grand immediately struck her as one of the most eccentric people she had ever met. He was wearing dark glasses, smoking through a long cigarette holder and sporting a red carnation in his buttonhole. He had 'all the paraphernalia of the spy master of popular fiction'.[15] Even his hair seemed to be playing a role, slicked with so much brilliantine that he looked like Errol Flynn in *The Perfect Specimen*. Although he was undeniably tall and good-looking, she couldn't help thinking to herself that, 'really, this chap's a bit mad'.[16]

He did, at least, take Joan into his confidence, telling her every-thing that Colonel Chidson had hitherto failed to reveal. He explained that she had been hired to work for a top-secret Whitehall depart-ment known as Section D. The 'D' stood for destruction and Grand and his staff had been tasked with conceiving a wholly new form of warfare. In the event of conflict with Hitler's Nazis, a small band of specially trained agents was to be dropped behind enemy lines in order to engage in murder, sabotage and subversion.

The work was to be done 'by undercover men, spies and sabo-teurs, who, if caught, would be neither acknowledged nor defended by their government'. They would be working outside the law and were to borrow their tactics from guerrillas and gangsters like Michael

Collins in Ireland and Al Capone in America. In signing up for Section D, they were effectively signing away their lives.

The work of Section D was highly contentious, which is why it was being orchestrated by the Secret Intelligence Service. Few in the government knew of its existence. Even the Treasury had been kept in the dark. Grand reiterated Colonel Chidson's warning to Joan that she must never breathe a word to anyone.

Section D was one of two organizations housed in that Caxton Street apartment block. Working alongside Grand's team was a second unit that was known as MI(R). This was a branch of military intelligence that dealt, somewhat euphemistically, with army research.

The boss of MI(R) was Joe Holland, to whom Joan was introduced later that morning. He made almost as much of an impression as Lawrence Grand, a tough-as-horsemeat soldier with the looks of a pin-up and the mind of a fox. He had made a name for himself as a fighter pilot during the First World War, leaning out of the cockpit and lobbing grenades on to the German trenches below. Although the war had ended more than two decades earlier, he had never quite shaken off the habit of hurling missiles through the air.

Many a visitor had found himself at the receiving end of a hail of books and files, thrown by an irate Holland. Joan was not immune to such attacks: she would later joke with her girlfriends about the 'quick downward movement by which I ducked the impact of a book flung at my head one day on opening the door of his office'.

She kept a wary eye on 'dear old Joe' as she typed up his letters, watching in appalled fascination as he sucked hard on his cigarette. He would stop breathing, 'holding in the smoke until the last wisp of nicotine had reached his boots'. Only when his face had turned vivid purple was it 'expelled with full force'.

Joan had plenty of gossip for her flatmate when she returned home later that evening. But it was neither Grand nor Holland who formed the principal subject of her conversation. There was a third man in the office, very different from the other two, and he left an even deeper impression. His name was Colin Gubbins and, from the very outset, Joan marked him down as someone quite unique – someone, she felt, who was 'destined for a distinguished career'.[17]

★

Colin Gubbins was a dapper little fellow who wore smooth suede gloves and walked with a silver-topped cane. He was 'dark and short, his fingers square, his clothes immaculate',[18] and was fortunate in having the looks to match the attire: 'slight and superbly built', wrote one, with 'beetling eyebrows, penetrating eyes and a gravelly voice'.[19] Some of his acquaintances were troubled by the sharp glint in his eyes, which seemed to hint at an icy ruthlessness. But Joan convinced herself that the glint was more of a twinkle, reflecting mischief and an inner playfulness.

In common with Lawrence Grand, Gubbins wore a fresh carnation in his buttonhole. But there the similarity stopped. Grand talked grandiosely, languidly, as if the last cognac at luncheon had left him in command of an elaborate soliloquy. Gubbins, by contrast, had a clipped speech, clipped moustache and clipped façade. He was as punctilious in his work as he was fastidious in his manners.

'Quiet-spoken, energetic, efficient and charming', at least that's how he appeared to Joan as she peeked at him from behind the keyboard of her Imperial.[20] He had the air of a perfect gentleman, one who bought his buttonhole from Solomons and his eau de cologne from Floris. But she had a sneaking suspicion, even on that first day at work, that Colin Gubbins would prove a gentleman full of surprises.

He had joined the Caxton Street office only a few weeks earlier and was still finding his feet. Forty-two years of age, and with the energy of a terrier, he had already lived more lives than most. Born in 1897 in Tokyo (his father worked for the British Legation), he had been shipped back to the Isle of Mull at a tender age and placed in the hands of a veritable clan of terrifying Scottish aunts. They had knocked him into what he was: tough, resourceful and independent of mind. His wicked sense of irony, deliciously wicked, was all his own.

Queen of the roost in that childhood home was Aunt Elsie, a formidable matriarch with 'rigid standards' and a fierce pride in her Scottishness. She didn't allow young Colin to be seated in her presence because, she said, 'it encourages indolence'. She instilled in him the notion that toughness was a uniquely Scottish virtue.

Killiemore House was a draughty Scottish manse with chill corridors and dimly lit parlours. 'Run round the house if you're cold' was Aunt Elsie's mantra.[21] As the sleet and drizzle tipped from the Killiemore gutters, Colin would slip on his sodden boots and perform yet another circuit of the property. Laughter was frowned upon and parlour games strictly forbidden in that austere childhood home. Such things, Colin was told, were frivolous. He would later write that jollity was seen as 'an unprofitable diversion from the more serious task of filling the larder and thereby adding some variety to the porridge and salt herring which seemed to be our staple diet'.[22]

The figure to admire in this dour household was old Grandpa McVean, a kilted ornithologist who spent much of his time studying H.E. Dresser's *History of the Birds of Europe*. On the occasions he ventured outside, it was invariably to blast his beloved birds out of the sky. In the evening, as the pale Highland sun slumped into the glacial waters of Loch Na'Keal, Grandpa McVean would settle into his armchair and pronounce judgement on all the issues of the day.

In 1913 Gubbins hatched his escape by signing up for the Royal Military Academy in Woolwich. He made a deep impression on the other new recruits, in part because of his utter recklessness. With Gubbins 'it was neck or nothing', wrote one of his contemporaries after watching him compete in sport. Another spoke of his 'wild, devil-may-care streak'.[23] The academy accepted him immediately and listed him as a gentleman cadet, one who was destined to fight a gentleman's war.

His comrades-in-arms found him 'a ripping little fellow' who displayed nerves of granite when fighting the Boche. His brigade soon found itself at the receiving end of a ferocious German artillery attack that left half his comrades blown to shreds. 'Gubby' dug his mutilated chums out of the Flanders mud, thereby earning himself a Military Cross. Aunt Elsie could finally be proud of him.

There followed such a 'beastly frozen nightmare of hardship'[24] that made life at Killiemore seem like a picnic. Gubby fell sick, got shot in the neck and shivered his way through trench fever. By the time he'd recovered, the war was over.

His pals called him Whirling Willie because he shared the same unbounded energy as the famous comic character. He certainly whirled his way through the armistice. He drank a skinful at the

Savoy and then shimmied up one of the restaurant pillars, thereby proving that even Highlanders could have fun. Then it was off to Ciro's nightclub in order to dance his way through the early hours.

Most Tommies who had lived through the Western Front had seen enough horror to last them a lifetime. Not so Gubbins. He spent a few listless months in London, taking his sister, Mouse, to a succession of West End reviews. But he had war in his blood and he wanted more. After a brief tour of duty in Murmansk, having a crack at Lenin's Bolsheviks, he offered his services in Ireland.

It was to change his life for ever. He found himself engaged in running street battles with Michael Collins and his band of Sinn Fein revolutionaries, a bitter, nasty and unpredictable conflict. Gubbins had previously experienced the trenches, shrapnel and shellshock, yet he had never experienced warfare like this. He complained to his superiors at 'being shot at from behind hedges by men in trilbys and mackintoshes and not allowed to shoot back'. But those men in trilbys taught him a lesson he would never forget: irregular soldiers, armed with nothing but homespun weaponry, could wreak havoc on a regular army.

After a tour of duty in India, Gubbins joined the London War Office where he was given a desk job in military intelligence. He was still at the War Office in the spring of 1939 when 'a cold hand took me literally by the back of the neck and a voice I knew said, "What are you doing for lunch today?"' It was Joe Holland inviting him to dine at St Ermin's Hotel in Caxton Street.

Gubbins declined his offer, explaining that he was about to head to his regimental races at Sandown. Holland stopped him mid-sentence. 'No, you are not,' he said. 'You are to lunch with me.'

Gubbins found himself whisked to a private suite in St Ermin's, a well-known watering hole, 'where I found the real host, who was waiting for us there'. It was Lawrence Grand of Section D.

Two hours later, over coffee and brandy, Gubbins accepted a new job. He was invited to join 'the left wing', as Holland liked to describe their work. Gubbins's task would be to plan a dirty, mischievous and thoroughly ungentlemanly war against Hitler's Nazis.

When he asked where the 'left wing' had its offices, Grand got up from his chair, walked over to the far side of the hotel room and with a theatrical flourish unlatched a hidden door.[25]

'The suite, true to the best Boys' Own Paper traditions, had a secret passage communicating with Section D's offices at Number Two, Caxton Street, next door.'[26]

Few in the regular army had any experience of fighting an ungentlemanly war. Gubbins's priority was to prepare an instruction manual in such warfare, setting out in terse prose how best to kill, incapacitate or maim the maximum number of people.

'My difficulty,' he later admitted, 'was that, strangely enough, there was not a single book to be found in any library in any language which dealt with this subject.'[27]

Gubbins had to look elsewhere, drawing inspiration from Sinn Fein and T.E. Lawrence (of Arabia), as well as from Al Capone and his Chicago gangsters. They had terrorized America with their audacious hit-and-run raids on nightclubs and their tommy guns had proved devastatingly effective. Gubbins wanted his band of men to be similarly armed. He felt that 'the whole art of guerrilla warfare lies in striking the enemy where he least expects it and yet where he is most vulnerable'. Guerrillas should not think of themselves as soldiers; rather, they were gangsters working outside the law and their task was to inflict 'the maximum amount of damage in a short time and then getting away'. Gubbins wanted them to be 'a running sore' that would confuse, exhaust and ultimately defeat Hitler's regular army.

As he began to prepare his instruction manual, he set down practical advice on everything from strangling sentries with piano-wire to contaminating water supplies with deadly bacilli. A pint or two of biological agent could wipe out an entire town. A carefully placed explosive could kill hundreds of people. There were also handy tips on such things as how best to destroy factories and ambush trains. 'It is not sufficient merely to shoot at the train,' he said. 'First derail the train and then shoot down the survivors.'[28]

He was already eyeing the bigger opportunity: destroying infrastructure so vital to the Nazi war machine that it could wholly change the nature of the conflict. But he also knew that such destruction could only be undertaken by specialists. It would require the services of men outside the military, men who understood how power plants worked and how viaducts were constructed. And it would require weapons that didn't yet exist.

Seated at the far side of the office, secretary Joan grew increasingly intrigued by Gubbins. Whenever she brought him his afternoon cup of tea, she found him hunched over his desk drawing neat diagrams of bridges and viaducts. They were no idle sketches. The arrows and crosses showed would-be saboteurs where best to plant their gelignite.

Joan couldn't help feeling that Gubbins's impeccable politeness masked a far more turbulent spirit. He was 'a still-waters-running-deep sort of man', she thought, who had 'just enough of the buccaneer in him to make lesser men underestimate his gifts of leadership, courage and integrity'.

She also found him darkly romantic in a way that Lawrence Grand and Joe Holland were not. For beneath the starched-collar exterior she could sense 'a man at arms, a campaigner, the fires banked up inside him as glowing as those round which his Celtic ancestors had gathered between forays for glen and brae'.[29]

Joan had a sharp insight into people's characters and she had read Gubbins to perfection. He was a curious blend of Scottish prudence and youthful recklessness. She duly typed up his guerrilla warfare texts on her Imperial; he called them *The Art of Guerrilla Warfare* and *The Partisan Leaders' Handbook*. He had stressed the importance of agents being able to dispose of the manuals quickly and quietly. Joan therefore took the decision to have them published on pocket-sized edible paper. Both manuals could be consumed in less than two minutes, if swallowed with a large glass of water.

2

Thinking Dirty

JOAN BRIGHT HAD lived in Argentina, Spain and Mexico City and the experience of life abroad had taught her an important fact: the British alone played by the rules. They formed orderly queues at the bus stop, they said sorry when there was no need to apologize. In her view, decency and fair play were integral parts of being British.

It was much the same with sport. In villages across the realm, well-spoken youths in whites and flannels spent their Sundays playing cricket, a game with so many rules that only the British were equipped to master it. Even more violent sports like boxing came with a book of regulations. In 1867 the 9th Marquess of Queensberry (though hardly a gentleman) had put his name to a set of rules that ensured boxing was fought in a spirit of decency. No longer could you hit a man when he was down: that was deemed to be underhand.

As international relations grew increasingly strained in the late 1930s, the question of what constituted gentlemanly combat became a subject of heated debate on the letters page of *The Times*. A certain Dr L.P. Jacks of Oxfordshire fired the opening salvo when he wrote to the editor expressing his belief that the sword alone was 'a gentleman's weapon'. His reasoning was quintessentially British. Attacking someone with a sword 'was more likely to give the other fellow a chance, and so make it more of a sporting affair between him and me'[1].

Not everyone agreed. Writing from his club in St James's, Mr Edward Abraham wanted to know how it could be considered gentlemanly 'to slash at a human being's jugular vein with a sword',[2] yet ungentlemanly to kill him with a bayonet. Where did Dr Jacks stand on less conventional weapons? Mustard gas, for example? Gentlemanly? Or ungentlemanly?

There followed a furious spat in which other readers entered the fray. Leslie Douglas-Mann confessed to not giving two hoots about the rules of the game. If you wanted to win – and win at all costs – there was no place for gentlemanly behaviour. Guns, gas or grenades; you should be prepared to get your hands dirty. 'A spiked mace smashed in the face,' he reasoned, 'is probably quite as unpleasant as poison gas.'[3]

The issue rumbled on for weeks until an exasperated Dr Jacks (who had started the fight in the first place) begged for a gentleman's truce. 'May I withdraw my rash description of the sword as a gentleman's weapon,' he wrote, 'and describe it, with greater caution, as less ungentlemanly than poison gas?'[4]

The epistolary spat would have been of little long-term consequence, were it not for the fact that it raised an important point. Was there any place for rules in the modern game of war?

The issue would eventually be debated on the floor of the House of Commons. Most members were rigidly conservative in outlook and spoke vigorously in defence of the rules. But one of them begged to differ. Robert Bower was the Conservative MP for Cleveland, a member whose ungentlemanly behaviour had already gained him notoriety in Westminster. Two years previously he had shocked his Tory colleagues by his use of unparliamentary language, insulting a Jewish backbencher with a nasty racist jibe. The backbencher in question, Emanuel Shinwell, was so incensed that he crossed the floor of the house and punched Bower in the face.

Now, once again, Bower was prepared to nail his ungentlemanly colours to the mast. He expressed shock at the manner in which his Tory colleagues continued to treat Hitler with kid gloves, even though he was breaking every international law in the book. He contended that there was no place for the rule book when dealing with the Nazis. 'When you are fighting for your life against a ruthless opponent,' he said, 'you cannot be governed by the Queensberry rules.'

He poured scorn on his frontbench colleagues for their outdated notions of fair play, claiming that most of them would rather lose a war 'than do anything unbecoming to an absolutely perfect gentleman'.

Bower's parliamentary colleagues were appalled by what they were hearing, but the honourable member for Cleveland was not yet finished. He warned them that Britain was doomed to destruction if it clung to the old ways. 'We must have a government which will be ruthless, relentless, remorseless,' he said. 'In short, we want a few more cads in this government.'[5]

Colin Gubbins's strict Scottish upbringing had instilled a powerful sense of morality in him, yet he was content to let others trouble themselves with the rights and wrongs of ungentlemanly warfare. He was more concerned with the practicalities of an effective guerrilla campaign against Nazi Germany.

It was clear that he could not do it alone. He would need an inner circle of experts who could help him plan how best to strike at Hitler's Nazi war machine. Such experts were unlikely to be found in the regular army. Gubbins needed rule-breakers: mavericks and eccentrics with a talent for lateral thinking and a fondness for making mischief.

He had been in Caxton Street for little more than a week when he was joined by Millis Jefferis, the gorilla-like officer who had first conceived the idea of a magnetic mine.

'Red of face, kind of heart', at least that's what Joan Bright thought when first introduced to the chain-smoking Jefferis.[6] He arrived in a cloud of tobacco, bringing yet more nicotine into her life. She was in awe of him during his first days in Caxton Street. He was gruff, impatient and rougher around the edges than the ever courteous Gubbins. His jacket was crumpled, his trousers creased: the overall impression was of someone with a complete disdain for military etiquette. His brother-in-law thought he looked 'more like a race-course bookie' than a soldier.[7] Joan wasn't so sure. She took one look at his ruddy cheeks and declared that 'he could never have belonged to any other branch of the Army but the Royal Engineers'.

Although he continued to intimidate her for weeks to come, she soon came to appreciate that he had a great deal more to offer than the typical British bulldog. He was inquisitive, wildly creative and, most impressive of all, entirely self-taught, 'an inventive genius, his dreams and thoughts linked with all forms of infernal machine – and the bigger the bang, the louder his ready laugh'.[8]

Jefferis's grizzled face was a result of too much exposure to the high-altitude sunshine of the Indian Himalayas. An engineer by training, he had started his career on the troubled North-West Frontier in the employment of the Madras Sappers and Miners. It quickly became apparent that he had a magician's hands when it came to designing bridges and viaducts. The *Royal Engineers Journal* described him as 'an outstanding man of rare inventive genius',[9] someone who was able to span impenetrable Himalayan ravines with his unique blend of algebra and imagination. His subaltern confessed to having never met anyone so driven by the will to succeed. 'Difficulties existed only to be surmounted, and there was no setback that a little thought and determination could not overcome.'

Jefferis had spent the bloody Waziristan campaign of 1922 hacking his way through impassable mountains until he had created a road of sorts that linked the strategic settlements of Isha and Razmak. It was a feat made all the more remarkable by the fact that he and his Afghan contractors were under constant gunfire from hidden snipers. 'Bet you never have another up to this level,' wrote his company major.[10] His bravado in the face of adversity was to earn him a Military Cross. More importantly, it earned him first-hand experience of guerrilla warfare.

Colin Gubbins was quick to see that Jefferis's craggy exterior masked a unique skill, one that had stood him in good stead during the Waziristan campaign. His floating bridges and concrete piles were merely the outward expressions of a passion for applied mathematics. For Jefferis believed that every problem could be solved by algebra – not the simple algebraic equations taught at school, but equations of staggering complexity. This, indeed, was his great discovery in life: everything conformed to an equation, if only you looked hard enough.

He had worked out the algebraic formula to explain how an albatross stayed aloft without flapping its wings. He had even found an equation that could predict the point at which a greyhound would capture a hare on any given racetrack, assuming that the hound was travelling at a slightly faster speed than its quarry. When Joan was first introduced to him in the spring of 1939, such matters seemed of trifling consequence. But Jefferis knew differently. For if you could predict when a greyhound would capture a hare, then you could also predict when a rocket would hit a plane. And that made both algebra, and Jefferis, very important indeed.

It was while serving on the North-West Frontier that Jefferis underwent a bizarre Damascene conversion. Hitherto, he had lived, breathed and dreamed of bridges. But as he trudged his way back to the town of Isha, depleted of men after a bruising campaign, he developed an overwhelming desire to blow them up.

Close friends had noticed the sudden change. 'Millis Jefferis had taken a dislike to bridges,' wrote one bemused observer, 'and was anxious to do them an injury.' There was logic to his antipathy. His Waziristan adventure had given him first-hand experience of the strategic importance of both railways and bridges. If you could cripple a bridge, you could stop an entire army in its tracks.

Jefferis's induction into Caxton Street was to mark a turning point in his life. He was given command of his own little unit called MI(R)c, an adjunct to Gubbins's team, with the task of 'designing and producing special weapons for irregular warfare'. These were the weapons on which Gubbins's guerrilla operations would succeed or fail.

Now, seated impatiently at his desk, his dark thoughts could be turned into an even darker reality. Others watched in awe as he scribbled numbers, letters and equations on to loose sheets of graph paper, systematically turning complex mathematics into diagrams of destruction. When the maths was done, he 'acquired some large drawing pads marked off in one sixteenth inch squares'[11] and began making detailed plans of viaducts in order to work out how best to reduce them to rubble. His finished work was to be published as a companion volume to Gubbins's edible pamphlets.

The title left little room for the imagination. *How to Use High Explosives* contained highly accurate advice for anyone who wanted to blow up a bridge, building, railway or road. It was illustrated with line drawings that showed 'how to fit a stick of gelignite under a railway sleeper or where to pack a lethal brown paper parcel under a bridge'.[12]

There were also handy tips on how to wreck train pistons, how to cripple points, how to blow up pylons (plant gelignite under three legs, not four, or it won't fall over) and how best to sabotage a factory. This little pamphlet, scarcely longer than a copy of *Science Illustrated*, was a historical first, the first manual in the history of the British Army to teach men how to wreak havoc on civilian targets with a small bag of explosives.

Not content with offering advice about weaponry, Jefferis began to design and build his own. Each chuckle from the far side of the office would announce the conception of some lethal new weapon. 'Blowing up railways appealed to him most,' wrote one colleague, 'but as a close second came the burning of pontoon bridges.' He took particular pleasure in designing a mine in which the train itself acted as the detonator. He also devised an ingenious floating fire-mine which would detonate itself when it hit a pontoon.

In his spare time, he invented booby traps intended to give a nasty surprise to any Nazi unfortunate enough to be on the receiving end. One of the most devious was the innocuously named Release Switch, 'which could be concealed under a book or a lavatory seat or something of that sort and cause a bang when it was lifted'. Men not in the habit of lifting the toilet seat at last had their excuse.

Most devilish of all was the aptly named Castrator, a concealed, spring-loaded striker that did exactly what it claimed. 'They were certainly a cheap and effective way of keeping down the birth rate of the Germans,' noted Stuart Macrae wryly, 'as they only cost 2/- each.'[13]

All these prototype bombs had to be tested. It was fortunate that the Caxton Street office had a secret stash of plastic explosive that was kept in a locked stationery cupboard. Only one man had the key, a roguish Cockney who 'habitually and quite naturally talked in rhyming slang'.[14] He had previously earned his living as a gun-runner and boxing promoter, thereby adding a further whiff of illegality to the activities of Caxton Street.

Some of Millis Jefferis's larger weapons were trialled at the Bedfordshire farm belonging to Cecil Clarke's brother. It was the ideal place for detonating his powerful incendiary bombs. But the working day was too short for constant trips to the countryside, so Jefferis began to use Richmond Park instead.

Keeping one eye on ramblers, dog-walkers and deer, he detonated increasingly large amounts of explosives. One mine, tightly packed with ammonal powder, caused such a massive explosion that it flung bags of earth into the Richmond skyline and created 'a most impressive crater'.[15]

It was one thing to build weapons for use in guerrilla warfare, quite another to find guerrillas who would be prepared to be dropped behind enemy lines. Gubbins was not immediately clear as to what sort of person would be willing to risk their skin on missions that would lead (as Colonel Chidson was always quick to point out) to certain torture if caught.

The British Army in 1939 was a volunteer force boosted by conscription; its men were poorly trained and not suitable for guerrilla fighting. The British Expeditionary Force offered more fertile recruiting. It had been established in the previous year, in the wake of Hitler's annexation of Austria, and some of the initiates had shown a reasonable degree of competence. But Gubbins knew that it could not spare any manpower in that fraught and uncertain summer.

He therefore elected for a rather more eccentric approach when seeking men for his guerrilla army. He decided to make use of the old public school network, turning to rugby-hardened alumni from schools such as Eton, Harrow and Winchester. In particular, he was keen to enlist school-leavers who had gone on to become polar explorers, mountaineers and oil prospectors, men who knew how to survive in a tough environment.

He had few contacts among the old school brigade: it stood at a far remove from the world of his Highland childhood. But he found himself receiving help from an unexpected quarter. Brigadier Frederick Beaumont-Nesbitt was an Old Etonian with an impeccable pedigree, 'tall and polite, an erect, good-looking man, his crisp moustache brushed up'. A well-connected Guards officer, the brigadier had been appointed head of the army's Intelligence Directorate. He had only recently drawn up a list of fearless, enterprising young men, anticipating their recruitment into his directorate. Now, with characteristic generosity, he handed the list to Gubbins and told him to take his pick.

The names on the list meant little to Gubbins and so he asked Joan Bright for help, since she knew this world far better than him. 'I was sent over to the War Office to make a preliminary sorting,' she later recalled, 'and then to pick out those whose qualifications seemed most suited to training in irregular warfare.'[16] There were some first-class candidates on Beaumont-Nesbitt's list. Peter Fleming (Eton and Oxford), Douglas Dodds-Parker (Winchester and Oxford) and Geoffrey Household (Clifton College and Oxford) were three of the six that Joan selected for her initial shortlist. They were soon followed by many more. All shared one thing in common: they had been given an education that, while expensive, had toughened them up and made them immune to hardship.

Once Joan had made her pick, she handed the list to Gubbins. He then embarked on a tour of London's various gentlemen's clubs, having learned that many of these men were members of either Boodle's, Brooks's or White's. One of his earliest potential recruits was Peter Wilkinson (Rugby and Cambridge), a young gentleman officer who had only recently joined the Royal Fusiliers. Wilkinson was lunching in the Army and Navy Club one day in the late spring of 1939 when he found himself engaged in conversation by an immaculately dressed, middle-aged stranger with a clipped moustache and a Scottish brogue.

Wilkinson found Gubbins most diverting company. The two of them chatted for a while about the Nazi occupation of the Sudetenland and then Gubbins spoke of his desire to learn German. Wilkinson recommended a newly published primer, *The Basis and Essentials of German*, which he had used to obtain proficiency in the language. Gubbins thanked him, drained his coffee and went on his way.

Wilkinson thought nothing more about the encounter until two days later, when he received an invitation to lunch at a private address in a mews off Marylebone Road. It came from the same Gubbins fellow and it piqued his curiosity. The invitation led him to the back entrance of a vast Regency mansion that faced on to Regent's Park.

Matters only got stranger when he was invited inside by a servant and led up the back stairs. He found himself 'faced with what looked like, and proved to be, Epstein's head of Paul Robeson'. Hanging above it was 'a magnificent *explosion de couleur* which on closer examination, proved to be a painting by Kokoschka'. Only later would he discover that the mansion belonged to the wealthy, art-collecting family of Edward Beddington Behrens.

There was no time to admire the art. Wilkinson was led into a vast drawing room where he found Gubbins chatting with two men, a subaltern in the Hussars and a captain in the Inniskilling Dragoon Guards, neither of whom he recognized. He still had no idea as to why he had been invited and Gubbins did nothing to enlighten him. The four of them ate a delicious cold luncheon washed down with Chevalier Montrachet, and then finished the meal with wild strawberries. It was not until the coffee arrived, and cognac was being sluiced into crystal balloons, that Gubbins finally explained why the three men had been invited. He told them that if war broke out, as seemed likely, 'large areas of Europe would be overrun by the Germans and that, in that event, there would be scope for guerrilla activity behind German lines'.

He confessed that 'he was a member of the secret branch of the War Office' and that he was looking to build an elite team 'for training in guerrilla warfare'. They would not have to plan their missions: that would be done by Gubbins and his inner circle. Nor would they have to concern themselves with weaponry. Such things would be dealt with by Millis Jefferis. Their training, too, would be undertaken by a special instructor who would teach them the dark arts of guerrilla warfare. Their task was to be at the sharp end: they were to be dropped behind enemy lines.

Peter Wilkinson listened to what Gubbins had to say, drained his cognac and signed up immediately, though not because he had any particular desire to be a guerrilla. 'It seemed to me that any job which involved cold luncheons washed down with Chevalier Montrachet and finishing up with *fraises des bois* merited careful consideration.'[17]

The other two men were also seduced by the lunch. They allowed themselves to be whisked back to the offices in Caxton Street in order to meet the fledgling team that was slowly being assembled. It marked the beginning of a whole new life, one that promised excitement, comradeship and danger. And it was to begin right away.

Joan Bright never ceased to be amazed by Colin Gubbins's energy and enthusiasm. He was driven by his work and would often remain in the office until long after midnight. But the day's work was merely the prelude to long hours of after-dark partying, for there was one rule to which Gubbins always adhered: if you worked hard, then you had earned the right to play hard. He put one of his staff, H.B. 'Perks' Perkins, in charge of after-hours entertainment. It was a job that Perks took very seriously.

One Caxton Street newcomer was surprised at how Gubbins 'would come and totally let his hair down'.[18] 'Great party-goer, great womanizer,' recalled another.[19] He would party long and hard, consuming impressive quantities of alcohol before 'going to bed at three or four in the morning'.[20] Then, somewhat sore of head, it was back to the office again at the crack of dawn.

Joan couldn't help but wonder if poor Mrs Gubbins had ever seen her husband at play. She doubted it, especially after being introduced to the shy, introverted Nonie. 'She was above all a home-maker,' she wrote, adding that homemaking 'was a quality which was stretched to its limit when she met Colin'.[21]

International tensions were on the rise throughout the long summer of 1939, leading to a frenzy of activity in Caxton Street. Gubbins made two hastily arranged trips to Warsaw, in order to build contacts with Polish intelligence. There were strong fears that Poland would be Hitler's first target if and when war broke out.

While Gubbins was away, Joan did her best to make space for all the new recruits. She found it a giddying experience to be surrounded by so many well-groomed young men. 'Our offices near St James's Underground became crammed with men and ideas.' She helped to set up basic courses in guerrilla warfare, with informal lectures by Joe Holland on subversion, wireless communication and local resistance. The venue for these talks was Caxton Hall, a building that was no stranger to subversion, having once been used by the suffragette movement for its 'Women's Parliament'. Joan had good reason for choosing it, aware that 'the constant comings and goings gave good cover to the small and highly secret groups of young men in plain clothes.'[22] She kept an eye on the new recruits as they were put through their classes and felt certain that, given time, they would prove a highly effective force.

But time was not on their side. On Saturday, 19 August, Gubbins received alarming news from the War Office. British intelligence had been tipped off about Hitler's intention to invade Poland before the end of the month. Three days later, the entire world was stunned to learn that Joachim von Ribbentrop and Vyacheslav Molotov had signed a German–Soviet Non-Aggression Pact. The fate of Poland now seemed sealed. It was surely only a matter of time before Hitler would send his troops over the frontier.

Gubbins knew that he had to act – and fast. He needed to get his 'left wing' into Poland in order that they might help to organize resistance to any invading German Army. He also wanted to renew the links he had made with senior Polish intelligence officials. It was unfortunate that his fledgling guerrillas had only undergone the most rudimentary training and had precious little idea about how to fight an underground war, let alone coach others in such warfare. But another trip to Poland would, at the very least, give them a better sense of the Polish will to resist.

Speed was essential. Gubbins had just three days to assemble his team and head for Warsaw. The men were to travel incognito and in the greatest possible secrecy. It was imperative that the Germans knew nothing of what was taking place.

Among those chosen to join the mission was Peter Wilkinson, who realized that his days of quaffing chilled Chevalier Montrachet were probably at an end. Not entirely sure as to what he should pack for guerrilla warfare against the Nazis, he sought the counsel of his ageing stepfather, a veteran of the First World War.

The old man had ready advice. Hunting wire-cutters and a liquid prismatic compass, those were the two essentials. He told Peter to take himself off to the Army and Navy Stores on Victoria Street and buy the best he could get. Peter did as instructed, somewhat puzzled as to how a liquid prismatic compass would help him defeat the Nazis.

The day for departure came soon enough. Joan made her way to Victoria Station to wave them off. 'Twenty men in civilian clothes, their passports identifying them as insurance agents, commercial travellers, entertainers, agricultural experts.' She was swept up by the excitement of it all: 'A deadly secret cell in a big body of naval ratings, soldiers and airmen.'

Yet as she handed the men their passports, she was shocked to learn that Caxton Street had made its first fundamental blunder. 'It was a sign of our immaturity in such matters that the numbers on the brand-new passports were consecutive.'[23] It was as if a school group were heading to the battlefront. In wartime, such a slip could cost them their lives.

If the mission began as farce, it rapidly turned into comedy. Peter Wilkinson had been warned of the importance of travelling inconspicuously. He was therefore a little dismayed when he met his fellow guerrillas at Victoria Station. Far from looking inconspicuous, they could have been heading to a fancy dress party.

Gubbins himself was wearing a bright green pork pie hat and clutching a diplomatic bag; Hugh Curteis was in tartan trews; 'Boy' Lloyd-Jones had chosen to disguise himself in a grey pin-stripe suit and seedy bowler hat. Wilkinson took one glance at him and decided that 'he looked like an absconding banker'.[24] Another member of the party, Tommy Davis, had made the effort to come in civilian clothes, but somewhat spoiled the effect by wearing a Brigade of Guards tie.

It was too late to change clothes: the train was ready to depart for Dover. As Joan wished them good luck, she happened to glance at the sky and noticed the first barrage balloons being installed, 'mute white forerunners of London's ordeal by raid'.[25] She felt suddenly depressed. Although she had spent the last four months helping to prepare for war, only now did the reality strike home. The barrage balloons reminded her of her frightening childhood during the First World War.

Gubbins and his team took an extraordinarily circuitous route to Poland so as not to arouse German suspicions. They travelled by train to Marseille, by boat to Alexandria and then by plane to Warsaw. By the time they arrived in Poland, it was all too late. German troops had stormed across the Polish frontier on the first day of September and the first bombs were already raining down on the suburbs of Warsaw.

Gubbins managed to renew contact with the brilliant Polish intelligence agent Stanislav Gano, head of Poland's Deuxième Bureau. He also snatched meetings with members of the fledgling Polish resistance. 'This tragic fortnight has been an unceasing rush, tearing round night and day in fast cars over primitive roads, trying to find out what is happening and why; rushing back to send wires to London and then dashing off to some new area of activity.'[26]

There was no time for guerrilla warfare: as the Germans pushed deeper into Poland, Gubbins realized that the game was up. He told his team to scatter and flee from the country in whatever way they could. Gubbins himself headed southwards in the company of Peter Wilkinson, who was somewhat disappointed by his first guerrilla mission. He had not even used his wire-cutters.

The two of them made it safely to Bucharest, where they got royally drunk at the infamous Colorado Club and flirted with a dancing bar-girl-cum-spy called Mickey Mouse. Wilkinson recognized her from a nightclub that he had once frequented in Prague. When he reintroduced himself, she seemed delighted to meet him again and reminded him of his 'nightly rendering of "I Can't Give You Anything But Love, Baby"'.

He and Gubbins finished their drinks and staggered off to the Nippon Club, where they got completely 'bottled'. They ended the evening 'with two very amusing girls and two bottles of fizz' – and all for less than a pound. It was a strange sort of guerrilla warfare.

Wilkinson kept a diary for his mother, who was longing to know if being a guerrilla was as romantic as it sounded. But he omitted the drinking, the womanizing and even the secret meetings with Polish intelligence officers. His mother was most disappointed and complained that his diary 'might have been written by a curate accompanying a party of Victorian spinsters'.[27] The truth was very different. Gubbins and Wilkinson had used their trip to create vital links with Polish intelligence.

Gubbins returned to London in October and found he had acquired a new nickname. Everyone in the office was now calling him Gubbski, on account of the friendships he had forged. Joan quizzed him about his Polish jaunt – not just the most recent one, but his previous two trips as well – but Gubbins proved reluctant to give anything away.

In the absence of hard news, wild rumours began to circulate throughout the office. There were stories that Gubbins had led secret discussions between Polish and British agents; that there had been a clandestine meeting in Poland's Pyry Forest; and most bizarre of all, that a heavily disguised British man (with the moniker of Professor Sandwich) had brought together a team of British and Polish cryptanalysts.

Joan would never get to the bottom of Gubbins's work in Poland; it was just one more mystery in an office whose *raison d'être* was subterfuge and deception. But others who scratched at the surface of the story began to suspect that the curious Professor Sandwich – facilitator of everything – had been Gubbins in disguise.

There are few certainties about Gubbins's three trips to Poland and the Professor Sandwich files – if they still exist – remain behind lock and key to this day. But one thing is clear: the rumoured meeting in Pyry Forest did indeed take place, and it ended with a British agent named Wilfred 'Biffy' Dunderdale being handed a bulky leather holdall. He was instructed to deliver it to London as a matter of urgency.

When Biffy peered inside the bag, he found that it contained a strange-looking machine built of rotors, cogs and an illuminated keyboard. Resembling some sort of futuristic typewriter, it was so valuable that the head of MI6, Stewart Menzies, turned up in person at Victoria Station to collect it.

Menzies had been making his way to a formal dinner when he was brought news of the machine's imminent arrival. He caused something of a stir on the station concourse by pitching up in full dress uniform, 'with the rosette of the Legion d'honneur in his button hole'.[28]

It was a suitably flamboyant welcome for a parcel that was to prove of supreme value to the British war effort. For the machine – filched from the Nazis and transferred to Britain with the aid of Gubbins's Polish contacts – was called Enigma.

Its destination was Bletchley Park.

3

Making Bangs for Churchill

COLIN GUBBINS HAD been right to stress to his staff the urgency of the work being undertaken by Caxton Street. At 11.15 a.m. on 3 September 1939, Prime Minister Neville Chamberlain informed the nation that Britain's ultimatum to Germany had met with no response. Hitler had refused to withdraw his troops from Poland, which meant that Britain was now at war. Later that day, King George VI made an emotional radio broadcast from Buckingham Palace. 'There may be dark days ahead,' he said, 'and war can no longer be confined to the battlefield. But we can only do the right as we see the right, and reverently commit our cause to God.'[1]

Everyone had their own reaction to the declaration of war. In Tavistock Road, Bedford, Cecil Clarke stood to attention in his living room as the National Anthem played on the wireless. His eldest son, John, was excited to hear the first air-raid siren of the war, set off (he presumed), 'in case German planes came over'.[2] He was disappointed when it proved to be a false alarm.

Sixty miles away in London, Joan Bright spent the afternoon answering the office telephone in a whisper, because everyone kept telling her that 'the enemy had ears'. Later that evening she almost became the first British casualty of the Second World War. She foolishly accepted a lift through the blackout with an Irish brigadier who was determined to display his machismo behind the wheel, driving his Rolls-Royce at reckless speed. As they hurtled down Tottenham Court Road in pitch darkness, the car slammed 'fair and square into a pedestrian island' and Joan was jolted violently forward.[3] She was lucky to escape with a cut lip.

The declaration of war had an immediate effect on life in Caxton Street. 'The work did not double,' wrote one of those in the office, 'it was at once multiplied by about four.'[4] Colin Gubbins suddenly found his team taken seriously by the few Whitehall officials who knew of its existence. On the same day that Chamberlain made his historic address to the nation, Gubbins was asked to move from Caxton Street to the War Office, so as to be closer to the heart of strategic decision-making. It was the first sign that ungentlemanly warfare might yet serve a purpose.

No removal men could be spared to shift the furniture, so Joan Bright had to arrange everything herself. She asked her close friend Lesley Wauchope to help with the move, packing up books, paperwork and the office desks. As the two of them 'staggered up Whitehall carrying files and typewriters', they were disappointed to see the men following behind them empty-handed. Joan amused herself with the thought that she was 'the vanguard of a revolution',[5] one that would be spearheaded by strong-willed women like herself. Working for MI(R) in the fraught summer of 1939, anything seemed possible.

The War Office was an austere, Edwardian baroque structure of imposing grandeur with a thousand rooms and two miles of corridors. Built at the height of empire, it gave the impression of solidity and permanence, flanking the east side of Whitehall like some vast baronial pile. It looked out on to a bronze equestrian statue of George, Duke of Cambridge, commander-in-chief of the Victorian army for almost four decades. Erect and proud – and decked in greatcoat and plumed helmet – he seemed to epitomize the old school of military thinking. He would have been appalled at the thought that two of the upstairs rooms of the War Office were being given over to a 'left-wing' band whose aims were to subvert the conventions of war.

Colin Gubbins was given an office on the third floor, while Millis Jefferis was allotted a first-floor office in Room 173. As Joan shuttled between the two, she couldn't help musing on the twist of fate that had landed her in a man's world of sweat, dirt and yet more nicotine. The War Office was a run-down labyrinth of a building, filthier than any boarding school, with 'the uneven watermarks revealing the length of the office-cleaner's arm'.[6] Gubbins's office looked like an abandoned prison cell: 'two chairs, a table, a very dirty inkwell and an ashtray made out of the lid of a cigarette tin'.[7]

As the first air-raid sirens wailed across Whitehall, Joan reconciled herself to long evenings in musty rooms that 'held the stale smell of scores of smokes and dozens of thick-cupped, thick-made teas'. The filth seemed indicative of a chronic lack of funding. If cleaners couldn't be afforded to wipe the floors, what hope was there of defeating the Nazis?

There was just one advantage to inhabiting a world of men. Each time Joan made her way to the lavatories, junior staff officers vied for her attention, cracking jokes about the clanking old tea trolley. One wag told her it was 'the only serviceable tank in the British Army'.[8] Everyone laughed nervously, aware that it wasn't far from the truth.

Colin Gubbins had been in his new office for just a couple of weeks when he informed Joan that he had to travel to Paris on urgent business. He was ostensibly being sent as the head of a War Office military mission, but the manner in which he spoke made her suspect that he was using this as a cover for something altogether more underhand. It would be some weeks before she would find out exactly what he was up to. In Gubbins's absence, the office baton passed temporarily to Millis Jefferis.

Jefferis's priority in Caxton Street had been to produce his pamphlet on high explosives. Now, his task was to put together a basic toolkit for any would-be saboteur. It needed to be an easily transportable case of explosives, detonators and limpet mines that could be used to blow up anything from bridges to transformers.

Jefferis knew from his experiences on the North-West Frontier that the most important item for any saboteur was the detonator and its accompanying fuse, the latter being used to trigger the explosive. He also knew that the army's Bickford fuse was hopelessly inadequate for targeted destruction. Specialist saboteurs required specialist detonators.

He had already begun this work in Caxton Street, where he had developed his miniature time vibration switch. Now, a new little beauty emerged from his design sheet. The pressure switch was a piece of consummate craftsmanship, combining the precision of a Swiss watch with the mischievous humour of a devious brain. As its name implied, it used the pressure of the train on the track to trigger the explosive. The humour was Jefferis's own: he relished the idea of the train itself setting off the charge.

Stuart Macrae had been working alongside Jefferis on an ad hoc basis and never ceased to be amazed at the way in which such a coarse-fingered individual could produce such finicky products. He tested the unfused prototypes on suburban railway lines and found them extraordinarily precise. The pressure switch worked by means of a spring-loaded striker, a steel rod hardened to brittleness and a sealed compression chamber: it took accuracy to new levels. 'When a train came along, the rail had to be deflected only a few thousandths of an inch to cause it to fire the mine.'

Jefferis was using advanced mathematical formulae to conjure up a whole new generation of weaponry. To Macrae's eyes, the algebraic logarithms scratched on to the office blackboard were 'an excellent example of how Millis had a gift for tackling a problem from a new angle'. An unfortunate by-product of his hyperactive imagination was his 'moody and irritable' temper, especially when confronted with a weapon that didn't work. 'When he had a problem on his mind, he did not wait to think about anything else.' But when he 'came up for air', as Macrae put it, the clouds passed and he was restored to good humour.

Other items in Jefferis's toolkit included his Castrator, his Camoflet mine and various specialist charges. Some were scarcely bigger than a matchbox, yet they allowed the operator to destroy anything from a sentry-post to a large railway junction. With the addition of a few of Cecil Clarke's limpet mines, 'the irregular soldier or saboteur was fully equipped to blow up absolutely anything in any way he chose'.

It was strictly forbidden to bring explosives into the War Office, but Jefferis couldn't develop sabotage weapons without the tools of the trade. Arriving each morning for work, he would park his Humber Snipe in the quadrangle and unload the wrapped packages on the back seat. The elderly lieutenant colonel guarding the main entrance would salute him, glance at the brown paper parcels tucked under Jefferis's arm and say: 'Ha! And what have you got there? Explosive, I suppose.'

Jefferis would let out a hearty guffaw. 'That's it, sir,' he would say. 'Very high explosive, this. We're trying to collect enough to blow this place up.'[9] He would then head straight to Room 173 and lock the blasting gelatine in the filing cabinet. At times he had as much as twenty pounds of the stuff stowed in the office cupboard, enough to bring down a sizeable chunk of the War Office.

There was the occasional mishap. Macrae was helping out one morning when he answered the telephone to an apoplectic admiral whose office was in a distant part of the building. He told Macrae that he had been seated at his desk when an explosive device had shattered through the floor and detonated under his chair. It had almost blown off his buttocks.

Macrae soon discovered what had happened. An officer, known personally to him, 'had been fooling about with some lethal weapon with which I had provided him'[10] when it had accidentally fired.

Just a few minutes' walk from the War Office, in the gleaming Shell Mex building on the Strand, sat a man who appreciated Millis Jefferis's talents even less than the irate admiral. Leslie Burgin, the recently appointed head of the Ministry of Supply, was a gaunt-faced bureaucrat (and Liberal MP) whose final Commons speech as a backbencher concerned mind-numbing details about the Selby bypass and toll bridge. His appointment as head of one of the key government ministries was memorably described as 'another horse from Caligula's well-stocked stable'.[11] The inference was clear: Burgin was not up to the job.

This would have had no bearing on Jefferis, had it not been for the fact that all new armaments had to be commissioned through Burgin's ministry. Burgin also held the keys to the Royal Ordnance Supply Factories, which had made a speciality out of bureaucracy and red tape. It could take months to complete the necessary ministerial paperwork and even longer for trials to be satisfactorily completed. Jefferis's saboteur toolkit, if approved, would not be ready for more than a year.

A few of Burgin's senior officers had come to hear about Jefferis's work and 'strongly disapproved of this pirate design section which had sprung up from nowhere'. So did Burgin himself. No sooner had war been declared than he implemented a vicelike control over the commissioning process for new weapons. Every large engineering company in the country was legally tied to his ministry 'and could accept orders only with its approval'.[12]

This was potentially disastrous for both Jefferis and Gubbins, for whom speed was the very essence of guerrilla warfare. To avoid such delays, Jefferis took the unprecedented decision to bypass Leslie Burgin and his Ministry of Supply. Instead of red tape, there would be no tape at all: henceforth, he would answer to one person alone and that would be himself. Every weapon he designed was to be built on the quiet – clandestinely and illegally – by small family-run companies whose owners were known to him personally.

One of these was Bob Porter of Boon and Porter, a Barnes-based engineering firm that specialized in upgrading Riley motor cars. Bob had always promised his local customers a service that was 'liberal in conception and speedy in execution'.[13] Now, anxious to help out his old friend, he got his entire team at the Castelnau workshop assembling Jefferis's detonators.

Next to be approached was Franco Signs in west London, whose owner was a friend of Stuart Macrae. Franco's was an electrical engineering company that made illuminated shopfronts for London stores. Macrae reasoned that they would soon be short of work, since 'illuminated signs were obviously not going to be much in demand' during the blackout. He tipped the wink to Franco's manager, who was delighted to keep his men busy making weapons. He put his main factory at Hendon at the disposal of MI(R)c 'and rapidly reopened one at Bristol which had been closed down'.

Jefferis's time vibration switch was a particularly complex piece of equipment, one that he contracted out to the Clerkenwell-based Kinematograph Engineering Company. This was run by a brilliant self-taught engineer named Mr Thomassen, whose eccentricities were such that even Macrae was left rubbing his eyes in disbelief. 'How Millis had run into him I never knew,' he said. 'His workshop was a decrepit old place equipped with very ancient machinery.' There were no safety procedures whatsoever. 'It looked as if it might fall down if a bomb exploded within a mile of it.'[14] Yet Mr Thomassen accepted the commission with enthusiasm and set to work immediately.

There was a faintly comic element to many of the workmen hired by Jefferis, one not lost on Macrae. While Hitler was using the industrial powerhouses of Germany – Siemens, Thyssen and I.B. Farben – Jefferis was forced to rely on men like Mr Thomassen of Clerkenwell. But ultimately, Jefferis was to have the last laugh. For those he hired were craftsmen of the highest order and were able to turn out complex weaponry with a speed and dexterity that not even Siemens could have matched. Mr Thomassen was to prove the most diligent of all, working throughout the night, even during the worst of the Blitz.

From the outset, Jefferis had recognized Cecil Clarke's limpet mine as a key weapon for any would-be saboteur. Now, he asked Clarke if he could build 250 limpets, using the workshop and facilities of LoLode. Cecil was more than happy to oblige, although he confessed to Macrae that he was unsure how much to charge for the mines. The basic materials were cheap enough: a Woolworths' bowl, an aniseed ball and a condom (plus the explosive charge). Since Clarke's Bedford overheads were also minimal, Macrae suggested that he ask £6 for each mine. Macrae (who was to help build the mines) added a whopping £2 commission that was to go to himself. He justified this on the grounds that he had found Clarke in the first place.

The first order yielded £500 for Macrae and a little less for Clarke. A second, much larger order earned them a further £2,000. Clarke was by now using aniseed balls at such a rate that it was no longer practical to buy them from the local sweet shops. Henceforth, he ordered them directly from Bassett's, the sweet manufacturers.

He had also amended the original design, considerably reducing the size of the striking mechanism. This meant that standard condoms were far too large. He therefore commissioned a rubber manufacturer to make special mini-condoms: 'So small,' noted Macrae, 'that they were useless for any other kind of protection.'[15]

Jefferis was never one to dawdle. As soon as the first toolkits were produced, they were boxed up in readiness for dispatch to the underground contacts that Gubbins had been establishing in the Balkans.

Gubbins himself was still in Paris and unable to oversee this, so

Jefferis stepped in to help. His explosives were sent in style, rushed to Belgrade aboard the Simplon-Orient Express and accompanied by two members of the MI(R)c team. The only hitch came when they reached Milan, where the train unexpectedly terminated. The two couriers 'had to sit on Milan station watching thirty-five parcels full of dangerous explosives and time fuses, and hoping the Italians would not declare war against us till they were inside Yugoslav territory'.[16]

The men eventually made it to Belgrade, along with the explosive packages; it was the first of many such deliveries sent to anti-Nazi resisters planning operations in southern Europe. A further three tons was sent to Egypt, a precaution against any military adventures that Hitler might be planning in the desert.

One Sunday afternoon, Stuart Macrae's phone rang and he found himself talking to a highly stressed Millis Jefferis, whose fourteen-hour days were clearly taking their toll. 'I just can't go on like this,' he barked down the phone. 'I must have your full time help.' Never one to stand on ceremony, he insisted that Macrae should hand in his notice at *Armchair Science* and join MI(R)c. 'Be up here tomorrow at ten o'clock,' he said. And then he hung up the phone.

Macrae had been keen to work alongside Jefferis from the very first moment they met, for he considered him 'an out and out genius'. But employment by MI(R)c meant he would no longer be able to claim his freelance commission on the limpet mines. This was indeed a blow. For months he had been promising Mrs Macrae that they were going to get rich. Now, he would be on the meagre pay of an army colonel. He drove back to London and reflected on his changing fortunes by downing half a bottle of Scotch. Then he took the half-finished bottle home to his wife and, 'tipping it into her' (as he put it), told her what had happened.

To his surprise, she declared herself proud to have a husband working on secret projects, even if it meant forgoing the Bentley that he had been promising. Macrae, his mind befuddled with whisky, could only conclude 'that women are far more patriotic than men'.[17]

He joined Millis Jefferis in Room 173 on the morning after the phone call, and his arrival was to transform the fortunes of MI(R)c.

Every genius needs a sidekick, and Macrae was the perfect prop to the ramshackle Jefferis. A jack of all trades, Macrae also happened to be master of one: cajoling unwilling partners into doing whatever was necessary to turn MI(R)c into a smooth-running machine that could properly exploit Jefferis's brain.

Macrae was tall and wiry, with a complicit smile and a twinkle in his eye. He wore his peaked service cap at the angle of a listing ship, as if the rakish tilt were a nod and a wink to his employment with 'the pirates', as he liked to call MI(R). His moustache was as fair as his hair, clipped in the fashion of a young Terry-Thomas. Disarmingly honest and witty to boot, he had the air of a benevolent racketeer. He kept the office well stocked with whisky and gin, and even better stocked with hangover cures.

He was the first to admit that he had been singularly ill-qualified for all his previous jobs. Just a few months earlier, he had accepted the editorship of *Gardening Magazine*. 'Nobody could know less about gardening than me,' he said. But it didn't stop him dispensing advice for his readers. 'I would solemnly give them my views on whether it were better to plant globe artichokes in September or March.'[18] Now, at last, he had fallen into a job for which he was extremely well qualified, one in which the only seeds to be planted were those of wholescale destruction.

He had been working just a few days at MI(R)c when he discovered that he and Jefferis shared a common interest in caravans, one fuelled by their discussions with Cecil Clarke. Shortly after the declaration of war, Jefferis had taken the decidedly eccentric step of cancelling the tenancy on his rented home in Farnham and moving his family into a luxury caravan parked in a field near Elstree, to the north of Edgware.

Now, Macrae joined him, manoeuvring his new caravan alongside that of his boss. Each evening the two of them would drive home together from work and park Jefferis's Humber between the two caravans, in order to afford them a little more privacy. It was an unusual arrangement but it had an important benefit. The two of them could talk until late into the night about hitherto undreamed-of weapons.

The MI(R)c team expanded within days of Macrae's arrival, for he hired a 'likeable, red-hearted fellow' called Gordon Norwood and a gruff sergeant by the name of Bidgood. With Gubbins still away, he saw much more of Joan Bright, who was spending a great deal of her working day in Room 173.

'God bless her,' said Macrae. 'She more or less ran the show.' She controlled the office purse, kept the four men equipped with supplies and even took the trouble of having the room carpeted. Macrae was so smitten that he decided to invite her out on a date. The others warned him that 'Joan was not that kind of girl' – and that *he* was married – but Macrae was undaunted. He proved so persistent that Joan eventually consented to be taken to lunch at Taglionis. But he also discovered that his colleagues were right: Joan was *not* that sort of girl. 'The whole thing was extremely platonic,'[19] he admitted with a tinge of regret.

The five members of MI(R)c were hard at work on the afternoon of 10 November when Jefferis's telephone rang unexpectedly. The caller did not identify himself and nor did he give any indication as to why he was phoning. He simply ordered Jefferis to attend an important meeting in Whitehall. When Jefferis pressed for further information, he was told that the meeting was 'with some naval officer'.[20] Perplexed, and not a little bemused, he duly attended the meeting and got the surprise of his life when he discovered that the naval officer in question was Winston Churchill.

Churchill had been appointed First Lord of the Admiralty on the day that war was declared. It was a return to the post he had last held a quarter of a century earlier, a tenure that had ended with the disastrous Gallipoli landings. Now, in very different circumstances, he was back in his former study. 'A few feet behind me,' he wrote, 'as I sat in my old chair, was the wooden map-case I had fixed in 1911, and inside it still remained the chart of the North Sea.'[21]

Churchill had known nothing of the work being undertaken by Millis Jefferis and his team, nor even of Colin Gubbins. But he was no stranger to dirty warfare. Two decades earlier, when serving as Minister for Munitions, he had taken the unprecedented decision to use chemical weapons against Bolshevik forces in northern Russia. He had also argued in favour of using chemical gas against the truculent tribes of the North-West Frontier. When his colleagues demurred, he told them he was 'strongly in favour of using poisoned gas against uncivilised tribes', and proceeded to lambast them for their 'squeamishness'.[22]

As First Lord of the Admiralty, Churchill's principal concern in the opening weeks of war was an underwater mine being deployed by the Germans to devastating effect. In one four-week period, almost thirty vessels had been sunk in British coastal waters. Churchill was particularly furious about the losses to shipping in the Thames estuary and was 'anxious to get his own back'.[23] His idea for revenge was to fill the Rhine with submersible mines. 'It seemed to me,' he later wrote, 'that the proper retort for indiscriminate sinkings by mines at the mouths of British harbours was a similar and possibly more effective mining attack upon the Rhine.'[24]

But there was a problem. When he asked senior military figures if they had any suitable weapons for such an attack, he was greeted with a negative. Such weapons did not exist.

Churchill persisted in his enquiries and, 'from somewhere or other, he learned that the War Office had a department dealing in special weapons'.[25] This was Millis Jefferis's team in Room 173. Now, he wanted to know Jefferis's thoughts on the possibility of a spectacular operation to mine the Rhine.

Once Jefferis had recovered from his initial surprise at the identity of his host, he told Churchill that such an operation ought to be feasible. He promised to report back within a fortnight, by which time he hoped to have outline drawings of how a prototype weapon might work.

Churchill felt an immediate affinity with Jefferis, whose positive stance was in striking contrast to Leslie Burgin's staff at the Ministry of Supply, whom he found 'dismally slow and unimaginative'.[26] Churchill promised Jefferis his wholehearted support, although he made it clear that such backing came at a price. He expected instant and tangible results.

Jefferis was rarely one to fluster. His work on the North-West Frontier had long ago taught him that a cool head was the key to success. But on this particular occasion, Macrae noticed that he returned from his meeting with Churchill 'in a highly excited state'.

He whisked the team to his gentlemen's club 'for a little fortification' before dropping his metaphorical bombshell. They had just two weeks to assist him in designing a technically complex mine, one that (according to Churchill's brief) could be dropped from a plane, must be no bigger than a football and had to float just beneath the surface of the Rhine. Most importantly, the W-Bomb – as Churchill had christened it (the W stood for water) – needed to detonate itself automatically before it was washed downstream into Dutch territory, in order to avoid inadvertently blowing up friendly shipping.

Jefferis had always been a workaholic and he expected his team to work a minimum of fourteen hours a day. They were often exhausted and unable to think straight, yet he continued to drive them hard into the early hours. Macrae thought him a tyrant, albeit a tyrant that he came to respect. 'If he had lived in Roman times, I am sure he would have become a chief flogger on one of those slave-powered galleons.'

Jefferis knew that the key component in any new weapon was the fuse. He flirted with the idea of once again using aniseed balls for the W-Bomb, before stumbling upon a far better solution. 'Because of our wearing work and the need to keep ourselves going with alcohol,' wrote Macrae, 'I kept in Room 173 a supply of Alka Seltzer tablets.'[27]

These, tested in conjunction with spring-loaded detonators, were found to dissolve with absolute regularity. The most challenging problem had been overcome. The W-Bomb was to be the first weapon of war that could both sink a ship and cure a hangover.

Churchill placed Jefferis under immense pressure during that second week of November. First, he demanded to see a scale model of the weapon before it was scarcely off the drawing board. Next, he began selling his idea of attacking the Rhine to the Cabinet. Long before Jefferis's W-Bomb was anything more than a prototype, he called for a demonstration in a specially made glass tank installed on a table in his Admiralty office. He was so excited by the results that he ordered Jefferis 'to get it into production right away'.

Within weeks of first meeting Churchill, Jefferis found himself in the extraordinary situation of being invited to join his inner circle.

He became a regular attendee at his 'Midnight Follies', the secret late-night meetings attended by senior generals and Cabinet ministers. Churchill sought Jefferis's advice on everything from detonators to dirty war, and treated him 'as a kind of wizard who could produce new armaments out of a hat in a hurry'.

Stuart Macrae often attended the Midnight Follies as Jefferis's assistant: on one notable occasion, he accidentally dropped the prototype W-Bomb. It fell apart, flinging antennae, rods and springs across the room. Churchill was furious 'and roared out something in which the words "bloody incompetence" occurred'.

Jefferis continually urged caution about the W-Bomb, warning Churchill that it was far from ready. But Churchill refused to listen. 'The trouble was that Winston was a born showman,' noted Macrae, 'and that the W-Bomb was his greatest act.'

Churchill soon decided to take his show on the road, travelling to Paris in order to sell Operation Royal Marine to the French. He insisted on taking Jefferis and Macrae with him, along with their half-finished W-Bomb. Macrae feared they would soon fall out of favour. 'I could think of no better way of ending a beautiful friendship than this one.'[28]

Churchill liked to travel in small groups and the trip to Paris was no exception. His party included Professor Lindemann (his old friend and scientific adviser), his then bodyguard Mr Hopkins, and a handful of others.

Travelling with Churchill was rather like travelling with an avuncular bachelor, or so it seemed to Macrae. Churchill's hunger for knowledge was matched by an accompanying thirst for alcohol. There was never any doubt as to who was to pay for the drinks. As the most junior member of the party, Macrae was made an honorary member of the mess, which meant that he 'was entitled to buy them drinks at around 8d per shot'.

When the little team arrived in Calais after a tense crossing of the English Channel (well lubricated with pink gins), they boarded a private night train to Paris. Macrae went to the bar for a final snifter, only to find himself in a tête-à-tête with Churchill. Another round of drinks was ordered and Macrae (somewhat nervously) recounted an anecdote of how he had once written an article about

Churchill's love of hats. Churchill exploded with laughter, ordered more brandy and was about to offer Macrae a cigar when he noticed that he only had three stars on his epaulettes. 'He then hastily changed his mind,' having decided 'that it would be wrong to waste a good cigar on a mere captain'.

Once in the French capital, the team was whisked to the Hôtel de Crillon in order to prepare for the morning's demonstration of the W–Bomb. Churchill had slept for less than two hours and drunk an ocean of cognac yet he was on irrepressible form. The W–Bomb demonstration was due to take place at Versailles in front of senior generals: Churchill insisted on being the principal showman, 'speaking mainly in schoolboy French'.

Rolling his Rs in true Gallic fashion, he spoke excitedly about Jefferis's miracle weapon and told his audience that the bomb was one of the most mischievous weapons ever invented. It primed itself as it floated downstream and then lurked for days just inches beneath the surface. When he reached the denouement, he pretended to be a German warship, performing the collision with Jefferis's W–Bomb with wild theatricality. 'Bang,' he shouted. 'C'est fini!'[29]

It was a remarkable performance and it impressed everyone in the room. Even the gravest French generals were heard to shout 'bravo'. But the chief obstacle to Operation Royal Marine was the French government. Prime Minister Edouard Daladier refused to countenance the idea of dropping 10,000 of Jefferis's W–Bombs into the Rhine, worried that it might provoke Hitler into launching retaliatory bombing raids on Paris.

Churchill was dismayed by such a defeatist attitude and heaped scorn on the French. 'Good, decent, civilised people, it appeared, must never themselves strike till after they have been struck dead.' He warned Daladier that the time for playing by the rules was over. Hitler was preparing 'a vast machine, grinding forward, ready to break upon us'.[30] And the French, it seemed, were prepared to allow themselves to be trampled on.

Operation Royal Marine was not given the French green light until May 1940, by which time it was far too late. Hitler's panzer divisions were already thrusting deep into France. Churchill felt a certain vindication when he was brought news that Jefferis's W–Bomb had worked to perfection. Some 1,700 were dropped into the Rhine and, for a brief period, caused absolute mayhem, sinking ships and blowing up bridges.

'Practically all river traffic between Karlsruhe and Mainz was suspended, and extensive damage was done to the Karlsruhe barrage and a number of pontoon bridges.' But even Churchill was forced to admit that it was too little, too late. 'The success of the device was however lost in the deluge of disaster.'[31]

But Millis Jefferis's work had one outcome that was both unexpected and fortuitous. It had brought the little team in MI(R)c 'to the notice of the man who was to become the most powerful in the land'. Churchill was already looking to the future and was fully aware of the potential value of Jefferis's work. He now vowed to protect him from the interference of ministers, generals and civil servants. Macrae saw it as a turning point. 'He was to save us from being abolished or swallowed up.'[32]

He was to do more than that. Within weeks of Operation Royal Marine, he fired off a memo to General Hastings 'Pug' Ismay, his chief military adviser. 'Report to me on the position of Major Jefferis,' he said. 'By whom is he employed? Who is he under? I regard this officer as a singularly capable and forceful man, who should be brought forward to a higher position. He ought certainly to be promoted Lieutenant-Colonel, as it will give him more authority.' Jefferis, he added, was a 'brilliant officer' with an 'ingenious, inventive mind'.[33] He refused to have such men quashed by the War Office and Ministry of Supply.

If they couldn't work within the strictures of Whitehall, then they would work directly for him.

4

Sweet Fanny Adams

COLIN GUBBINS HAD spent the autumn of 1939 in Paris. The French authorities were told that he was working for the War Office's Military Mission, but they soon suspected he was 'more concerned with covert activities than with normal military liaison'.[1] This was absolutely correct. Scarcely had he arrived in Paris than he took himself off to the Hôtel Regina, a luxurious *fin de siècle* pile just a stone's throw from the Louvre. This was the temporary home of Stanislav Gano, head of the Polish Deuxième Bureau.

Gubbins had last met Gano in Warsaw three months earlier. Since that meeting, Gano had found himself dragged through a series of unwelcome adventures. He had been seized by the Gestapo and interned in a prison camp, but he had outwitted the Nazis by escaping their grasp and making his way overland to Paris. Now, he was attempting to orchestrate resistance inside occupied Poland.

He spilled a woeful tale of the guerrilla activities being attempted by his compatriots. They were hampered by a lack of equipment and stood in desperate need of radio transmitters and automatic pistols. Gubbins promised to help and immediately contacted the War Office in London. The response was hardly encouraging. There were only two spare transmitters in the whole of England, and these would not be available until the following spring. As for automatic pistols, the War Office didn't have any at all. All they could offer were some old revolvers, weapons that were totally unsuitable for guerrilla warfare.

General Gano found it hard to believe that the British had no spare supplies and concluded 'that it was more likely due to unwillingness than inability'.[2] He was absolutely correct. Gubbins's request for weapons had been blocked by the Secret Intelligence Service,

49

whose senior officers had come to view guerrilla warfare as a blunt-edged tool that risked compromising their undercover agents. According to one of those agents (and later, double-agent), Kim Philby, they 'resisted bitterly the whole idea of letting a lot of thugs loose on the continent'.[3] Just as Leslie Burgin was intent on under-mining Millis Jefferis and his work, so the Secret Intelligence Service was determined to put Gubbins's team out of business. It was another warning that not everyone in the establishment was as enthusiastic about ungentlemanly warfare as Winston Churchill.

Gubbins found himself in a quandary as he attempted to help Gano's efforts to build a Polish resistance. He was living in great comfort in a top-floor apartment on the rue de Varenne, with a view over the garden of the Musée Rodin. He had a housekeeper (who also happened to be a gourmet cook) and the use of a large Renault saloon. But he was unable to put any of his theories about guerrilla warfare into effect.

In the evenings he would take himself off to one of the city's White Russian nightclubs where he and other expatriates found consolation in magnum after magnum of pink champagne. When the band's leader came to play at their table, Gubbins would jump unsteadily to his feet and give 'a lusty performance of *Ochi chornye* and *Stanka razin*, to the astonishment of the other patrons'. It was an enjoyable enough existence, but it was hardly the life of a guer-rilla leader.

Joan Bright was in regular contact with Gubbins and could sense that he was starting 'to feel restless'.[4] He was not alone in having such feelings. Peter Wilkinson, back in the office after his Polish jaunt, felt as if he should be doing something constructive for the war effort, even if it was 'digging trenches on the Franco-Belgian frontier'.[5] Instead, he was having a ball in his bachelor pad in Clarges Street, off Piccadilly.

If the war seemed unreal to those in MI(R), it was even more so to the population at large. One expat returning to London after a spell in Germany was astonished by the general lassitude. He had witnessed the Third Reich's 'massive preparations and mobilisation of her youth'. Yet here in London, his friends were 'blissfully inter-ested in cricket, tennis, gold and the results of the four-thirty'.[6]

On the far side of the Atlantic, seasoned American observers began saying it was a war that didn't exist. Senator William Borah spoke for many when he attacked the European powers for their lack of action. 'There is something phoney about this war,' he said.[7]

Phoney. The word stuck. It was a Phoney War. The British Expeditionary Force had dug itself into the trenches on the borders of eastern France, yet there was nothing to be done except to wait for the Germans to attack. Officers got so bored that they imported foxhounds and beagles from England so that they could spend their time 'in the open air with the music of hounds and the clean fresh smell of the countryside reminding them that there still existed the old traditions of sanity and justice'.[8] If they weren't able to kill any Boche, then they could at least slaughter a few foxes.

The Phoney War came to an abrupt end at a few minutes before midnight on 8 April 1940. Captain Leif Welding Olsen, commander of the Norwegian patrol boat *Pol III*, was scanning the moonlit horizon when he noticed a group of silhouetted warships entering the mouth of Oslofjord. He immediately recognized them as German and fired a warning shot.

When the vessels continued to steam into the fjord, Captain Olsen took the momentous decision to attack. He stoked his engines to full throttle, hurtled across Oslofjord and then rammed his patrol boat hard into the German torpedo ship, *Albatros*. It was a brave act of defiance but a fatal one. 'He was sprayed with machine gun fire, both his legs pierced by bullets.'[9] He died from severe blood loss, earning himself the dubious distinction of being the first mortality of the German invasion of Norway.

News of the invasion reached Whitehall within hours, causing outright panic. Clement Attlee, Leader of the Opposition, immediately called up the War Office file on Norway, only to find that it was completely empty. On the cover were the cryptic letters SFA. 'I suppose it means Sweet Fanny Adams,' he said to Winston Churchill when the two of them met later that day. 'I sincerely hope there is no other interpretation to be placed on those letters,' replied Churchill.

Two expeditionary forces were rushed to Norway in the vain

hope of blocking the Nazi drive towards Narvik. This was a key objective for the Germans, as it was the winter outlet for all the iron ore mined in neutral Sweden. The British landings proved a farce. None of the officers spoke Norwegian and they were wholly unprepared for the hostile terrain. 'You can really do what you like,' was the instruction that one officer gave to his men after a briefing at the War Office, 'for they don't know what they want done.'[10]

Colin Gubbins had returned to London shortly before the invasion of Norway. He was relieved to be back, for his time in Paris had been a disappointment. The office in London, by contrast, was abuzz with men and ideas. There were now more than a dozen staff working for MI(R), all of them sniffing at the danger ahead. Secretary Joan felt that everyone was driven by the same motivation, 'the taut thread of adventure and desire for individual action'.[11]

Two days after the landings in Norway, Gubbins attended a sherry party in the typists' room at the War Office. Joan had managed to lay her hands on a couple of bottles with which to toast the first birthday of MI(R). Gubbins was in no mood for celebrating. Indeed his mind was on other matters entirely. The German invasion of Norway at long last provided him with the opportunity to put guerrilla warfare to the test by sending elite companies of men deep into the country in order 'to conduct small harassing operations on the enemy'.[12]

He confided his idea to Joan, who by now knew more about guerrilla warfare than any other woman in the country. He told her that he envisaged sending in hit-and-run teams that 'would be independent and self-sufficient, and know where and how to use the explosive they brought with them'.[13]

Gubbins was never one to hang around. He proposed his idea to the War Office on 13 April, four days after the German invasion. Two days later, he was given permission to form specialist units that were to be known as Independent Companies. Five days after that, he was given overall command of four of these companies, which were to be known as Scissorforce. He was also given permission to establish a guerrilla warfare training centre in Scotland: 'A bit late in the day,' he noted in his office diary, 'but it was something to get the thing pushed through.'[14]

There was no time to give specialist training to the guerrillas heading to Norway. Scissorforce was scraped together with volunteer units that had completed their training and were waiting to be sent to France. On paper, they sounded impressive. Each company comprised 20 officers and 270 men, including sappers, signals experts and infantry. They were issued with Alpine rucksacks, snow-shoes, Arctic boots, leather jerkins and woolly sheepskin coats, essential protection against the sharp chill of a Norwegian spring.

The kit turned out to be rather more impressive than the men. One officer was surprised to discover that 'no one knew how to use the snow-shoes', a serious oversight given that they were to be operating in an area where the snow lay more than two feet deep.[15] That same officer was no less alarmed to be told that the sheepskin coats were too bulky to be transported and were to be left in England. As compensation, the men were offered extra supplies of pemmican, a gumlike mixture of animal fat and protein. At its best, it tasted like salt-pork chewing gum. At its worst, it was like rancid whale blubber.

Gubbins could do nothing about equipment, but he was shrewd enough to realize that a guerrilla force is only as good as its leaders. There was no one in London (with the exception of himself) who was fit to lead the troops on the ground. Even men like Peter Wilkinson had only undergone the most rudimentary training. He therefore wired Indian Army headquarters in Lahore and asked for twenty of their finest officers to be dispatched to England with immediate effect. He specifically requested officers with experience of guerrilla warfare on the troubled North-West Frontier.

The twenty officers were sent to Karachi, where they boarded an Imperial Airways flying boat named *Cathay*. It was only designed to carry seventeen passengers, requiring three of the men to spend the entire voyage squashed into the freezing luggage compartment, half buried under kit-bags. 'This was noisy, smelly and dark,'[16] wrote one of the unfortunate three, who humoured himself by naming it the 'Black Hole of Cathay'.

Gubbins was under few illusions about his guerrilla mission to Norway. He could not stop Hitler's invasion and nor could he reverse the German advances. At best, he could slow their drive towards the three key towns of Bodø, Mo and Mosjøen. His War Office orders reflected this reality. He was given free reign to destroy roads, railways and communications and was told to 'ensure that all possible steps are taken by demolition and harrying tactics to impede any German advance'. In short, he was to make Hitler's drive northwards 'slow and costly.'[17]

For this, he needed the help of Millis Jefferis.

No sooner had Colin Gubbins's Norway mission been given the green light than Jefferis found himself under intense pressure. On Thursday, 25 April he received a memo to the effect that Gubbins's men – all 1,200 of them – needed to be fully equipped with sabotage weaponry by the following Tuesday. They required Camoflet mines, pressure switches and time vibration switches, the last two to be used to blow up railways being exploited by the Nazis.

Jefferis's decision to stockpile these weapons while Gubbins had been in Paris now proved to have been a wise one. Bob Porter's team at Riley Motors, along with Mr Thomassen of Clerkenwell and the specialists at Franco's, had all been hard at work and Jefferis had managed to assemble a significant arsenal. But more was needed. Stuart Macrae dipped deep into his 'bag of gold' – the limitless supply of funds that fell outside any Whitehall accounting system – in order to encourage these freelance artisans to work even harder.

Once the commissioning was set in motion, Macrae headed to Edinburgh in order to instruct two of Gubbins's Independent Companies in the use of these strange new weapons. Sergeant Bidgood meanwhile went to Dymchurch in Kent and then on to Suffolk, where the other two companies were billeted. 'We took some of the gear with us,' said Macrae, 'whilst the rest followed by road or passenger train.' He had hired more staff in order to keep Room 173 running smoothly, yet there was a palpable sense of urgency in the air. Macrae confessed to having never worked so hard in his life. 'I flattered myself that I was working myself to death and was chastened when I realized that these others were working even harder.'[18]

Once Jefferis was satisfied that production was proceeding smoothly, he made a surprise announcement to the team: he was taking a short overseas break. Macrae was never in any doubt as to his destination. He was heading to Norway in order 'to get some practical experience in blowing up railway lines'. He had been keen to try out his weaponry ever since he joined MI(R). Now, 'his wicked face lit up with joy'[19] as he helped himself to 1,000 pounds of high explosive, along with pressure switches, time delays and enough blasting gelatine to blow up half of Norway.

He arranged for the RAF to fly him from Hendon airfield to Scotland; from here, he was to board a Sunderland flying boat that would drop him into occupied Norway. His intention was to stage a lightning, hit-and-run operation on the Western Railway that ran through the centre of the country. If all went to plan, he would be back in London before Gubbins's men had even set sail.

The War Office's car pool was so busy on the morning of his departure that Jefferis had to drive his own car to Hendon. Delayed by traffic, he was obliged to make up time by driving at breakneck speed down the Finchley Road. He drove so fast, indeed, that he got 'pinched' by the police for speeding. Next morning, an officer from Hampstead police station appeared at MI(R) and announced that Jefferis had been summoned to appear in court.

Macrae expressed his indignation in no uncertain terms. 'Speed limits, I pointed out, were admittedly very necessary in peace time, but in wartime it must be understood that army officers in the course of their duty were entitled to disregard them.'[20] He told the officer that Jefferis could not attend because he was busy blowing up Nazis. His protest fell on deaf ears. Jefferis was fined a hefty £6 for his failure to appear in court.

Jefferis landed safely at the snowbound fishing port of Åndalsnes, some hundred miles south-west of Trondheim. He followed the railway out of town until he reached a pre-agreed rendezvous with Brigadier Harold Morgan, commander of one of the hapless platoons sent to Norway in the wake of the Nazi invasion. The brigadier spilled a sorry tale. His men had come under sustained attack from shells and machine-gun fire from low-flying German aircraft. Jefferis found them chastened and scared. 'The moral effect of seeing the aircraft coming, of being unable to take cover, of being able to observe the bomb dropping, and of the terrific explosion, had been overwhelming.'[21] *He* felt rather differently, smelling the cordite with relish. He had not been in a combat zone since his battles in the Himalayas almost two decades earlier. There was a sense in which he was returning home.

Selecting a sergeant and two privates, he picked his way through the German front line 'in order to lay his recently invented protracted delay action explosive charges'. These were set to detonate at various intervals over the next few months, in order to give the Germans a string of unwelcome surprises. He had been tipped off about two key targets, one in Øyer and the other in Lillehammer. He first made his way to Øyer, where he blew up the strategically vital bridge and caused major problems for the German thrust northwards. Once this was done, he pressed on to Lillehammer, where he 'placed an electrically fired mine and an anti-tank trap',[22] both of them wired to one of Mr Thomassen's detonators.

By the time this was done, the Germans were advancing so rapidly that Jefferis had no option but to take flight. He reached the port of Åndalsnes under heavy bombardment and took shelter on a sloop. Thirty high-explosive shells fell around him, 'a third of these within a ship's length'. Jefferis had always enjoyed mathematical puzzles, but this one had an answer that was altogether too uncomfortable. 'He calculated that his life would probably not be more than three days.'[23] He was fortunate to be plucked from Åndalsnes soon afterwards; he was back in London on the last day of April.

He was immediately asked to write a report for the Prime Minister, Neville Chamberlain, informing him of the military situation in Norway. This was discussed at length at the following day's Cabinet meeting. Everyone present came to the same conclusion: that the remaining British forces in Norway were doomed and that 'it was quite impossible for land forces to withstand complete air superiority'[24] on the part of the Nazis.

The last remaining hopes were now pinned on the pioneering guerrilla force under the command of Colin Gubbins. On Sunday, 5 May they set sail aboard the *Orion*, the *Royal Ulsterman* and the *Ulster Prince*. Their destination was the as yet unoccupied area of Norway, but they were aware that the Nazi invaders were driving north at alarming speed under the command of one of Hitler's most experienced generals.

General Nikolaus von Falkenhorst played the game of war with the same attention to strategy as a grandmaster of chess. He was the principal architect of the Norwegian invasion and had plotted each move with care, aware that losing the game would almost certainly mean losing his head.

A patrician aristocrat from eastern Prussia, Falkenhorst had all the verve and mettle of a Teutonic knight. 'A soldier first, second and last,' was the opinion of one who served with him.[25] At an early age he had changed his patronymic from the Slavic, Jastrzembski, to the more Germanic-sounding Falkenhorst. It meant Falcon's Eyrie, a fitting name for a military commander with a hawk's eye for detail.

Hitler had placed him in charge of the invasion in the third week of February 1940, demanding that he produce a battle plan that would guarantee victory. When the general asked how long he had got, the Führer said he wanted it by 5 p.m. that same day.

General von Falkenhorst knew absolutely nothing about the country he was to invade. 'I went to town and bought a Baedeker, a tourist guide, in order to find out what Norway was like,' he later confessed.[26] He read the relevant chapters, studied the maps and was back in Hitler's office later that afternoon with a workable battle plan.

Now, just eight weeks later, his life had changed for ever. His new home was Oslo (he had taken modest lodgings in the Royal Norwegian Automobile Club) and his troops were punching north-wards at an astonishing speed. Southern Norway was already in their grasp and they were rapidly approaching the coastal town of Mosjøen, equidistant between Oslo and Tromsø, when they found themselves confronting a wholly unexpected enemy.

Colin Gubbins and his Scissorforce guerrillas had set sail from Scotland after breakfast on 5 May, equipped with their snow-shoes, their pemmican and a growing sense of unease. They knew little about the enemy and even less about Norway. No one had thought to pack a Baedeker.

The atrocious weather made them realize what a mistake it had been to discard their sheepskin coats. They shivered into their sou'westers and cursed the biting North Sea gale. It flung fine sheets of salty spray across the poop, along with 'a mixture of sleet and snow'.[27] As the metal deck turned to a slick of ice, some of the men began to question the wisdom of signing up for their Norwegian adventure.

Shortly after midnight on the third day at sea, one of the crew sighted the snow-covered hills of Norway, lit by the glancing sheen of an Arctic moon. It might have made a romantic sight, were it not for the fact that those hills were already under the control of Nazi storm-troopers.

The *Ulster Prince* and her two-ship escort reached land in the chill of dawn, dropping one group of men at the port of Bodø while Gubbins and the rest headed eighty miles further south to Mosjøen. Here, they were met by a company of French Chasseurs Alpins led by Captain Coche. The captain warned Gubbins of the perilous situation into which he was landing. German storm-troopers were just twenty miles away and Norwegian resistance was crumbling fast, having been 'stunned by the rapidity of the enemy advance'. Gubbins had been promised that Captain Coche and his skiers would fight alongside his guerrillas. But when he asked the captain for support, he was met with a Gallic shake of the head. Coche said he was getting out while it was still possible, 'on direct orders from Paris'.

Gubbins and his men were in an acutely dangerous situation. They were in an exposed port with no air cover and little winter equipment. 'In a panic,' noted Gubbins tersely in his war diary. The captain of the *Ulster Prince* was also in a panic. 'Get to hell off this ship,' he shouted to the men. 'I've got to get moving before the bombers arrive.'[28]

Gubbins had spent many months studying the theory of guerrilla warfare and knew the strengths of a good leader. 'Bold in action and cool in council, of great mental and physical endurance, and of strong personality.'[29] Now, he proved himself up to scratch by taking command of a potentially catastrophic situation.

His Indian Army officers were deeply impressed by his energy. Few on the North-West Frontier displayed such bravado in the face of adversity. Yet Gubbins 'moved unceasingly by car, by bicycle, walking and even swimming in order to reach all detachments'.[30] That tough Highland upbringing was paying dividends. Not many commanders would be prepared to swim a fjord in order to issue instructions to their troops.

The dapper little officer with a freshly cut buttonhole had transmogrified into 'a brute in a khaki shirt with the sleeves cut off, snoring prodigiously in a twenty-minute squirt of sleep, then waking up alert and talking coherently'. Even his physical appearance seemed to have changed: dressed in army fatigues, he seemed 'very short and thick, with vast heavy arms that looked as if they could crush rocks and hung down to his knees'.[31]

Gubbins was under no illusions that he could stop the relentless German advance. Nor could he even prevent the capture of Mosjøen. But he could put his guerrilla tactics to the test, if only to see how his men performed under pressure. Even if they didn't kill a single German, it would provide him with invaluable experience.

Norwegian partisans brought news that the German Army was making a lightning advance along the main road to Mosjøen and that the main body of troops was preceded by a large scouting party of soldiers on bicycles. Gubbins's guerrilla mantra was blunt: 'shoot, burn and destroy'.[32] Now, he placed the defence of the Mosjøen road in the hands of one of his finest Indian Army experts, Captain Prendergast, along with a platoon of men. They were to prepare a nasty little surprise for the advancing Germans.

The choice of Prendergast was wise. He was an expert in Pathan guerrilla tactics, which utilized ambush to devastating effect. He knew that success would be entirely dependent upon his men being able to hide, strike fast and then blend back into the snowy land-scape. He spent the night reconnoitring the best place to attack.

The snow on these bleak hillsides was waist deep and as soft as cream, quite different from the icy crusts of the North-West Frontier. It had clotted in the hollows, wiping contours and making every step slow and treacherous. 'Exceedingly difficult going,' wrote Prendergast, who tried hard to avoid sliding into drifts. 'I had twice to be dug out of the snow with bayonets.'[33]

After several hours of reconnoitring, he found the perfect place for attack. The main road narrowed to single-track as it crossed a fast-flowing river just a few miles from Mosjøen. There was a fresh-water lake on the left side and an ice-blown ridge on the right. If the Germans could be ambushed here, while they were crossing the long bridge, they would have little chance of escape.

There was an additional reason why Prendergast selected the bridge. It had small roadblocks at either end, requiring the cyclists to dismount in order to lift their bikes over the blocks. If Prendergast got his timing right, they would be desperately exposed.

He told his novice guerrillas to bivouac themselves into the snow as he reminded them of the rules of a successful ambush. Surprise was the key factor, but speed was also important. It was kill or be killed. If his men didn't shoot the Germans as they crossed the bridge, the tables would rapidly be turned.

It was just after 5.30 a.m. by the time the last of the men were in position. The sky held the sullen grey of a spring dawn and a knife-blade wind was rasping across the snowfields. The mercury was far below zero. The men shivered uncontrollably as they awaited the German cyclists.

Captain Prendergast had been monitoring the upper stretch of road for the better part of an hour when he detected a distant noise. A minute or so later, he spied the first of the cyclists. They were approaching in pairs and were separated by ten-yard intervals. They were oblivious to the imminent danger.

Prendergast had been expecting them to be dressed in Arctic combat gear and was surprised to see that they were in uniform, 'very smartly dressed in short tunics and high boots'. He was also surprised by how many there were: he counted sixty in total.

He watched them intently as they approached the bridge. They braked, slowed to a standstill and then dismounted from their bikes and began lifting them over the roadblocks. They had no idea that they were being watched by fourteen pairs of eyes.

Captain Prendergast had stressed to his men the importance of patience. If they opened fire too early, they risked missing their target. Too late, and they would expose themselves to unnecessary danger. It was nevertheless agonizing for the men to watch the Germans clamber back on to their bikes and start pedalling across the bridge.

Still Prendergast held his fire. Indeed it was not until the first of the cyclists was halfway across the bridge that he shouted the order. A split second later, the two hidden machine guns let rip, spraying a lethal rain of bullets into the German cyclists.

'At the first burst, from all arms, the majority of the cyclists seemed to fall.' They crashed into each other, and then fell to the ground. 'As they were lying spread-eagled on the crown of the road, [they] were clearly killed outright.'

A few at the rear had time to react. They leaped off their bikes and threw themselves into a ditch at the side of the bridge. But Prendergast had planned for that. 'As we could see right into that at different angles, we were able, by deliberate fire, to mop up the rest.'

Prendergast had insisted that ruthlessness was the key to success: Germans were no different to the jihadist tribesmen of the North-West Frontier. He certainly displayed no squeamishness about killing in cold blood. He spotted several stragglers trying to make their escape and 'was myself able to shoot one in such a manner'.[34] His men brought down the rest.

The Germans managed to fire just two rounds of ammunition before the engagement was over. A body count revealed that all sixty cyclists were dead. 'The first burst of fire killed many and the rest, shouting Heil Hitler!, rode jinking through the dead to their own destruction.'[35] The attack had been swift, brutal and effective. It was textbook guerrilla warfare, the first action of its kind since the outbreak of war.

Gubbins's hopes of repeating the attack proved impossible. The German drive northwards was unstoppable and the collapse of organized Norwegian resistance left his men dangerously exposed. Captain Prendergast himself warned against further action. The recruits were untrained in winter warfare 'and quite unsuitable for the task'. He reminded Gubbins that to be successful, guerrilla forces needed to be immune to hardship. Yet these men 'were exhausted and it is doubtful that they could have fought another day'.[36]

Gubbins's men retreated northwards to Bodø, blowing up everything they could, and then rejoined the comrades they had left a few days earlier. They clung to their precarious positions, but the shortening nights left them at a huge disadvantage. Just a few weeks earlier, Millis Jefferis had warned the Cabinet that the Germans had complete mastery of the skies. Now, General Nikolaus von Falkenhorst threw all his aerial firepower against Gubbins's men as they awaited rescue from Bodø.

The German pilots were determined to exact revenge for the ambush against their cycling comrades. Their attack began just as Captain William Fell arrived with a rescue fleet of six trawlers. Hearing a low throbbing noise, he turned his head to the sky. 'At first, one reconnaissance plane circled high over the town, then came wave upon wave of bombers till the roar of the engines filled the air. Then that sinister whistle and scream and double crack as the bombs fell.'

The destruction was meticulous, methodical and total. 'From end to end and side to side bombs crashed. In half an hour the whole lovely innocent little town was blazing to heaven.' A hundred planes took part in the raid and bombed the town for a further three hours. They even targeted the hospital, forcing its evacuation. Then, when the patients were being wheeled through the streets, they were machine-gunned from the air. Captain Fell was staggered by the ruthlessness of the Germans. 'At the end nothing was left of Bodø but a blazing inferno of hell.'

The British soldiers were no less dazed by the ferocity of the attack. 'Gaunt, exhausted, they had despair stamped all over them.' Yet Gubbins himself gave every appearance of enjoying himself. Captain Fell could scarcely believe the pluck of 'the amazing little general who never slept but grinned enchantingly'.[37] He seemed to be living entirely off adrenalin. 'How and when he slept I can't remember, but it was seldom for more than half an hour and was never in or on a bed.'

Gubbins would not return to London for another fortnight, but when he did, he was received as something of a hero. The success of the Norwegian campaign had been limited in both scope and destruction: sixty dead cyclists was never going to stop an invasion. But it had shown – in a small way – that guerrilla warfare could be a highly effective form of fighting back at the Nazis.

First to congratulate him was Joan Bright, who listened with pride to the stories from the battlefront and declared that he had 'made a very respectable showing'.[38] She said that his first guerrilla command had seen him 'at the very top of his form' and that his experiences 'had left him full of confidence in his ability to handle major units in battle'.

More important was the praise from General Auchinleck, overall commander of Allied forces in Norway. Gubbins, he said, had been 'first class'[39] and recommended that he should be given command of 'the New Army', as he dubbed the guerrillas. The mission also brought Gubbins a medal. Just days after landing back in Scotland, he was awarded the Distinguished Service Order.

There was an important lesson to be learned from the Scissorforce campaign, one that Gubbins would never forget. If British guerrillas were to defeat the Nazis, they needed to be properly trained and equipped. The difference between his own men and those of General Falkenhorst was striking. 'The German infantry, who needed machine-carbines, had them; those who had snow-shoes could use them; they were specialists in Norwegian warfare, not just Poor Bloody Infantry.'[40]

Above all else, his guerrillas needed to be the most elite force ever sent into battle. 'We must see that our officers are properly selected and trained, and weed them ruthlessly so that only those who have a real devotion to duty and fighting spirit can achieve command.' There was no room for slackers. 'Officers who are useless must be reduced to the ranks and made to fight in the ranks.'

The Norway campaign had also sharpened Gubbins's concept of guerrilla fighting. Against the Nazis, he was prepared to use 'hitherto unthinkable methods of warfare', justifying it on the grounds that 'this was total war, and total war is a very cruel business indeed'.[41]

He suspected that he would have further business in Norway. For even as his men had been doing battle against the Germans, alarming intelligence reached London – intelligence that was handed to him on his return. Among the many Norwegian installations captured by the Nazis was the Norsk Hydro heavy water factory at Rjukan. One of their first acts was to order the factory 'to increase the production of heavy water (deuterium oxide) at Vermork to 3,000 lbs'. This was ominous indeed, for heavy water was – as Gubbins well knew – 'a basic requirement in her attempts to produce the atomic bomb'.[42]

Such intelligence caused deep alarm in Whitehall. And it made Norsk Hydro a most important target for future sabotage.

5

The Wild Guerrillas of Kent

S IXTY MILES FROM London, in rural Bedfordshire, Cecil Clarke
had developed a theory about how to defeat the Nazis, one that
might have been dismissed as fantasy were it not for the fact that it
was a theory shared by Hitler.

In his leisure time, at weekends and late in the evening, Cecil
put his caravans to one side and indulged his passion for the theory
of war. Quietly, obsessively, he embarked on a study of scores of
historical battles, from Arsuf and Crécy to Gandamak and Majuba.
In each case, he investigated the weapons used by the victors, be
they muskets, wire guns or lyddite shells. His findings were startling
and formed the subject of a brilliant little thesis he wrote entitled
The Development of Weapon Potential.

Clarke contended that Captain Henry Shrapnel's revolutionary
spherical case-shot had swept the British to victory at the Battle of
Vimeiro, and George Koehler's newly invented Depressing Carriage
had helped defeat the Great Siege of Gibraltar. The Sussex-made
breech-loading guns of Elizabethan England had proved decisive in
countless sea battles, while the Duke of Marlborough's greatest
triumphs had been possible only because of the precision flintlock
muskets made by Messrs R. Brook of Birmingham. Clarke concluded
that in a thousand years of conflict, 'it is difficult, if not impossible,
to find an instance in which British forces achieved victory except
with a novel weapon in their hands'.[1]

He had long argued that Hitler's downfall would at some point
necessitate an Allied attack on the heavily defended western frontier
of Nazi Germany. And this posed a significant problem. The
Siegfried Line was an impregnable system of 18,000 interlocking
bunkers, tank traps and ditches. According to one report, 'the

ground is chequered with little forts, machine-gun nests and strong points'.[2]

Clarke's experience of trench warfare in the First World War had taught him that infantry was at its most exposed when advancing towards fortified bunkers. Any assault on the Siegfried Line was certain to provoke a deluge of fire from the German defenders, making a conventional attack doomed to failure. Technology alone could be guaranteed to breach the German defences, but it would have to be technology so strikingly original that it would catch the Germans completely unawares. With this in mind, Cecil began to sketch the design of a hydraulic excavating machine of such immense power that it could plough a deep trench through the Siegfried Line, uprooting topsoil, tank traps and bunkers.

Clarke's digger was a veritable beast of a machine, the like of which had never been seen in the history of mechanized transport. It was 90 feet long, weighed 140 tons and was equipped with a revolutionary pump system that propelled it relentlessly forward. At full thrust, it could advance at a rate of approximately four miles in a single night, carving a trench that was ten feet wide and eight feet deep.

Clarke was so proud of his design that he took the unusual step of writing a letter to the War Office, enclosing plans of his invention. 'I envisage a machine which would, by hydraulic means, more or less row itself through the ground. This is rendered possible by the use of the latest hydraulic pump gear.'[3]

Officials in Whitehall were astonished by Clarke's drawings, not least because they had also been trying to work out how to cut a swathe through the German defences. More than £100,000 had been earmarked for their project and a replica of the Siegfried Line had been built on Salisbury Plain. They had got so far as to build a prototype machine, but it was discovered to have a major flaw: it got stuck whenever it hit a large concrete obstacle.

Clarke had foreseen this problem. His digger was armed with a multitude of cylindrical ammonal charges powerful enough to shatter any concrete obstacles that lay in its path. The machine would then plough through the broken remnants until it had forced a passage across to the far side of the line.

Clarke's idea was so groundbreaking, in every sense, that it was taken directly to Winston Churchill, whose fondness for unconventional machinery was well known. He immediately wanted to know the identity of this maverick inventor. He then ordered the government's leading scientific adviser, Professor Lindemann, to go and meet Cecil Clarke. He also sent a personal letter to 171 Tavistock Road, Bedford, praising Clarke for his work.

Events now proceeded swiftly. After his meeting with Lindemann, Clarke was summoned to Whitehall for a more thorough interview. The notes of this interview were later filed in a box labelled 'Most Secret: to be kept under lock and key'.[4]

> Mr Clarke called to see me by appointment this morning. I formed a very good opinion of him. He is frank, direct, obviously knowledgeable, very keen to put his whole weight into the war effort . . . Mr Clarke is accustomed to secret work and has access to a special naval school [Bedford swimming pool] where certain experiments have been carried out by him.

The official who interviewed Clarke also paid a visit to Millis Jefferis, who was known to have utilized Clarke's talents for the creation of the limpet mine. Jefferis gave his assurances that Clarke was a staunch patriot, 'absolutely reliable' and in possession of a febrile imagination when it came to the design of unorthodox weaponry. He was the sort of person who could create weapons for the most elaborate sabotage operations.

Clarke was immediately offered the job of assistant director of the Naval Land Section, in charge of developing his monstrous digging machine. He accepted that same day and wrote a second letter to Churchill thanking him for his support. 'You can rely upon me to push forward this project with all possible speed.'[5]

Clarke's letter arrived in Whitehall on 10 May, a momentous day for Churchill, for the country and for Colin Gubbins's staff at MI(R). Joan Bright was seated at her desk when the 'ticker-tacker' telegram machine began spitting out an urgent message. It had been sent in such a hurry that it contained a typographic error that might have been amusing were it not so serious. 'Hotler's troops have overrun Luxembourg; Dutch and Belgian Cabinets appeal to France; Hotler proclaims fall of Belgium and Holland; Hotler says he will crush Britain.'

One of Gubbins's team read the telegram to everyone in the room and then turned to Joan and wryly remarked that if Hotler was replaced with Hitler, 'the meaning will immediately become apparent'.

The invasion of Belgium, Holland and Luxembourg was grave indeed, but it was not the only big news that day. In the early evening, Neville Chamberlain resigned as Prime Minister and Britain had a new wartime leader.

'Winston is in!' wrote Joan that night. She also made a note of Churchill's conviction that the country's future was entirely dependent 'on winning this battle, here in Britain, now, this summer'.[6] In her opinion, there was only one man who could win it, and that was Colin Gubbins.

Colin Gubbins did not arrive back in London from Norway until Monday, 10 June, a day of unremittingly bleak news. Italy had declared war on Great Britain and German panzers were thrusting westwards to Paris. Although more than 300,000 Allied troops had been plucked from the beaches of Dunkirk, an entire division of 51st Highlanders – 10,000 men from Gubbins's home turf – were trapped in the town of Saint-Valéry-en-Caux. There was no hope of rescuing them.

Gubbins had long warned the War Office that Hitler's Polish blitzkrieg tactics might be repeated against the French. He had even put his warning into writing after returning from his mission to Warsaw. But his words had been received 'with various degrees of scepticism' and even downright mockery. Whitehall officials had told him it was 'inconceivable that the German panzer tactics could succeed against such a sophisticated defence as the Maginot Line'.[7]

Now, those same officials were forced to eat their words. Hitler's panzers had swept to the north of the Maginot Line, avoiding it altogether as they thrust deep into eastern France. As the key Channel ports fell into German hands, War Office officials changed their tune about Gubbins. On Saturday, 22 June they took a decision that was unexpected, secret and immediate.

Gubbins knew nothing of what was taking place until he found himself summoned to a private meeting in Whitehall. Once there, he was left in no doubt as to its importance, for there was none of the usual preamble and small talk. 'The briefing was brisk and to the point,' he later wrote. 'I was told: "We must expect the German invasion at any time."'[8] Hitler was poised to attack by air and sea and was likely to use the same blitzkrieg tactics that had proved so successful in Poland, France and the Low Countries. Every human resource was to be thrown against the Nazi invaders as they sought to land on British beaches, but no one doubted the stark reality of the outcome: Hitler's panzer divisions would almost certainly succeed in creating a beachhead.

Those same forces also looked set to seize strategic positions right across southern England, for military intelligence suggested that extensive parachute drops would 'put areas behind the lines in German hands'.[9] It was not just possible, but probable, that large parts of Kent and Sussex would be under Nazi occupation within hours of the invasion.

During Gubbins's five-week absence in Norway, the task of planning how to sabotage any Nazi-controlled beachhead had fallen to his old Caxton Street colleague, Lawrence Grand of Section D. Grand had begun the process of hiding secret caches of explosives in areas close to the expected invasion zone. But as with everything done by Grand, there was an element of fantasy to his work. He had refused to liaise with police or local authorities, leading to a string of unfortunate incidents. One Section D agent 'in pin-striped trousers and dark coat turned up in a village and asked the bewildered postmaster, whom he had never seen before, to hold a store of explosives for him'.[10] Not surprisingly, the postmaster phoned the village constable who promptly arrested the man.

Lawrence Grand was far too mercurial to be entrusted with the nation's defences, which was why Gubbins had been summoned to Whitehall. The Chiefs of General Staff had decided to place him in charge of the defence of southern England. He was 'instructed to form an organisation to fight the Germans behind their lines'.[11] This secret guerrilla force was to operate inside the envisaged German beachhead, wreaking havoc on supply lines.

Gubbins's specific task was to cause such destruction that the Nazi advance on London would become impossible. He was told he could recruit anyone he wanted, including his comrades at MI(R), and could call upon any of the weaponry being developed by Millis Jefferis. He was also promised unlimited financial resources in this life-or-death struggle. Indeed, he was offered 'a blank cheque', although his Scottish prudence prompted him to question whether 'there was any money in the bank to meet it'.[12]

Security was paramount. Neither the Germans, nor the country at large, were to know about this clandestine army. He was 'to report directly to General Ironside' – the newly appointed Commander-in-Chief of Home Forces – 'and the Prime Minister'.

Gubbins accepted the post immediately, even though he had misgivings. 'As I left the room,' he later recalled, 'I realized it wasn't going to be a particularly easy task.'[13] Yet it was an exhilarating one. He was to be in command of his own private guerrilla army charged with defending the realm. The army was to be known as Auxiliary Units, a bland name that was suitably vague. Gubbins felt that it covered 'a multitude of possible lines of action and wouldn't create too much suspicion'.[14]

He was fired by the sense of urgency, aware that Hitler's generals were working day and night to prepare the invasion. 'At the shortest, we had six weeks before a full scale invasion could be launched.'[15] Six weeks was not long to train and equip a guerrilla army: his first decision was to poach Peter Wilkinson from MI(R). Wilkinson had shown himself to be professional, creative and quick to learn, all valuable skills in guerrilla warfare. He accepted the job with alacrity and then asked what he would be expected to do. Gubbins gave him a typically forthright response. 'Blowing up bridges, slashing car tyres and creating a pretty uncomfortable situation.' He added that they had been given carte blanche to act in whatever way they saw fit, a freelance approach to warfare that particularly appealed to Wilkinson. 'Walking across the park in London with Gubbins that afternoon,' he said, 'we started making it up, and continued making it up for two months or more.'[16]

Next to be hired by Gubbins was Bill Beyts of the Rajputana Rifles, 'a deceptively mild-mannered regular'[17] who had been one of the twenty officers serving under his command in Norway. The Kent coastline had none of the geographic features of the North-West Frontier, but Beyts was a master of guerrilla warfare and was placed in charge of training.

Gubbins's MI(R) room at the War Office was too small to accommodate his growing staff. He was therefore allotted new offices at 7 Whitehall Place, an anonymous white stone building close to Downing Street. One of his early recruits, Donald Hamilton-Hill, was struck by the clandestine nature of the organization. All the other rooms had 'not only the designation of the department, but also the names, ranks, regiments and decorations of those who inhabited them'. But Gubbins's office was completely anonymous, with 'nothing on the door, not even a number'.[18]

Gubbins intended his Auxiliary Units to be an elite force of highly trained specialists: 'very small units, locally raised, and able to melt away after action'.[19] They were to be quite different from the Home Guard, whose amateurishness had become apparent within weeks of it being established. He divided the British coast into twelve sectors, each of which was to have its own field commander. Of the twelve, Kent was by far the most important. It was widely believed that Hitler would land his invading army on the east Kent coast, where the broad beaches and low-lying grassland favoured the invader. The beachhead – and the fight for survival – was likely to be in Thanet, close to the little villages of Guston, Woodnesborough and Great Mongeham. If the invaders pushed further inland, then the critical battles would take place in the Kentish farmland between Canterbury and the coast. It was essential that the commander of this stretch of territory should be of the highest calibre.

Gubbins never had any doubts as to who that person should be. Peter Fleming belonged to that rare breed of gentleman who seemed to have it all: movie-star looks, a glamorous wife (Celia Johnson, of *Brief Encounter* fame) and a patrician grandeur that had been finely honed at Eton. 'Tall and slender, rich and urbane,' wrote one, 'he would appear on duty in well cut riding breeches and highly polished riding boots.'[20]

The older brother of Ian (of James Bond fame), he had found celebrity after hacking his way through the Amazonian jungle in search of the lost explorer, Colonel Percy Fawcett. His account of the trip, *Brazilian Adventure*, had become an immediate best-seller.

Fleming was a close friend of Joan Bright, who was so impressed with his disdain for physical comfort that she had first suggested his appointment to MI(R) almost a year earlier. 'He was a four-square, basic, solitary sort of person,' she wrote, 'immune to luxury, to heat or to cold, with a rock-like quality which made him the most staunch of friends.'[21] He had already proved his mettle in Norway, where he had served with the expeditionary force: now, he relished the idea of playing dirty in Kent.

Gubbins provided him with a detailed brief on the sort of men required for his Kentish guerrilla army: men 'who knew the areas in which they would operate as well as their own homes' and men 'who could move about from coppice to coppice, in darkness and daylight, making use of every bush and ditch'. In particular, Fleming was to hire local people 'who could appear from nowhere, hit hard and then vanish as mysteriously as they came'.[22] They were to work at night, under the blanket of darkness, and were to be armed with specialist weaponry.

Gubbins was quick to see the importance of hiring people who were intimately connected with the areas of land they were charged with defending. 'Poachers and gamekeepers, fishing and shooting ghillies, stalkers, Verderers in the New Forest, farmers and farm labourers, tin miners and coal miners, market gardeners and fisher-men.'[23] Knowledge of underground caves and abandoned cellars 'would be particularly valuable for the siting of caches and hideouts we visualized for storing arms and rations'.[24]

The defence of each of his twelve sectors was to require very different skills. To this end, Gubbins travelled around England personally recruiting suitable individuals. In Lincolnshire, he sought out Fenmen 'who knew every foot of their marshes and tricky fens'. They could strike invading paratroopers with lightning speed 'and then return to their muddy hideouts where any following soldiers would have been quickly lost, drowned or trapped in the mud'.

Next stop was Hampshire, where he recruited forest rangers, 'men who could appear and vanish in the forest as silently and swiftly as their own red deer'. And then it was off to the vitally important south coast, where he hired lobstermen and fishermen. 'From boyhood days they knew every creek and nook from which fishing boats might be able to glide silently out and lob explosives at landing enemy units.'[25]

After a hectic fortnight of recruiting, Fleming felt confident that his own strike force would be able to cause serious damage inside any German beachhead. 'The guerrillas would have a sporting chance, not merely of inflicting one suicidal pinprick, but of remaining a thorn in the enemy's flesh for weeks or perhaps even in some cases for months.'[26]

Colin Gubbins had been in his new job less than four weeks when the threatened invasion became a dramatic reality. On 16 July 1940 Adolf Hitler issued Directive No. 16, the Nazi invasion of Great Britain. Even Churchill felt that the final showdown was now just days away. 'The scene has darkened swiftly,' he wrote in a letter to President Roosevelt. 'We expect to be attacked here ourselves, both from the air and by parachute and airborne troops in the near future and we are getting ready for it.'[27]

Hitler's Operation Sealion was as grand in scale as the War Office had feared: an amphibious landing of 67,000 men, supported by an airborne division that was to be parachuted into Kent and Sussex. The aim of this first wave was to seize and fortify a beachhead before pushing outwards towards their first major operational objective, a front line stretching from the Bristol Channel to Maldon in Essex.

The plans were meticulous – far more so than for the Norwegian invasion – and covered details of the occupation itself. The former German ambassador, Joachim von Ribbentrop, was being widely touted for the job of Reichskommissar: his appointment was to be followed by a 'cleansing' operation undertaken by one of Dr Franz Six's Einsatzgruppen death squads. Some 3,000 notable people were to be arrested, including Noël Coward, Bertrand Russell and Virginia Woolf. Britain's 300,000 Jews were to be interned, with an even darker fate awaiting them.

A further plan envisaged the deportation of vast numbers of people. 'The able-bodied male population between the ages of 17 and 45 will, unless the local situation calls for an exceptional ruling, be interned and dispatched to the Continent.'[28] Britain was to be treated far more harshly than other occupied countries. Not even Poland had hitherto been subjected to such a brutal regime.

Within hours of Hitler's issuing of Directive No. 16, Gubbins summoned a meeting of his twelve newly appointed guerrilla commanders, with Peter Fleming as the first among equals. Others included the veteran Greenland explorer Andrew Croft, and Donald Hamilton-Hill, whose forebears had fought with distinction against Napoleon in Egypt.

His briefing reflected the depressing reality of the situation. 'In clear, concise terms,' said Hamilton-Hill, 'he described the situation in Britain as it then stood.' Gubbins reminded his twelve appointees that they were guerrillas, not regular soldiers, and had been selected because they had 'a non-military and independent approach to life'.[29]

Peter Fleming was to display a professionalism sorely absent in the regular army. He studied every nook and hollow of the Thanet countryside before deciding to establish his guerrilla headquarters in a half-timbered farmhouse called the Garth in Bilting, a village some fifteen miles inland from the east coast. It was likely to fall just outside the initial German beachhead, making it the ideal place for him to mastermind his operations. It also became his principal weapons' dump, with the big barn next to the house stashed 'from end to end and from floor to roof with explosives, ammunition and weapons, including half a dozen longbows'.

Fleming had good reason for acquiring the longbows. He intended to teach his men to use them 'to hurl incendiary charges into German petrol dumps'.[30] Without fuel, Hitler's tanks and jeeps would be trapped inside their beachhead.

Fleming was shrewd enough to realize that his men would need underground cells if they were to fight a sustained dirty war against the occupying Nazis. 'A guerrilla without a base,' he told them, 'is no better than a desperate straggler.'[31] He also knew that cells would need to be well stocked if the guerrillas were to continue their operations over many weeks. Each one was to be self-sufficient and stocked with food rations, chemical Elsan toilets, wireless sets and large quantities of explosives.

It was essential that they should remain undiscovered by the Germans. To this end, the men concealed the entrances and exits with gnarled, ivy-clad roots, while the ventilation funnels and water supply pipes were interwoven with branches, leaves and man-made camouflage. One of the key cells in the Kent area set the gold standard for the rest: anyone wishing to enter had to drop a marble down a mouse-hole. The marble rolled down a twelve-foot-long pipe and into a tin can, a signal to the men below ground to open the trapdoor concealed in the roots of a tree.

The planning of the cells was combined with an upper-class *savoir faire* about the finer things in life. One group of army officers was invited to a meal in one of these cells and expected to be served powdered rations in an earthen hole. But when they slipped down through the trapdoor, 'they were faced with a long dining table covered with a crisp damask cloth. The candles were in candelabra and the cutlery on the table gleamed.'[32] Even when training for ungentlemanly warfare, Gubbins's guerrillas remembered to dine as gentlemen.

While Gubbins was busy directing the Auxiliary Units, his colleagues in MI(R) found themselves caught in a whirl of energy. They embarked on what one of the staff described as 'a whole series of Scarlet Pimpernel missions', crossing the English Channel in great secrecy in order to secure limited but vital objectives. Colonel Chidson succeeded in smuggling himself into Amsterdam and 'returning to London by the skin of his teeth with many thousands of pounds of industrial diamonds'. Louis Franck made it to Brussels and returned with a stockpile of Belgian gold. Tommy Davies took himself to Calais 'and stripped Courtauld's factory in the town of several hundred thousand pounds' worth of platinum'.[33] He was almost caught red-handed.

Other members of the extended team were sent to Albania, Greece, Hungary and Egypt in order to prepare anti-Nazi patriots for guerrilla warfare. There was an overwhelming desire to ensure that the previous year's debacle with Poland – too little, too late – would not be repeated.

Millis Jefferis and his team were meanwhile working hard to

supply the Auxiliary Units with all the weaponry they needed. The persistence of Stuart Macrae had enabled MI(R)c to move out of its cramped quarters at the War Office: it was now based in the former headquarters of the International Broadcasting Company at 35 Portland Place. Here, in a veritable rabbit warren of underground rooms, he had installed lathes, workbenches and specialist engineering tools.

'I could never have achieved this impressive result by myself,' confessed Macrae. 'It became possible only because Joan Bright' – who seemed to know every general in town – 'took pity on me and dropped the right words in the right ears.' It enabled the team to speed up production of their booby traps, phosphorus bombs, Molotov cocktails, detonators, Castrators and delayed-action fuses.

They also produced a prototype anti-tank grenade that was a triumph of homespun engineering. The Sticky Bomb was invented for a specific purpose: to knock out German tanks as they thundered through the Kent countryside. It consisted of a glass flask filled with nitro-glycerine. This was then wrapped in a sleeve (to prevent it from fragmenting on impact) and coated in toffee-like glue. The glue was a unique concoction created by Mr Hartley, the chief chemist at a Stockport-based chemical manufacturer called Kay Brothers.

The Sticky Bomb was thrown by means of a glue-free handle. On hitting the target, the glass shattered inside the sleeve and fused the nitro-glycerine to the tank. It then exploded, creating a deadly inward blast that flung high-velocity shrapnel into the interior of the tank.

A prototype of the bomb mistakenly found its way to the Ordnance Board, whose officers expressed revulsion that such a dirty weapon could have been conceived by a civilized human being. They told Macrae that it 'broke all the rules of the game and just could not be permitted'.

Churchill thought otherwise. After weeks of frustrating hold-ups in production, he wrote a blunt note to Jefferis. It was scribbled in his own hand 'on 10 Downing Street notepaper' and its message was perfunctory: 'Sticky Bomb. Make one million. WSC.'

Within hours of getting the green light, Jefferis's freelance contractors set to work. The flasks were made by a specialist glass-blowing company run by a certain Hugo Woods of Leeds, while the glue was supplied by Kay Brothers, who were also tasked with assembling the grenades. But the order was so huge that Macrae found it necessary to call upon the help of other craftsmen and small businesses. 'Our contractors' service was operating so well that it was no trouble at all to arrange this production work,' he said. 'One firm made the handles, another the metal covers, another the glass flasks, and another the wool socks.' Once this was done, the Sticky Bombs were transported to ICI's outpost factory at Ardeer on the west coast of Scotland, where they were filled with explosive.

Gubbins's guerrillas were trained to use the Sticky Bomb and found that it exceeded all expectations. It was better than any defensive weapon available to the regular army. The Americans would later put the bomb through a series of stringent tests before accepting it for their army. There was to be just one change. The name – Sticky Bomb – was deemed too homespun. Henceforth, it was to be known as MKII No. 74 Grenade. Stuart Macrae was delighted with the outcome. Years later, he would write that 'although the W-Bomb started us off . . . it was the Sticky Bomb that first brought us fame'.[34] It was a fame restricted to a tiny clutch of people, but it included the Prime Minister and his chiefs of staff.

Winston Churchill constantly expressed concern that the Auxiliary Units didn't have enough weapons. 'These men must have revolvers!'[35] he scribbled in the margin of one memo. They got them soon afterwards, along with American .32 Colt automatics acquired from the New York Police Department. Each underground cell was also equipped with at least one tommy sub-machine gun.

Colin Gubbins's office-based work came to an end shortly after five o'clock each Friday afternoon when he and Peter Wilkinson clambered into their Humber and drove down to Kent. Here, they spent the weekend helping to train Peter Fleming's guerrilla unit. The work was exhausting and physically demanding. 'Into this short time,' wrote Gubbins, 'we had to cram rifle and revolver [training], hand grenades, Molotov and sticky bombs, mock ambushes and raids, night work, penetration of defences including barbed wire, hide out construction.'

Colonel 'Billy' Beyts of the Rajputana Rifles led these weekend sessions. His speciality, perfected on the North West Frontier, was the art of silent killing. He had learned how to move through the darkness without making any noise; now, he stressed upon Gubbins's men the importance of moving with stealth rather than speed. 'If you have eight hours of darkness, then use four to reach your objective and four to get away again. Don't hurry and be killed.'[36]

As the guerrilla army grew in strength, Gubbins needed a larger base that could serve as a professional training centre, preferably somewhere in remote countryside. He procured the services of a Home Guard captain, the Honourable Michael Henderson, and sent him on a tour of suitable properties.

Henderson knew just the place. Coleshill was a Wiltshire country estate whose sprawling grounds lay adjacent to those owned by his brother. The house itself was a large Palladian manor designed by Inigo Jones. It was the home of Miss Molly Pleydell-Bouverie and her elderly sister (members of the Earl of Radnor's extended family), who were somewhat surprised to be told that their home had been commandeered by the War Office. The two ladies were permitted to remain in the house, even though it was to be overrun by guerrillas. They soon regretted their decision to stay, for their beloved dogs were so petrified by the constant explosions that they had to be put on a diet of aspirin and brandy.

Coleshill's private parkland with its unploughed fields and fast-flowing streams made it the ideal training camp for Gubbins's private army. The coursework taught the men how to kill, with special emphasis on the most vulnerable points of the body. It was not for the faint-hearted. 'Mouth-slitting, ear-trapping to break ear drums, eye-gouging, the grallock (or disembowelling), rib-lifting, "lifting the gates" – temporary dislocation of the jaw – ear-tearing, nose chopping, shin-scraping with the edge of a boot, shoulder jerking.' The hands-on training included practising killing 'on a stuffed dummy mounted on a doorway with elastic bands'. The men were told that once the victim had been disembowelled, he was to be castrated.

Castration was to be an important element in Gubbins's game of psychological warfare against captured Nazis. His men were 'to cut off their "knackers" to demoralise the rest'.[37] If all went to plan, Kent's trees were to be festooned with German testicles.

Security at Coleshill House was tight and all new recruits reported for duty at the country post office in the nearby village of Highworth. Here, they were given instructions by the white-haired postmistress, Mabel Stranks, who would demand to see their identity papers, ask for a predetermined password and then disappear while she made a phone call. 'Somebody's coming to fetch you,'[38] she would tell them if everything was in order. Soon after, a civilian car would sweep up outside and take the new recruits through the parkland to the mansion itself. Mabel Stranks prided herself on security. On one notable occasion, she kept General Montgomery waiting in his car while she undertook a thorough identity check on him.

By late summer, Gubbins had established the rudiments of the first guerrilla army in British history. The 3,000 recruits being trained at Coleshill were a quixotic mix of men, most of whom had been hired because they had a particular skill. Not all were gentlemen: the War Office referred to them as 'scallywags' and many were indeed men of dubious repute. A criminal past was no hindrance; in fact it often provided a fast track to employment. Peter Wilkinson cast his eye over one batch of new arrivals and couldn't help but smile at the social mix in the dormitories, with 'peers of the realm owning broad acres kipped down happily with poachers and convicted burglars, the latter criminals recruited for the dexterity in handling explosives or in picking locks'.[39]

Gubbins faced frequent complaints from the regular army, whose commanding officers abhorred the very idea of guerrilla warfare. Their fears were rarely allayed by the behaviour of Gubbins's more exuberant leaders. One of them, John Gwyn, decided to test the defences of General Montgomery's headquarters, which the general had declared to be impregnable. He was soon proved wrong. Gwyn crept through the perimeter fence and buried a number of Jefferis's explosive charges in the lawn, with the fuses set to detonate just as Montgomery was giving his morning lecture. The resulting explosion was the Full Monty, with Peter Wilkinson there to witness the fall-out. Montgomery 'was never one to forgive these sorts of pranks,' he said, 'and he never reconciled himself with irregular operations for the rest of the war.'[40]

Winston Churchill kept a close eye on Gubbins's work and praised him for organizing the Auxiliary Units 'with thoroughness and imagination'. He also expressed his hope that the guerrillas would fight to the death inside the German beachhead and 'perish in the common ruin rather than to fail or falter in their duty'.[41]

But that fight to the death was unexpectedly put on hold. Hitler's invasion had always been predicated on two factors: air supremacy and naval superiority. As the summer wore on, it became apparent that Germany had neither. Luftwaffe pilots had failed to wipe out the Royal Air Force and the Kriegsmarine was hindered by the loss of ten destroyers in the invasion of Norway. The Kriegsmarine commander, Erich Raeder, insisted that German naval strength was insufficient for an invasion to be undertaken that summer. 'A German invasion of England would be a matter of life and death for the British,' he warned, adding that it was certain to be 'an all-out fight for survival'.[42]

On 17 September a reluctant Hitler ordered the indefinite postponement of the invasion, having been convinced by his senior generals that it was not viable in the foreseeable future. Although Gubbins's guerrilla units had not been put to the test, they had been 'a triumph of improvisation'. Gubbins had said from the outset that 'their usefulness would have been short-lived, at the longest until their stocks were exhausted, at the shortest when they were caught or wiped out.' But this was their *raison d'être*. 'They were designed, trained and prepared for a particular and imminent crisis: that was their specialist role.'[43]

They had also given Gubbins a taste of things to come. He knew that it was now only a matter of time before full-scale guerrilla operations would commence against the enemy. By the autumn of 1940, his work with the Auxiliary Units was at an end. But his association with Winston Churchill was only just beginning.

6

The Enemy Within

MILLIS JEFFERIS INCREASINGLY came to resemble one of his own weapons in the summer of 1940, or that's how it appeared to Stuart Macrae. Just as butchers develop sausage-shaped fingers and wine merchants get port-stained cheeks, so Jefferis had acquired a short fuse and an explosive temper. Too much pressure and he was in danger of detonating.

Macrae was increasingly concerned by the way in which his boss was rubbing people up the wrong way. Jefferis's cavalier approach to the rule book was not passing unnoticed in Whitehall. Macrae repeatedly warned him that the Ministry of Supply 'resented our not coming under their jurisdiction' and that Leslie Burgin was furious at their illicit trade in weaponry. A showdown was not just likely, but inevitable. Amazingly, Jefferis didn't care one jot.

The troubles began with a telephone conversation. A certain Brigadier Wyndham called the Portland Place workshop to express his disapproval about the uncivilized weapons they were producing. Macrae retorted that no one else was in a position to design sabotage weapons. Nor, for that matter, could anyone else have supplied Gubbins's Auxiliary Units with such a supply of explosives. He said that 'the vitally important work we were doing at 35 Portland Place could not readily be taken over by anyone else'. If it had been left to Leslie Burgin to equip Gubbins's men, he would still be doing the paperwork.

Wyndham was unmoved. 'With a slight snort, the brigadier announced his intention of paying a state visit to our establishment to see for himself if there was any truth in my suggestion.'

Macrae was the first to realize that 'the situation was serious'.[1] Brigadier Wyndham was a senior figure in military intelligence and had a wealth of connections. The Ministry of Supply, the Director of Military Administration and the Armaments Design Department were all backing his move to hurl a bureaucratic sticky bomb into the workings of Portland Place.

Jefferis rarely concerned himself with office matters, for experience had taught him that such things were best left to Macrae. But on this occasion, his anger got the better of him. The stress of a fourteen-hour day coupled with a production line close to breaking point led to an unprecedented outburst. 'I refuse to waste my time trying to argue or excuse myself with any of these bodies,' he fumed. 'My contention is that I have a better brain for the purposes of producing warlike weapons.' He lambasted Burgin's halfwits at the Ministry of Supply, who were absolutely devoid of creative talent. 'What it boils down to is that if I am left alone, I might produce something.'[2]

And produce something he did. At the very moment of Brigadier Wyndham's Portland Place inspection, Jefferis plucked a rabbit from his magician's hat. It was a rabbit with very sharp teeth.

His conjuring trick had only been possible because of a surprise encounter that took place some weeks earlier. A self-styled Irish inventor named Stewart Blacker had pitched up at Portland Place with a strange-shaped package and an even stranger story. He introduced himself to Jefferis as the country's only freelance inventor of experimental weapons, one who had begun work at an early age, drawing inspiration from the revolutionary mortars used in the Sino-Japanese War. 'Procuring some black powder, a stock of cigarette papers and a croquet ball as a projectile, he built his first mortar,' while still a schoolboy in the Lower Fifth. It proved a triumph. 'He carried out a spectacular bombardment of the headmaster's greenhouse at a range of 300 yards!'[3]

Blacker conformed to all the stereotypes of a madcap inventor. He kept a monocle clamped to his right eye and had a bulging, size eighteen neck on account of breaking his vertebrae when shot from his plane by a German fighter ace during the Great War. He shared many things in common with Jefferis: he had served on the North-West Frontier, spoke Pashto with the same degree of fluency and had a 'pathological hatred of officialdom'. He particularly despised civil servants, referring to them as the 'abominable no-men of Whitehall'.[4] There was good reason for his antipathy. When he had presented his new wonder weapon to the War Office, they had politely shown him the door.

For two years, Blacker had persisted in petitioning to get his weapon adopted; for two years, the War Office had shown no interest. 'In Millis's eyes,' said Macrae, 'this was certain proof that it must be a good idea.' Jefferis's opinion of the War Office remained unchanged: 'he had never known them to be right yet.'[5]

Jefferis watched with interest as Blacker proceeded to unwrap a bizarre, tubelike barrel that he called his Bombard. He had co-built it with the local clockmaker in Petworth, the village in which he lived, and described it as an anti-tank gun. Jefferis immediately recognized it as a work of consummate creativity. Instead of firing a shell from a gun barrel, the barrel itself was fired at the tank, with the explosive charge at the front and stabilizing tail fins at the rear. It was like a primitive missile.

There were problems with the Bombard, just as there were problems with Blacker himself. 'He had no mathematics,' said Jefferis bluntly, a failing he took very seriously indeed.[6] Yet Blacker's home-spun weapon – a spigot mortar – was a masterpiece of explosive malice and Jefferis devoted many weeks to correcting its deficiencies. By late summer, he had perfected it to such an extent that it could blow a hole in any advancing German tank.

With Blacker's agreement, he now took it back to the Ordnance Board in order to show them how wrong they'd been in rejecting it. His words fell on deaf ears. 'If God Almighty had sponsored the spigot mortar,' he was told, 'I tell you it would still be turned down by the Ordnance Board.'[7]

When this news reached Professor Lindemann, he called for a demonstration at Chequers, the Prime Minister's country residence. Macrae thought this a high-risk strategy. 'We were still in the experimental stage with this weapon,' he said, 'and the workshops at 35 Portland Place had to work 24 hour shifts before we got everything sorted out and could take to Chequers a weapon which we felt might work without blowing up and injuring the PM and his retinue.'

When Jefferis's team arrived at Chequers, they were alarmed to see that Churchill had invited along General de Gaulle and General Smuts. No one seemed terribly impressed with the weapon, with its stubby tube and splayed metal legs. Even Macrae thought it 'looked nothing at all like a gun, but rather like something thought up by Heath Robinson'. Yet that tubelike exterior concealed a conical-shaped missile with a massive explosive charge.

Jefferis chose the two most competent members of his team to fire the weapon. Ralph Farrant was a gunner with a rare genius for hitting distant targets, while Norman Angier had played a key role in constructing the mortar. There was a great deal at stake. Although the Sticky Bomb had already been issued to the Auxiliary Units, the country stood in urgent need of more powerful anti-tank weapons.

Farrant elected to fire the mortar at one of the trees in the garden of Chequers, selecting one that, to Macrae's eyes, 'seemed an awful way off'. Norman Angier was in the process of adjusting the alignment of the weapon when disaster struck. It accidentally fired. There was a piercing screech as the explosive charge spun through the air, almost whipping off the heads of the attending dignitaries.

'The missile very nearly wiped out General de Gaulle,' said an alarmed Macrae. He knew of Churchill's antipathy towards the leader of the Free French and added that 'unkind people afterwards suggested that the Prime Minister had in some way bribed Norman to have a go at this.' Miraculously, having narrowly missed de Gaulle, the missile struck the tree right on target, shattering its branches and incinerating it. 'A roaring success,'[8] was the conclusion of everyone in attendance.

Churchill was deeply impressed that Jefferis had produced yet another winner. He turned to him and said, somewhat formally, 'as Prime Minister, I instruct you to proceed with all speed with the development of this excellent weapon.' He offered an initial sum of £5,000, and promised a great deal more once 'proper financial arrangements' had been made.

When he learned of the problems being caused by the Ministry of Supply, he took an important decision. Alongside his many official titles and duties, Churchill had named himself Minister of Defence, even though there was no Ministry of Defence. Now, he decided to turn Jefferis's team into a Ministry of Defence department to be known as MD1. 'In order to secure quick action,' he wrote, 'free from departmental processes, upon any bright idea or gadget, I decided to keep under my own hand, as Minister of Defence, the experimental establishment formed by Major Jefferis.'

Professor Lindemann was to be the go-between between Jefferis and Churchill, while the Prime Minister's personal military adviser, General 'Pug' Ismay, was to shield Jefferis from any further interference. MD1 was to be answerable solely to Churchill. 'I used their brains,' he later wrote, 'and my power.'[9]

Macrae was delighted by the outcome and soon received even better news. The Prime Minister told the Ministry of Supply 'that they must give us everything we wanted and look after our well-being, without having any say at all in what we did'. Brigadier Wyndham had been silenced for ever. He 'retired hurt'[10] and was never heard from again.

Millis Jefferis faced other troubles in that long summer of 1940, ones rather closer to home. Ruth Jefferis's enthusiasm for caravans never quite matched that of her husband and it took a decisive knock when her portable stove spectacularly malfunctioned and she came home to find 'everything covered with a thick film of black soot'. Stuart Macrae's wife, Mary, was also tiring of life in a caravan and so the two wives hatched a plot to settle into a more routine existence, taking themselves house hunting in north London. They soon found a comfortable little place for rent in Mill Hill, one that was affordable, cosy and relatively safe from the Luftwaffe.

The new surroundings made the routines of life easier for the two couples, but did little to calm the simmering discontent between the respective husbands and wives. Macrae was the first to admit that 'the ladies had a poor time', but even he underestimated the resentment caused by them coming home at midnight each night reeking of whisky.

Jefferis's approach to marital discord was the same as his approach to the Nazis: it was to be confronted with every heavy weapon available. When Ruth and Mary complained about never receiving any flowers, Jefferis launched a floral blitzkrieg. He and Macrae drove to a flower shop in Hendon Central and bought the ladies a bouquet they would never forget. 'We want to buy the contents of the shop, please,' said Jefferis to the astonished florist as he pulled out his chequebook, 'and will you have them delivered to this address.' At first the lady thought he was joking – it was wartime, after all – but Jefferis was most insistent. 'When we got home that night, we had great difficulty getting into the little house,' said Macrae. 'There were flowers, flowers everywhere, including a palm tree in the lavatory, which made it impossible to sit down.' Jefferis's solution seemed to work, for both Ruth and Mary were completely silenced. 'Flowers,' said Macrae, 'were never mentioned again.'[11]

Problems came in twos and threes as summer drifted into autumn in that first full year of war. First, the MD1 storehouse at Hendon was burned to the ground by German incendiary bombs, destroying Jefferis's entire stockpile of sabotage weaponry. Next, the main office at Portland Place received a direct hit and was 'put completely out of action'. It was a miracle that no one was hurt. Jefferis himself seemed to relish the bombing raids, viewing them as only marginally more inconvenient than an unexpected rain shower. 'Nothing pleased him more than to strut down the middle of some London street when alarming whistling noises and bangs were going on all around.'

Professor Lindemann had promised to be a 'very powerful string-puller' and so he proved to be. Jefferis's team was assigned a civil servant named Mr Rose, who arrived at the bombed-out offices with a blank requisition warrant. He told Macrae he was permitted to acquire any building that might be of use to the new MD1.

Macrae took Mr Rose off to Buckinghamshire in order to search for a safe house in the countryside that could become their new headquarters. He soon found the perfect place. The Firs was a half-timbered, mock-Elizabethan manor that stood in secluded grounds on the outskirts of Whitchurch village. It was the country residence of a gentleman squire by the name of Sir Arthur Abrahams, who spent his leisure hours touring the Buckinghamshire countryside in his magnificent Rolls-Royce. The Firs had brick outbuildings, extensive stabling and several little cottages in the grounds. Macrae noted that the secluded garden at the rear would be perfect for experimental demolition work.

Sir Arthur had only recently put the mansion on the market and was delighted to learn that he had viewers from London. 'The impeccable butler who had first shown us round the place had been under the impression that we were potential purchasers,' said Macrae. It was therefore 'a bit of a shock to him when Mr Rose whipped out his requisitioning form and informed him that the place was ours'.[12] Macrae added that Sir Arthur was 'not very happy'[13] – something of an understatement, as it transpired – but there was nothing he could do. It was wartime and everyone had a role to play in defeating the Nazis.

The Firs now became the country headquarters of Jefferis's team and Macrae was put in charge of giving the place a make-over, a task made easier by the fact that Churchill proved extremely generous with funds. Macrae found himself custodian of 'a bottomless bank account' and this enabled him to hire many more staff – not just inventors and engineers, but also carpenters, builders and roofers, who were tasked with converting outbuildings into lodgings. Macrae already had his eye on turning the place into a major weapons-building establishment and was privately delighted to learn that Jefferis fully supported this idea, telling him that 'it was vital for The Firs quickly to be converted into a sizeable research organization so that he could run a number of projects at once.'

Local villagers began to wonder what on earth was going on in Sir Arthur's old house. Lorries arrived from London with heavy machinery, lathes and workbenches. The house was converted into offices, the lawn resembled a firing range and two vast swimming pools were rumoured to be under construction, an unusual luxury in wartime. And then one day the villagers awoke to discover that the house had sprouted antennae, pipes and wires. 'The electricity people supplied a whacking great transformer to give us power,' wrote Macrae, 'and the telephone people ran in new lines.'

Whenever anyone made enquiries as to the new owners of the Firs, they were met by a wall of silence. In common with the government code-breaking centre at Bletchley Park, just twelve miles to the north-east, the Firs was surrounded by a cordon of secrecy.

With MD1's move to the countryside, Jefferis's enemies finally conceded defeat, although they continued to smart over their wounds.

Macrae overheard a number of them referring disparagingly to the Firs as 'Winston Churchill's Toyshop'. He had a quick rejoinder for anyone who cared to listen. 'The toys we produced,' he said, 'were rather dangerous ones.'[14]

Colin Gubbins returned to London from Coleshill House to discover that he had just missed the best job in town. On the very day that Hitler had announced his intention of invading Great Britain, Winston Churchill had called one of his midnight meetings at Downing Street. On this occasion there was only one person invited and only one item on the agenda. Hugh Dalton, the Minister for Economic Warfare, was being placed in overall charge of guerrilla warfare.

Churchill was characteristically blunt when speaking with Dalton, informing him that there was no hope of conventional military action against the Nazis for the foreseeable future. Hitler's war machine had kicked its iron boot through the Low Countries and France and was now so powerful, in terms of both men and weapons, that Britain's Dunkirk-shattered forces could not hope to compete. Sabotage and subversion represented the only possible way of striking back and Churchill instructed Dalton to establish – as he called it – a Ministry of Ungentlemanly Warfare.

If its name was amusing, its role was anything but. It was to subvert the conventions of war – punch below the belt – and it was to work in tandem with Jefferis's team at the Firs. Any German target, however soft, was to be considered fair game, and no weapon was to be considered off limits. 'This form of activity was of the very highest importance,' said Churchill.

The Ministry of Ungentlemanly Warfare was to be 'a special organisation',[15] as well as a clandestine one. The remnants of MI(R) and Section D were to be amalgamated into this new body whose purpose 'was to coordinate all action by way of subversion and sabotage against the enemy overseas'. Its official name was the Special Operations Executive, but that was to remain secret and was never to be used, not even on internal memos. In Whitehall it was to be known by its cover name, the Inter-Services Research Bureau. To its employees it would be known simply as Baker Street, after the location of its headquarters.

Churchill stressed that knowledge of its work was to be kept 'within a very restricted circle'. Even members of the Cabinet were not to be informed of its day-to-day activities, partly because most of them disapproved of the envisaged ungentlemanly antics. One minister quipped to the Foreign Secretary, Lord Halifax: 'You should never be consulted because you would never consent to anything. You will never make a gangster.'[16]

Hugh Dalton was a strange choice to be the ministerial head of an organization in which personal loyalty was to count for so much. His nickname was Dr Dynamo, a moniker that suggested unceasing energy and dependability. Yet his benign façade masked an altogether more devious interior. His staff thought him an abrasive bully with a penetrating voice and weird eyes that, as one of them put it, 'used to roll around in a rather terrifying way'.[17]

'The biggest bloodiest shit I've ever met,' was how one ministerial rival described him. Churchill agreed. 'Keep that man away from me,' he once said. 'I can't stand his booming voice and shifty eyes.'[18] But the Prime Minister and Dalton shared one thing in common: both believed that the Nazis would only be defeated by playing an even dirtier game of war than them. Dalton accepted the job with alacrity, privately exhilarated by the thought that he now had a 'black life' so secret that not even his family knew what he was doing.

As he turned to leave the Prime Minister's study, Churchill issued him with one final, famous instruction: 'And now set Europe ablaze.'[19] Those who knew Dalton's lack of personal skills said that he was more likely to set Whitehall ablaze.

Colin Gubbins was the most obvious candidate to direct the operational wing of the new organization. But Gubbins was preoccupied with the Auxiliary Units in the summer of 1940. Dalton turned instead to Frank Nelson, a former Conservative backbencher who had resigned from Parliament some years earlier in order to devote his working life to pneumatic tube delivery systems. These were used by department stores for transporting money from cash registry to accounting office.

It was not an exciting job, but then Nelson was not an exciting person. A fastidious workaholic with a gaunt forehead and lavishly oiled hair, he struck Joan Bright (who met him that summer) as 'an austere and somewhat remote figure'[20] who lacked Gubbins's panache, vision and bonhomie. Even his friends admitted that he was 'a man of grim but unshakeable determination'.[21] One of his early recruits to Baker Street was alarmed to learn that he had moved into a government service flat so as to be closer to his office. 'He seemed to have no family life and was in the office seven days a week from about a quarter to nine until very nearly midnight.'[22]

What few knew about Nelson was that he had been living a secret double life. Alongside his business interests, he had been working as an intelligence agent in Basel, an important listening post in the late 1930s. It was this intelligence work – and not his interest in pneumatic tube delivery systems – that had led to his employment by Hugh Dalton.

That summer, Dalton hired scores of men he knew through personal contacts: bankers, accountants and international lawyers. 'Before long,' said one recruit, 'we were employing one or more representatives of most of the merchant banking houses in the City.' Dalton also hired most of the partners working for the legal firm Slaughter and May. As summer drifted into autumn and the tally of attempted guerrilla operations remained stubbornly at zero, one office wag joshed that 'we seemed to be all "may" and no "slaughter".'[23]

Dalton's appointments puzzled many, yet they were not without logic. He believed that resistance to the Nazis would come from civilians not soldiers. If so, his high-flying team would be well placed to foster that resistance. But after a year working for Gubbins's inner circle, Joan Bright felt that Dalton was living in fantasyland. 'In these early days, most people in Occupied Europe were still stunned by defeat and, except for a few ardent patriots, asked for nothing except to be left in peace.'[24] If there were to be resistance to the Nazis, it would have to be spearheaded by British-trained guerrillas.

Dalton realized his mistake within two months of starting his new job and immediately turned to Gubbins, newly returned from Kent, offering him the post of Baker Street's Director of Operations and Training.

Gubbins might have been expected to jump at such a job, but he hesitated as he eyed up the well-heeled bankers employed by

Dalton. They were hardly the sorts of people he would have recruited for a dirty war against the Nazis. His hesitation led to the offer of sweeteners. He was to be promoted to brigadier and given a salary considerably higher than his contemporaries in the regular army. He was also allowed to rehire everyone who had worked for him in Caxton Street. These sweeteners may have enticed him, but he eventually accepted because of his unswerving belief that 'guerrilla warfare on the mainland of Europe might prove decisive in what might otherwise be a single-handed struggle against Hitler.'[25]

The office to which he arrived for work on Monday, 18 November was very different to the grimy MI(R) rooms at the War Office. Number 64 Baker Street was a gigantic stack of a building that sprawled over six floors. He was accompanied by Peter Wilkinson, who had served him so well in the Auxiliary Units. The two men found the atmosphere decidedly frosty when they were introduced to Dalton's bankers. Wilkinson immediately realized why: the two of them had come to work in military uniforms, whereas everyone else in the office was wearing open-necked shirts. The unsmiling faces said it all: they viewed Gubbins's arrival 'with considerable suspicion', said Wilkinson, and feared that 'it heralded a military take-over'.[26]

Gubbins had been expecting to be housed in the main building, but he was told this was not possible. His fledgling department, codenamed SO2, was to be relegated to two dingy flats in Berkeley Court, opposite Baker Street Tube station. Neither he nor Wilkinson was impressed when they were escorted to this backstreet building. The office was in 'one of the rather glum warrens of Edwardian flats which cluster around the northern end of Baker Street'.[27] Even the furniture looked like cast-offs. To Wilkinson's discerning eye, the rooms looked as if they'd been fitted with 'pretty nasty furniture from the cheaper end of the Tottenham Court Road'. Far worse, from his point of view, was the fact that Berkeley Court was situated on the outer fringes of the civilized world. 'Too far to go and lunch at one's club,' he noted sadly.[28]

Gubbins relished the position of the underdog: it was precisely what guerrilla warfare was all about. When he learned that Dalton had already hired several members of his former team from MI(R), he had them immediately transferred on to his own roster. They included his Polish expert, H.B. 'Perks' Perkins, the 'larger than life'[29] colonel who had proved so gifted at organizing post-work parties. Perks had developed a new party trick over the long summer months: 'The only man I had ever actually seen bend a poker in his hands,' remarked one of his astonished colleagues.[30]

Gubbins also retained the services of Colonel Chidson, the terrifying recruitment officer who had originally warned Joan about the Nazis sticking pins in her toes. The intervening months had done little to soften his interviewing technique. When a young banker named Bickham Sweet-Escott arrived for an interview, Chidson set out 'with steely precision the blood-curdling aims of the organisation'. He also warned of the need for secrecy. 'For security reasons, I can't tell you what sort of a job it would be. All I can say is that if you join us, you mustn't be afraid of forgery and you mustn't be afraid of murder.'[31] Sweet-Escott was taken aback. He thought he was going for a regular day job at the War Office.

Once new recruits had signed on Chidson's dotted line, there was no turning back. They were given codenames, fake identities and fictitious jobs, for everyone 'who worked here had cover stories to fit the work they were doing'.[32]

Gubbins's first task was to find a secretary to replace the redoubtable Joan Bright, whose services had been retained by the War Office. He was sorry to part company with her, for she had done sterling work. He vowed to remain in touch and proved true to his word. He continued to see her several times a week and she was one of the few people with whom he trusted the secrets of his work.

Joan's replacement was Margaret Jackson, a bewitchingly glamorous thirty-three-year-old who had first worked alongside Gubbins in Paris. She had fled her post in the wake of the Nazi invasion, making a dash to the coast alongside 'cars with mattresses on their roofs and machine-gunned windscreens'. Gubbins had immediately rehired her to work at Coleshill House, where her cool pragmatism left him deeply impressed. In a crisp assessment of her qualities, he noted that she had 'a strong sense of responsibility, plenty of initiative and competent'.[33] Margaret was Scottish, like him. She was also a first-class organizer who spoke both French and Spanish and prided herself on her loyalty. On occasions she could be frivolous: she later confessed that she had focused her life on four objectives: 'ambition, being admired, captivating people and doing my best to attract glamorous young men'.[34] One of those young men, Leo Marks, told Gubbins that Margaret 'had everything we sought for in a woman except availability'.[35]

Margaret was the first to admit that she was fascinated by her boss. Indeed, she found it hard to take her eyes off him as he paced restlessly around the office in a trail of pale blue cigarette smoke. 'He was always quick in all his movements and he had this quality of dynamism.'[36] Everyone worked hard in Berkeley Court, but Gubbins seemed to be on triple-speed. He was, she said, 'like an electric current'.

His fastidious attention to detail could be tiresome, especially at the end of a long working day. He insisted that she fold the office maps in the correct fashion, with 'the annexes neatly flagged', and he dictated his memos in precise staccato (telling her where to place each comma and colon). It was some months before it dawned on Margaret that Gubbins's precision was not gratuitous. It was the very essence of guerrilla warfare.

Just occasionally she would find the pressures of work too much. In these moments, he would encourage her to have a tea break. '*Festina lente*,' he would say. 'Hasten slowly.' It was an expression he had learned during his childhood in the Scottish Highlands when out stalking deer. 'Pursuits,' mused Margaret, 'in which it is necessary to pause and think of the quarry's next move.'[37]

Security was a prime concern, even in these early days. Gubbins constantly reminded Margaret that they would soon be sending saboteurs into Nazi-occupied territories. These would be dangerous undercover missions with no room for mistakes. 'Symbols and code-names were always used [and] telephone numbers and extensions memorised,' she said. 'Ours was an operational service headquarters where security was crucial.'

Some rules were never broken. The office had to be cleared of paperwork each evening and documents locked into the steel safe. Margaret even had to empty the wastepaper baskets, a tiresome task. Once she had gathered all the disposed papers, 'the contents were shredded so that there was nothing left by the time the cleaners came round.'[38]

The last job before heading home was to remove blotting paper from the various blotters, lest the imprint on their surfaces betray the identity and whereabouts of an undercover agent.

Colin Gubbins took two key decisions at an early date. The first was to divide the entire Baker Street organization into country sections, with each occupied territory having its own department and staff. Every department was to be entirely independent, to the point of having its own training schools for sabotage, explosives and endurance. The security was not gratuitous. It was vital that a saboteur being sent into Norway should know nothing about the work of a fellow saboteur being sent to Greece or the Balkans, lest he be induced to reveal details of their mission under torture.

The second decision was taken by Gubbins alone. He decided to employ women – lots of them – and not just as secretaries. They were to be given key positions of responsibility. Margaret had been the first to note that Gubbins 'didn't have any discrimination against women', yet even she was only dimly aware of the growing number of young ladies working in Baker Street until one day she looked up from her desk and realized that she was surrounded by dozens of female faces.

The most important of the administrative jobs was that of country registrar. The registrars controlled all the secret files, including what Margaret called 'the nerve centre' of the country sections. This 'centre' contained highly sensitive information about all the saboteurs, along with plans of factories and installations targeted for destruction. As such, it contained many of the secrets of Baker Street.

Gubbins insisted that the registrars were women, for he found them more trustworthy than men. He also insisted on a strictly hierarchical structure, with a formidable operator on the registrars' throne. 'Lesley Wauchope was queen of the registry,' said Margaret. One of Joan Bright's closest friends, she was proud, sharp and blessed with 'the face of an untroubled Madonna'. She certainly knew how to knock men into shape. Margaret said she had 'a wicked wit' and was 'no respecter of others' pretensions'.

Equally formidable was Joan Armstrong, the owner of an interior decorating business, whom Gubbins had promoted to head of the Scandinavian Section. It was not just the men who admired her model-like allure. 'Very attractive,'[39] confessed Margaret as she watched young Joan filing the paperwork of her Scandinavian empire.

Entering this brave new world, where women were on equal terms to the men, was a bewildering experience for gentlemen of the old school. Even the younger chaps found themselves thrown into turmoil. One uniformed recruit, Jack Robertson, confessed to being totally intimidated when introduced to one of Gubbins's senior managers named Annabel, a feisty young sophisticate. She looked him up and down and admonished him in a fashion he hadn't experienced since prep school. 'Larks, young man!' she said, 'what on earth induced you to come here in uniform? Can't have chaps like you mucking around here in uniform.'

Robertson confessed that 'she frightened the life out of me', but he soon discovered that Baker Street contained scores of Annabels, 'refined, chatty, intelligent gentlewomen' of impeccable pedigree, who hailed from large mansions in the Home Counties. 'They all had names like Claudia and Bettina and Georgina, they all called their bosses by their Christian names, and were crisply efficient and nineteen-twentyish, enervated by turns.'[40]

Gubbins also hired the services of the all-female First Aid Nursing Yeomanry, employing its members as drivers, telegraph operators and signals experts. One of those who worked for him, Sue Ryder, got to know Gubbins well: she said his conviction that 'women were better at doing this work than men' won him few friends in the Whitehall establishment. He was 'highly disliked by people in the War Cabinet and Foreign Office. They couldn't stick his guts.'[41]

As the dreadful year of 1940 drew to a close, Gubbins encouraged everyone to attend what was to become his annual New Year's Eve party. It was an all-ranks dance for both sexes – a time to party, drink too much and snatch a moment of romance.

Gubbins wore his kilt 'and led the Scottish dancing until the small hours of the morning'. The frisky young Annabels and Georginas were presided over by the imperious Mrs Phyllis Bingham, who behaved like a Victorian chaperone-cum-governess. Under her chill gaze, the girls remained on their best behaviour. 'It was,' said Joan Bright, 'as decorous as an end of term party at a girls' school.' But Joan also knew that end-of-term parties do not necessarily come to an end when the headmistress retires to bed.

Gubbins enjoyed himself to the full, leading the party-goers through late-night jigs and Highland reels, caring little for the conventions that 'senior officers were not expected to enjoy all-rank dances'. He was 'an exception', said Joan, adding that 'in staff relations, as in much else, he was ahead of his time.'[42]

Gubbins had started his new job with very little: two gloomy rooms and a handful of staff. Within weeks he had hired so many people that he 'annexed another flat'.[43] Within months, he had moved his team into Norgeby House on Baker Street, a grand modern office block. 'Every time we visited the place,' said one, 'partitions seemed to be going up or coming down.'[44]

A makeshift Operations Room was established on the first floor, 'absolutely sealed off from everybody'. As the first major missions entered the final planning stage, the tight security was made tighter still. Even Margaret found that she was 'only ever told what you needed to know'. She was under strict instructions not to chatter with her female friends, an instruction she took with a weak smile. 'It was unthinkable to visit people in offices. There wasn't time.'[45]

Gubbins knew that he needed to strike – and strike soon – if he was to stifle the criticism being levelled at him by many in Whitehall. 'Constant pressure was put upon us to show results,' said one of those working alongside him.[46] But Gubbins also felt that events were at long last being propelled forward. As he cast his eye over his staff, he saw 'tremendous enthusiasm, everyone working day and night, feeling that here was a start to enable us to get back at the enemy again quickly and show that the Allies could still hit back'.[47]

Now, all he needed to do was attack. And for the particular mission he had in mind, he needed the help of Cecil Clarke.

7

The First Big Bang

Cecil Clarke had been putting the finishing touches to his monstrous hydraulic digger when Hitler's army swept through France and the Low Countries. The Nazi victory meant that there was no longer any need for such a machine, at least not for the foreseeable future, as the Siegfried Line had become an irrelevance. But there was most definitely a need for Clarke himself. He was immediately poached by the Intelligence Corps and sent to work at Aston House, a Hertfordshire research station.

Cecil always managed to cause a stir and his arrival at Aston was no exception. The station's commanding officer, Lieutenant Colonel Langley, was a stickler for security and had surrounded the place with barbed wire, sentry boxes and armed guards. All visitors had to report to the gatehouse, where they were interrogated and frisked for weapons. 'It really was most impressive,' said Stuart Macrae after visiting the establishment.

Most visitors accepted the security as a necessity. Clarke saw it as a challenge. He 'contrived to avoid all security measures', inching his substantial frame through the coils of barbed wire, dodging the guards and then pushing through the phalanxes of rhododendrons. In just a few minutes, he was knocking on Lieutenant Colonel Langley's door.

Langley was incandescent at such a breach of security and immediately blamed Macrae, 'deploring this conduct on the part of an officer for whom I was responsible'. Macrae pointed out that Clarke alone was responsible for his conduct, leading to yet more fuming on the part of Langley. He said that while he was unable to evict Clarke from the property, 'in no circumstance would he be allowed inside the house and he could not be served meals.'[1] It was a punishment more appropriate to a boarding school than a government research station.

Clarke cut a strange figure at Aston: jovial to the staff, yet solitary and absorbed. His idiosyncratic habits rarely passed without comment. He was constantly muttering 'what–what–what'[2] and spent his rare moments of leisure writing doggerel verse. The rag that he clutched, oil-smeared and in tatters, was used for everything from cleaning spark plugs to blowing his nose.

He had left Mrs Clarke in the driving seat at LoLode, where the luxury caravans, parked out front in Tavistock Street, seemed like symbols of a happier era. Now, LoLode's small roster of staff was preoccupied with producing limpet mines and army trailers. Clarke occasionally cycled home for an evening with the family, but it was a tiring and costly journey. He jokingly told Dorothy that he cycled eight miles to the pint, which meant that the round trip involved at least four stops in local pubs. By the time he arrived back at Aston, he was decidedly merry.

The purchasing officer at Aston, Cecily Hales, had got used to buying all manner of strange supplies for the researchers working at Aston, including 'molybdenum, stainless steel, mild steel and piano wire'. Yet Clarke himself required even stranger materials. One day she peeked into his drawer and found it contained 'masses of condoms', probably on account of a new limpet mine he was developing. She began to suspect that he was obsessed with contraception, a suspicion confirmed when Max Hill, the head of supplies, confessed that Clarke had asked him to go to 'the condom manufacturers, Durex', and purchase 'various sizes and thicknesses'. Cecily felt sorry that Mr Hill had had to undertake such an embarrassing task. 'They must have imagined that he was a dirty old man.'[3]

Clarke found time to write a practical guide to sabotage during those autumn months at Aston. His *Blue Book* offered advice on everything from disguise to explosives and bore many of his literary hallmarks: explosives were 'sweets' and detonators were 'toys'. But as always with Clarke, the clownish tone was a veneer. The advice he offered was rooted in a deep understanding of sabotage. 'A job is a good one,' he said, 'if it looks like an accident, act of God or has no explanation.'[4] Leaving no traces allowed the saboteur to flee from the scene undetected, as well as reducing the chance of reprisals.

Colin Gubbins had been keeping a keen eye on Clarke's work and was most impressed by what he saw. His approach was so strikingly original that it seemed the perfect counterfoil to the Nazis. Gubbins was intent on poaching him from the Intelligence Corps and approached him shortly before Christmas 1940 with the offer of a new job. He was to be promoted to acting major, given the codename D/DP and made the commanding officer of Brickendonbury Manor, a country mansion that Gubbins was intending to transform into his principal training centre for all would-be saboteurs. It was to be modelled on Coleshill House, only he wanted it to be far more professional. Clarke was to be responsible for teaching new recruits the fine art of sabotage.

He signed up immediately, an acceptance that came as no surprise to Stuart Macrae. 'It was just Nobby's cup of tea,' he said, 'and enabled him to become a bigger menace than ever.'[5] It also lifted him into Gubbins's elite inner circle, one whose single-minded pursuit was ungentlemanly warfare.

Brickendonbury Manor was a Jacobean mansion of imposing grandeur, one that had been extended and enlarged by so many generations that its echoing chambers had become a burden rather than a pleasure. Its most recent owners had been the Pearson dynasty, whose titular head, Sir Edward, had rebuilt the south front, added yet more rooms and contrived a Jacobean-style banqueting hall. But Sir Edward had died more than a decade earlier and his widow, Lady Susannah, found the place too large for comfort. In the summer of 1939 she sold the estate to a wealthy businessman named Ernest Gocher, who had just taken possession of the keys when he was informed that it had been requisitioned by the government.

For the first few months of the war, Brickendonbury had been used by Lawrence Grand's Section D. When Grand's section was disbanded, the future of the house looked uncertain. Gubbins was aware of this and visited the place soon after his appointment to Baker Street. According to Kim Philby, who was living there at the time, he arrived 'with a posse of fresh-faced officers, who barked at each other and at us'.[6] Gubbins liked what he saw and had Brickendonbury Manor swiftly transferred into his fiefdom, renaming it Station 17.

In common with the Firs, it was to become one of the country's most secret addresses, a house that even its owner, Mr Gocher, would not be able to enter until the war was over. In the intervening time, neither he – nor any of the local villagers – was to have any idea what was taking place behind its dense screen of foliage.

Within days of taking control of Brickendonbury, Gubbins handed Cecil Clarke the keys to his new domain. He immediately stamped his idiosyncratic personality on the establishment. No sooner had his first sabotage students arrived from London than they realized that theirs was to be a training unlike any other. One of them, Peter Kemp, couldn't work out if Clarke was mad or brilliant or both. 'He had a disquieting habit, during lectures, of exhibiting to us one of his pets [he means an explosive device] with a large charge attached, placing it on the desk in front of him, cocking it, and announcing: "This will go off in five minutes."'

He would then proceed with his lecture, unconcerned by the ticking bomb, while his students nervously counted the minutes. 'During the last half of the last minute the sound of his voice was almost drowned by the shuffling and scraping of chairs, especially from the front rows. When only five seconds remained, and every head in the class was down, he would suddenly remember, pick up the infernal machine, look at it for a moment, thoughtfully, and toss it nonchalantly through the window to explode on the lawn with barely a second to spare.'[7]

Kim Philby described Clarke as having a 'rumbustious sense of humour'.[8] This quickly became apparent to all who visited Brickendonbury. 'He had no guards on the gates to his magnificent estate. One just drove in and then found the vehicle being battered by rounds fired from spigot mortars set off by trip wires.' Happily for the occupants of the cars in question, these rounds were blanks. 'Nobby [Clarke] would emerge smiling and point out that if they had been live rounds, the occupants of the vehicle would no longer be in this world.' This was all very well, 'but it was of little consolation to the driver, who had to explain how the bodywork of his vehicle had been badly bashed.'[9]

Clarke's tree spigot was his latest invention, one specially designed for use by saboteurs. It was a clever adaptation of the mortar that

Millis Jefferis had first demonstrated at Chequers. Clarke had equipped it with a special silencing rod that held gases, flames and smoke inside the tail of the bomb, making the point of firing almost impossible to locate. The Americans later bought large quantities of the weapon and produced an army training film to show how it worked. 'The initial acceleration arms the special fuse, so that when the bomb hits its target, the impact drives the fuse firing pin into a detonating cap which ignites the booster charge.'[10] Its three-pound explosive charge was powerful enough to destroy any vehicle.

There were times when Clarke used live mortars in his demonstrations, especially when he wanted to impress visiting dignitaries. He would have an old car 'towed down the drive with a suitable length of rope, giving the driver some protection'. Then, without warning, one of his spigots would be fired by a tripwire. In a blinding flash of light, it would strike the vehicle side-on. 'It was a nice avenue of trees down the approach to Brickendonbury and these were prettily heavily decorated with bits of old car as a result of these demonstrations of the spigot mortar.'[11]

In happier times, the flower gardens of Brickendonbury had been featured in horticultural magazines, with lavish photographs of the Dutch gardens, climbing roses and the spectacular weeping ash tree that overhung the moat. Now, the trees and flowering bushes served as targets for Clarke's various mortars.

His favourite trick was to lead visitors to the chalk pitt, which he used for testing the most powerful explosives. Here, he would demonstrate 'what could be accomplished with a fertile imagination, a range of devices and a bit of plastic'. He particularly excelled himself on the occasion of a visit from Hugh Dalton and a select group of Whitehall officials. 'Various booby traps had been laid for them, with bangs going off and grenades rolling out at their feet, so that they arrived at their bomb-proof observation redoubt walking stiff-leggedly like cats on miry ground. The guests, who had had a day off in the country and had met the Jolly Roger boys, expressed themselves as highly impressed.'[12]

The head of Baker Street, Frank Nelson, may have been a workaholic, but those long hours in the office had not translated into action. Bickham Sweet-Escott had regular mid-week meetings with all the county section heads and then drafted the seven-day progress reports. 'The meetings were grim,' he confessed, 'and we always looked forward to Wednesdays with a sinking feeling.' As the new year dawned, he was able to record a few acts of sabotage in the Balkans and several more in Norway. 'But elsewhere the work was slow,' he admitted, 'and my reports were gloomy documents.'

The gloom had been lifted by the arrival of Gubbins, who injected life and purpose into the machinery of Baker Street. At last, there was a feeling that someone had switched on the power. Within days of Gubbins taking his place at Berkeley Court, the veteran saboteur Tom Masterman was smuggled into Belgrade in order to establish an underground network of saboteurs. Another agent, 'a likeable and busy barrister' named George Pollock, was dispatched to Cairo in order to build a team that could strike throughout the Middle East. Pollock delighted in underhand work – it was not so different from being a lawyer – and exceeded his brief by planning a series of spectacular assassinations of pro-Nazi Middle Eastern politicians. He was disappointed to learn that Whitehall refused to sanction them. 'We had to infer that cold-blooded murder was not part of our code,' wrote Sweet-Escott.[13] Not yet, perhaps, but Gubbins was already eyeing the possibilities of assassinating leading Nazis.

Agents were dispatched to Gibraltar, Malta, Lisbon and even Cape Town. A large group of Balliol graduates were sent to join Pollock in Cairo. Gubbins even established a mission in French West Africa, under the auspices of a man named Louis Franck. He was recommended as 'a good athlete and excellent linguist'.[14] More importantly, he was a personal acquaintance of General de Gaulle. His orders were to keep an eye on Vichy collaborators.

Lastly there was the 'brilliant and ruthless' George Taylor, who was smuggled into the Balkans. He was said to have 'a mind of limpid clarity'.[15] He also had a job on his hands. His task was to arrange groups of saboteurs who could hide out in the mountains.

Gubbins had been working as hard as his agents, planning his first sabotage mission within weeks of joining Baker Street. Intelligence had revealed that German pilots of Kampfgeschwader 100, a bomber squadron in France, were driven to Vannes aerodrome each evening in two coaches. Gubbins's idea was to parachute a small team of guer-rillas into Brittany, ambush the coaches and shoot all the pilots inside.

The planned operation soon hit a snag. Charles Portal, Chief of the Air Staff, was vehemently opposed to such ungentlemanly conduct and refused the use of RAF planes. 'I think that the drop-ping of men dressed in civilian clothes for the purpose of attempting to kill members of the opposing forces is not an operation with which the Royal Air Force should be associated.' He said that there was a big ethical difference between smuggling a spy into a country 'and this entirely new scheme for dropping what one can only call assassins'.

Gubbins pressed ahead regardless and managed to parachute a small group of French saboteurs into France. But the mission came too late: the German pilots were no longer travelling to the aero-drome by coach and Operation Savanna, as it was known, had to be abandoned. But it had not been entirely in vain: the returning saboteurs brought back to England 'a mass of intelligence about living conditions – curfew rules, bicycle regulations, cigarette prices, identity papers, ration cards'.[16] Such details were to prove of vital importance in the months ahead.

A larger and more enticing target on Gubbins's list of targets was the huge electrical transformer station at Pessac, close to Bordeaux. This stretch of coastline, along with the rest of the Atlantic littoral, fell inside the German occupied zone of France, for it was deemed too strategically valuable to entrust to the Vichy government. Pessac had been an early goal for the German invaders, whose commanders were quick to see the importance of the power station. Its eight transformers supplied power to the principal factories in the coastal area between St Nazaire and Bayonne. They also provided energy for the chemical manufacturers in the Bordeaux area, now in the hands of the Nazis. But for Gubbins, these factors were completely overshadowed by the fact that Pessac was supplying all the power for the massive German submarine base outside Bordeaux. If his men could knock out the transformer station, they would strike a crippling blow to German U-boat operations in the North Atlantic.

An air attack on Pessac was initially considered, but quickly ruled out on the grounds that aerial bombardment was highly inaccurate.

If the pilot missed the target, his bombs stood a high chance of landing on a civilian area. The only other option was to parachute a small team of saboteurs into Pessac. They would have to find their way to the transformer station, scale the perimeter fence, dodge or kill the sentries and then force an entry into the main building. If they managed to get inside without being caught, they would need to locate the key components of the plant machinery and wire them with explosives.

It sounded hard enough on paper, but there were additional obstacles. Pessac was on such an industrial scale, and so important to Germany's submarine campaign, that it had been surrounded by a heavily fortified wall that was believed to be under twenty-four-hour guard. These guards would kill the saboteurs if they caught them.

Gubbins was enough of a realist to know that an attack on Pessac could only be undertaken by French saboteurs. He therefore turned to his newly formed Free French Section and asked for volunteers for Operation Josephine B, the codename given to the mission. Three men immediately offered their services: Sergeant Jean-Pierre Forman, Sub-Lieutenant Raymond Cabard and Sub-Lieutenant André Varnier.

There was never any doubt as to who was best equipped to lead the mission. Sergeant Forman had already proved his worth during training: he was a man 'of courage, initiative and resource of the highest order'.[17] He also had the perfect profile of a saboteur. He was patient, ruthless and abhorred the Nazi occupation of his homeland, yet his hatred was carefully measured. In common with Gubbins, he believed that clinical strikes were the best way of hurting the German occupiers.

Gubbins had initially handed over the planning of the mission to two of his colleagues, Major Hugh Barry and Eric Piquet-Wicks, head of the Free French Section. Major Barry displayed an alarmingly breezy approach to a mission that was certain to land the men in extreme danger. 'All we had to do was provide them with the explosives and they had to cut their way through the wire fence and attack the things and go.'[18] He made it sound like an afternoon stroll in the park.

Cecil Clarke took a less cavalier view of the perils facing Sergeant

Forman and his comrades. He put together a two-month programme of intensive training at Brickendonbury Manor, one that revealed a commitment to professionalism that placed Clarke in a different field from Barry and Piquet-Wicks. His programme had two principal goals that were to become the hallmark of all future missions: destroy the target and get out alive. The ultimate success of any mission was rated on whether or not the saboteurs made it back to England.

The French volunteers arrived at Brickendonbury Manor in the spring of 1941, by which time Gubbins's team in London had discovered a great deal about the transformer station. Aerial reconnaissance photographs revealed the layout of the plant and the position of the various buildings. They even showed up the eight transformers. This information was to prove crucially important to Clarke as he prepared to train the men.

The transformer station stood some two miles from Pessac village, in heavily wooded countryside. This would afford the men good cover as they prepared themselves for the attack. Their greatest difficulty would be in entering the plant, with its sixteen-foot perimeter wall topped with wire. The saboteurs would have to scale this wall without attracting the notice of any workers at the plant.

Clarke knew more than most people about transformers. They usually had thin steel casings that housed the winding machinery. These casings contained oil, which was used as a coolant. It was clear that 'maximum damage will be inflicted by damaging the windings, letting out the oil and igniting it.'[19] If Sergeant Forman and his men could start a fire, Pessac could conceivably be knocked out for six months or more.

Clarke was in no doubt as to how best to blow up the transformers. His limpet mine was the ideal explosive. It would stick to the steel, be almost invisible if placed in the right position, and give the men ample time to make their escape.

He began by teaching the men the rudiments of sabotage and demolition. 'Know every detail backwards.' That was his mantra. 'Remember that within five minutes of landing at your destination, you may be questioned by a hostile official.' He was particularly insistent that the three men have an understanding of exactly how a transformer station functioned. Indeed he felt it was 'very important that these foreign enthusiastic volunteers should get some "hands on" experience of trying to carry out an attack'.

There was an obvious means of getting this experience. Luton Power Station was just twelve miles from Brickendonbury and it resembled Pessac in many respects. It had a high perimeter fence, was guarded by the military and had sentries who patrolled the site at night. Its transformers, too, were similar to those at Pessac. This made it the perfect place for Sergeant Forman and his men to undertake a trial run for their forthcoming act of sabotage.

Cecil's son, John, watched in puzzlement as his father faked a pass on War Office paper that read: 'The holder of this pass, Major C. V. Clarke, has authority to inspect Luton Power Station.' Equipped with this pass and a sack of blank limpets, he took the three saboteurs to Luton. He was preparing a little nocturnal surprise for the power station's general manager.

Night had fallen by the time they reached the station. Clarke and young John hid in the damp undergrowth in order to monitor the progress of the three saboteurs as they crept towards the perimeter fence. 'They used scaling ladders to get over the walls,' recalled John, who was pleased to see them scale the outer fence without drawing attention to themselves. The three Frenchmen then forced an entry into the main building and placed their magnetic limpets on to the metal transformers, just as Clarke had instructed. Once done, they crept out of the transformer station, rescaled the perimeter fence and rejoined Clarke and his son in the undergrowth. They hadn't triggered a single alarm. It was a job well done.

Clarke was impressed and now decided to have some fun. 'He walked up to the front door of the power station and asked to speak to the Officer of the Guard. He then flourished his fake pass and said: "I want to do a routine inspection."'

The officer was taken aback by this unannounced inspection but had little option but to allow Clarke inside: after all, he was equipped with an official War Office pass. 'So he went round with a very big torch' and began flashing light on to the transformers. 'He said: "What's that?" And this young subaltern who was in charge of the guard said: "I'm not quite sure what this is, sir. It looks to me like an explosive charge."'

Clarke pressed on with his inspection, revealing to the nervous subaltern each of the dummy charges. The subaltern was appalled that such a breach of security could have taken place on his watch. He expected to be roundly punished.

But Clarke had no wish to land him in trouble and said he would take no further action. "'Alright old man", he said. "You say nothing about this and I'll say nothing about it. But you've learned your lesson.'"[20]

So had the saboteurs. A practice run could mean the difference between life and death.

Sergeant Forman and his team set off from Stradishall Aerodrome in Suffolk at around 9 p.m. on 11 May, flying to France in a specially converted Whitley bomber. There was a sharp frost in the late evening air and the men knew it would get even colder once airborne. Over the previous days, pilots had been complaining of temperatures dipping as low as minus 25 inside their cockpits, so cold they had to scratch away the ice from the inside of the glass.

The Pessac mission had been timed to coincide with a full moon, an important consideration for men being dropped blind into the French countryside. Their equipment and explosives had been carefully packed into a rigid capsule: this, too, was to be parachuted from the plane.

Clarke had planned Operation Josephine B with surgical precision, intending it to be the antithesis of the sort of raids being undertaken by Bomber Command. Just twenty-four hours earlier, the Royal Air Force had undertaken its heaviest bombardment to date on Nazi Germany, dropping 'load after load of high explosives and incendiaries'[21] on to the cities of Hamburg and Bremen. The raid had come at a high cost: eleven bombers had crashed or been shot down and no one could be certain if the bombs had hit their target. Clarke, like Gubbins, had long believed that bombing was a blunt-edged weapon, one that killed more civilians than soldiers. Sabotage, at its best, was clinically precise.

The men had been equipped with specialist weaponry. Forman carried an automatic pistol, four grenades and a fighting knife to be used against German sentries if caught in close combat. He also had wire-cutters, a compass, a torch and a rope ladder. His principal explosive charge was the limpet mine. Cecil Clarke's wonder weapon was about to be put to the test.

The mission began like clockwork. The Whitley bomber reached the Bordeaux area at shortly after midnight and all three men jumped into the night, closely followed by their precious metal container. They landed some five kilometres from the target area, in an area of woodland, but managed to avoid getting their parachutes snagged in any branches. They didn't locate the container until dawn, when they noticed it dangling in a tree. They hauled it down and then buried it, just as Cecil Clarke had instructed.

Forman led them to a safe house in Bordeaux, only to discover that their contact was not at home. This was a setback, but they successfully checked into a hotel without arousing any suspicion and on the following morning acquired bicycles and used them to travel to Pessac. Forman wanted to stake out the ground before launching his attack.

Their reconnaissance of Pessac brought both good and bad news. The transformer station was surrounded by a nine-foot concrete wall – lower than expected – but the wall itself was topped by a high-tension wire that made scaling it almost impossible. More disquieting were the sentries on constant patrol inside the perimeter fence. Their presence put Forman in a quandary. He was under specific orders that 'fire will not be opened unless sentries of the transformer station interfere'.[22] Yet it was inconceivable that he and his men could get inside the plant without a firefight that would almost certainly leave all three of them dead.

Forman decided to postpone the attack in order to consult with Joel Letac, one of the men parachuted into France for the abortive assassination of the Kampfgeschwader bomber pilots. Letac had remained in France in order to work for the fledgling French resistance. He persuaded Forman to stake out the ground more carefully, informing him that the occupying Germans were becoming increasingly complacent in their attitude to security. He even volunteered to join him for the mission, an offer that Forman was more than happy to accept.

Sub-Lieutenant Raymond Cabard was selected to investigate the site more carefully and he displayed considerable bravado by walking up to the main gate and chatting with the French sentry on duty. From him, he learned a crucial detail. The night sentries had indeed become lax in their work and were in the habit of knocking off duty shortly before midnight. He also discovered that they slept in a billet in the north-east corner of the transformer station, leaving the main building unguarded.

Equipped with this knowledge, the saboteurs decided to attack on the following night, setting off from Bordeaux by bike under the cloak of darkness. Cabard and Varnier arrived first, at around 10 p.m., and made their way into the dripping woodland where they had buried their limpet mines. The loamy earth squelched underfoot, for it had been raining hard, and Varnier found that moisture had penetrated into the time fuses of the buried explosives. But he managed to cut out the spoiled section and rewire the detonators.

Forman and Letac joined their two comrades in the woodland at around midnight. A quick reconnaissance confirmed the information about the sentries. There was no one patrolling inside the site.

Forman followed his instructions to the letter, moving 'as rapidly as possible, following the line of pylons to the small wood, 300 yards west of the transformer station'. He scaled the wall without the use of a ladder, swung himself over the high-tension wire and clambered on to a pylon that stood just inside the perimeter fence. He then jumped down on to the soft ground in the yard and crept towards the main gate of the station, which he was able to unlatch from the inside. 'This made a considerable noise, but did not appear to attract any attention at all.'

His fellow saboteurs entered in absolute silence, slipping through the dark shadows towards the transformer building. It stood as a neatly defined silhouette in the pale spring moonlight. It was unlocked – amazingly – and the men got inside without difficulty. The place was deserted. The workmen were asleep. The only sound was the low hum of the transformers.

There was no light inside the factory, but the men's night training had not been in vain. They had no difficulty in locating the eight transformers and it took just seconds to attach their limpet mines to each of the metal casings. The only slight hitch came when they discovered that some of the transformers were wet, causing the mines to slide on the surface. Yet even this problem was overcome. In the operational report, written after the event, the men expressed satisfaction with their progress. 'During the whole period of half an hour in which the party were in the station, no one was seen and there was not the slightest attempt at interference.'[23]

They had no intention of hanging around. As soon as the limpets were secure, they skipped back through the main gates and retrieved their bicycles from the dense woodland close to the perimeter fence.

They had just mounted their bikes 'and were pedalling with all their might' when a series of hollow booms shook the stillness of the night. The booms were followed by 'resounding explosions and flames reaching to the sky'.[24] As the men glanced backwards, these flames could be seen towering more than 150 feet upwards. 'Seven other explosions were heard,' all timed like clockwork.[25] Cecil Clarke's limpet mines had worked to perfection.

The four of them pedalled hard, light-headed with success. They 'rode back to their digs by the light of the burning oil and of searchlights hunting for the bomber the Germans supposed to have passed'.[26] Forman knew that the searchlights brought good news. The Germans clearly thought the attack had come from the air.

Forman and his team later learned that the damage caused to Pessac was every bit as devastating as they had hoped. Six out of the eight transformers had been crippled, cutting all power supplies to the German submarine base. The wreckage was on such a grand scale, indeed, that it would take more than a year to repair the facility.

The Germans immediately tried to restore power by rerouting electricity from the power station at Dax, some seventy miles to the south. But it 'merely resulted in the blowing of numerous fuses, and this attempt had to be abandoned'.[27] The coastal railway from Bordeaux to Spain was also seriously disrupted, hampering the service. The electric locomotives eventually had to be abandoned and replaced with decommissioned steam trains.

When the Abwehr (military intelligence) discovered that the attack on Pessac had been carried out by saboteurs, and not aircraft, the

German sentries carried the blame. All twelve were arrested and were later said to have been shot. The local French population was also punished, but not severely. Some 250 people were arrested and a fine of 1 million francs imposed on the community.

Colin Gubbins was delighted by the success of the first major act of sabotage undertaken on his watch. It triumphantly vindicated his belief in playing dirty. 'The operation showed what could be done by a couple of gallant, well-trained men, trained for the job and equipped with the proper devices.'[28] The best news of all came when the three original saboteurs pitched up in England in the third week of August after a daring escape across Spain and Portugal. Their safe arrival was one cause for celebration. Another was the fact that Forman had managed to establish the first significant network of undercover agents in France. He was awarded the Military Cross for having 'contributed materially to the growth of resistance to the enemy'.

Hugh Dalton was as delighted as Gubbins with the success of Operation Josephine B and wrote a 'most secret' memo to Winston Churchill informing him that the scale of the destruction caused by eight small limpet mines 'strongly suggests that many industrial targets are more effectively attacked by Special Operations methods than by aerial bombardment'.

Dalton added that the operation had fully justified the existence of a dedicated sabotage unit, as well as Cecil Clarke's Brickendonbury training programme. 'It is indeed most encouraging that our first action of this kind (which reflects great credit on Brigadier Gubbins, my Director of Training and Operations) should have succeeded.'[29] Churchill was inclined to agree.

8

Killing School

COLIN GUBBINS'S DECISION to attack the Pessac transformer was at one level blindingly obvious. Deprive the U-boat base of power and you deprive the enemy of his ability to function. But it was also a clever piece of lateral thinking, one that opened up a whole new realm of possibilities. Military factories, aerodromes and industrial docks: suddenly, the Nazis' soft targets looked enticingly vulnerable.

The only problem with Operation Josephine B was that it failed to address the fleet of German U-boats that were already at sea. Admiral Donitz had almost a hundred in service and they were wreaking a terrible toll on shipping. Nearly every day brought news of another catastrophe. On 1 March the *Cadillac* was sunk by U-552. On 2 March the *Augvald* and *Pacific* were sent to the bottom. Five days later saw the sinking of no fewer than seven ships, including a huge whaler that had been converted into a supply vessel. It was attacked by the veteran U-boat commander Günther Prien, the first to win the Knight's Cross for mastery of submarine warfare.

Deep in his bunker below Whitehall, Winston Churchill kept a grim tally of the statistics. 'My mind reverted to February and March 1917,' he wrote, 'when the curve of U-boat sinking had mounted so steadily against us that one wondered how many months' more fighting the Allies had in them.'[1] It was these U-boats – the scourge of the Atlantic – on which Millis Jefferis now set his sights.

He was well equipped for planning sabotage at sea, for his country establishment, the Firs, had expanded greatly over the previous months. The tumbledown brick outhouses, once used to store flowerpots, had been converted into specialist labs and Macrae had set up a fledgling weapons' factory, 'snatching a dozen automatic machines and a raft of other machine tools from under somebody's nose and putting Leslie Gouldstone' – a gifted radio sound-recordist – 'in charge of the outfit'. Two huge water-pools had also been dug in the back garden, raising hopes among the staff that they would be able to go swimming in their leisure time. Macrae soon put them right, informing them that the pools were 'not for bathers but for underwater experiments with various devices'.

New staff arrived each week, many of them specialist mechanics and engineers who were hired by Macrae in order to fine-tune Jefferis's more exuberant weapons of war. Some of these recruits were decidedly odd. One, known only as Mr Wilson, had previously worked at Portland Place, where he had chosen to live 'in a cell about six feet square'. To Macrae's eyes, he resembled a fish in an aquarium. 'In this cell, he just had room for a drawing board, on which he produced really beautiful work remarkably quickly.'

Macrae also set up a small factory in the extensive grounds, in order that the Firs could start building weapons as well as inventing them. This required manual labour, which he sought in the surrounding villages. The elderly and unemployed were delighted by the prospect of paid work and Macrae soon found himself in the position of employing so many locals that he had to rent a fleet of buses to shuttle them back to their homes at the end of each shift.

Millis Jefferis strode around the sparsely furnished rooms of the Firs like some ill-kempt pasha, while Macrae played the role of ever faithful vizier. He had become the self-styled manager of a station whose production line was already working with remarkable efficiency. 'The experimental workshop was running full blast, we had compiled temporary stores and trucks were whistling in and out with our products.'

The most tangible sign of their importance was the splendidly polished limousine that Macrae had managed to scam from the War Office. Parked up front for everyone to see, it was the ultimate symbol of success. 'The kind of vehicle reserved for the use of generals, and was complete with glass partition, speaking tube and all mod cons.'

As the output of sabotage weaponry increased, Macrae began to assemble a small fleet of trucks and drivers to enable the explosives to be transported more efficiently to Gubbins's operatives. He also established a building team, in order to construct more labs in the extensive grounds. And he opened a 'special Number 2 account' at the Midland Bank in Aylesbury, into which development money gushed like a waterfall. 'Nearly one million pounds,' he noted with a mixture of surprise and satisfaction. There were distinct advantages to having Winston Churchill as benefactor.

As the conflict spread across Europe, saboteurs were dispatched to Gubbins's furthest-flung outposts – Cairo, Belgrade, Albania and Greece – and began ordering large supplies of explosives in preparation for the fight ahead. Even Macrae expressed surprise when he saw the destinations of their wares. One night, a consignment was sent to Bombay. The next, his team were loading trucks 'to take our stores to the docks to catch a ship for Australia'. Just a few days later, 'there was a top priority shipment to the Middle East'.

The only person who seemed unhappy with the progress was Jefferis himself. One day he summoned Macrae to his office and issued a blunt warning. 'He solemnly told me that he was now working a minimum of sixteen hours a day and that he thought I and everybody else in the establishment should do the same.'[2] Macrae tried to talk him out of such a punishing regime: men like Mr Wilson were already working so late into the night that their complexions were ashen grey. But Jefferis wouldn't budge. His only concession, he told Macrae, 'was to allow entertainment on the last Saturday of every month'. Macrae vowed to make that entertainment worth the wait.[3]

Colin Gubbins was a regular visitor to the Firs, noting each meeting (though never its contents) in the office diary in his scratchy little handwriting. Professor Lindemann was also a frequent guest and he often arrived with inventors and scientists. One of these scientists was Charles Goodeve, a lecturer in thermodynamics at University College and author of publications with titles like *Cataphoretic Measurements on Visual Purple and Indicator Yellow*. They were not for the casual reader.

Goodeve was an inventive genius with a lofty forehead and an oversize brain. 'In my time I have met many cranks,' said one who met him at the beginning of the war, 'and this man bore all the external hallmarks.'[4] Yet he was a crank with a mind so sharp that he had been placed in charge of an experimental naval outfit known as the Department of Miscellaneous Weapons' Development. It was in this role that he was brought to the Firs in order to meet Millis Jefferis.

The two men shared much in common. Both were workaholics. Both had what Goodeve liked to describe as 'a novelty of outlook'.[5] And both knew that the Royal Navy's anti-submarine depth charge, whose technology had remained unchanged for years, was hopelessly out of date.

Goodeve had been toying with the possibility of devising a weapon that could somehow fire depth charges into the water. But now, as the two men sparred ideas, Jefferis suggested an altogether more radical approach. He proposed transforming his spigot mortar into an underwater missile.

Goodeve was at his best when given the crumbs of an idea. Quick as lightning, he envisaged an even more devastating weapon. 'Do you think we could use this spigot mortar of yours to fire a whole ring of bombs?' His idea was to create a multi-firing launch-pad that would send several dozen spigots into the sea, all entering the water simultaneously. If these could be propelled downwards and inwards, the spigot could be transformed into a truly lethal weapon against Hitler's U-boats.

The viability of such a weapon was contingent on the mathematical configuration of the mortars. Jefferis took his spigot 'back to the drawing board' and made a series of calculations. Within a few days, he showed Goodeve 'a design which seemed distinctly promising'.[6] On paper it looked unlike any weapon ever invented: two dozen spigots with state-of-the-art fuses, thirty pounds of explosive packed into each nose and tubular tail-fins to guarantee stability in both air and water. Jefferis intended his mortars to fire upwards to the sky, where they would form themselves into a perfect ellipse before plunging into the sea in an ever decreasing diameter. If the maths was correct, they would strike their target when it was deep underwater.

Goodeve was as impressed with Jefferis's maths as he was with the Firs. He had been granted 'indifferent research and development facilities', quite inadequate for developing new weaponry. Jefferis, by contrast, had everything: 'facilities for filling projectiles, detonators and fuses, a special electronic apparatus was available for measuring velocity and there were large water tanks'.[7] Goodeve tentatively asked Macrae if he might 'attach some of his people'[8] to the Firs. Macrae immediately agreed, hoping that an influx of yet more staff would bring about the cross-fertilization of more clever ideas.

These new recruits found that life at the Firs was never dull. Bombs exploded unexpectedly, sheds caught fire and, on one memorable occasion, an entire corner of the building 'containing some lethal liquid' blew up in a spectacular explosion. It was hastily repaired, before the owner of the property, Major Abrahams, got to hear about it.

One of Goodeve's underlings noted that 'the least concerned observer present when things went wrong was the impresario of this unusual establishment, Jefferis.' He impressed everyone with 'his habit of walking around with his pockets crammed full of detonators, small batteries and pieces of wire'.[9] It was a miracle he never blew himself up.

The anti-U-boat mortar was the first in a new generation of sophisticated weaponry and both men knew it would take a great deal of time to perfect. When it came to building a prototype, Jefferis turned to the trusted craftsmen who had hitherto served him so well. The weapon's complex mounting was made by a firm of specialist boilermakers in Bristol, while the spigots were built by a gifted artisan who worked for Boosey and Hawkes, the musical instrument makers.

There was one issue yet to be settled. Goodeve offered a bottle of sherry to the person who came up with the best name for the weapon. The prize went to Ian Hassel, one of his team, who said it should be called a Hedgehog. It was a name that gave 'a splendid suggestion of prickly hostility'. It was also an accurate description, since the rows of spigot mortars 'bore a striking resemblance to the quills on a hedgehog's defiant back'.[10]

The prototype reached completion in the late spring of 1941, just when Jefferis was due to stage a demonstration of his latest weapons for the Prime Minister. The demonstration took place in a chalk pit near Chequers and proved to be 'a spectacular show' that brought such delight to the Prime Minister that he asked if he could fire some weaponry himself. 'Taking a tommy-gun, he fired a long burst at the tyres of a derelict Army lorry.' He showed such cavalier regard for safety that the spectators took shelter behind the Prime Minister's substantial girth. Churchill was enjoying himself so much that he 'turned his attention to the lorry's Triplex screen on which he cut his initials with bullets'. When all the ammunition was finished he called for more and then gave the tommy gun to his young daughter, Mary, 'who blazed away enthusiastically at the battered lorry'.

Seeing the Prime Minister in such high spirits, Goodeve approached him and suggested that he spare a few minutes to visit the Firs, in order to inspect the Hedgehog. Churchill was interested in this new project but he was also hungry. He said he would see the Hedgehog another day. But young Mary had been listening to one of the team, Jock Davies, telling her amazing tales about this strange wonder weapon with its amusing name and devastating power. She grabbed her father's arm as he was getting into his car. 'We must see Captain Davies's bomb-thrower,' she pleaded, 'of course there's time.'[11]

Churchill was putty in his daughter's hands. He ordered his fleet of cars to head to the Firs, where the prototype Hedgehog was primed and made ready for action. Aware of Churchill's enthusiasm for dramatic displays, Jefferis and Goodeve pre-programmed it to fire twenty-four rounds in quick succession. The result was spectacular. The villagers of Whitchurch were accustomed to fireworks' displays on Guy Fawkes Night, but they had never seen anything quite like this. 'Climbing the blue sky, they formed a strangely graceful pattern, and as they reached their zenith they turned lazily over, like well-drilled marionettes, before starting their swift dive to earth.' The mortars landed in perfect order around the shape of a submarine that had been pegged out on the lawn.

Churchill was enthralled by this experimental weapon. He asked for a second salvo to be fired and then a third. Everyone watching shared the same opinion, that 'here at last, it seemed, was the instrument which could turn the tide of the U-boat war.'[12]

★

While Millis Jefferis was concentrating his efforts on sending large numbers of Germans to a watery grave, Colin Gubbins was focused on a more clinical approach to death. His experiences in Norway had taught him that men don't find it easy to kill in cold blood. Many soldiers hesitated before pulling the trigger, even when they couldn't see the face of their target. Many more found it difficult to shoot at close range. Yet Gubbins would soon be asking his men to undertake operations that would possibly require them to kill with their bare hands.

Such work could only be undertaken by men trained in what he called 'the stalkers' instinct'. They needed to be as skilled as snipers, with 'absolute confidence in their weapon', and they also needed to learn how to operate as a band of brothers. Gubbins wanted nothing short of 'complete reliance on one's comrades to stand and fight'.[13] Training men in the art of killing had been one of the biggest problems he faced at the outbreak of the war, but by the spring of 1941 he thought he had found the solution. And on Easter Sunday, 13 April, he boarded the express train to Scotland in order to see that solution with his own eyes.

He was glad to escape the office, for the previous few days had brought a flood of relentlessly depressing news. Belgrade had surrendered to the invading Nazis less than twelve hours earlier. Salonika had also fallen to Hitler's storm-troopers. Gubbins's hope of a sustained guerrilla campaign inside Yugoslavia and Greece was looking increasingly unlikely.

More encouraging was the news that three Polish agents had been successfully parachuted into Poland. The flight had been a triumph of logistics, for few planes were equipped to fly such long distances. The Whitley aircraft had to be extensively remodelled with an auxiliary fuel tank in the fuselage in order to make the fourteen-hour return flight. Dropped alongside the men was a cylindrical metal container filled with sabotage equipment and explosives. Both it, and the saboteurs, made it successfully to Warsaw.

A second piece of good news came from Tom Masterman in Belgrade. When he had left London, his parting shot to Bickham Sweet-Escott had been a promise to bring down the pro-Hitler government of Dragisa Cvetkovic. Now, he had spectacularly succeeded – not on his own, as Sweet-Escott was quick to point out, but he had played an important behind-the-scenes role in helping General Simovic to power. His work raised spirits in Baker Street, for it was 'the first reverse of this kind which Hitler had so far received'.[14]

The news about Masterman came just two weeks before Gubbins's trip to Scotland, where he hoped to be greeted with more encouraging news. He made a brief stop at Inverness, where he had a meeting, and then continued his journey to the town of Fort William. Here, he changed trains and boarded 'the puffer', as it was affectionately known – the quaint little steam locomotive that chugged along the empty shores of Loch nan Uamh before swinging north towards the fishing port of Mallaig.

Gubbins relished the opportunity to return to the Highland wilderness of his childhood. This was where he felt truly at home: a land where the lead-grey lochs carved gashes into the fractured coast, where the offshore isles of Eigg and Muck showed up as lilac smudges in the mist. But Gubbins had not come for the scenery. He was here to meet two idiosyncratic individuals, neither of whom was a soldier, nor even in the military. Both were portly gentlemen of a certain age who shared lodgings in an austere Victorian hunting lodge on the edge of Loch nan Ceall.

Eric Sykes and William Fairbairn had first come to the attentions of the War Office a year earlier when they pitched up unannounced in Whitehall, having just arrived from the Far East. Both were close to retirement age and had come to offer their services in the fight against Nazi Germany. At first glance they were an unlikely couple of recruits, best suited, perhaps, to patrol duty in the Home Guard. Dressed in khaki, and striding suburbia with pitchfork and spade, they would have at least been made to feel they were playing a part in the war against Hitler.

But they arrived in London with such an incredible story (and curriculum vitae to match) that they could not be easily ignored. The first of the men, Eric Sykes, was known to his friends as Bill, a reference to Dickens's famously shady character. He was stocky, with pebble-glass spectacles and a dimpled smile: he looked as if he couldn't hurt a fly. One acquaintance said he had the 'manner and appearance of an elderly, amiable clergyman'. Others were 'lulled by his soft tones and charmed by his benevolent smile'.[15] But Sykes was neither benevolent nor a clergyman. He was an expert in silent killing – chilling, ruthless and clinical – and a man whose every sentence was said to end in the words, 'and then kick him in the testicles'.[16]

His previous employment had been in Shanghai, where he had worked as the representative of two American firearms companies, Colt and Remington. He was a crack shot, arguably the finest in the world, and his speciality was shooting from the hip. One who watched him in action was astonished to see him spin round, gun in hand, 'with his back facing the target and hit the bull's eye from between his legs'.[17]

Sykes's comrade-in-arms was William 'Shanghai Buster' Fairbairn. Similarly portly, and myopic to boot, he gave the impression of being 'smaller than he really was, with his long arms and the slight stoop that gave him the aspect of a monkey having learned to walk like a man'.[18] Like Sykes, he had the air of a Church of England chaplain. 'His horn-rimmed spectacles and benevolent expression earned him the nickname "The Deacon".'[19] Yet he was a deacon whose sermons had a nasty sting in the tail: 'Kill or be killed,' was his catchphrase.

Fairbairn's conversation was generally limited to two words, 'yes' and 'no', and he didn't allow his discussions on human anatomy to stretch his vocabulary unduly. 'He had never attempted to find out the names of the various bones or muscles, and throughout his short, jerky explanations he would merely refer to "this bone" or "that muscle" and point it out or touch it with his finger.'[20]

His friends knew him as Delicate Dan, but he referred to himself as Mister Murder-Made-Easy. He would smile benevolently as he taught his pupils 'how to break a man's neck or smash his spine across your knee'.[21]

Fairbairn was the elder of the duo, a fifty-eight-year-old miscreant who had run away from the family home at the age of fifteen and lied his way into the Royal Marines. Initially posted to the British Legation in Seoul, he won himself a place on the bayonet fighting team and then honed his skills in contests against Japanese experts in martial arts. The Japanese taught him that the butt of a rifle was every bit as effective as a bayonet. Smashed hard into an opponent's face, it caused such severe internal bleeding that death would rapidly follow.

Fairbairn had been headhunted for employment by the Shanghai Municipal Police in 1907, a position he was to hold for the next thirty-three years. The city was infamous for its armed gangsters, drug runners and violent criminals. Not for nothing was it known as the toughest city in the world. Fairbairn's job was to quell gang warfare, a task he set to with such relish that there were some who wondered if he wasn't a gangster himself. He rapidly established his Riot Squad, a team of 120 hand-picked men who were trained in what he called 'Gutter Fighting'.

All his men were crack shots, but Fairbairn himself favoured close-range physical combat over the bullet. 'His system is a combination of ferocious blows, holds and throws, adapted from Japanese bayonet tactics, ju-jitsu, Chinese boxing, Sikh wrestling, French wrestling and Cornish collar-and-elbow wrestling, plus expert knowledge of hip-shooting, knife fighting and use of the Tommy gun and hand grenade.'[22]

A lifetime of fighting had left its mark. He had a broken nose and a long scar that stretched from ear to chin. Yet most people were struck by 'his flashing white teeth that no amount of punching had ever loosened'.[23]

His principal interest in life, apart from fighting, was his prize goldfish. He had the finest collection in China – more than 100,000 in total – which he kept in specially constructed pools.

Fairbairn came to know Eric Sykes through his work with Colt and Remington. By 1926, he had drafted him into his Riot Squad, where Sykes swiftly proved himself a valuable addition to the team. The two men shared a passion for dirty killing and together wrote the seminal work on pistol shooting, *Shooting to Live*. This was followed by other books: *All-in Fighting*, *Get Tough* and *Self-Defence for Women and Girls*.

When Sykes and Fairbairn explained their skills to the War Office, it was immediately apparent that there was no place for them in the British Army. The idea of a good clean fight was anathema to them.

They were brought to the notice of Colin Gubbins, who immediately hired their services and sent them briefly to Brickendonbury Manor before dispatching them to the Highlands of Scotland. By the spring of 1941, they had become key members of his inner circle and as important to his forthcoming operations as Millis Jefferis and Cecil Clarke.

On first arriving at the sparsely populated west coast of Scotland, they found themselves entering a secret zone, one that was forbidden to anyone without the requisite military permission. The Protected Area had been established within a few weeks of Gubbins's Independent Companies returning from their Norwegian adventure. Gubbins himself had been sanctioned to requisition a vast slab of Scottish wilderness, along with a dozen or so country properties.

Lord Lovat, whose residence was not far from Gubbins's childhood home, was sent north to take possession of 'all available premises astride the Fort William–Mallaig road and railway line'. He also requisitioned the surrounding moorland and mountains, including 'six deer forests and their lodges, covering a land mass for training purposes of not less than 200,000 acres of wild country'.[24]

And wild it certainly was. Gubbins's childhood stamping ground was a land of lochs, watery bogs and mountains of sparse beauty, where the shadows of clouds scudded at speed over the empty landscape. Such wilderness was perfect for honing skills in stalking, endurance, orienteering and small boat work.

The first property to be commandeered was Inverailort House near Lochailort, a Victorian shooting lodge that stood at the head of Loch Ailort. Inverailort was where Gubbins's Independent Companies were billeted after their bruising experience in Norway.

While still nursing their wounds they were given lessons in fieldcraft by David Stirling (who went on to found the SAS) and Lord Lovat (who was to become captain of the Lovat Scouts). They were also taught survival techniques by the polar veteran George Murray Levick, who had accompanied Captain Scott's expedition to the South Pole and survived to tell the tale.

'I know a man who always cut a hole in the skull of a seal as soon as he had shot it and sucked out the nice warm brains,' he would tell his students. 'Young foxes and dogs are quite palatable, but they are improved with Worcester Sauce or Tomato Ketchup.'[25] He neglected to tell them how to find Tomato Ketchup when fighting behind enemy lines.

Inverailort House was to remain an endurance training centre for the duration of the war, while nearby Arisaig was to be the principal killing academy for Sykes and Fairbairn. This was their private domain, a Victorian lodge whose gabled ends stood solid against the blustery shores of Loch nan Ceall. There was no architectural frivolity to be found in Arisaig's hewn walls, no baroque twirls and fancies. On the rare fine days of the year, the Sound of Arisaig would reveal a Spartan beauty of scoured rock and glassy water. But when the wind whipped at the chimneys and lashed the stunted trees, the sombre austerity was all-pervading. Bonnie Prince Charlie had fled to France from this remote outpost, his whereabouts kept secret by the loyal local fishermen. 'A price was put on his head of thirty thousand pounds,' said one local, 'and nobody gave a whisper away.'[26] Now, those same locals had another secret to keep.

Gubbins ordered Sykes and Fairbairn to set up a training school unlike any other. Indeed he gave them complete freedom to teach whatever methods they thought necessary. 'Take no bloody notice of anyone but me,' he said.[27]

True to his word, the two trainers informed their pupils that the rule book had been cast into the dustbin. 'We were to be gangsters with the knowledge of gangsters,' said one, 'but with the behaviour, if possible, of gentlemen.'[28]

Sykes and Fairbairn switched between Arisaig and Inverailort on a daily basis, preparing men for the most dangerous missions of all. New recruits were given a typical Fairbairn welcome. 'In this war,' he would say, 'you can't afford the luxury of squeamishness. Either you kill or capture or you will be killed or captured. We've got to be tough to win and we've got to be ruthless.'

He would recount eyebrow-raising anecdotes from Shanghai before glaring at the men through his pebble glasses. 'What I want you to do is get the dirtiest, bloodiest ideas in your head that you can think of for destroying a human being.' He told them to forget all notions of fair play. 'The fighting I'm going to show you is not a sport. It's every time, and always, a fight to the death.'

New recruits were toughened up with a gruelling regime of physical training: endurance runs over empty moorland, hiking with heavy packs and lessons in the martial arts. The men were told how to induce a heart attack, snap the coccyx and strangle a sentry. It was not for the faint-hearted. Fairbairn would teach each new recruit 'a dozen edge-of-the-hand blows that break a wrist, an arm or a man's neck; twists that wrench and tear; holds that choke and strangle; throws that break a leg or a back; kicks that crush ribs, shins and feet bones'.[29] He bragged that he could kill a man with a folded newspaper, and his finger-jab to the eye had blinded many a Shanghai gangster.

Fairbairn particularly relished his dining room routine, showing them how to whisk up a tablecloth as you dived over a table and then 'wrap it round your opponent's head as he crashes down under you and, finally, how to push it into his mouth with the remains of the bottle meanwhile smashed over his skull'.[30]

Knife-fighting was one of the great specialities of Arisaig: Fairbairn and Sykes had designed their own double-edged commando knife – an eight-inch blade with a cross-piece and a ribbed centre on both sides. Now, their recruits were taught to slash and stab. But Fairbairn knew that it was one thing to stab a straw-filled dummy, quite another to plunge a blade into flesh. 'We've got to get you bloodied,' he would say with a devilish grin as he led the men to the local slaughterhouse.

'Each of us had to plunge a knife into a recently killed animal to get the feel of human flesh that was still quivering,' said one new recruit. There was a reason for this practice. 'It was to make us realize that when you put a knife into any living creature, the contractions of the sinews is such that it's very difficult to get it out.'[31]

Such training was vitally important for the missions that lay ahead. Gubbins's goal was to produce the most elite guerrillas in the world. In Sykes and Fairbairn, he had the best tutors in the world.

The two men faced constant criticism from the War Office, but Gubbins always championed their cause. This became more difficult when the criticism came from senior generals, as it often did. On one occasion, Fairbairn had taken his best pupil, William Pilkington, to a Home Guard training session in Glasgow. They had just been teaching their audience how to sever someone's carotid artery with a sharpened trowel when there was a furious cry from the back of the room: 'Stop this at once!'

Unbeknown to anyone, the training session had been brought to the attention of Major-General Sir Edward Spears, a senior army officer of the old school. He was appalled by what he had just heard.

'This is monstrous,' he bawled. 'Don't pay attention to this dreadful teaching. Remember, we are British. We do not stoop to thug-element tactics. We do not stab in the back. We fight as men. We do not slash. Now this must cease.'

Fairbairn was furious. He had never respected authority and was so angered by Major-General Spears's outburst that he answered back in the most colourful terms, hurling abuse at the general and telling him he was an idiot. He might have been court-martialled on the spot, had it not been for the arrival of someone of even greater stature. Unseen by anyone, Winston Churchill had slipped into the room just after Major-General Spears: the two men had been visiting Glasgow together. Churchill was grinning widely, very much the worse for wear, with saliva dripping from his cigar. Steadying himself with a walking cane, he called out: 'Come on Teddy, for Christ's sake, you've said enough. Come and have a drink.' He then grabbed Spears and pulled him outside.

'Good work,' he shouted to the room at large. 'Keep it up.'[32]

Winston Churchill knew something that Major-General Spears did not. Four months before Gubbins made his trip to Arisaig, he had been sanctioned to form his own private strike force: a small group of men who could be used for private hit-and-run attacks. The idea was that they should never number more than twelve. In the event, Gubbins was to settle on eleven. The size of the force was perhaps no accident. Eric Sykes always liked to tell his men that they were in Arisaig to unlearn the rules of a game of cricket. Eleven was indeed the same as the number of players in a cricket team, but cricket was the very last game that Gubbins's men were going to be playing.

Gubbins interviewed the potential captain of the team shortly before Christmas 1940, and was immediately struck by his towering self-confidence. Gustavus ('Gus') Henry March-Phillipps was a thirty-two-year-old survivor of the Dunkirk catastrophe, a man with guts of granite and a contempt for rules. He had previously served with a remote hill battery on the North-West Frontier, fighting a dirty war against rebellious tribesmen. The long hours spent staring into the Himalayan sunlight had left their mark. 'His eyes, puckered from straining against tropical glare, gave him an enquiring, piercing and even formidable expression.'[33]

Twelve months earlier, he had joined the newly formed commandos, an elite force being created out of Gubbins's Independent Companies. Churchill himself had encouraged the formation of such a force, calling for 'specially trained troops of the hunter class, who can develop a reign of terror' along the northern coastline of France.[34]

March-Phillipps had always been the first among equals and his unremitting professionalism soon brought him to the attention of his superiors. He was appointed to lead B Troop of 7 Commando. But his drive for perfection was such that even the commandos failed to satisfy him. Within weeks, he began to gather a small team of like-minded professionals who he hoped to forge into an elite brotherhood.

No one who met March-Phillipps ever forgot the experience. His young wife found him 'frightfully good looking, if you got him at the right angle, and very beaky if you got him at the wrong one, and this marvellous, scarred, beautiful mouth'. He practised everything to extremes, even his faith, having an unshaken belief in his Roman Catholic god. He prayed for ten minutes every night, fervently, yet he was at heart an iconoclast with 'a complete contempt for small regulations that sometimes make life in the army tiresome'.

Slothfulness offended him, as did obesity. He had 'great scorn of anyone who was carrying an ounce too much fat'. His friends saw him as an archetypal Renaissance man, bold, quick-witted and highly cultivated. 'By tradition an English country gentleman,' said one, 'he combined the idealism of a Crusader with the severity of a professional soldier.'[35] In reality, he was a freelance adventurer who secretly hoped to strut the globe like some lineal descendant of Sir Francis Drake. Gubbins interviewed him in Baker Street and was deeply impressed. 'Full of initiative, bursting to have a go, competent, full of self-confidence.'[36] He hired him on the spot and put him in charge of the eleven-strong band.

March-Phillipps's second-in-command was Geoffrey Appleyard, a man who sailed through life trailing an embarrassment of riches. He gained a first at Cambridge, where he was Head of Boats (at Caius College), and he was also a skiing blue. He was one of the great skiers of the age, leading Britain to an unprecedented victory against Norway in the winter championships of 1938.

Appleyard had originally been appointed section commander to March-Phillipps in 7 Commando. Now, hired by Gubbins, he became second-in-command of the as yet unnamed strike force. He loved the freelance approach to warfare as much as the piratical element of their work. 'No red tape, no paperwork, none of all the things that are in the army,' he wrote. 'Just pure operations, the success of which depends principally on oneself and the men one has oneself picked to do the job with you. It's terrific! It's revolutionary and one can hardly imagine it happening in this old Army of ours.'[37]

One by one March-Phillipps hired men for his elite band. By the late spring of 1941, there was just one place left vacant. Gubbins knew that March-Phillipps was looking for an eleventh member and, while visiting Arisaig, asked Sykes and Fairbairn if they had a suitable candidate for a mission into uncharted territories. The two men had no doubts as to their best student. Anders Lassen, 'the Viking', was one of the ten Danish recruits currently being put through their training programme. Pale-eyed, aristocratic and alarmingly wild, he shared March-Phillipps's contempt for army rules. 'The most remarkable aspect of Lassen was the strength of his self-belief,' said his childhood friend, Prince Georg of Denmark. 'Indeed, it was more than self-belief.'[38] He had a vaunting air of invincibility.

He had certainly made an impression on everyone at Arisaig. One day, he was out on the moors with his fellow trainees when he spotted two huge stags in the distance. 'I want that one!' he roared, as he set off in hot pursuit, his Fairbairn-Sykes dagger at the ready. Fleet of foot and spurred on by hunger, he was soon bearing down on the unfortunate beast. His comrades watched on aghast. 'He stabbed it with his knife,' said one, slaughtering it in an instant. 'It was a fine, big animal and the next few days we had lovely roast.'[39]

Bold, fearless and fast — they were the very attributes Gubbins most appreciated. Indeed, his behaviour was more like a pirate than a soldier. Gubbins informed Sykes and Fairbairn that he was taking Lassen back to London. A pirate was exactly what he needed.

9

Gubbins's Pirates

THE ANTELOPE HOTEL in Poole was an Elizabethan coaching inn that served a decent array of ales and, considering it was wartime, a reasonable selection of food. Its proprietor, Arthur 'Pop' Baker, had wisely stocked up on supplies in the months before the outbreak of war. Now, in the second summer of conflict, he still had luxuries in his cellar.

Colin Gubbins arrived at the hotel just after 10.30 a.m. on 10 August 1941, having made an early start from London. The news that morning had been as grim as ever. Just seven weeks after Hitler's spectacular invasion of the Soviet Union, his forces had reached within striking distance of Leningrad. Further south, in Ukraine, two entire Soviet armies had just been crushed, with the capture of 100,000 prisoners. Marshal Semyon Timoshenko, the Red Army's most senior battlefield commander, found the situation so desperate that he issued a call for outright guerrilla warfare. 'Join guerrilla detachments, attack behind the lines and destroy German convoys and supply columns,' he said. 'Wreak merciless, complete and continuous vengeance on the enemy.'[1] They were sentiments that could have been uttered by Gubbins.

Gubbins had travelled down to Poole in order to bid farewell to a pioneering mission destined for tropical waters. Gus March-Phillipps and his team were about to set sail on the biggest adventure of their lives.

From the outset, Gubbins had conceived of his private strike force as one that could conduct coastal raids, amphibious sabotage missions and hit-and-run attacks on Nazi bases. Such operations required a vessel, one that would arouse no suspicions when under sail. March-Phillipps had found just the craft at anchor in Brixham harbour. *Maid Honour* was a fifty-five-ton local trawler ideally suited to such missions. Her hull was wooden, rendering her immune to magnetic mines, and her dark brown sails meant that she was almost invisible at night. She looked like what she was: an unremarkable fishing vessel.

March-Phillipps now 'pulled off a feat that only he could have got away with'. He requisitioned the vessel from its owner and then, once it was done, telegrammed Gubbins and asked for the necessary authority. Gubbins was no stranger to breaking rules, but he was nevertheless impressed at the panache with which March-Phillipps had overstepped the mark. According to one of the team, he immediately sanctioned March-Phillipps's actions and 'won the everlasting gratitude of the crew by backing us up through thick and thin'.[2]

Once the *Maid Honour* was acquired, Gubbins enlisted the services of Millis Jefferis and Cecil Clarke to help transform her from fishing ketch to special operations' vessel. Although she continued to look like any other trawler in the harbour, she was equipped with weaponry designed to catch rather more than fish. Her plywood deckhouse concealed a formidable arsenal that included a Vickers Mark two-pounder gun, four Bren light machine guns, four tommy guns and a stockpile of hand grenades. She was also well stocked with specialist detonators supplied by the Firs, along with a large supply of plastic explosive. More importantly, she carried four spigot mortars designed by Jefferis and perfected for use at sea by Clarke.

The *Maid Honour*'s inaugural combat mission had been planned some four weeks earlier, when Gubbins invited March-Phillipps to luncheon in London. His team was to head from Poole to equatorial West Africa, where they were to 'undertake subversive operations on both sea and land'. In particular, they were to target Admiral Dönitz's U-boats that were prowling the coast of West Africa and had sunk no fewer than twenty-seven Allied merchant ships over the previous months. The U-boats had been spotted lurking in the muddy creeks and mangrove swamps of Vichy-controlled territory there: this was where they came to refuel and re-victual. This, too, was where they were most vulnerable to attack. March-Phillipps declared that if he so much as sighted one, he would 'blow a hole in her with the spigot mortar'.[3]

Gubbins warned March-Phillipps that hunting U-boats was merely 'a general direction'[4] as to what his men were to do. It was quite possible – indeed probable – that their mission would change. Flexibility, as he was always reminding them, was the key to everything.

The *Maid Honour* was fully kitted out by the time Gubbins paid his lunchtime visit to Poole. He was joined at the waterfront by Cecil Clarke, who had travelled down from Brickendonbury Manor in order to watch the first test firing of the spigot mortars at sea. His workload had increased dramatically since taking up the reins at Brickendonbury, with more than a hundred agents from a dozen countries currently undergoing training. But the adapted spigot mortar remained his special project and he was so keen to film the test firing on his hand-held camera that he took the time to travel down to Poole.

The firing took place in Poole harbour and revealed that the spigot was every bit as powerful on sea as it was on land. One of March-Phillipps's team, Graham Hayes, was seated on the deck of the *Maid Honour* calmly smoking his pipe when the firing took place. There was a flash, a roar and, for Hayes at least, an unwelcome surprise. The force of the blast lifted him clean off the deck and hurled him into the water, from which he emerged, concussed and bedraggled, minus his pipe, shorts and pants. March-Phillipps's men were astonished by the spigot's power. Not many weapons could relieve a man of his underwear.

The firing was followed by a farewell luncheon at the Antelope Hotel, with Gubbins seated at the head of the table like a much loved warlord presiding over a band of gangsters. The Antelope's proprietor, Pop, lived up to his nickname by producing a few bottles of champagne from his well-stocked cellar. When the last of the desserts were finished, the men wandered down to the harbour and boarded the *Maid Honour*. Gubbins betrayed his Scottish sentimentalism by pinning a lucky sprig of white heather to the foremast. Anders 'the Viking' Lassen felt they would need more than luck to keep them alive. 'He's mad, our commander,' he confided to one of his fellow team members. 'We are doomed.'[5]

The voyage to West Africa was remarkably trouble-free, despite gale-force winds and big seas. The route took them across the Bay of Biscay, past Madeira and west of the Canary Islands before heading for Freetown in Sierra Leone. They might easily have been spotted by U-boats or even German planes, yet their only problems came when the *Maid Honour*'s engine seized up with rust. One of the team, 'Buzz' Perkins, stripped it down and repaired it.

Anders Lassen supplemented their meagre rations by means of an old nautical trick. He pierced a tin can, placed pieces of carbide-laced bait inside and then tossed it into the water. Swallowed by one of the many sharks that tailed the vessel, the can exploded when the carbide mixed with the acid contents of the fish's stomach. The next few hours were spent pulling floating chunks of shark meat from the water.

After a six-week voyage and having covered more than 3,000 miles, the *Maid Honour* arrived in tropical Freetown on 20 September. The men now awaited precise orders from Gubbins. They felt as if they were on vacation rather than at war. 'Really, this camp is for us a sort of holiday,'[6] wrote Geoffrey Appleyard as he struggled up from his sun-lounger and undertook another bout of spear-fishing.

Colin Gubbins had already hinted that the focus of their mission might change. This was indeed the case, for within weeks of the *Maid Honour* arriving in tropical West Africa, he received intelligence of a most alarming nature. His informant was Louis Franck, whom he had sent to Lagos – capital of the British colony of Nigeria – almost a year earlier. Operating under the codename 'W', Franck's task was to keep a sharp eye on the Vichy French territories on this stretch of African coastline and report on anything untoward taking place.

In order to undertake this work efficiently, Franck had built his own network of spies and informers whose tentacles reached right across the tropics. One of them was Victor Laversuch, W4, a Spanish-speaking operator based in Lagos. Another was Richard Lippett, or agent W25. And there were many more, all of whom operated under codenames.

It was from one of these informers, Colin Michie, that there came startling intelligence. Michie was the British Vice-Consul on Fernando Po, a steaming hothouse of an island that lay some twenty-five miles off the West African coast. It was a soporific place dominated by its pyramid-shaped volcano and tangled mantle of tropical rainforest. When the explorer, Sir Richard Burton, had come here half a century earlier, he described it as 'the abomination of desolation'.[7] Most of its inhabitants lived in the diminutive port of Santa Isabel, a colonial Spanish backwater with its cluster of white-washed houses and a horseshoe volcanic bay. Here, at a far remove from the world, the war seemed impossibly remote. Yet in this very bay – warned Michie – there lurked a vessel that spelled grave danger for Allied shipping.

The *Duchessa d'Aosta* was a large Italian liner that had dropped anchor more than a year earlier, claiming shelter in the neutral, Spanish-controlled port. Michie had reasons to doubt this claim. He knew that the Spanish governor of Fernando Po, Captain Victor Sanchez-Diez, was by no means neutral. He was 'violently pro-Nazi'[8] and would do anything to help the Axis powers in their fight against the Allies.

More alarming, the *Duchessa d'Aosta*'s radio had not been blocked by Captain Sanchez-Diez, as it should have been. Michie had been informed that she was a listening vessel, tasked with supplying the Abwehr with precise details of Allied shipping movements. This information was being sent to a German fishing company in Las Palmas, from whence it was being forwarded to Berlin.

This was a grave matter indeed and it was made even more worrying by the fact that the *Duchessa d'Aosta* had recently been joined by two German ships, the *Likomba* and *Burundi*. The three captains had become close drinking companions, carousing long and hard at the Casino Terrace Restaurant. They made for a dangerous and unholy trio. Scores of Allied vessels, and thousands of lives, were being put at risk by the presence of these enemy vessels in Santa Isabel.

Gubbins thought long and hard about how to combat this threat. His Lagos-based agent, Louis Franck, warned that Captain Sanchez-Diez had greatly increased the strength of the local garrison, with sentries at the harbour mouth and an efficient Guardia Colonial. 'Action,' he said, 'was almost impossible.'[9]

Almost. But not entirely. Gubbins's most obvious course of

action would have been to use March-Phillipps's team to sabotage all three vessels. Equipped with collapsible canoes and Cecil Clarke's limpet mines, they could have sunk them without too much difficulty. But such an operation carried huge risks, for it was certain to provoke outrage in Franco's pro-German Spain. Worse still, it might tip Spain into the war as a pro-Axis combatant. This would be a disaster, especially for all the British Crown Colonies in West Africa: Sierra Leone, the Gold Coast, Nigeria, British Cameroon and others.

There was one other option, one that was infinitely more appealing to Gubbins's mischievous mind. He had often spoken of his desire 'to strike the enemy and disappear completely, leaving no trace'.[10] Now, he began planning a piratical raid of the sort not seen since the days of Sir Francis Drake's attacks on the Spanish Main. Only on this occasion, instead of singeing the Spanish beard, he intended to leave no mark whatsoever.

The plan was for March-Phillipps and his men to perform one of the greatest nautical conjuring tricks in history, causing the three enemy vessels in Santa Isabel to vanish into thin air. It was a trick that would require neither a magician nor even a magic wand; rather, it would need guile, pluck and a tiny quantity of plastic explosive.

Having determined his course of action, Gubbins ordered his West African network into action. Louis Franck was to use every intelligence tentacle at his disposal as he planned a mission that was given the codename Operation Postmaster.

Franck's first port of call was Colin Michie, who had originally warned of the danger posed by the *Duchessa d'Aosta*. Michie did much of the intelligence groundwork and even talked a local pilot into giving him an aerial tour of the island, enabling him to take reconnaissance photographs of the three vessels in the harbour. This showed their precise positions and their alignment with the shore. Michie also managed to acquire highly revealing photographs of the Spanish governor, naked, cavorting with his equally naked African mistress. He conspired to get these shown to the governor, who was so concerned about being exposed to blackmail that he offered to relax the tight surveillance on the tiny British community on Fernando Po. Michie graciously accepted.

Soon after Gubbins received the aerial photographs, he was supplied with even better intelligence. In the previous March he had hired the services of Leonard Guise, or W10, a talented servant of the Nigerian colonial government. Now, Guise lived up to his name by landing in Fernando Po in the guise of a diplomatic courier. He was able to undertake a highly precise reconnaissance, right down to the strength of the *Duchessa d'Aosta*'s mooring chains.

While he was on the island, Guise enlisted the services of the local English chaplain, the Reverend Markham, whose devotion to God came second only to his devotion to country. In heavy disguise, he managed to slip aboard the Italian liner during a party and discovered that the crew were extremely lax in their approach to security. They were also shockingly debauched. 'At least four have been sent to Spain sick,' wrote Reverend Markham, 'and a large number suffer from venereal disease.'[11]

The gathering of intelligence took time, but by Christmas Gubbins had his mission fully planned and March-Phillipps knew exactly what was expected. The final task was to inform Sir George Giffard, the army's commander-in-chief in West Africa. His permission was needed for an operation due to take place on his patch.

Giffard was appalled when he learned of the intended piratical mission. He vociferously refused permission to allow Gubbins to send his men to Fernando Po, regarding them as little better than a band of wayward hooligans. 'They are not round pegs in round holes,' he said.

Giffard's hostility was seconded by the Royal Navy's Commander-in-Chief, South Atlantic, Vice-Admiral Algernon Willis. He described Gubbins's mission as 'unnecessarily provocative' and sent a telegram to London that arrived a few minutes after midnight on Christmas morning. It was a present that Gubbins could have done without. He and Giffard had 'suspended operations'[12] on the grounds that they were too underhand. Operation Postmaster was over before it had even begun.

Gus March-Phillipps and his men were blissfully unaware of the hostility to their mission. They spent Christmas up-country in Nigeria, at an enchanting lodge called Olokomeji, the former holiday home of the colonial governor, Sir Bernard Bourdillon. Here, far from prying eyes, they let rip with their machine guns and blew clearings in the jungle with plastic explosive. March-Phillipps's second-in-command, Geoffrey Appleyard, thought it the best Christmas ever. All around there were 'luscious fruits which we picked straight from the forest trees – oranges, grapefruit, coconuts and tangerine as big as grapefruit, no pips and full of juice'.

Sir George Giffard and Vice-Admiral Willis continued to block Operation Postmaster until they learned that Gubbins had succeeded in winning the backing of the Foreign Office and Admiralty. Now, reluctantly, they agreed to support it. 'I tell you frankly, I do not like the scheme,' said Giffard, 'and I never shall like it.'

March-Phillipps had taken two decisions during his Christmas break. First, the *Maid Honour* was not suitable for the mission ahead. He needed powerful tugs, not a Brixham trawler. To this end, he approached Governor Bourdillon, who graciously offered two craft, *Vulcan* and *Nuneaton*.

March-Phillipps's second decision was to hire more men, for he was concerned about being outgunned by the Italians and Germans in Santa Isabel. Once again, Governor Bourdillon offered to help. March-Phillipps was allowed to choose as many men as he wished from the Nigerian Colonial Service.

He picked seventeen tough, military-trained individuals with a keen hunger for action. When Gubbins's agent, Leonard Guise, met them, he was impressed. 'As choice a collection of thugs as Nigeria can ever have seen.'[13]

On 10 January the mission was given the green light. On the same day, March-Phillipps received a telegram from Gubbins: 'Good hunting. Am confident you will exercise utmost care to ensure success and obviate repercussions.'[14]

March-Phillipps telegrammed back: 'Will do our best.'[15]

He meant it.

At a few minutes before dawn on Sunday, 11 January the *Vulcan* and *Nuneaton* slipped unnoticed out of Lagos harbour on the four-day voyage to Fernando Po. As they crossed the bar, the swell of the open sea pitched the tugs from wave to trough, causing intense seasickness. It was like setting sail in a floating bottle. No one complained, aware that 'the wrath of Gus would have descended upon them like an avalanche.'[16] The breeze was as damp as a face-flannel and the tropical sun was soon burning with such intensity that sweat dripped from the brow at the slightest exertion.

March-Phillipps intended to use every hour of the voyage for additional training in target practice and marine assault. It was particularly important that his newly recruited 'thugs' familiarize themselves with the weaponry. When night fell after the first day at sea, the crew of the *Nuneaton* lowered their Folbot canoes into the water and undertook a practice raid on the *Vulcan*. 'Highly successful,' noted March-Phillipps. 'The Folbots approaching within a few yards without being seen.'[17] It was vitally important for everyone to be a master of their appointed role.

There was still much to be done. The men cleaned their weapons, sharpened their fighting knives and practised firing their Bren and tommy guns. 'When possible, intimidate,' said March-Phillipps. 'If not, use force. Speed is essential.'[18]

As a tropical dawn cut through the sky on 14 January, a faint emerald smudge was discernible on the horizon. A few hours later, it began sharpening into focus and the men caught their first glimpse of Santa Isabel's pyramid-shaped peak, its tangled upper slopes enveloped in a soupy mist. The warm mist also hung low over the water, a blessing for March-Phillips and his adventurers: it rendered their two vessels invisible to even the sharpest-eyed lookout on Fernando Po.

A cold lunch was served that noon, because the galley areas were being used to boil and mould the plastic explosive. In the afternoon, tommy guns, torches and pistols were issued to each of the men, along with truncheons designed for silent killing: twelve-inch metal bolts encased in sheaths of rubber.

The men spent the rest of the afternoon waiting for dusk, when their mission would begin in earnest. Their greatest concern was the troubled state of the *Nuneaton*'s engines. They had already faltered on several occasions since they'd been at sea. If this happened in Santa Isabel harbour, the men would be sitting ducks.

The mist lifted with the approach of evening and with it came an improvement in the weather. At 10 p.m. both tugs lay some four miles offshore and the town lights of Santa Isabel twinkled on the water like specks of phosphorescence. March-Phillipps kept glancing anxiously at his watch, counting down the minutes. Soon it was 11.15 p.m., time for the engines to be fired.

The vessels quickly closed on the lighthouse of Cap Formoso, which was to give them a steer on Santa Isabel harbour. Their raid was timed for just after 23.30 hours and March-Phillipps was a stickler for punctuality.

The *Nuneaton* was the leading vessel, but she was creeping towards the harbour mouth at an agonizingly slow speed. March-Phillipps, who always stuttered when stressed, called through the darkness: 'Will you get a b-b-bl-bloody move on or g-g-get out. I'm coming in.'

It was only now, just as they prepared to enter the harbour, that March-Phillipps realized he had made a disastrous mistake in the planning. The island generator was always switched off at 11.30 p.m., extinguishing the harbour lights, which was exactly when he was intending to strike. He had assumed Fernando Po kept the same time as Nigeria. It didn't. The island was on Spanish time, one hour behind Lagos, which meant they had arrived an hour too early.

He was so fired by adrenalin that he wanted to press on regardless, even though it meant risking a firefight in the well-lit harbour. This would have been insane and it earned him a stern reprimand from Leonard Guise, who had joined the mission in Lagos. 'Gus himself struck me as completely intrepid, almost to the point of overdoing it, because this was not really a military operation. It was a burglar's operation, and burglars don't go in shooting.' He convinced him to linger for an hour, until the lights went out.

After a tense wait, the island's generator finally snapped off, plunging the town into darkness. 'Very dramatically the blackout arrived,' recalled Guise, 'and what had been a well-illuminated display became utter darkness.'[19] He felt vindicated. Only a few faint lights remained: the flashing buoys, a pier light and a bulb on the foreshore of the *Duchessa d'Aosta*. In the night sky, there was not even a whisker of moonlight.

The *Vulcan* and *Nuneaton* crept into the harbour with stealth, unseen by anyone. The *Duchessa d'Aosta* was visible as a dark gleam, with two lit portholes suggesting that there were people on board. The *Likomba* and *Burundi* lay in darkness, their bulky hulls wallowing low in the water. The men prepared themselves in absolute silence, aware that even whispers carry noisily on a nocturnal breeze. It was time for them to perform a conjuring trick unlike any other.

The Casino Terrace Restaurant in Santa Isabel was unusually busy that evening. A dinner had been arranged for twenty-five people, including Captain Umberto Valle of the *Duchessa d'Aosta* and eight of his officers. Also present was Captain Specht of the *Likomba*. As far as the two captains were concerned, the dinner had been arranged by Abelino Zorilla, a well-connected local fixer. His services were often used to arrange evenings such as this one. They had no idea that Zorilla was actually working for Richard Lippett, one of Colin Gubbins's locally based agents in Santa Isabel. Lippett had paid Zorilla to arrange the casino dinner, aware that it would provide exactly the distraction March-Phillipps needed to pull off his heist.

Zorilla was more than happy to help, for he was deeply opposed to fascism and also disliked the presence of Germans on his island home. Now, he excelled himself in preparing a dinner the two captains would never forget. His attention to detail was particularly impressive. His seating plan for the Casino Restaurant ensured that all the officers had their backs to the windows that overlooked the harbour. He also made sure that the alcohol flowed in unusually abundant quantities. And he supplied the restaurant with Tilley Paraffin lamps, so that the party need not be disrupted when the town's generator was switched off at 11.30 p.m.

On the evening scheduled for Operation Postmaster, Richard Lippett sauntered down to the Casino Terrace Restaurant in company with the town's Spanish bank manager. Here, they had a few drinks. When Lippett settled his bill at around 9 p.m., he feigned innocence and asked the manageress about the dinner party upstairs. She said she knew only that it had been booked in advance and that an unusually large quantity of alcohol had been bought. Lippett smiled inwardly: Zorilla's dinner was going according to plan.

Lippett next wandered down to the harbour and was pleased to see that the Colonial Guard had no inkling of what was set to take place that night. 'There were no preparations of any kind, in fact several of the sentries were sleeping.'[20]

He looked up at the evening sky and noted with satisfaction that it was punctuated with flashes of lightning and there was the occasional drum-roll of thunder. With luck, the thunder would mask the sound of the explosions to come.

Gus March-Phillipps's two tugs, *Vulcan* and *Nuneaton*, were inside the harbour within minutes of the main town lights snapping off. The *Nuneaton* came to a stop some ninety metres from the harbour-mouth to enable the Folbot canoes to be lowered. The *Vulcan*, meanwhile, nudged slowly towards the *Duchessa*. The tugmaster, Mr Coker, managed to align the port side of the vessel with the starboard side of the *Duchessa*. Although a few lights were still shining from the portholes, no one had noticed their approach.

As soon as the two vessels were in contact, March-Phillipps and five of his team leaped aboard, their movements covered by the Bren guns on the *Vulcan*'s bridge. The *Vulcan* recoiled slightly as she nudged the *Duchessa* and had to be inched forward again to allow another six men to board. A third manoeuvre enabled the last of March-Phillipps's team to clamber on to the ship. There was 'no resistance worthy of the name', or so March-Phillipps later wrote in his report.[21] In fact, the only casualty occurred when one of the men tripped over a pig that was waddling around on deck.

Securing the vessel proved easier than expected. Lassen 'the Viking' lashed a rope to one of the *Duchessa*'s bollards and then threw the other end to his comrade Robin Duff. 'Pull, Robin! Pull like fuck!'[22]

March-Phillipps and 'Haggis' Taylor had meanwhile reached the bridge, 'knife in one hand and pistol in the other'.[23] They found it deserted. The rest of the team headed below decks and took prisoner all the Italians who had not been invited to the Casino Restaurant. A few tried to resist, but March-Phillipps's men were ready with their truncheons, or 'persuaders', as they called them. One 'had to take his persuader and play a quick arpeggio on their heads'.[24] It quickly persuaded the resisters to surrender.

The only surprise of the night came when the boarding party kicked down one of the locked doors and found a woman stewardess,

Gilda Turch, cowering inside the cabin. When confronted by a band of distinctly ungentlemanly commandos, with truncheons and black-ened faces, she fainted.

While March-Phillipps secured the bridge, Geoffrey Appleyard was laying explosives on the ship's cables. This was the crucial moment of the entire operation, when it would either succeed or fail. None of the men could be sure that the plastic explosive would sever the heavy metal hawsers.

When the charges detonated, they did so with massive explosive force. Leonard Guise described it as 'a titanic roar and a flash that lit the whole island'.[25] Even so, one of the chains failed to be cut by the charge and Appleyard had to lay a second charge on a very short fuse. There was another flash as the last cable was broken. Further explosions cut the chains that were securing the *Likomba* and *Burundi* to the harbour wall.

The *Duchessa* had by now been roped to the helm of the *Vulcan*. As the tug's propellers started churning the water, her skipper, Mr Coker, performed a deft nautical manoeuvre. He 'gave the Duchessa two slews, one to starboard, one to port, like drawing a cork out of a bottle'.[26] Appleyard watched transfixed as 'the huge liner lurched and began to slide forward.' He leaped on board just in time. The *Duchessa*, 'without the slightest hesitation, and at the speed of at least three knots, went straight between the three buoys to the open sea'.[27]

Moments later, the *Nuneaton* was also heading out to sea with both the *Likomba* and *Burundi* in tow. In less than a minute, March-Phillipps's two vessels, together with their towed prizes, had been swallowed by the night.

All hell had broken out on shore. The series of explosions had echoed throughout Santa Isabel and caused absolute panic. Bugles sounded the alarm and people were running through the town screaming, '*Alerto! Alerto!*' Most townsfolk thought that the harbour was under attack from raiding aircraft. 'Immediately after the deto-nations were heard, the anti-aircraft guns went into action and blazed into the sky.'

No one realized that the harbour, still blacked out and moonless, had come under attack from the sea. Local Spaniards dashed across to the Guardia Colonial to arm themselves with rifles. The guard's captain was also seen running towards the building shouting, '*Que pasa?* [What's happened?]'[28]

In the Casino Terrace Restaurant, the explosions and anti-aircraft fire had caused confusion rather than panic. Most of the men were so drunk they could scarcely walk. Some had taken themselves off to the local brothel, only to find their dalliances disturbed by the mayhem outside. Now, all of them staggered down to the harbour only to find their ships were missing. Blurry-eyed and still dazed by the heady fumes of cognac, they rubbed their eyes and looked again. They were not deceived: the ships had gone.

The ensuing uproar was witnessed by the British consul, Peter Lake, and his new deputy, Vice-Consul Godden. They overheard peals of laughter coming from both local Africans and Spaniards as they realized what had happened. Altogether less amused was Captain Specht of the *Likomba*, who, at around 1.30 a.m., marched over to the British Consulate and burst through the unlocked front door. 'Where is my ship?' he screamed.

'He was very drunk and quarrelsome,' wrote Consul Lake, who promptly ordered him out of the building. 'In reply, he struck me in the face.'[29]

Vice-Consul Godden was more attuned to the fine arts of diplomacy than late night pub brawls, but on this occasion he proved himself a master of the left hook. He 'rushed to the affray and put some heavy North of Scotland stuff on Specht, and literally knocking the s—t out of him'. When Specht realized that Godden was about to shoot him, 'he collapsed in a heap, split his pants and emptied his bowels on the floor.' Godden called for his steward, who handed the soiled and 'dilapidated Specht over to the police'.[30]

By the following morning, the news of the stolen ships had spread far and wide. When Richard Lippett went to the badminton courts in order to play a game with his Spanish friend, Senõra Montilla, he found the place surrounded by soldiers. They told him what he had known for hours: that three ships had been seized from the harbour and spirited away. Senõra Montilla said to him: 'Well done, the English are very smart.' Lippett replied: 'No, the English would never do such a thing like that, especially in a Spanish port.' Señora Montilla smiled. 'Just wait and see,' she said.

Consul Peter Lake was delighted to discover that no one had been able to pin the blame on the British. 'The following day was full of rumours,' he recalled. 'Free French, Vichy, USA, British and even anti-Falange Spanish pirates were all equally possible culprits.' He added that the sheer bravado of the perpetrators was causing a sensation. 'Admiration and amusement for the way in which the job was performed and timed was shown openly by many Spaniards.'[31]

The German shipping agent Heinrich Luhr contended that it was such a masterful operation that only the Germans themselves could have pulled it off. If so, he felt sure that each man would be awarded the Iron Cross. But the discovery of Free French caps floating in the harbour – a little parting gift from March-Phillipps – suggested that it had perhaps been a Gaullist operation.

March-Phillips had conducted a textbook cutting-out operation, one that had left absolutely no trace. The hours that followed the seizure of the ships were not without their difficulties. The *Nuneaton* had scarcely left the harbour, towing the *Likomba* and *Burundi*, when the stolen vessels began smashing into each other. The *Nuneaton* was forced to cut her engines while the *Burundi* was secured at the end of a longer rope. But this soon frayed, prompting a dazzling display of acrobatics from Anders Lassen. Using skills learned from Sykes and Fairbairn, he performed a tightrope walk along the line that joined the *Nuneaton* to the *Burundi*. 'With a heaving line tied around his waist, he swarmed across the fraying tow rope.'[32] Several times he was flung into the air and was lucky to regain his balance. But he eventually made it to the *Burundi* and attached a new rope to the ship.

The *Duchessa d'Aosta* had been placed under the command of Geoffrey Appleyard and a skeleton crew, who were so delighted with their prize ship – and their Italian prisoners now locked below decks – that they hoisted a skull and crossbones from the mainmast. March-Phillipps exploded when he saw it fluttering in the dawn breeze. 'We all got a rocket and we were told we weren't to fly the Jolly Roger,' recalled Leonard Guise. 'He was a great stickler for etiquette, old Gus.'[33]

The *Duchessa d'Aosta* had been theoretically untouchable while she lay at anchor at Santa Isabel, for she was sheltering in a neutral harbour under the protection of international law. But now that she was out on the high seas, albeit unwillingly, she was fair game for any Allied vessel that happened to chance upon her. And this is where the second part of March-Phillipps's mission came into play. It had been previously agreed that the HMS *Violet* would intercept the *Duchessa d'Aosta* while she was at sea. She would then be seized and impounded as an enemy vessel. If all went to plan, the Italians would have been worsted for the second time in just a few hours.

The HMS *Violet* was late for her rendezvous with March-Phillipps's flotilla, not closing with them until the afternoon of 20 January. But her lateness made no difference to the outcome. Soon after being captured, at just after 6 p.m., all six ships sailed into Lagos harbour, where March-Phillipps and his men were given a hero's welcome.

'We had a tremendous reception,' said one of the men.[34] They were met by His Excellency Governor Sir Bernard Bourdillon, who stood at the end of his private landing stage cheering wildly, whisky and soda in hand.

A more surprising welcome came from General Giffard. He had done everything he could to scupper the mission, but now that it was a success he was keen to claim the credit. '[He] came down and looked upon us as his chaps, having pulled off a successful operation.'[35]

As March-Phillipps surveyed the cheering crowds, he felt deep pride in his men. They had worked 'almost without sleep for a whole week, under difficult and dangerous conditions, with the utmost cheerfulness and disregard for themselves'.[36]

News of the mission's success was rapidly sent to Colin Gubbins, setting it out in bold terms. 'Casualties, our party, absolutely nil. Casualties enemy, nil, except a few sore heads. Prisoners, German, nil; Italians, men, 27, women, 1, natives, 1.'

Gubbins immediately sent a telegram back to Lagos. 'Best congratulations to all concerned on complete success of a well-thought out, carefully planned and neatly executed operation.'

As congratulatory telegrams arrived from the Foreign Office and even the Cabinet, General George Giffard saw fit to compose his own, somewhat embarrassed message, addressing it to one of the principal agents involved in the planning. 'For reasons which I was unable to explain to you, I felt I had to oppose our project,' he said. 'It does not lessen my admiration for skilled [word missing], daring and success with which you have succeeded.' He added his 'hearty congratulations, and hope in the event of similar projects in future, circumstances may permit me to assist and not oppose'.[37]

There remained one outstanding issue that had to be tackled head-on. It was imperative that the Spanish should never discover that a British raiding party had flagrantly breached their neutrality by cutting out three vessels. March-Phillipps's first task on arriving at Lagos was to silence the Italian prisoners. To this end, all those aboard the *Duchessa d'Aosta* were marched to an internment camp situated deep in the jungle, more than 150 miles inland from Lagos. They were to languish there for the rest of the war.

The next thing was to propagate a series of lies that would mask what had taken place. Hugh Dalton began this process with a message to Churchill. 'There is reason to suppose that the Spanish authorities are aware that a large tug of unknown nationality entered the harbour and took the vessels out; but that is probably all they know.' He said that March-Phillipps had covered his tracks with such skill that 'we do not believe they will be able to *prove* that the tug was British, and the greatest precautions have been taken to see that no information leaks out at Lagos.'[38]

Britain's first official response came within hours of the operation having taken place: it was a masterpiece of dissimulation. A communiqué was issued at midnight on 19 January spelling out the British position. 'The British Admiralty considers it necessary to state that no British or Allied ship was in the vicinity' of Fernando Po. It added that German accusations of British involvement were of such a serious nature that the British commander-in-chief in West Africa had dispatched reconnaissance vessels from Lagos in order to search for the real culprits.

In Spain itself, there was outrage at what had taken place. Although there was no proof that the British had conducted the operation, the pro-Nazi Foreign Minister, Serrano Suner, pointed the finger of blame squarely at Britain. Long before March-Phillipps's vessels reached Lagos, he was calling the cutting-out operation an 'intolerable attack on our sovereignty'. He added that 'no Spaniard can fail to be roused by this act of piracy committed in defiance of every right and within waters under our jurisdiction.'[39]

The Nazi press was no less indignant, with the *Völkischer Beobachter* openly accusing the British of undertaking an illegal and outlandish act of piracy.

The British consul in Madrid, Sir Samuel Hoare, rose majestically above the fray, expressing deep disappointment that the Spanish government 'should so readily have assumed that His Majesty's Government were concerned with any events which may have taken place in Santa Isabel or on the *Duchessa d'Aosta*'. He reiterated that the British government was 'in no way responsible for what happened prior to the capture of the enemy vessels on the high seas'.[40]

This, like all the other British communiqués, was completely untrue. After two years of war, the British government and its servants were finally learning to behave like cads.

10

A Deadly Bang

COLIN GUBBINS'S WEST African triumph led to a subtle change in the way he was treated by his enemies in the War Office. For more than a year, senior generals had spoken to him as if he were 'a somewhat disreputable child', one whose goals were 'not deemed worthy of serious attention'. Some had even dismissed his team as 'harmless, back-room lunatics'[1] and argued that the entire Baker Street organization should be dismantled. Only now did they awake to the fact that Gubbins had been steadily establishing a network of agents and saboteurs that stretched from tropical Africa to the Arctic Circle.

Operation Postmaster was one success. Another, less spectacular, was the so-called Shetland Bus. Gubbins had succeeded in establishing a regular link between the Shetland Islands and Norway, using fishing skiffs to smuggle agents and explosives into Nazi-occupied territory. By the spring of 1942, almost a hundred saboteurs and 150 tons of explosives had been infiltrated into the country. An array of bold sabotage operations was now being planned.

But there was one Norwegian target that Gubbins's men were unable to attack, even though it lay at anchor in a coastal fjord. The *Tirpitz* was the latest addition to Hitler's fleet and she also happened to be the most powerful warship in the world. A veritable leviathan of 52,600 tons, she was bristling with torpedoes and anti-aircraft guns. If ever she were to be deployed in the North Atlantic, she would be able to wreak havoc on convoys already suffering massive losses from German U-boats.

'No other target is comparable to it,' wrote Churchill in a memo circulated to his chiefs of staff on 25 January. 'The whole strategy of the war turns at this period on this ship.' As far as he was concerned, 'the destruction or even crippling of the ship' was a matter 'of the highest urgency and importance'.² To this end, he called for active cooperation between Bomber Command, the Fleet Air Arm and the Royal Navy's destroyers, but he was also prepared to consider any scheme that might prevent the *Tirpitz* from being deployed in the North Atlantic. And that included sabotage.

The *Tirpitz* herself could not be sabotaged, not even by Gubbins's Norwegian agents, for she was heavily defended, surrounded by support vessels and too large to be easily sunk with limpet mines. But her greatest strength – her size – was also her most significant weakness for it left her vulnerable and exposed. Every captain knows that a battleship is only as good as the docks in which she is serviced, and the only Atlantic dock large enough to service the *Tirpitz* was the Normandie Dock at St Nazaire. Admiralty officials had long believed that Hitler would not dare to deploy his greatest battleship in the Atlantic if the Normandie Dock were to become unavailable, for she would have to return to Germany for repairs, and that meant exposing her to unacceptable risk as she made her way up the English Channel. Sabotaging the Normandie Dock now jumped to the top of the agenda and Colin Gubbins was tasked with planning his most daring adventure to date: an amphibious assault on the biggest dry dock in the world.

Targeting this immense dock was one thing, destroying it quite another. The statistics alone suggested it would be an operation of staggering complexity, for it was more than 1,200 feet in length and built of huge blocks of reinforced concrete. An even greater challenge was presented by the giant steel caisson gates situated at each end. Any successful sabotage operation would have to break open these caissons, but they were widely held to be indestructible. Constructed as sectional boxes and locked into deep underground sockets, the gates stood higher than a house and were built of reinforced steel that was fully thirty-five feet thick.

Reconnaissance photos revealed further bad news. St Nazaire was of such importance to the Nazis that it was heavily defended, with gun emplacements, anti-aircraft guns and heavy mortars. Many of these had been installed to protect the dredged channel that led directly to the dock gates. This channel passed within a few metres of the shoreline, exposing any attacker arriving by sea to unacceptable risk.

Gubbins studied all the available diagrams and photos of the Normandie Dock and concluded that it would require a minimum of thirty-eight men and 900 pounds of specially designed explosive to bring about 'complete destruction of the lock gates'. He also warned that 'such a large body of men could not enter the dock area without fighting'.[3] An assault on St Nazaire could not be undertaken without the additional support of several hundred professionally trained guerrillas.

It was not entirely clear who might undertake such a suicidal mission. One possibility was to send in Gus March-Phillipps and his team. They were back in London after their West African jaunt and itching for renewed action. In the aftermath of Operation Postmaster, Gubbins had been permitted to expand them into a force of some one hundred men who were henceforth to operate under the name of No. 62 Commando. March-Phillipps certainly had enough of a death wish to have a crack at the Normandie Dock, but Gubbins felt that his team was as yet too small to send into St Nazaire.

A second option was to parachute saboteurs into the port: this, after all, had been brilliantly successful at Pessac. But Pessac had required just eight small limpet mines to wreck its machinery. The destruction of St Nazaire's caisson gates required so much explosive that it simply wasn't feasible by air. Gubbins ruled out a parachute drop as logistically impossible and reluctantly concluded that the destruction of Hitler's biggest dock complex was 'outside the capabilities' of Baker Street, at least for the foreseeable future.[4]

And there the matter might have rested, had it not been for a brilliant piece of lateral thinking. Gubbins had long argued that the enemy must always be struck in the most vulnerable places, and in late January 1942 the most vulnerable point on the *Tirpitz* was not on the ship itself, nor even in the Normandie Dock, but inside the head of an up-and-coming naval commander named John Hughes-Hallett. He and a friend, Dick Costobadie, were idly glancing at a nautical map of the French Atlantic coastline when Hughes-Hallett was struck by what could only be described as a eureka moment. And as with Archimedes, so John Hughes-Hallett's solution to a seemingly insurmountable problem was predicated upon a surfeit of water.

As Hughes-Hallett studied the water depths in the Loire estuary, he realized that there was a significant flaw to the defences of St Nazaire, one that had hitherto been completely overlooked. In springtime, when there was the conjunction of a full moon and a rare flood tide, water levels rose to such a height that a shallow-draught vessel could reach the southern caisson without having to use the dredged channel. This meant that a ship could approach the dock gates without having to run the gauntlet of the coastal defences. For just a few hours each year, the Normandie Dock was tantalizingly exposed.

Captain Hughes-Hallett mentioned his discovery to his friend, Captain Charles Lambe, who in turn talked it over with Lord Mountbatten, the head of Combined Operations. Mountbatten realized that this was an opportunity to be seized. That very afternoon in late January he called together his staff at their headquarters in Richmond Terrace and repeated what Captain Lambe had told him over luncheon. 'Let's get out something unconventional,' he said.[5]

The unfolding plan was not just unconventional, but breathtaking in scope and audacity. The attacking force was to be drawn from Mountbatten's commando units while the explosives and specialist training were to be provided by Gubbins. Unlike most senior army commanders, Mountbatten had a deep respect for Gubbins and was 'quick to note' that he offered 'a unique and apparently inexhaustible source of special arms, explosives and other technical supplies which Combined Operations had neither the funds nor the facilities to manufacture for themselves'.[6]

Gubbins set to work with gusto, calling for a meeting with Captain Hughes-Hallett within days of his nautical discovery. A plan rapidly took shape. The idea was to ram the southern caisson at high speed with an old destroyer packed with delayed-action high explosive. It was to be the dirtiest bomb ever devised, one encased in so much steel and concrete that it would explode with devastating force. Mountbatten described it as a 'terrifying solution'[7] to a hitherto intractable problem, one that would turn the Normandie Dock into a twisted, mangled wreck.

There was just one potential difficulty. Success would be entirely dependent on the bomb's detonator and fuse, which would need a delay of at least seven hours to allow the men to fight their way off the ship, sabotage the docks and then escape from St Nazaire.

Gubbins had long recognized the need for a simple but reliable delayed-action fuse. 'In the conditions under which our men were often working, dark, wet nights, scaling barbed wire and broken glass, it was essential to keep our devices to the simplest, smallest and most fool-proof.'[8]

Millis Jefferis had taken heed of his words and was currently working on his L–Delay, a cunning little fuse that was designed to perform with hitherto unknown accuracy. The L stood for lead: Jefferis had discovered that lead wire crept with absolute regularity under tension. His idea was to use this 'creep' to produce a time-delay fuse with accuracy down to the last milli-second. The problem was that the L–Delay was still at the prototype stage and was never going to be ready in time for the spring tide at St Nazaire.

Other delay fuses relied on mechanical clocks, which were extremely vulnerable, or slow-burning mechanisms that were only suitable for very short delays. Neither could be adapted for use in a vessel whose engine vibrations would play havoc with accuracy.

The only option was to rely on the Time Pencil, a fuse that had an alarmingly poor track record. 'A very dodgy device indeed,' was the opinion of Stuart Macrae. 'One had to be very brave to use it.' Its most striking feature was its simplicity. A spring-loaded striker was held under tension by a piano wire. The wire was surrounded by a fragile glass tube filled with acid. When this tube was broken, the acid began to eat away at the wire. When the wire broke, it released the striker that detonated the explosive.

And herein lay the flaw: no one could predict how long it would take for the wire to break. 'In very hot weather, a theoretically long delay fuse might go off in a few minutes,' said Macrae, who tested hundreds of them. 'In very cold weather, it might not go off at all.'[9]

But there was no alternative. The success or failure of the attack on St Nazaire would be dependent on a highly inaccurate fuse that was little bigger than a pencil. If it went off too early, the commandos would be blown to the heavens, along with their ship. But there was also a chance that it wouldn't go off at all.

The St Nazaire attack was to be on such a grand scale that it would require the services of more than 600 men, many of them veterans of Gubbins's Norwegian escapade. But three of them were to shoulder much of the responsibility, for they had vital roles to play in a mission that was to break all the rules of war.

The first of the three was Stephen Beattie, the thirty-four-year-old son of a Hertfordshire parson. Everyone liked Stephen: he had 'a charming personality, a serene and even temperament, a sound and sensible judgement and a retiring manner'. His friends thought him the very epitome of an English gentleman, 'tall, slender, black-bearded, blue-eyed',[10] and he was devoted to his wife, Philippa, and their three small children. He also happened to be a gifted sea captain, one with just enough of the buccaneering spirit for him to jump at the chance of leading a piratical raid on the French coastline.

Beattie had previously commanded the HMS *Vivien*, guarding the Arctic convoys as they made their perilous crossing of the North Sea. It was said that 'nothing rattled or ruffled him', which was just as well, for he was about to take command of a ship with four and a half tons of high explosive packed into her bow. It was his first sea command in which the goal was to cripple his own ship.

Second in importance to the mission's success was the explosives expert, Nigel Tibbits, a highly gifted naval student 'with a long, sensitive and intelligent face and a slow, quiet smile'. Just twenty-eight years of age, he had already notched up more qualifications than most acquire in a lifetime. He was a prizeman cadet who had obtained five firsts in his naval exams and won an Ogilvie medal for torpedo gunnery. If fate had not taken him to St Nazaire, he might have been adopted by Millis Jefferis's team at the Firs, for he was a genius at pure maths, 'the higher abstractions of which he would discuss with verve and gusto and often with great bursts of laughter'.[11] He had already spent several months working with Charles Goodeve, the oddball scientist who was helping to develop the Hedgehog mortar.

The principal aim of the attack on St Nazaire was to destroy the Normandie Dock's caisson gate. But there was a recognition that the dirty bomb might not explode. It was therefore decided to land a team of saboteurs whose task was to wreck as much of the winding and pumping machinery as possible. These saboteurs were under the command of twenty-eight-year-old Captain Bill Pritchard, the third member of the unholy trio of leaders. Pritchard was a hard-drinking Welsh mischief-maker with a keen interest in targeted destruction. He, like Gubbins, had long since dismissed aerial bombing as a blunt-edged tool. 'You make a lot of big holes and create a lot of nuisance, but you don't stop the dock from working.' The only way to guarantee the destruction of the pump machinery and winding mechanisms was to 'send chaps in and place explosives right on the vital parts'.[12]

Pritchard looked every inch the saboteur: tall and powerfully built, he had mischievous brown eyes that 'glinted with humour' when planning 'the pranks or rags that he enjoyed'. He was now charged with orchestrating the biggest prank of his life: he had to lead his team ashore and blow all the impeller pumps and hydraulic winches.

Pritchard had the pick of all the best explosive devices so far invented, including firepots, tar babies and 'sausage-charges' for cutting gun barrels. But the key explosives were to be limpets and clams, the latter being a miniature version of Clarke's limpet. It had been developed by Macrae in response to a request for smaller explosive charges. 'Although the explosive content was only about eight ounces,' he said, 'ICI produced some very high speed stuff for us and the design was such that the explosive was almost in contact with the target over a considerable area.'[13]

The commandos selected to undertake the mission were based at Lochailort, close to Arisaig, in the Scottish Highlands. They were told nothing about their goal, although they got some inkling that it was going to be tough when they were sent to be trained by Eric Sykes and William Fairbairn.

They were surprised to be taught by 'two benevolent square-shaped padres', but soon learned that their lives would depend on the tricks of these experts. One of the recruits, Lieutenant Corran Purdon, was led down to the cellars at Arisaig House and taught how to kill in the dark, including 'close-contact shooting in their sandbagged basement range where moving targets suddenly material-ized from the gloom'.

Purdon and his comrades learned how to kill with every conceivable weapon, 'including the Boyes anti-tank rifle, standing, and the two inch mortar from the hip', weapons that would blow a man apart. The commandos were warned that they risked getting 'shattered shoulders' and 'broken hips' if such guns were incorrectly fired.[14]

They were also reminded that attacking a heavily fortified dockyard in darkness meant that their guns would most likely be of little use, as Fairbairn knew from his experience of busting gangsters in night-time Shanghai. 'There always comes a point where you have to go over the top and at 'em,' he said. 'And when you're in that close, it's the best fighter that wins.' He now taught the commandos close-contact knife-fighting and stressed that confidence was the single most important factor in success. 'When you're confident, you instinctively attack. And whatever your opponent's weight and strength, you can overcome it if you attack. To stay on the defence is fatal.'[15]

The training for St Nazaire was intense and gruelling. Lieutenant Purdon and his fellow trainees 'splashed through hip-high freezing sea-loch estuaries, forded icy torrents holding boulders to combat the force of the rushing spate, climbed seemingly interminably high mountains and ran down steep scree slopes'.[16] By the third week of March, they were ready for action.

The ship that was to be used to ram the steel caisson was the HMS *Campbeltown*, a relic of the First World War. She was an American lend-lease vessel that was to have one last opportunity for glory. In order for her to pass over the St Nazaire shoals, she needed to be substantially lightened. To this end, all her heavy gear was cut away, along with her torpedo tubes. Her heavy deck guns were also stripped down and her fuel oil reduced to a minimum.

She even had two of her funnels removed, a modification that was not only done to lighten her. It was hoped that any German sentry seeing her as a dark silhouette from the shore would mistake her for a German destroyer of the Möwe class, especially if she was flying the swastika. Deception and subterfuge were to be important elements of the attack on St Nazaire.

Once her deck had been shielded with armoured sheeting, she was taken for a test-drive by Captain Beattie. She handled like 'a bitch', he thought, and would need to be treated accordingly if he was to have any hope of slamming her into the southern caisson of Normandie Dock.

Her final modification was the most important of all. A gigantic bomb was winched deep below decks, where it would wreak maximum damage. The explosive itself weighed four and a half tons, the same as a large lorry, and was enclosed in steel and then encased in cement. When it blew – *if* it blew – it would cause utter devastation.

Stephen Beattie had overheard a great deal of chatter about the unreliability of the Time Pencil detonators and voiced his fears to Nigel Tibbits, the explosives expert. 'What happens if we run into heavy fire and the fusing system gets shot up?' he asked. Tibbits said he hoped that it wouldn't. 'Or the chap responsible, that's you, gets shot up?'[17] Tibbits shrugged. They were indeed taking an enormous gamble. His own concern was that the force of ramming the ship into the caisson would trigger the fuses and blow them all to an early death. It was a concern shared by his beloved wife, Elmslie. She was filled with anguish about his mission and 'could not dispel the dread feeling that they would never meet again'.[18]

Not until the eve of departure were the officers provided with details of their adventure, which had been given the codename Operation Chariot. Colonel Charles Newman, the operational commander, gave them their briefing. 'Gentlemen,' he said, 'I know jolly well you have all been wondering what we are up to down here and now I'm going to tell you. You will all be delighted to know that we have been selected for a really lovely job – a saucy job – easily the biggest thing that has been done yet by the commandos. You could say it is the sauciest thing since Drake.'[19]

The *Campbeltown* set sail from Falmouth at two o'clock in the afternoon on 26 March, accompanied by two naval destroyers, a torpedo boat, a gunboat and twelve motor-launches carrying many of the commandos. The window of opportunity for the attack was extremely slight. It had to occur between midnight and 2 a.m. on the night of 29–30 March, when the full moon and spring tide would theoretically allow the *Campbeltown* to slip through the shoal-waters of St Nazaire, thereby avoiding the shipping lane close to the shoreline. If the tidal calculations were wrong, she would get stuck in the estuary mud.

Although the officers had been informed of their mission, the commandos themselves were still unsure of their goal. Now that they were at sea and there was no possibility of information being leaked to the enemy, Stephen Beattie gathered them on deck and gave them a briefing. The men were pleased to have been selected, masking their nervousness with laughter and backslapping. 'They broke into broad grins and returned to their stations with pert little jokes and a quickened pulse.'[20] They then raised a swastika and took photographs of themselves giving mocking salutes.

Shortly after nightfall on 29 March, the flotilla regrouped for a final rendezvous at sea. The ships were now forty nautical miles from the French coast and it was time to bid farewell to the two naval destroyers. They would remain offshore throughout the night, with the aim of making a rendezvous with the motor-launches on the following morning. In the intervening time, the *Campbeltown* and her accompanying motor-launches, gunboat and torpedo boat would be without their heavily armed escort.

At exactly eleven o'clock in the evening, Nigel Tibbits clambered down into the gloomy bowels of the ship to where the huge explosive charge was situated. It was stiflingly hot, a factor that could affect the working of the fuses, and the rumbling vibration of the ship's engines was a further cause for concern.

Tibbits groped his way towards the vast block of concrete and steel that filled much of the bow of the ship. With extreme care he now activated the three eight-hour Time Pencil fuses that were designed to detonate at seven o'clock the following morning. It was the most stressful moment of his life. From the moment he released the acid on to the piano wire, the men aboard the *Campbeltown* would be sitting on a massive suicide bomb. A single fault in either the acid or the wire would trigger the detonator.

There were countless other dangers to be faced before the Time Pencils were due to detonate, as all the men knew. They were hoping to sneak through the mouth of the Loire in the guise of a German destroyer, but that guise could not hold for ever. At some point they would surely be identified as enemy shipping.

As midnight approached, the *Campbeltown* reached the point at which the estuary met with the sea. After a further thirty minutes the men on the bridge sighted the half-submerged wreck of the *Lancastria*, sunk two years earlier during an aerial attack by German junkers. They were now just seven miles from their goal and were entering the dangerous shallows.

As the commandos shivered on deck, they could feel the ship 'churning and shuddering through the mud'.[21] At one point her keel scoured the bottom of the estuary. But Captain Beattie kept a cool head under pressure and managed to drive her relentlessly through the silt.

It had been a dull night for Korvettenkapitän Lothar Burhenne, commander of the Naval Flak Battalion on the east bank of the Loire estuary. He had spent much of the night with his eyes clamped to his night-vision binoculars, watching English bombers circling in the sky above. Their behaviour was most unusual. They were flying in strange formations and dropping very few bombs. It was almost as if they were there to divert attention.

Shortly after 1 a.m., Burhenne turned his binoculars towards the charcoal-grey estuary. He had to pinch himself, such was his astonishment at what he saw through the light of a dim moon. A flotilla of vessels appeared to be heading in the direction of the docks.

Burhenne snatched at the telephone and fired off this news to the harbour master. He was told not to be so idiotic. He then called his commanding officer, Captain Mecke, and informed him of what he had seen. Mecke's suspicions had already been aroused by the behaviour of the English bombers overhead. Now, as a precaution, he flashed a warning to all the troops guarding the estuary: *Achtung landegefahr!* Beware landing. A minute or so later, one of the dockyard searchlights was snapped on to the estuary, illuminating what appeared to be a German destroyer. She was accompanied by a dozen or more smaller vessels.

On board the *Campbeltown*, Signalman Pike had been anticipating this moment for hours. Now, in this moment of tension, he flashed a message in German: 'Two damaged ships in company – request permission to proceed in without delay.'[22] The message caused surprise on shore and deceived the Germans for a further five minutes. But at 1.28 a.m., after a rush of hasty phone calls, the ruse was unravelled. The ships in the estuary were not friend but foe.

Seconds later, a dozen searchlights lit the flotilla and every gun on the shore began blazing fire on the *Campbeltown*. Quick-firing cannon, machine guns and the coastal batteries unleashed a lethal rain of metal on to her exposed upper decks. If the vessel had been using the dredged channel, she would have been sunk in an instant.

As Captain Beattie cranked the *Campbeltown* to eighteen knots, a staccato of bullets hit the bridge, puncturing the thin steel. The side of the ship was 'alive with bursting shells'[23] that sprayed shrapnel and freezing seawater across the deck. The shells alarmed Tibbits. If a single one landed on the bow of the *Campbeltown*, it risked detonating her bomb with devastating consequences.

Chief Petty Officer Wellstead clutched at the wheel, desperately trying to steer a course through the glare of searchlights and flying tracer. He ducked and dodged the machine-gun fire, but the fire was so intense that he was eventually hit and killed. His place was taken by the quartermaster, who was trying to catch Captain Beattie's steering directions when he was also struck by a bullet.

One of the saboteurs, Bob Montgomery, was about to step forward to steer the ship when Nigel Tibbits tapped him on the shoulder. 'I'll take it old boy,' he said.

The *Campbeltown* was now taking direct hits on all sides. Her funnel and bridge were shot out and machine-gun bullets had penetrated all the way through to the boiler room. At one point there was a terrific explosion on deck, 'like the noise of someone banging a steel door with a sledgehammer'. A shell had burst next to Stuart Chant, another of the saboteurs, sending shrapnel deep into his flesh. He stretched out his arm in the darkness and was shocked. 'My leg was wet and sticky and my right arm was spurting blood down into my hand.'[24]

The shellfire was so intense that Captain Beattie was finding it hard to locate his target. The great steel caisson of Normandie Dock was lost in the drifting smoke and even the adjacent Mole was no longer visible. As he peered through the smoke and tracer fire, a German searchlight fell on the Old Mole for a second, giving him the perfect steer. He shouted to Tibbits, telling him to crank the vessel to port. They had 500 yards to go.

Beattie gave the engine a final blast. As she thrust towards twenty knots she began to judder violently. Less than sixty seconds to go. They were on course. The caisson lay directly ahead.

The ship's bells pealed through the gunfire, a warning for the men to brace themselves. They felt her snag slightly as she dragged the torpedo nets on the sea bottom. And then, at exactly 1.34 a.m., she smashed headlong into the caisson.

Major Copland, one of the commandos, was thrust forward on deck. He had the feeling that Beattie 'had applied super-powerful brakes to a very small car'. Debris rained backwards from the shattered bow of the vessel, spilling on to the deck. 'Sparks, dirt and planks seemed to be flying everywhere.'[25]

Captain Beattie dusted himself down, checked his watch and smiled. 'Well there we are,' he said in a cool voice. 'Four minutes late.'[26]

Captain Stephen Beattie's most urgent task was to examine the damage to the caisson, but this was not easy in the half-light of flares, searchlights and burning petrol. He inched his way forward and was satisfied to discover that he had scored a direct hit. The bow of the *Campbeltown* had crumpled back some thirty-six feet, leaving her stuck to the caisson in a tangle of shredded metal.

Now, urgently, he ordered the valves to be opened in order to flood the stern of the ship. This would prevent the Germans from towing her off the caisson before she exploded on the following morning. While he was examining the damage, the commandos and saboteurs began leaping ashore and advancing towards their targets through smoke, searchlights and sustained machine-gun fire.

The key goal for Bill Pritchard's saboteurs was the pump house. This was known to contain four massive impeller pumps situated in a fortified chamber some forty feet below ground. After the caisson itself, the pumps were the single most important target for destruction. Without them, the Normandie Dock could be neither filled nor emptied of water.

Stuart Chant was the nominated leader of the four men assigned to destroy the pumps. In spite of severe wounds caused by the exploding shell, he led his fellow saboteurs through the fire-swept dockyard towards the pump house. The men were weighed down with sixty-pound rucksacks filled with specially designed explosives. They blew the locked steel door with one of Cecil Clarke's limpets and then clattered down the circular iron staircase in near darkness.

Chant's wounds were bleeding profusely, yet he hauled himself down into the echoing chamber of the pump house, followed by his little team. Here, deep below ground, the only noise was the distant boom of explosions until one of the saboteurs, Arthur Dockerill, started singing: 'There'll be blue birds over the white cliffs of Dover.'[27] It was a surreal moment, even for Dockerill, but it broke the tension.

The men set their charges in the gloom. Chant and Dockerill then ordered the others back upstairs while they primed the detonators. These were timed to explode within ninety seconds, leaving them precious little time to race back up the spiral stairs. They had just reached safety when 150 pounds of high explosive shattered through the main impeller pumps, an explosion so loud it 'cracked our ear-drums'.[28] A huge concrete block was tossed through the air, the windows were shattered and the ground juddered violently as the inside of the pump house was ripped apart.

Bill Pritchard and his team were meanwhile destroying the machinery that operated the northern caisson. As they went about their work, the commandos kept up covering fire, shooting at the German gun emplacements. The dock area was by now a vision of hell, lit by ghastly flares of burning oil. Sirens and alarms were overlaid with bursts of tommy-gun fire and the agonized screams of wounded and dying men.

Many of the commandos were still in their motor-launches. Trapped in the flare of German searchlights and unable to get ashore, they were sitting ducks. Half the launches had already been shot to pieces and the water was strewn with gruesome, half-submerged corpses.

The dockyard battle raged until about 3 a.m., when the ferocity of the shoot-out began to abate. Three out of every four men were now dead or injured and the Germans were starting to round up survivors. Escape had proved impossible, for just two launches and the motorized gunboat had survived the onslaught. These were now heading back to the destroyers waiting out at sea.

Scores of wounded had been left behind in the dockyard. Colonel Charles Newman was still in overall command and attempted a break-out with a few of the men. It was no use. The Germans had thrown a cordon around St Nazaire and Newman, like most of the other survivors, was to find himself a prisoner of war.

Survival that night was a question of luck. Stephen Beattie had been conferring with Nigel Tibbits aboard one of the motor-launches when the deck was raked with machine-gun fire. Beattie was unscathed but Tibbits was hit and collapsed into the water. He was never seen again.

Beattie himself was eventually captured as he struggled ashore, wet and naked but still counting the hours until the *Campbeltown* was set to explode.

As dawn broke above St Nazaire, a scene of utter carnage was revealed to the captured survivors. The ground was strewn with corpses and twisted metal and smoke was drifting listlessly through the chill morning air. Beattie knew that the ship was set to explode at 7 a.m. and passed a tense few hours as a prisoner of war, waiting for the church clock to strike the hour. It eventually rang seven. And then there was silence. Nothing.

Tibbits had warned that there could be a delay of up to two hours. He had also warned that if the bomb hadn't blown by 9.30 a.m., then the Time Pencils would have been fatally damaged in the collision with the caisson. As the hours passed – first eight, then nine – Beattie feared an even more humiliating outcome: the bomb had been discovered and defused by the Germans.

By 10 a.m. the *Campbeltown* was awash with German military personnel – naval officers, gunners and submarine commanders, along with scores of soldiers who had taken part in the previous night's battle. They could be seen clambering below decks, poking their heads into the mess decks, the cabins and even the wheel-house. It was not long before there were 150 men on the upper deck of the ship and many more below.

Beattie continued to count the minutes, but when another hour had passed he reluctantly concluded that the Time Pencils had failed. The bomb was not going to detonate.

He tried to put a brave face on the outcome. The impeller pumps had been destroyed − a reason for optimism − and the dock had been badly damaged. But the caisson was still intact and that, in his eyes, made the mission a failure. Nigel Tibbits had sacrificed his life for nothing.

The final insult came when Beattie was interrogated by a German intelligence officer, who began gloating in English. 'Your people obviously did not know what a hefty thing that lock-gate is,' he said. 'It was really useless trying to smash it with a flimsy destroyer.'

At that very moment, exactly as he spoke those words, St Nazaire was hit by an earthquake of such magnitude that the ground felt as if it were being ripped apart. 'An explosion of unbelievable violence', was how it felt to the town's assistant mayor, Monsieur Grimaud. The *Campbeltown*'s funnel was sent spinning into the clear morning air and a forty-foot chunk of steel hull was flung into the gardens of the Santé Maritime. It was as if a giant were playing havoc with a Dinky toy.

Beattie heard the explosion with quiet satisfaction. Cool as ever, he smiled at his interrogator. 'That, I hope, is proof that we did not underestimate the strength of the gate.'[29]

The impact of the blast was even more devastating than Beattie had dared to hope. As the *Campbeltown* ripped herself to pieces, the impregnable steel caisson was thrust inwards by the force of the blast, turning it into a 160-ton chunk of flying debris. The collapse of the caisson was followed by a tidal wave of water that smashed into the dry dock, sweeping the mangled remnants of the *Campbeltown* along with it. The two tankers inside the dock, *Schledstadt* and *Passat*, bore the full force of the onrush of water. They were plucked upwards by the deluge and dashed against the wall of the dry dock.

Those who rushed towards the Normandie Dock were greeted by a scene so macabre that it would be for ever imprinted in their brains. The wharves, cranes and storehouses were festooned with human remains, the grisly remnants of the hundreds of German sightseers who were on the vessel when she blew out her bowels.

The exact death toll was never discovered: some reckoned it was as high as 400.

Hitler was furious when he learned of the sabotage. He ordered Field Marshal von Rundstedt to conduct an immediate inquiry. Not satisfied with its findings, he ordered General Jodl to undertake a second inquiry. This didn't satisfy him either. The facts were indeed difficult to accept: the saboteurs and commandos had successfully carried out an operation that even Lord Mountbatten had considered 'absolutely impossible to undertake', yet 'brilliantly achieved'.[30]

Winston Churchill was gleeful when he learned of the destruction of the Normandie Dock. A 'brilliant and heroic exploit', he said, and called it 'a deed of glory intimately involved in high strategy'. The men who had taken part won their share of glory. Five Victoria Crosses were awarded, including one for the cool-headed Stephen Beattie. Four men won the Distinguished Service Order and seventeen were awarded the Distinguished Service Cross, including the deceased Nigel Tibbits. But the operation had come at a heavy price: 169 men dead and a further 215 taken prisoner.

The Normandie Dock was to remain a ghostly ruin for the next decade. It was so badly damaged that repair was impossible in wartime. As for the *Tirpitz*, she didn't venture into the Atlantic for the rest of the war.

Three years earlier, Gubbins had written that successful sabotage operations required surprise, speed and mobility. He added that the most effective operations were those undertaken in stealth and at night. 'When the time for action comes,' he said, 'act with the greatest boldness and audacity.'[31]

This is exactly what his men had done. It was a textbook guerrilla operation, one that had been lifted straight from the pages of the little pamphlets written by himself and Millis Jefferis.

II

Masters of Sabotage

RUTH JEFFERIS FELT increasingly like a war widow in the late spring of 1942. She had moved the family to Buckinghamshire shortly after her husband's appointment to the Firs, renting a tumbledown little lodge, Rose Cottage, in Cudlington, a village some three miles from Whitchurch. It was ideal for her three young sons, John, David and Jeremy, and might have made the perfect family home, were it not for the fact that one member of the family was constantly missing. Millis was never at home.

Ruth had been genuinely touched when he had filled their Mill Hill house with flowers: it had been an unexpected gesture that partially compensated for his long absences at work. But the flower episode had been two years ago and was little more than a memory. Now, on the rare occasions when he did pitch up at home, he was morose and silent for 'his thoughts were directed on his work'.[1] The worst moment of all came when he offered to take Ruth on a forty-mile drive through the countryside. She was hoping to catch up on his news and share stories about the boys, but he didn't say a single word for the entire journey. His head was so filled with weaponry that he wasn't able to speak.

One night a bedtime argument got out of hand and Ruth stormed out of the house, suitcase in hand. She had only gone a few yards when she heard bare feet on the pavement behind her. It was Millis coming after her, offering to carry her suitcase. Ruth melted when she heard this and forgave him for his distracted mind. It was wartime and her husband had a vital role to play.

She eventually took matters into her own hands, applying for a job at the Firs in order to be closer to her husband. By the beginning of summer, she was working in the explosives unit, helping to pack specially designed shell-cases with deadly concoctions. She found herself working alongside 'a dozen or so little Welsh girls' who had been hired by Stuart Macrae. He had followed Gubbins's initiative and hired female staff in a bid to keep one step ahead of the increasing workload. The first influx of girls was soon followed by a second, and then a third, until there were scores of them working alongside the growing ranks of inventors and engineers. The girls were overseen by a stiff-collared welfare officer named Miss Wond. She was known, inevitably, as Fairy.

The girls were initially unhappy to have been dispatched to the Firs and complained incessantly to Macrae. 'They just hated it at the start and were longing to get back to Wales.' But the generous measures at the mess bar coupled with the full-blooded male company soon caused them to change their minds. One of the girls had to be repeatedly hauled from the sentry box, where she spent her evenings in the arms of one of the guards. 'What was surprising,' said Macrae, 'was that although quite a big girl, she favoured a little sentry.' He asked what made this particular sentry so special and was told, with a nudge and a wink, that he 'was not built in the normal proportions'.

As the workload grew heavier, even occasional staff found themselves building weaponry. Mr Bridle was a hairdresser by profession, with a particular skill at blending oily concoctions for damaged hair. After clipping everyone's hair and oiling the heads of those who wanted his tonics, he would help to fill shells with high explosive. Macrae watched him at work, surprised by his fearlessness. 'Although Mr Bridle appeared to be a quiet and courteous fellow who would treat even a small firework with great respect, he showed no signs of fear whatever in his new profession and the thought that the slightest mistake on his part might blow not only himself, but also the rest of us to kingdom come, never seemed to enter his head.'

Many of the staff kept to Jefferis's sixteen hours a day rule, working so hard that they often forgot what day of the week it was. 'We would discover it was Sunday only when we tried to ring up some other department,' said Macrae. Jefferis had limited entertainment to one Sunday a month but Macrae overruled him, aware of the need for in-house entertainment. He established a permanently open bar, a cinema with 35mm projector and even launched the Firs magazine.

One of the more clownish members of staff, Gordon Norwood, was invited to stage a series of regular theatricals, 'which were put on at his carpenter's shop under the title of "Woodchoppers Balls"'. The pun was most definitely intended.

Stuart Macrae worked hard to keep the Firs running on schedule, but he was driven to distraction by Jefferis, who was constantly side-tracked by matters of no relevance to the war effort. 'When we were in the heat of the fray at Whitchurch,' said a frustrated Macrae, 'he got involved in producing a theory of prime numbers and it became very difficult to get him to think about anything else.' Matters were scarcely helped by the fact that Professor Lindemann encouraged him in these lofty abstractions. Macrae watched in despair as Jefferis got 'involved in these mathematical problems and, in the middle of devising some new weapon, would write a treatise on the formulae governing the calculation of compression spring movement under varying loadings'.

Gubbins drove out to the Firs on a monthly basis in order to consult with Jefferis. He was delighted to learn that his L–Delay fuse was almost ready for use. After much experimenting, Jefferis had discovered that the purest lead wire from the Broken Hills Mines in Australia, when blended with 5 per cent of tellurium, crept with absolute uniformity under tension. It was the breakthrough he had been seeking for so long and meant that a highly accurate fuse could now become a reality. Constructing the prototype was a complex process that required the latest automatic lathes. The lead had to be stretched to an accuracy of one-tenth of a thousandth of an inch, a process that initially involved much trial and error. But when it worked, and was linked to a striker, it performed with an accuracy never previously achieved in the history of warfare.

Even Jefferis's harshest critics at the Ordnance Board were forced to concede that his L–Delay was a work of genius. They ruled that henceforth it was the only fuse to be used in all army, sabotage and guerrilla operations. Within days of this ruling, the first of more than 5 million L–Delays were rolling off the Firs's production line. 'They were used everywhere in the world,' wrote Macrae at the war's end, and yet 'there was not a single report of a failure with them, or an accident.'

Macrae continued to be surprised by the size of the orders coming from both the commandos and from Baker Street. He was no less surprised by the fact that they were expected to supply the weapons free of charge. Ever the racketeer, he politely suggested that Gubbins's Baker Street agents should start paying for the weaponry: after all, 'they had bags of money'. A deal was struck, a delivery arranged and Macrae 'walked off with £500 in cash in payment for 500 limpets, for which they did not want a receipt'. He was delighted and said that this money 'started off my new bag of gold very nicely and enabled us to take on new staff right away'. Macrae kept 'most careful accounts covering these highly illegal transactions',[2] lest he should ever be challenged by the War Office, but he kept the paperwork well away from Jefferis, who was so morally upright that he would have been horrified.

Winston Churchill demanded frequent updates on the rates of production at the Firs and was most impressed by the growing output of weaponry. In one six-month period between the autumn of 1941 and spring of 1942, Jefferis's ever growing team of workers, now organized into a production line, produced 15,000 limpets, 10,000 clams and 600,000 detonators. These were now being shipped to saboteurs around the globe, not just Occupied Europe, but as far afield as Cairo, Alexandria, New Zealand, Rangoon and Bombay.

Professor Lindemann reminded the Prime Minister that Jefferis's inventions were also being used by the regular army. 'I believe the value of the orders placed approaches £18,000,000,' he said. 'Considering that the cost of the experimental work is only about £40,000 a year, I think this can be considered a very satisfactory yield.'[3]

The quality of the weaponry produced by the Firs was in striking contrast to the other development stations up and down the country. The experimental base at Welwyn, known as Station IX, was producing all manner of prototype machines, yet few of them ever entered production. There was also the Thatched Barn in Hertfordshire, Station XV, that produced such curiosities as exploding rats and self-detonating camel dung, the latter designed for use in North Africa. Such items produced much laughter among the staff, but were dismissed by Jefferis and Macrae as gimmicks that were never going to turn the tide of war. They contended that the Firs alone was producing all the most effective weapons of sabotage.

Churchill agreed with this assessment and rewarded Millis Jefferis by making him a Commander of the British Empire in the 1942 New Year's Honours list. Macrae at last saw an opportunity to drag his boss away from his work. He arranged a celebratory dinner at the Bull's Head Hotel in Aylesbury, inviting Mrs Jefferis, Norman Angier and a couple of other members of Jefferis's senior staff. The hand-printed menu bore all the hallmarks of Macrae's ready wit. The main course was *faisan roti à la bombarde*, a reference to the Bombard mortar, and the pudding, *bombe sticky*, referred to another of Jefferis's inventions. At the bottom of the menu he recycled an office joke: the menu, he said, was 'subject to revision or amendment at any moment'.[4]

Colin Gubbins had also established a formidable little inner circle of talent by the spring of 1942. Cecil Clarke was one of his rising stars, working around the clock at Brickendonbury Manor as he trained a growing number of would-be saboteurs. The numbers passing through his classes were impressive: 667 Norwegians, 258 Poles, 209 Czechs and 118 British, along with men from eight other countries. Most had arrived in Britain in the spring of 1940, but some – particularly Norwegians – continued to trickle into the country after making perilous journeys across the North Sea in the so-called Shetland Bus. Men were now starting to be sent back into Nazi-occupied Europe. Clarke had already seen off 80 Norwegians, 65 French and 151 other nationalities. They were tasked with building underground networks and creating weapons' dumps in preparation for forthcoming strikes.

Cecil Clarke was by no means the only cog in Gubbins's machine. Six hundred miles from London, Sykes and Fairbairn had increased the scope of their activities and were now training hundreds of would-be guerrillas in the fine art of killing. Gubbins had also established a specialist parachute training school at Ringway, near Manchester, along with a 'finishing school' at Beaulieu. This was where men and women were trained in how to live undercover in occupied territories.

The team working in Baker Street had also expanded rapidly. Just two years earlier, when Gubbins was still in Caxton Street, his outfit had consisted of four men, one secretary and an office not much larger than a living room. Now, hundreds of staff were working for him, plotting guerrilla operations in almost a dozen countries. These operations were being planned without any of the constraints placed on the regular army. They were discussed only at the highest level, directly with Churchill and the Chiefs of Imperial Staff, and Gubbins was already eyeing the day when they could be undertaken without discussing them with anyone at all.

One of his more efficient members of staff, Bickham Sweet-Escott, returned from a trip to the Middle East to find everything changed. 'We were now in close and constant touch by wireless with the nucleus of resistance organisations in Norway, Holland, Belgium and France, as well as Poland and Czechoslovakia.' When Gubbins had joined Baker Street, there had not been a single wireless set operating in Occupied Europe. Within eight months, more than sixty agents had been trained and dropped into the countries of north-west Europe, along with sophisticated wireless equipment.

A shortage of aircraft remained a constant headache and Gubbins fought a tenacious battle to be given more. They were needed for dropping both saboteurs and supplies. The Air Ministry and Bomber Command did their best to block his requests, informing Churchill that all available planes were needed for the bombing offensive. Gubbins argued his corner with skill, reminding the chiefs of staff that 'a hundred bombers can fail to hit their target, but one aircraft could drop a party of saboteurs who might make certain of it.'

His persistence eventually won the day. He was granted the use of ten Halifaxes 'which could cover the whole of Western Europe, and which could take up to fifteen containers of 300 lbs each'.[5] He was also given a fleet of Lysanders, smaller planes that could be used for pick-up operations in France. After much arm-twisting he was even granted the use of Tempsford airfield in Bedfordshire. It was to become a vital component for operations into Occupied Europe.

Gubbins's change of office, from the back rooms of Berkeley Court to Norgeby House, enabled him to establish a centralized Operations Room. This allowed him to keep an overview of all the missions being planned at any given time. As director of both training and operations, Gubbins had become, in the eyes of one observer, 'the mainstay of the Baker Street organisation'.

Hugh Dalton and Frank Nelson were both quick to recognize his vital contribution and placed him in direct control of the two French sections, along with the Belgian, Dutch, German and Austrian sections. This was in addition to the Polish and Czech sections, for which he had been responsible from the outset. He also continued to take a keen interest in Gus March-Phillipps and his No. 62 Commando, which was engaged in a series of spectacular hit-and-run raids on the coastline of northern France. One of these, Operation Basalt, involved an attack on one of the German-held Channel Islands. It so infuriated Hitler that he issued his Commando Order, instructing that all captured commandos were to be shot.

Some of the bankers and accountants in Baker Street were unhappy about Gubbins's growing control: they clung to the idea of mass civilian uprising against Nazi rule in the occupied lands. In order to help 'smooth feathers ruffled by the extension of Gubbins's empire',[6] Frank Nelson instituted a weekly council in order that everyone could express their opinion about missions that were being planned.

In spite of these consultations, Gubbins's personal responsibilities grew with every month that passed and he found himself invited to participate in consultations with the army top brass. According to Joan Bright, who saw him regularly in her new job as secretary to General Hastings 'Pug' Ismay, he was by now at the very heart of decision-making. 'Not only was he involved in discussions of policy and future strategy at the highest levels with the Chiefs of Staff and with many of the leaders of the allied governments-in-exile, but in an organisation which was rapidly expanding and recruiting often inexperienced and untrained officers, he was frequently obliged to supervise the detailed work of the country sections.' By the spring of 1942, 'it was no exaggeration to say that he had become the mainspring' of Baker Street and had transformed it into a body to be taken seriously.[7]

Gubbins's ever faithful secretary, Margaret, often worked until the early hours as she tried to keep pace with her boss. He spent much of each day in meetings and didn't return to the office until late evening, when she was required to type up all the most important decisions of the day. She was constantly exhausted and needed strong tea to keep herself awake. Yet she was happy to be 'doing her bit', even when she found herself 'wrestling with manual typewriters and carbon copies that wrinkled'.[8] Only when everything was typed up and the office cleared for the night did the two of them join the rest of the team for liquid refreshments at the Nut Club.

On the afternoon of Saturday, 21 February Gubbins heard the first whiff of a rumour that later turned out to be true. Hugh 'Dynamo' Dalton, the ministerial head of Baker Street, had been removed from his post. Churchill had decided to move Dalton to the Board of Trade, a job that he was reluctant to accept. Indeed, he was deeply upset at the prospect of leaving Baker Street and confessed that 'it twanged my heart-strings'.[9] He tried to negotiate with Churchill, but the Prime Minister was adamant. Dalton had little option but to accept his new job: he was quick to inform his parliamentary colleagues that he had been promoted.

His place was taken by the Earl of Selborne, one of the more unlikely candidates to spearhead a guerrilla outfit. 'A small, stooping figure with a deceptively mild appearance',[10] or so thought Joan Bright, who liked to keep tabs on all the senior figures in Whitehall. Selborne was a bureaucrat, a grey man in a grey suit who even friends found to be entirely lacking in chutzpah. 'I dare say it will work, but he is not very inspiring,' was the comment of one Whitehall insider.[11]

Just a few weeks after this unwelcome surprise, Gubbins was handed an even bigger bombshell. Frank Nelson, operational head of Baker Street, had tendered his resignation. 'He had worked himself almost to death,' said Joan, who had been alarmed by his steady decline.[12] He had been working for sixteen hours a day, seven days a week, for eighteen months. Now, he was suffering from burn-out.

Gubbins was the most obvious choice to replace Nelson and was certainly the most qualified candidate for the job. But the old school network closed ranks and promoted the international banker Sir Charles Hambro, originally hired by Dalton on account of his financial connections. A former captain of the Eton cricket eleven, Hambro had a quick brain, an oil-slick of charm and scores of important contacts across Europe. 'He kept more balls in the air than any man I knew,' said Dalton, in justification of the appointment.[13] Others quipped that Hambro had so many balls in the air that he was unable to concentrate on any single one of them.

Gubbins was 'suspicious of Hambro's charm' and confessed to his colleagues that he was 'slightly resentful of the easy assurance with which the latter delegated the too difficult problems'.[14] He was not alone in wondering if Hambro's overweening self-confidence would be enough to keep him in such a demanding job. 'He lives by bluff and charm,' noted one.[15] An additional drawback to his appointment was the fact that he already had three full-time jobs. He was a director of the Bank of England, a managing director of Hambro's Bank and chairman of the Great Western Railway Company.

He certainly had no intention of continuing his predecessor's habit of working sixteen-hour days. Bickham Sweet-Escott noted that the new boss would make a leisurely start to the day, coming in 'for an hour or two in the morning'. He would then pursue his business interests for the rest of the day, 'and not return till late at night, when he would work till the small hours'.[16] Even these long nocturnal stretches at his desk were few and far between. Each time the Luftwaffe hit the Great Western Railway, which was often, he left the office in order to inspect the damage. The prevailing opinion in Baker Street was that he would be out within a year.

All eyes were already focused on Gubbins, who was being openly talked of as Hambro's replacement. Even Hambro himself recognized Gubbins's unique talent and promoted him to a position – Deputy for Operations – that gave him effective control over all the sabotage and guerrilla warfare being planned.

The prominent civil servant Gladwyn Jebb had been watching Gubbins in action for more than a year and was one of those who predicted that he would soon be head of his own empire. 'I have seldom met a man more vigorous and a more inspiring soldier, or incidentally possessing a more political sense. There is no doubt that he is the lynch pin of the existing machine.'[17]

Lord Selborne agreed, saying that there was no one 'who is more vital to the continuance of the work of this organisation than Brigadier Gubbins'. He added that Gubbins had been the principal architect of guerrilla warfare since the very beginning and was now the undisputed master of the Baker Street machine. 'He has acquired a technique, a knowledge and experience which are really irreplaceable . . . It is a truism that no one is irreplaceable, but for the many reasons which I have explained, Brigadier Gubbins comes very close to it.'[18] Winston Churchill gave Lord Selborne's assessment a stamp of approval. 'Indispensible to Baker Street,' he said.[19]

Gubbins increasingly found himself surrounded by devoted acolytes who admired his two principal qualities: sharp intelligence and relentless energy. 'An outgoing, energetic, gung-ho sort of chap', was the opinion of one of many.[20] Yet Gubbins had an additional quality that captivated those close to him, one they found impossible to pin down. 'There was something about him that made him somehow different,' said his friend Peter Colley.[21]

That 'something' was almost certainly the fact that he was an outsider. The names of his acolytes spoke volumes: Alfgar Hesketh-Prichard, Edward Beddington-Behrens, Douglas Dodds-Parker and Bickham Sweet-Escott: all had been educated at the same universities and all had known each other since prep school. Now, they found themselves working for a boss who came from a world at a far remove from the silver-spooned squirearchies of the Home Counties. Gubbins had left school at sixteen, he had not gone to university and had none of the old boy connections of those who now served under him.

If they admired him at work, they positively worshipped him at play. In the Nut Club, their brains infused with whisky, his junior staff stood in awe of his stamina. 'A great party man', noted one exhausted follower.[22] Not until the most youthful were dropping on their feet would Gubbins summon his 'marvellous and devoted' batman[23] and be driven home to Notting Hill, slipping into the marital bed an hour or so before dawn.

His longest-standing admirer was Nonie, his childhood sweetheart, whom he had married at the age of twenty-three. But now, as the working day increased from fifteen to eighteen hours, Nonie Gubbins began to feel much the same way as Ruth Jefferis. Her elder son,

Michael, was based in Arisaig, working alongside Sykes and Fairbairn. Her younger Rory, was away at boarding school and only returned during vacations. The family home in Campden Hill Road felt desperately empty in the evenings, when the lights were dimmed and blackout blinds secured.

War placed strains on many marriages, but Colin and Nonie's relationship was dangerously close to breaking point. The camaraderie of Baker Street only served to accentuate their differences. Nonie was the very opposite of her gregarious husband. She disliked sports (which he loved) and dreaded grand social occasions (at which he excelled). She was the first to admit that she lacked her husband's 'blythe spirit',[24] but she had her reasons. Her mother had died when she was seven and her father three years later. Now, it looked as if she were to lose her husband as well, not to his secretary or a mistress, but to a band of public school-educated guerrillas.

Much of Gubbins's working day was spent in the Operations Room at the very heart of the Baker Street headquarters. He had placed the strategic planning in the capable hands of Douglas Dodds-Parker, one of the first people he had recruited almost three years earlier. 'He had not only an extraordinarily wide acquaintance,' wrote Joan Bright of Dodds-Parker, 'but his manipulation of the old boy network was exceptional.'

Efficiency was Dodds-Parker's byword. Everything he ran 'was reminiscent of a bracing north Oxford preparatory school',[25] which was just as Gubbins wanted it to be. But to the select few who were allowed into the Operations Room, the overall impression was one of unstudied calm. Dodds-Parker had installed it in the drawing room of one of Norgeby House's Edwardian apartments: it was spacious and high-ceilinged, the sort of room in which (in happier times) Dodds-Parker and his chums might have retired for cigars and brandy.

The room had internal windows overlooking the central staircase of Norgeby House, but Gubbins insisted that these were blacked out in order that no one could peer inside. He felt that 'it was essential to have the highest possible security on all our hundreds of individual operations.'[26] This security had to begin and end in the Operations Room. Every inch of wall was covered in maps, many of them festooned with little coloured pins. Each pin denoted an agent who had been dropped into Nazi-occupied territories.

As an additional layer of security, Dodds-Parker had the maps themselves covered in black curtains. These were only opened when a particular country was due for scrutiny. Then, once an operation entered the planning stage, scores more maps would be brought out, as well as large-scale plans of towns and cities. These would be laid out on the long wooden table that ran down the middle of the room.

One of secretary Margaret Jackson's work colleagues, Daphne Maynard, was excited to be given a peek inside the Operations Room and noticed a large map spread out on the table. 'Everyone was bent down over it,' she said, 'pushing little bits of stuff across.' There was a hushed silence, as if it were the reading room of a private library. The electric lights were burning brightly, even though it was daytime, and everyone was studying the maps in concentrated silence, 'planning where the plane was going to land and take off'.[27]

Gubbins and Dodds-Parker were assisted in their work by serving pilots, who were brought in to give advice on airstrips, landing grounds and potential dropping sites. Daphne was appalled to see the terrible battle scars on these men. 'One of them, Bill Simpson, had no hands and no eyelids.' She didn't dare to ask what had happened, but it brought home to her the dangers of guerrilla warfare. 'He had a hook on one hand and could get the telephone off, the other hand was covered in leather.' She later learned that the hook had been made by specialists at Queen Victoria Hospital, which was pioneering primitive plastic surgery.

A second pilot, also working in the Operations Room, was more forthcoming about the occupational hazards of his work. He told her an extraordinary tale of how his parachute had failed to open as he bailed out of his stricken plane. 'He heard this noise and realized that it was himself screaming. And then he had a feeling of euphoria, laughing and throwing things out of his pocket.' He had a miraculous escape from death, landing in a tree with no injuries. He had been posted to the Operations Room 'while he got his nerve back'.[28]

It was not the best place to unwind, for this was the most stressful place in Baker Street. The pressures of work got to everyone, even

Gubbins. On one occasion, he emerged from his office and noticed that a member of staff had left a bicycle in the atrium outside his door. He 'took one look at this bicycle, jumped on it and went off at high speed round the fountain about six times'.[29] He then replaced the bike against the wall and calmly returned to his desk, his stress levels marginally reduced.

Although the work was exhausting, Margaret found it exhilarating. 'Things were moving terribly fast,' she said. 'It was like a fast train and you had to get aboard. There was a sense of urgency.'[30]

There was also a sense of heady excitement, for Margaret had just discovered something that almost no one else knew: a spectacular assassination was in the offing.

12

Czech–Mate

IN THE NINE months that Margaret Jackson had been working for Colin Gubbins, she had come to realize that there was something extraordinary about her job. Unlike everyone else in the country, who were 'dependent on newspapers or what had been censored' for their daily news, she was 'in direct touch with what was happening abroad'.[1] She also knew of decisions being taken at the highest level, for it was she who typed up the notes about the work being undertaken at the secret stations and she who kept the records of Gubbins's meetings with the chiefs of staff. Indeed she was privy to all the undercover operations being planned across Europe. If ever she had been abducted by the Nazis, she could have revealed priceless information.

One of Gubbins's responsibilities was to liaise with the Czech government-in-exile, which Winston Churchill had recognized as a representative body in the summer of 1941. Baker Street had already agreed to start training the Czech soldiers who had fled to Britain more than a year earlier and had also accepted 'that an essential pre-condition of any future operations was the establishment of a secure radio link with the Protectorate'.[2] A Czech volunteer was trained for this role, but it took many months and 'several false starts' before he was finally dropped into the country by air. He was accidentally landed in Austria, instead of Bohemia, but eventually managed to slip across the border. Henceforth, London and Prague were in radio contact.

As early as September 1941, the Czechs had revealed to Gubbins that they were planning a mission of such secrecy that neither MI6, nor any senior British politician, was to be informed. The secret came directly from Colonel Franticsk Moravec, the wily head of

Czech intelligence, who was based in London and working alongside his government-in-exile. Moravec and his staff had fled their native Czechoslovakia eighteen months earlier, flying out in the teeth of a blizzard at the very moment Hitler's storm-troopers were marching across the frontier.

Moravec had been deeply depressed to flee his native land, for he was leaving everything behind. 'My wife and children were lost to me, abandoned in the stricken country below, somewhere under the swirling flakes, left to the mercies of the invaders.'³ There was just one cause for optimism. He had spent several months directing the activities of a German double agent who was working against the Nazis: the experience had taught him that 'even a brutal police state like Hitler's could be penetrated'.⁴

The penetration he was now planning was little short of spectacular, as he confessed to Gubbins at their September meeting. The Czech president-in-exile, Eduard Beneš (who was nominally running Czechoslovakia from a suburban villa in Gwendolen Avenue, Putney), 'had sanctioned a terrorist attack on some prominent personality'⁵ in the Nazi government in Prague. When Gubbins pressed Moravec further, he learned that this prominent personality was none other than the Reichsprotektor, Reinhard Heydrich.

Heydrich was a spectacular target, as Gubbins well knew. Appointed Reich Protector of Bohemia and Moravia – the lands incorporated into the Third Reich in the spring of 1939 – he was proving utterly ruthless. 'Intelligent, ambitious, cunning and cruel', is how Moravec described him. Heydrich was one of the principal architects of the extermination of the Jews and was in the process of undertaking the racial cleansing of his fiefdom 'with sadistic zeal'.⁶

Within days of taking office, he vowed to 'Germanize the Czech vermin',⁷ but he was only intending to Germanize those who had been confirmed, by X-ray screening, to be Aryans. The rest were to be liquidated. Ever since arriving in Prague, his rule had been 'an unbroken chain of murders' and his ruthlessness fully justified the Führer's description of him as 'the man with the iron heart'.⁸

Gubbins was enthusiastic about the plan to assassinate Heydrich, aware that it would be a much needed coup for the beleaguered President Benes. He was facing constant criticism from the Russians for not doing enough to sabotage the factories in Bohemia that were mass-producing weaponry for the Third Reich. Assassinating Heydrich would show that he meant business.

Gubbins told Moravec that 'he had no hesitation in agreeing', but he expressed a word of caution. Assassination was frowned upon by many in Whitehall and ministers had previously objected to a Baker Street plan to murder Nazi-supporting leaders in the Middle East. Anthony Eden went so far as to call it 'war crimes business'. Gubbins suggested that Moravec should 'restrict the knowledge of the Czech approach, and above all of the identity of the probable target, to a very small circle'.[9] Moravec agreed. 'The fewer persons involved the better,' he said, especially if the assassination 'was to be regarded as a spontaneous act of national desperation'. The hope was that 'the spontaneity would become genuine when Heydrich was dead'.[10]

Gubbins also warned of the likely cost of the assassination, even if it were unsuccessful. It would provoke 'wholesale reprisals'[11] that could cost the lives of thousands of innocent Czechs. Moravec had a ready answer. Heydrich was already killing civilians on an unprecedented scale. Some 5,000 people had been arrested since his arrival in the country and all the principal resistance leaders had been 'swiftly and systematically eliminated'. Moravec also told Gubbins that he was receiving regular news from undercover agents, thanks to the wireless link, and their reports made for grim reading. 'Police cars drove daily out of the grim Pankrac prison in Prague on their way to the shooting range in Kobylisy and the airport fields at Kuzyn where German execution squads waited.'[12] In short, mass killings of civilians were already taking place.

Colonel Moravec now had a question for Gubbins, one on which the entire operation was to depend. He asked whether he 'would help in this project by providing facilities for training and supplying special weaponry that was required'. Moravec knew that without access to the specialists, the assassination stood very little chance of success.

Gubbins 'had no hesitation about agreeing',[13] giving Moravec the green light he needed. Within weeks, Eric Sykes and Cecil Clarke would become involved in the assassination project, along with a small number of other individuals. These included Gubbins's secretary, Margaret Jackson, who found herself writing reports of a most surprising nature.

'The object of the operation,' she typed on to notepaper headed MOST SECRET in red ink, 'is the assassination of Herr Heydrich, the German Protector in Czechoslovakia.' Initial research suggested that there were several possible means by which he could be killed, including blowing up his private train or 'shooting him when he is appearing at some ceremony'.[14] But further study suggested a rather different option, one that was far more enticing. Heydrich had elected to live on the baroque country estate of Panenské Břežany, which lay some twelve miles to the north of Prague. The estate was guarded by an SS company stationed in the nearby village. Although Heydrich liked to work on his official papers at Panenské Břežany, he was obliged to travel into Prague on most days. He always refused an escort on the grounds that it would damage German prestige: he had no wish to give the impression that he feared for his safety. Instead, he travelled to Prague accompanied only by his driver, Oberscharführer Johannes Klein, 'a strapping six-footer'.[15]

As Margaret typed up the various intelligence reports, she learned that an attack on Heydrich's car, while en route between Panenské Břežany and Prague, had become the favoured option for the assassination. 'Practical experiments proved that such an anti-personnel attack on a car must be carried out at a corner where it is forced to slow down,' she wrote.[16]

Colonel Moravec managed to lay his hands on a large-scale map of the road from Panenské Břežany to Prague and this was studied 'in minute detail'.[17] There was one obvious place to strike. As Heydrich's Mercedes entered the Prague suburb of Holešovice, there was a crossroads with a sharp bend on a hill that led down to Troja Bridge. The car would be obliged to slow down as it approached the crossroads, leaving Heydrich dangerously exposed.

Holešovice offered an additional advantage: it was at a considerable distance from the SS garrisons in both Panenské Břežany and at Prague Castle in the centre of the city. In theory, the assassins would have time to get away.

Gubbins offered to have these assassins trained at the killing school in Arisaig, an offer that Moravec was only too happy to accept. But first, he had to find two men willing to undertake an operation of extreme danger.

There were some 2,000 Czech soldiers in England, most of whom were based in barracks at Leamington Spa. A small group of these had already formed themselves into an elite. Moravec interviewed them all and selected two dozen of the most promising men for special training. They were given no information about the proposed mission: all Moravec told them was that they would need 'all the qualities of a commando, such as physical fitness, mental alertness and various technical aptitudes', along with one additional quality. When the men asked what this was, he said: 'Are you ready to die for your country?'[18]

The men who signalled their agreement were taken by train to Arisaig in order to be taught the art of silent killing. William Fairbairn was absent at the time of their arrival, leaving the training in the hands of Eric Sykes. He was quick to recognize that Moravec's men were professionals, 'a disciplined lot' who were 'a very different ball-game to the French section'.[19] Yet he nevertheless said that they would require a minimum of six weeks' training in fitness, killing and shooting practice.

Colonel Moravec watched as the bespectacled Sykes put them through their paces. He was impressed by what he saw. 'The men were kept in isolation from the outside world, taught the use of small arms of every kind, manufacture of hand-made bombs, ju-jitsu, survival in open country on synthetic foods, topography and map-reading and concealment devices.' Even by commando standards, Sykes's programme was 'very exacting' and pushed the men to the very limits of their endurance.[20]

They undertook punishing training in rock climbing and were then thrown headlong into unarmed combat. 'Stretched to the utmost, harried, prodded, tested, the trainees were probed for any hidden physical or psychological weaknesses which might cost them their lives.' Sykes pushed them 'to their psychological limits', not because he was a sadist but because he wanted to know the point at which each man would crack. It was the only way to weed out those 'who could not function under the crushing pressures they would face in the field', when they would be at constant risk of exposure by informers.

At the end of six weeks, it became clear that two of the men were outstanding. Josef Gabčik was short, tough and 'absolutely reliable', with a fine sense of leadership. Just twenty-eight years of age and an orphan since he was a small boy, he could be provoked into a fury by the most trivial things, such as spilling a drink. 'Up he soared like a rocket, spurting rage, to burst effectively, briefly and brightly at a high altitude; then, with a wry appraisal of his own ridiculousness, he would laugh himself down to ground level again.' His temper might have proved a handicap, but it was offset by his bravery and determination. If anyone could be trusted to kill Heydrich, it was Gabčik.

The second candidate was Jan Kubis, 'a shy and softly spoken man who never lost his temper'. He was the perfect counterfoil to Gabčik: 'well disciplined, discreet and dependable'. He was also an ardent patriot who told his superiors that he wanted 'to help the Czechoslovak cause as much as I could'.[21] If that meant being dropped into his native land on a near-suicidal mission, then he was keen to take part.

Colonel Moravec wanted to be absolutely sure that he had got the right men for the job and had a private chat with Eric Sykes. Sykes had trained hundreds of men over the previous twelve months, yet he had rarely come across such a talented pair. 'He said that in ju-jitsu they were almost perfect. They had passed their discretion test with flying colours.' Moravec himself had watched them on the shooting range. 'I could see that they were artists with pistols, rifles and sub-machine guns.' More importantly, 'they threw hand grenades with precision at a hundred yards.'

Moravec was satisfied that he had found the right men: now, he had to be certain that they were undertaking the mission of their own free will. He took them to one side and spoke to them individually, explaining that they were the favoured candidates for an assassination attempt that would place them in grave danger. 'If they were lucky enough to escape death during the attempt,' he told them, 'they would have two alternatives: to try to survive inside the country or try to escape abroad and return to their London base.'

He said it was most likely they would be killed. 'I thought they deserved complete honesty.'

Both men answered without displaying any emotion. Gabčik told Moravec that 'he viewed the mission as an act of war and the risk of death as natural.' Kubis simply thanked Colonel Moravec 'for choosing him for a task of such importance'.[22]

Colin Gubbins had been helping to organize the technicalities of the Czech mission while the assassins had been training in Arisaig. He had recently appointed the brilliant young Cambridge graduate Alfgar Hesketh-Prichard to head his Czech Section. It was a wise choice. Hesketh-Prichard had previously lived in Prague and knew the city well. Now, his task was to help with the detailed planning of the assassination.

It soon became clear that the principal problems were technical ones. 'Chief among these was the difficulty of providing a bomb which could be concealed in a briefcase, used at short range without killing the operator, but which was nevertheless sufficiently powerful to penetrate the armour-plating of the Reichsprotektor's official motor car.'[23]

Heydrich's car was likely to be within range for just four or five seconds as it slowed down at the Holešovice crossroads. The fuse on a standard grenade was too long for an attack where speed would be essential. Nor could a grenade be guaranteed to pierce the armour-plated Mercedes. Alfgar Hesketh-Prichard realized that an explosive device would have to be specially designed and built. Millis Jefferis's team at the Firs would have been well placed to construct such a weapon, but they were deluged with work in the final months of 1941. Hesketh-Prichard turned instead to Cecil Clarke, who had shown considerable mastery at blowing up cars with his specially adapted spigot mortar.

Clarke agreed that a standard grenade would not puncture the armour-plating of Heydrich's car. He also knew that an anti-tank grenade, which would blow a hole in almost anything, was far too cumbersome to be thrown across a road. It was almost a foot long and weighed some four and a half pounds. It was not a weapon for assassination. What was needed was some sort of hybrid grenade, powerful enough to pierce armour-plating but also light enough to be thrown. Clarke now began sketching a uniquely destructive explosive device, modelling it on the cylindrical No. 73 Anti-Tank percussion grenade. With its screw-on cap, it looked like a thermos flask. Cecil decided to streamline it still further, packing its top end with a pound of nitro-glycerine explosive. This reduced the weight by a third, making it a great deal easier to throw. He then fitted the grenade with a No. 247 fuse made of black bakelite that was 'designed to function on impact, irrespective of how the grenade landed'.[24] It would detonate, come what may.

The explosive was held *in situ* by adhesive tape, which lent a Heath Robinson touch to the grenade. But Clarke's weapon was anything but makeshift. When it exploded, it was designed to shatter with such force that shards of metal shrapnel would tear through the bodywork of the car with unbelievable force, inflicting devastating injuries on anyone inside. It was so lethal that the two assassins were warned to take great care 'to avoid the powerful blast'.[25] They needed to take cover within seconds of throwing the device.

There was perhaps another reason why Clarke warned them to take cover, one that needed to remain absolutely secret. It is possible that he had laced his grenade with botulinal toxin, a deadly poison that had been developed at the biological warfare wing of Porton Laboratories and given the codename X. The Porton scientist who developed substance X, Paul Fildes, was a genius in biological warfare. He later confided to two scientists that he 'had a hand' in the death of Heydrich. Indeed, he told the American biologist Alvin Pappenheimer that Heydrich's murder 'was the first notch on my pistol'.[26] There are no other records to substantiate his claim and Clarke himself never admitted to using any biological agent. Yet he was certainly interested in biological warfare and at one point had even managed to acquire his own supply of poison gas from a ship in Barry docks, exchanging it for a large box of plastic explosives. 'No one thought it much of a swap,' said Eveleigh 'Dumbo' Newman, who had been training at Brickendonbury Manor at the time.[27]

Newman and his comrades never ceased to be amazed by Clarke's capacity to invent dirty weapons, unaware that he was fighting an intensely personal battle against the Nazis. It was a battle born out of an experience on the Italian Front in the final hours of the First World War. As he crossed the corpse-strewn River Piave in November 1918, he had stumbled across a shot and dying Austrian soldier who stretched out his arm, imploring, quizzical, looking at him 'with composure, with an enquiring and kindly expression'. Clarke felt a surge of emotion unlike anything he had experienced before. 'As I shook his hand,' he wrote, 'a feeling of newness spread over me, and the scene appeared brighter and more intense. It was as though the illumination of the sun had been intensified, and I became unconscious of the presence of my body.' The mysterious glow in his soul 'lasted probably two seconds', before being replaced by an icy chill as he watched the man die at almost same moment as the armistice.[28] More than a year later, Clarke was still replaying the scene in his head.

That poignant encounter was to trigger a complete mental collapse in the aftermath of the war. Indeed, it caused him such anguish that he refused to talk about it with anyone, preferring to commit his most intimate feelings to a private notebook. Yet it was ultimately to change his life, for when he eventually emerged from his breakdown, he had developed his own theory about how to fight a war with a minimum of human casualties. Sabotage and targeted killing – eradicating individual monsters like Heydrich – was better by far than the slaughter of conscripted civilians.

The effectiveness of his Heydrich grenade, and therefore of the assassination itself, was to be entirely dependent on the accuracy of the person throwing it. This was deemed so important that the two assassins were taken to Aston House in Hertfordshire where they were given intense training under the auspices of Cecil Clarke, Alfgar Hesketh-Prichard and Peter Wilkinson, who, like Hesketh-Prichard, had previously lived in Prague. The men 'spent several Arcadian afternoons in the autumn sunshine carrying out field trials on an ancient Austin saloon'. To make the trials as accurate as possible, the vehicle 'had been rigged up with armour-plated panels and was towed behind a tractor'. A second car was also used, a Canadian Buick, that had a colourful history. It was one of two Buicks owned by King Edward VIII and had taken him to Windsor Castle to make his abdication speech. Clarke had bought the car shortly before the war and loaned it to Brickendonbury, where it was used for military trials.

The Czech assassins and their trainers practised with the car travelling at various speeds. Hesketh-Prichard was the first to throw the grenade and was surprised how easy it was to hit the target, although he reasoned that this was probably because he came from a long line of keen cricketers. His father had played for the Gentlemen versus the Players at Lords before the First World War and Alfgar, too, was a skilled bowler. Indeed he had 'no difficulty in hitting the moving target at speeds of up to 25mph', the maximum that Heydrich's car could conceivably be travelling as it approached the Holešovice crossroads.

Gabčik and Kubis found it rather harder to throw the grenade, 'not having been reared in a cricketing tradition'.[29] The two of them were so concerned about missing their target that they decided to carry a veritable arsenal of additional weaponry. In addition to Clarke's six percussion grenades, they also took two Colt.38 Supers, four spare magazines, four Mills bombs, one of Clarke's tree spigot mortars, a Sten gun, ten pounds of gelignite and 'one lethal hypodermic syringe'.[30] No explanation was given for this last item. As with Clarke's grenade, any mention of biological weaponry was carefully expunged from the records.

The two men were kept apart from everyone else during their stay at Brickendonbury Manor. Secrecy had always been Cecil Clarke's priority and this mission was the most secret of all. When Sue Ryder arrived at Brickendonbury shortly before Gabčik and Kubis, she was told to keep her ears and mouth closed. 'Anybody who comes here is not expected to ask questions. You will find out what you need to know, but always keep your own mouth shut.'[31]

Back in London, secretary Margaret had one last memo to type, one that set out the precise details of the killing. Gabčik and Kubis were to be disguised as street cleaners and 'were to begin sweeping the road at a selected corner. Their explosives and arms were to be concealed in their dustman's barrow.' If Clarke's grenade failed to kill Heydrich, they were to shoot him 'at close quarters with their Colt .38 Super'.[32]

Once the two men had undergone their parachute training and

learned every last twist and turn in the road layout of Prague, they were taken for a night at the theatre with Alfgar Hesketh-Prichard and Peter Wilkinson. Their behaviour took both of them by surprise. When the actors on stage embraced, 'they thought it screamingly funny and roared with laughter.' But during all the jokey parts, 'they remained stolidly glum.' To inject a note of cheer, the four went off to the Criterion afterwards for 'a slap-up supper'. Wilkinson found them 'utterly reliable, utterly fearless, absolutely devoted to their cause'. He was most impressed. 'I could not have admired them more.'[33]

They were taken out again on the eve of their departure, this time by Colonel Moravec. He escorted them to an Italian restaurant in Bayswater where they enjoyed the food, cracked jokes and made no comment about the final item of equipment that Moravec handed to them as they ate their meal: 'two capsules of quick-acting poison to be used on themselves in the event of unbearable torture'.

The men were driven directly to Tangmere aerodrome in Sussex, arriving there in the deep winter twilight. They were met by Flight Lieutenant Ron Hockey, whose task was to fly his Halifax to the Protectorate and drop them into the night sky.

As the men boarded the plane, Gabčik turned to Colonel Moravec. 'You can rely on us, Colonel,' he said. 'We shall fulfil our mission as ordered.'[34]

Nothing was heard from the two assassins for more than a month. In London, it was assumed that something had gone seriously awry. This was indeed the case. The men had been dropped far from Plzen, their intended landing point, and Gabčik had injured himself on landing. But the men were fortunate that local villagers had heard the Halifax overhead and guessed that it was dropping agents. They went in search of the two men and found them hiding out in a quarry.

Gabčik and Kubis accepted assistance with great reluctance, for in doing so they were breaking the first rule of their mission: no contact with the local resistance. Yet they also realized that those locals had almost certainly saved the operation from being aborted. For the next six weeks, they were hidden in safe houses as they planned where and when to strike.

They finally settled on a date for action on receipt of crucial information from a member of the resistance, Josef Novotny. He was responsible for the castle clocks in Prague Castle and he over-heard precise details of Heydrich's travel arrangements for 27 May, including the exact time at which his car would be travelling into Prague. Gabčik and Kubis decided to wait no longer: the assassination was set for that day.

Both men were confident in every aspect of the attack except one. They still did not trust Cecil Clarke's percussion grenade. When they headed to Holešovice crossroads on the morning of the attack, they took the precaution of packing their Sten gun and Colt pistols, in addition to Clarke's grenades. The weapons were placed in an old case and then covered in a thick layer of grass as a precaution against any police inspection. This was not as bizarre as it sounded. There was such a shortage of food in Prague that many people had started to breed rabbits. To feed them, they collected grass and weeds from the local parks.

Gabčik and Kubis took a train to the suburb of Žižkov, where they collected bicycles that had been left for them at a prearranged spot. They then cycled to the junction at Holešovice and made contact with an accomplice, Josef Valcik, who was to stand at the top of the hill and flash a mirror when Heydrich's car came into view.

The two assassins now took up their position at the very point at which Heydrich's car was expected to slow to walking pace. Gabčik assembled the Sten gun while Kubis prepared Clarke's percussion grenade. Both men kept their eyes fixed on Valcik at the top of the hill, waiting nervously for the signal.

Heydrich was late. The clock sounded ten o'clock and then ten fifteen. Unbeknown to the assassins, the Reichsprotektor had decided to take a stroll around the castle gardens with his wife and three children. It was much later than usual when he finally climbed into his vehicle, sitting in the front seat beside his chauffeur, the six-foot Johannes Klein.

Kubis and Gabčik were by now growing jumpy. They had been loitering in the street for almost half an hour and were in danger of arousing the suspicions of passers-by. They were wondering how much longer to remain in wait when, at precisely 10.32 a.m., Valcik's mirror flashed a signal. Heydrich's Mercedes had swung into view.

The assassins had spent weeks training for this very moment. Gabčik released the catch on his Sten and rushed across to the sharpest point in the bend. Kubis pulled one of Clarke's grenades from his briefcase. Both men could see Heydrich's car as it approached. It was travelling quite fast, but dramatically decelerated as it approached the bend and prepared to make a wide sweep. It was now or never. As it slowed to walking pace, Gabčik raised his gun. For a split second he had Heydrich at point-blank range. He squeezed the trigger.

Nothing happened. There was just a faint click. The Sten had failed to fire, possibly because there was grass caught in the mechanism. Gabčik was left standing at the side of the road, fatally exposed, with a gun that was jammed.

Johannes Klein, the chauffeur, had been trained for just such a scenario. His duty was to accelerate sharply away from trouble and whisk Heydrich to safety. But Heydrich was furious at the attempt on his life. Seeing that Gabčik's gun was jammed, he ordered Klein to stop the car and then pulled out his automatic pistol as he prepared to shoot his would-be assassin. As he did so, Kubis stepped from the shadows and hurled Cecil Clarke's bomb at the car. He had practised for this moment so many times during his training but now, in the heat of the moment, he missed his target. Clarke's percussion grenade exploded against the rear wheel of the Mercedes, detonating with unbelievable violence and flinging shards of glass and shrapnel through the body of the car. It was so powerful that Heydrich's and Klein's SS jackets, folded on the back seat of the soft-top vehicle, ended up draped on the high wire of the nearby tramway.

Kubis had been hit by the flying shrapnel and blood was streaming into his eyes. Through a veil of blood, he saw Klein jump from the car and run towards him, pistol drawn. Gabčik had managed to avoid the shrapnel, but he was horrified to see Heydrich drag himself from the vehicle and level his gun. He was lurching forward, shouting wildly as he prepared to fire. Gabčik ditched his jammed Sten and drew his Colt, taking pot-shots at Heydrich from behind a telegraph pole.

Kubis wiped the blood from his eyes, dodged Klein's bullets and jumped on to his bicycle. Klein took aim once again and tried to bring down the fleeing Kubis with a hail of bullets. But his gun also jammed, enabling Kubis to get away. Less than ten minutes after hurling his grenade, Kubis had made it to a safe house.

The situation was more desperate for Gabčik. He was caught in a shoot-out with Heydrich and risked being either shot or captured. But as he was ducking the bullets – suddenly – the unexpected happened. Heydrich staggered to the side of the road and collapsed in agony. Unbeknown to either of his assassins, Cecil Clarke's grenade had done precisely what it had been designed to do. As the shell fragmented, it had driven metal, glass and fragments of horsehair from the car's upholstery deep into Heydrich's spleen.

'Get that bastard,' shouted the Reichsprotektor to his chauffeur, pointing at the escaping Gabčik.[35] As Klein chased after the assassin, Heydrich clutched at the bonnet of the smoking, mangled Mercedes. He was in agony. Not a single eyewitness went to his help.

Colonel Moravec was the first person in England to learn news of the attack, picking it up on Prague radio. 'So that was it,' was his first reaction. 'Gabčik and Kubis had done it.'[36] He immediately informed Gubbins, who began dictating a memo for Margaret to type up. It was to be circulated to just one person, Lord Selborne. 'I would ask that this report be treated with the utmost secrecy,' he said, stressing that it was 'absolutely essential' that no one knew about Baker Street's involvement in the assassination.

'Even should Heydrich not die,' said Gubbins, 'and it is to be sincerely hoped that he will, he must obviously be incapacitated for a very long time.' He was delighted that Gabčik and Kubis had managed to strike at such a high-ranking Nazi. 'This is a most important matter on which we can congratulate ourselves, as even in Germany there is a limit to the number of men of his type who combine both the special aptitude and the special degree of brutality required.'

After praising his Czech Section and the wily Colonel Moravec, he also praised his own team: Eric Sykes, Cecil Clarke, Alfgar Hesketh-Prichard and Peter Wilkinson, 'for the meticulous care with which they prepared the operation and the necessary stores'.[37]

If Gubbins himself was impressed with the professionalism of the attack, then so were the Gestapo. Gubbins managed to acquire their official report into the assassination, which admitted that 'the attack was carried out in a most skilful manner.' The extraordinary grenade had been crucial to its success. 'It was an extremely powerful bomb,' read the Gestapo report, 'for only the fuse and a few pieces remained of it.'

They soon found the assassins' abandoned briefcase containing two more of Clarke's grenades. These were immediately sent for analysis. The experts who defused the weapons had never seen anything quite like them. It was clear that they were 'of British make' and also clear that 'they have the same kind of fuses as the anti-tank shells used by British troops in North Africa.' Yet they had been skilfully modified by an expert, someone who was intent on wreaking maximum damage to an armour-plated car.

Clarke's grenade had indeed done its deadly worst. It had broken one of Heydrich's ribs, ruptured his diaphragm and flung shrapnel deep into his spleen. The Reichsprotektor was rushed to hospital and underwent emergency surgery, but Clarke's grenade was to prove a very dirty weapon indeed. Septicaemia soon took hold and Heydrich breathed his last on the eighth day after the attack.

His doctors blamed the dirty bomb for his death, saying that it had been caused 'by bacteria and possibly by poisons carried into [the vital organs] by the bomb splinters'.

Hitler was furious about the assassination. He initially blamed Heydrich himself, saying that driving around without outriders and SS bodyguards was 'just damned stupidity'.[38] But he quickly transferred his fury to the assassins, whose identity and whereabouts were still unknown.

Unless or until they were found, Czech civilians were to pay the price for Heydrich's death in a series of random, brutal and senseless killings. The village of Lidice was the first to be targeted, on the spurious grounds that it had links to the assassins. The village was cordoned off and 199 male inhabitants shot by the Gestapo. The 195 women and 95 children were arrested and sent to Ravensbruck concentration camp where most were gassed to death. The village of Ležáky was next to be targeted. All thirty-three villagers were shot and most of the children exterminated.

Gabčik and Kubis had made a lucky getaway, sheltering in a number of safe houses before being offered refuge in the dank catacombs of the St Cyril and St Methodius Orthodox Church. They took shelter with five other resistance fighters who feared being captured in the extensive house-to-house searches that were now taking place. All seven were hoping to make their escape.

What they did not know was that they were about to be betrayed by one of their fellow agents, Karel Curda. His revelations led the SS to their hiding place and the church was stormed at 4.10 a.m. on 18 June. The SS fought their way up to the choir loft in a ferocious two-hour gun battle: when they reached the top of the spiral staircase, they found two of the fighters dead and a third, Kubis, mortally wounded. He was rushed to hospital, for the SS were desperate to keep him alive, but he died of his wounds some twenty minutes later.

The other four fighters, including Gabčik, were still hiding out in the catacombs of the church, but their whereabouts were eventually revealed to the SS by the terrified preacher, Vladimir Petrek. First, the SS tried to flood them out, ordering the Czech fire brigade to fill the catacombs with water. When that failed to work, they threw hand grenades through the vents. Eventually, in a cloud of tear gas, masked SS soldiers stormed the catacombs, opening the main entrance with explosives.

As they waded through waist-deep water, they faced heavy gunfire from the four Czech survivors. The German troops fell back for a moment, in preparation for a renewed attack, but were halted by the sound of four shots. The defenders had used their last bullets on themselves.

Colonel Moravec and Colin Gubbins always knew that Czech civilians would pay a high price for the assassination. Several thousand were killed in the aftermath of Heydrich's death and there was a renewed reign of terror throughout the country. But Moravec remained convinced that the assassination was justified, arguing that the Nazi killings would have happened even if Heydrich had not been assassinated. 'The eradication of the Czech nation and its amalgamation into the Reich, including the systematic murder of its leaders, was the assignment with which he came to Prague.' He wrote a personal letter to Gubbins expressing his 'congratulations and admiration' for a job well done.[39]

Winston Churchill expressed his full approval when he learned news of the attack: he was untroubled by political assassinations. When President Roosevelt asked him if the British had been involved in Heydrich's death, Churchill winked but said nothing. There were some secrets too sensitive to be revealed, even to the American President.

13

Sabotage in the Mountains

COLIN GUBBINS REALIZED that he had one significant advantage over the Nazis in the aftermath of Reinhard Heydrich's assassination. The use of underhand tactics had transformed the game of war into an exhilarating game of risk. If he played his hand with skill, he could elevate himself from underdog to master of strategy. And that would leave him, rather than the Nazis, calling the shots. 'If we could surpass them in design, in cunning, in surprise, in boldness,' he said, 'then the fruits of our labours might begin to show effect, in time, to have some influence on the war.' He had learned an important rule from Sykes and Fairbairn: to play the game well meant always being on the offensive. He now saw his role as 'waging a constant battle of wits against the Gestapo' and recognizing the vital importance of retaining the initiative, 'always with something new in preparation'.[1]

Gubbins had been quick to see that Greece presented fertile territory for sabotage, with an underground resistance that had sprung into action within weeks of Mussolini's invasion in the autumn of 1940. Peter Fleming had smuggled himself into Greece as soon as his work with the Kent Auxiliary Units was over: he managed to establish a small group of saboteurs who played merry havoc with the Italian and German armies. A few months after Fleming's arrival in the country, Bickham Sweet-Escott was seated in the Baker Street office when he received a 'stirring' and characteristically colourful telegram from Fleming 'with news that he was holding the Monastir gap' – a valley in Macedonia – against the might of the Nazi war machine.[2] As the Germans advanced, so Fleming retreated, but he did so in a trail of destruction, blowing up bridges and railways as he went.

Fleming was not Gubbins's only operator in Greece. His comrade David Pawson had based himself in Athens, from where he supplied Baker Street with up-to-the-minute news. The Nazi advance left him with little option but to flee the country, but not before delivering a wireless set to a trusted Greek colonel. This colonel vowed to continue Pawson's work using the codename Prometheus, the bringer of fire.

Prometheus was soon in regular contact with Gubbins's office in Istanbul, whose staff arranged for the delivery of explosives. These were sent from England to Palestine and thence to Izmir, in Turkey, before being transferred by caique to Greece. Thus it was that the weapons assembled by Fairy Wond's team of Welsh girls at the Firs ended up in the remote mountains of Thrace.

Prometheus's work eventually came to the notice of the Nazis and he was forced to flee for his life in the summer of 1942. But he managed to hand over his wireless to a young Greek naval officer who was to continue relaying information under the codename Prometheus II. Gubbins's operatives in the Middle East had by this point delivered significant quantities of explosives to Greece and managed to create 'a valuable fighting front organisation'.[3]

This organization was soon to take part in a most spectacular act of sabotage, one that had its roots in North Africa. Here, the British Eighth Army's advance on El Alamein was being hindered by the massive quantities of supplies being delivered to Field Marshal Rommel's Afrika Korps. The supplies were transported by rail from Germany to Greece – forty-eight trains each day – and then shipped from Piraeus to Tobruk and Benghazi. Each train was packed with hundreds of tons of weaponry, vital tools for Rommel's army.

The route through Greece used a single-line standard-gauge railway that meandered across the baked plains of Thessaly before weaving upwards into the wilderness of the Roumeli Mountains. Here, miles from anywhere, was a sparse backland that looked from afar like a vast sheet of hammered pewter, beaten into sharp clefts and ridges. Roumeli was harsh enough in the summer months, when the grass-tufted lower slopes were inhabited by itinerant shepherds. But in winter, when the mercury plunged, it was transformed into a forbidding zone of frozen scree and waterlogged gorges. The icy mountain torrents had scoured sinkholes, tunnels and caverns the size of cathedrals. Such terrain was a regular army's nightmare. Conversely, it was a guerrilla army's dream.

Colin Gubbins had long argued that motorized armies such as Rommel's Afrika Korps presented 'a particularly favourable opportunity for guerrilla warfare', especially if sabotage was 'directed against their communications'.[4] He was also quick to realize that the Afrika Korps was at its most vulnerable not in North Africa itself, nor even in the Mediterranean, but high in the Roumeli Mountains, where the Piraeus railway traversed three large viaducts. If any one of these could be destroyed, the principal supply line between the Third Reich and North Africa would have been spectacularly cut.

Such an operation presented formidable challenges, as Gubbins knew only too well. It would require dropping a team of saboteurs into wholly unknown terrain that was under occupation by the Italian Army. The saboteurs would have to find their way to the viaducts and kill the Italian sentries before laying their explosive charges. To achieve this, they would require the support of the Greek *andartes* – guerrillas – known to be hiding out in this empty wilderness.

In spite of the difficulties, Operation Harling was given the green light. A small team was to be parachuted into Greece with enough explosives to wreak havoc on Rommel's vital supply line. Gubbins decided from the outset that the mission should be undertaken by his team in Cairo, which had been overseeing action in Greece and the Balkans for the previous two years. Although he was to keep a sharp eye on unfolding events, the baton was temporarily handed to Cairo.

Cairo was awash with British officers. Some had been posted to the city as intelligence agents; many more had fled there in the wake of the Nazi invasion of Crete. Among this latter group was Chris Woodhouse – known to his friends as Monty – an accomplished young Oxford graduate who had gained a double first in classics along with a clutch of the university's most prestigious prizes.

On Friday, 18 September 1942 Woodhouse was summoned to an interview at Rustrum Buildings, Baker Street's Cairo headquarters, where he found himself being grilled by a mysterious individual who declined to introduce himself. 'In the room to which I was directed sat a lieutenant-colonel behind a desk at right angles to the window. In the blinding light through the window I could only see his profile. I never learned his name. He looked up from the papers on his desk simply to say: "Would you be willing to be parachuted into Greece next week?"'

Woodhouse thought about it for a moment. 'There seemed no reason to say No, so I said Yes.'[5] He reasoned that it would be a good opportunity to practise his Greek.

He was better qualified than most to be dropped into Greece, yet he was nevertheless a strange choice for an undercover mission. He was 'tall and conspicuously un-Greek looking'[6] with a mop of ginger-blond hair that made him look more like a Scandinavian fisherman than a Greek shepherd. But he had the advantage of knowing classical Greek and he also had the stamina of a mountain goat. He was delighted by the idea of becoming a thorn in Rommel's flesh.

Woodhouse was to be one of the principal players in Operation Harling, but the leadership role itself went to Eddie Myers, a thirty-six-year-old Jewish sapper who had earned his spurs in Palestine during the Arab Revolt. Myers gave the impression of being gifted in everything. A fine horseman and skilled pilot, he had a 'forceful personality'[7] that was frequently deployed against his superiors. He was initially reluctant to accept the post of guerrilla leader, for he had just been granted his first annual leave in years. But his commanding officer persuaded him to have a crack at an operation that offered danger, glory and exhilaration. 'You are just the sort of chap we are looking for,' he said. 'How would you like to take command of the show? It is frightfully important.'

Myers agreed and began to gather other members of his twelve-strong team. It was to include three trained saboteurs led by a New Zealander, Tom Barnes, who was 'fair-haired, stickily built and immensely strong'.[8] There were also three wireless operators, three commandos and an officer named Thermistocles Marinos, the only Greek member of the team.

Accurate intelligence was everything for a mission of this complexity. Gubbins's Athens-based wireless operator, Prometheus

II, had managed to keep Baker Street informed about the destruction of oil installations and army supply ships. Now, he offered to help with arrangements for Myers's saboteurs to be parachuted into the Roumeli Mountains, assuring Cairo that Greek guerrillas would light fires on the night of the drop in order to guide the men to safety.

This sounded promising in theory, but Prometheus II's wireless transmissions were often faulty or corrupted. It would only take one miscommunication for Myers and his men to be landed in the wrong place, in a remote mountainous wilderness where there was no local support.

There was an additional problem that threatened to scupper Operation Harling before it even began. Gubbins's team in Cairo had precious little information about the three mountain viaducts in Roumeli. There were no plans, nor even photographs, until someone managed to lay their hands on an old postcard of the Simplon-Orient Express crossing the Gorgopotamos viaduct.

Shortly afterwards, Baker Street succeeded in acquiring drawings of both the Papadia and Gorgopotamos viaducts. These were sent to Cairo and handed over to Eddie Myers, who felt a thrill of excitement when he saw pictures of the Gorgopotamos gorge and viaduct. The gorge itself was a gaping limestone fissure of such depth that the racing torrent at the bottom appeared as little more than a thinly traced line. It was spanned by one of Europe's more spectacular viaducts, an awesome feat of structural engineering that was almost 900 feet in length and spanned the gorge at a dizzying height. Rommel's army in North Africa depended on this vulnerable structure.

Myers now began planning his mission in earnest. It was to require specialist equipment, for the men would be working during the rigours of a mountain winter. They would need to be dropped with stores, supplies and food, along with a large quantity of weaponry. The weapons included Sten guns, hand grenades and detonators, as well as Cairo's entire stock of plastic explosive.

Each man was also to be given a personal supply that included a revolver, a Fairbairn-Sykes commando knife and field dressings, along with the standard Baker Street kit: 'a compass disguised as a button, a map disguised as a silk scarf, a leather belt containing two sovereigns', together with rations, torches and poison pills in case of capture.[9]

Myers divided his teams into three groups of four men who were to be dropped into Greece by three American Liberator aircraft. There was no time to lose, for the fight in North Africa was reaching a critical stage. By the third week of September, Myers's men were ready for action.

Their first attempt at dropping into the country, on 29 September, gave some inkling of the problems ahead. After a four-hour flight over the Mediterranean, the planes found themselves circling over the Roumeli Mountains in a vain search for the landing flares promised by Prometheus II. The dark folds of the mountains revealed no welcoming beacons and the men were reluctantly forced to return to Cairo.

On the following evening they made a second attempt, having decided to land even if there were no flares. As they circled over the frozen peak of Mount Giona, gleaming milky-white in the moonlight, Myers thought he spotted a group of three fires in the valley below. 'I spoke to the pilot on the intercommunication telephone and said that I was prepared to have a go there if he agreed.'

The pilot dropped low from the cloud until the plane was flying alarmingly close to the surrounding peaks. He made a final arc across the valley and then signalled for Myers and his saboteurs to jump. Operation Harling was finally under way.

It was only as Myers floated downwards, struggling with his heavy pack, that the difficulties of a blind drop into unknown terrain become apparent. His parachute was caught in a sharp mountain updraught that sent him whirling towards a towering forest of fir trees.

'I fell into the middle of a tall mountain fir, which opened and parted its arms and had some rudely broken as I crashed through it.' He tumbled downwards through the branches, falling uncontrollably as they parted beneath his weight. 'The next thing I knew, I was sitting on the ground on an extremely steep slope, with my parachute caught up above me.'

His pack was dangling from the tree like some overgrown Christmas decoration and the rest of his supplies, dropped in separate metal containers, were nowhere to be seen. As he shook off the dirt, he heard the valedictory throb of the American Liberators heading back to Cairo. There was no sign of his comrades. He was alone and lost on a near-vertical mountain slope. His goal of blowing up the Gorgopotamos viaduct seemed very remote indeed.

Gubbins had always stressed that the hallmark of a professional guerrilla was to keep a cool head under pressure. True to this creed, Myers acted with commendable calm. First, he lit a flare to attract the attention of his comrades. When this had no effect, he lit a bonfire. This, too, failed to solicit any response. Eventually he managed to stumble down the slope, using the trees for support, until he emerged into a moonlit valley. Here, he bumped into two Greek shepherds. 'After a roundabout sort of deaf-and-dumb conversation, including a lot of pointing to the sky, we mutually agreed that we would stay where we were for the next three hours until dawn broke.'

As soon as it was light, Myers led the two Greeks back up the mountain slope to his rucksack and parachute, both of which had mysteriously vanished. He was wondering what to do when, 'from a parting in the trees, emerged Tom Barnes'.[10]

Myers was relieved to discover that Barnes was unhurt and even more delighted when he learned that Barnes had picked up a signal from Len Wilmot. The two of them went off to look for him, while the Greeks went in search of the fourth member of Myers's team, Denys Hamson, the only one who spoke Greek. At the pre-agreed midday rendezvous, the Greeks returned with Hamson, whom they had found in the forest, while Len Wilmot appeared soon after, having heard the sound of voices. The first of Myers's three teams was miraculously intact.

Chris 'Monty' Woodhouse and his group had jumped from the second Liberator and had fared rather better. Woodhouse himself had landed with scarcely a bump, 'not harder than stepping off a table',[11] while the others had also dropped without mishap. There was a moment of panic when they were surrounded by Greek soldiers who suspected them of being Germans, but Woodhouse was quick to put them right. He called out: 'I am a British officer.' To which one of the Greeks replied: 'I am a Greek officer.' He then rushed towards Woodhouse 'and kissed me on both cheeks'.

Woodhouse's most urgent task was to locate the other two teams, but first he and his men were led to a nearby mountain village. Here, they were alarmed to see that a group of children had found their supply canisters and taken out the plastic explosive. Assuming it was fudge, they were cramming it into their mouths. 'This was disastrous for them,' said Woodhouse, 'but it was also disastrous for us, because it was reducing our essential explosives.'[12] In fact, the explosive did no harm to the children other than to make them sick.

One of the Greek villagers, known as Barba [Uncle] Niko, had lived in America and spoke broken English. He warned that the mountains were patrolled by Italian soldiers and suggested they should hide out in a concealed cave on the eastern slopes of Mount Giona. It was large enough to house all three teams, if and when the others were located, and was unknown to the Italians. Woodhouse agreed to be led there, hoping that the others would indeed be brought to the same cave.

The hike was extremely arduous, involving a three-day march across bleak mountain passes, with a relentless icy blast knifing in from the north. Scuds of snow lay in the hollows, wind-blown and grey with dirt, and the men were cold and miserable. 'Some of us had lice and some had fleas. The first rains had ended, but the snow-line was creeping down towards us.'

Their misery was soon tempered by good news. Eddie Myers's team arrived at the same cave just two days after Woodhouse and his men, having been led there by Greek shepherds. When Woodhouse thanked Uncle Niko for his support, he replied: 'I heard that God had sent us Englishmen from heaven, so it was my duty to help them.'[13]

And help them he did. When he learned that Italian troops were searching the vicinity, perhaps because they had heard the circling Liberator aircraft, he found an even more secure cave at the foot of a rocky escarpment. Now that they were safe, their priority was to locate the whereabouts of the third team.

Back in London, Colin Gubbins had no idea of the fate of the teams dropped into Greece. It had been the same with the Czech assassins.

Once the men jumped from their planes, they were invariably out of contact. Myers's wireless transmitter had broken on landing. The men were on their own.

Yet Gubbins nevertheless continued to pull the strings of Operation Harling, albeit from a distance. His *Partisan Leaders Handbook*, widely distributed in Cairo, had been written with exactly such a mission in mind: a bold strike in rugged countryside with the active support of local guerrillas. Now, Eddie Myers followed this manual so closely that he was to adhere to all seven points of Gubbins's guerrilla creed, including the use of stealth, nocturnal cover and the recruitment of local mountain experts.

Gubbins had long believed that war against the Nazis would eventually reach a tipping point, the moment at which the local population would rise up against the occupying army. 'As the war progresses and the enemy's hold begins to weaken owing to successful sabotage,' he said, 'the conditions will become ripe for the formation of partisan bands.' In Greece, and especially in the Roumeli Mountains, those conditions were already in place.

Gubbins also said that operating in familiar terrain gave the local guerrilla the upper hand, for he was 'fighting in his own country, among his own people, against a foreign foe who has invaded his land'. Unlike the enemy, he was not constrained by rules, command structures and centralized barracks. And although the occupying forces retained the use of the road and railway system, the mountain guerrilla always held the trump card in hit-and-run raids. 'By the judicious selection of ground, and by moves in darkness to secure surprise, the guerrilla can enjoy relatively superior mobility for the period necessary for each operation.'[14]

Uncle Niko warned Myers that a great swathe of the Roumeli wilderness had become the fiefdom of a local chieftain named Napoleon Zervas. He controlled a large band of partisans who roamed the Roumeli like lawless bandits, ambushing Italian sentries and dispensing summary justice: Zervas's cooperation was essential for any sabotage operation. Myers agreed and asked Uncle Niko if he could lead Woodhouse to the chieftain's mountain headquarters in an attempt to gain his support.

The two of them hiked for more than a week, crossing snow-blasted ridges and forlorn valleys as they went in search of Zervas. At one point they were stopped by an elderly woman who asked Woodhouse what he was doing. 'Boldly I told her I was a guerrilla.' She was intrigued and said 'she had never met one before'. She then asked where he was from. 'For want of anything better, I named the neighbouring village which I had passed through twenty minutes earlier. The woman nodded knowingly. "Ah, I knew from your accent you were a foreigner."'

After a gruelling trudge over the mountains, they finally located the feared Napoleon Zervas. Woodhouse had been expecting an imperious braggart, lording it over his mountain fiefdom like some self-styled satrap. The truth was rather different. Zervas was short, comically rotund and perennially smiling. 'He greeted me with a kiss on both cheeks, which was prickly for both of us. "*Kalos ston Evangelon!*" he said with quiet satisfaction. "Welcome to the Angel of Good Tidings!"'[15]

Zervas was a godsend: efficient, cheerful and devoted to expelling the hated Italians from Greek soil. 'When he laughed, as he so often did, his whole body vibrated, and the merry sparkle in his eyes belied the black, hairy fierceness of a heavily bearded face.' His eyes were large and brown, his lips full and generous. He was dressed in an old khaki smock, without any insignia, with breeches and over-large riding boots. 'An unpolished Sam-Browne belt around his ample waist supported a small automatic pistol and jewelled dagger whose sheath was liable to stick out from his stomach at a jaunty angle when he sat down.'[16]

Zervas controlled a band of a hundred guerrillas, whose enthusiasm for action was rather more impressive than their equipment. 'Few had any military uniform. Even fewer had boots: leather slippers, strips of goat-string tied around their ankles, slices of rubber tyre fastened with wire, in some cases nothing but threadbare socks.'[17] They had one tommy gun, one machine gun and a few Mannlicher rifles dating from the First World War.

Zervas agreed to help with the sabotage operation, but there was a problem. He was not the only chieftain in these mountains. There was a second band of guerrillas led by Aris Velouchiotis, a notoriously violent partisan with a penchant for summary justice. It was unthinkable for any attack to take place on the viaducts without Aris's active involvement, but herein lay a problem. Aris's men were Communists while Zervas's were Republicans. The two leaders and their men were bitter rivals.

When Woodhouse learned that Aris's base was just a few hours' march away, he used all his persuasive powers to induce Zervas to meet his Communist foe, arranging a rendezvous in the village of Viniani, in the holiday villa of a Greek-American expatriate.

Aris cut a very different figure from the genial Zervas. Small and wiry, he had a long black beard and a Cossack cap of black fur that gave him a benign, monklike look. 'But his eyes were deep-set and, except when he smiled, there was much hardness in his features. Only when mellowed by alcohol did he ever relax.'[18]

He conformed to the stereotype of a bandit chieftain, with 'two bandoliers loaded with cartridges and a large knife in his belt'.[19] The knife was often used to slit the throats of captured Italians, as well as against those in his own ranks who disobeyed his authority. 'Silent and inclined to be dour, he always gave the impression of being on guard against someone or something.'

His men displayed a rare professionalism and were 'tougher and more determined than those of Zervas'.[20] Woodhouse realized that Aris's support would be crucial for their attack on the Gorgopotamos viaduct and was therefore delighted when he agreed to join forces.

Aris had one piece of news that was both unexpected and welcome. He told Woodhouse that his men had rescued the third group of British saboteurs from the Italians. The men had misjudged their landing and dropped into the Karpenisi valley, close to an Italian garrison town. They would certainly have been captured had they not been plucked from danger by Aris. Woodhouse was now able to send a message to them, with instructions on how to join Eddie Myers and the rest of the men. After four weeks on the ground, the entire team was reunited.

Eddie Myers had not been slacking in Woodhouse's absence. He had undertaken a reconnaissance of the three Roumeli viaducts, in order to be certain that Gorgopotamos was the best target. It was every bit as spectacular as in the photographs. The gorge itself resembled a yawning jaw, open to the sky and spanned by a single line of railway track. Most of the viaduct's piers were built of masonry, but the two at the southern end were constructed from steel. Myers studied them through his field glasses and then made drawings of them. He decided that these steel girders presented his best hope of bringing down the structure, even though they would be extremely hard to destroy. In his pamphlet, *How to Use High Explosives*, Millis Jefferis had warned that girder structures like Gorgopotamos presented unique complications for the would-be saboteur. 'Steel girders *may* be cut with explosives, but this is the most difficult kind of demolition to tackle and should not be attempted by men who have not had experience.'[21]

Myers was aware of this. His powerful binoculars enabled him to make a detailed study of the steel piers. He concluded that the legs were L-shaped in cross-section, an important detail. It meant that his men could mould their 400 pounds of plastic explosive in advance, 'pressing the separate sticks into a wooden mould, which we had made for our charges, to fit the believed cross section of the legs of the steel piers'.

Myers returned to his hideout with a strategy already in place. He knew that it would be hard to destroy the viaduct without first killing the Italian sentries. This was unlikely to go unnoticed by the rest of the garrison, for the Italians had entrenched positions at either end of the viaduct. Both of these would also need to be attacked.

The success or failure of the mission would ultimately depend on Tom Barnes's demolition party, which would need to descend into the deep gorge and place charges on the girders. Myers reckoned this would take up to four hours, time enough for the Italians to call up reinforcements. But there were no other options. An assault on the Italian positions, followed by a spectacular sabotage operation, was the only viable one.

Myers hoped to launch his assault on the night of 25 November, although he knew the exact timing would be dependent on the weather. He formed an advance party that set off on the afternoon of 23 November: they were to be joined by the rest of the men on the evening of the attack. It was a gruelling six-hour trudge through the snow to their forward position, a shepherd's hut perched high on the wooded upper slopes of Mount Oiti. Once here, they were within striking distance of the viaduct. The ground was blanketed in soft snow – it was more than a foot deep – and the evening clouds were so low that the fir trees were enveloped in mist.

Myers snatched a few hours' sleep and awoke at dawn in order to crawl to his lookout position. But there was nothing to be seen except banks of mist. 'A bird's eye view of the approaches to the Gorgopotamos viaduct proved to be impossible.' Later that morning, it began to rain and great clods of melting snow slid from the trees. But the mercury soon plummeted and the rain turned to snow. 'As we lay in the bleak and draughty hut, with our eyes sore from the smoke of the fire that we kept going in the middle of its earth floor, we seemed strangely isolated from the rest of the world by the low-lying clouds.' Darkness came early and Myers prepared for a second night without much sleep.

When he awoke on the following morning, the clouds had lifted and the sky was bright. It was perfect reconnaissance weather. Accompanied by a couple of companions, he cautiously descended the mountain until they were less than a thousand yards from the railway. 'There, crawling on our hands and knees from cover to cover, through gaps in the slowly moving clouds, we got some excellent glimpses of the viaduct. Several hundred feet below us, it looked like a toy bridge.' He studied the vast structure through his field glasses, then watched the sentries as they scurried around like ants. He set the attack for that night.

The main body of guerrillas arrived later that day, at about four in the afternoon, 'silently winding its way in single file out of the clouds which now clung again to the sides of the mountain'. The men crouched down in the misty dampness of the forest and ate their last meal before the attack: cold meat, a hunk of bread and a flask of icy water cut with ouzo. They were about a mile from Gorgopotamos and some 4,000 feet above the viaduct. Myers divided his men into their respective teams and made sure that those who had watches synchronized them. Then, as dusk approached, he ordered the men to their feet. At shortly after six o'clock, the guerrillas began winding down through the wet snow in single file. The low cloud was once again clinging to the side of the mountain, enveloping everything in mist.

The men split into their prearranged groups, with two of them heading north and south to cut the railway tracks. The rest were to be engaged in the attack. The most treacherous task of the night was to be undertaken by Tom Barnes and his saboteurs. In pitch darkness they had to clamber down the near-vertical gorge accompanied by eight mules carrying all the explosives. They then had to cross the raging torrent by way of a rickety plank bridge before unharnessing their mules and strapping the explosives to the girders.

Each group said its farewells and the men headed their separate ways. Within less than a minute, they had been swallowed by the darkness. The four commanders – Eddie Myers, Chris 'Monty' Woodhouse, Napoleon Zervas and Aris Velouchiotis – went directly to their forward command post, crawling to within 150 yards of the viaduct where there was a hollow that afforded them protection from stray fire. Myers was pleased to note that 'the mist was now thinner and the full moon, trying to get through, lit up the surrounding country sufficiently for our purpose. Conditions, in fact, were ideal.'[22]

The four of them lay there in silence, glancing nervously at their watches. They had a long wait. At a few minutes before eleven, to everyone's surprise, a train rumbled past. 'That'll be the last for a long time,' whispered Woodhouse.[23]

Myers once again checked his watch. The attack was set for eleven o'clock. Two minutes to go. He inched himself forward through the snow in order to get a better viewing position. 'Through the light mist we could clearly see the viaduct ahead of us. It looked huge and gaunt.'

Zero hour. It was eleven o'clock. Myers was anticipating the opening crackle of gunfire as his teams went into action at either end of the viaduct. But there was only silence. It was as if the mountains had gone to sleep.

For fourteen agonizing minutes he waited at the edge of the ridge, trying to work out what might have gone awry. And then, 'when we began to think that something had gone seriously wrong, that all the parties were late, or that in the darkness they had gone astray, pandemonium was let loose right in front of us around the north end of the viaduct.'[24]

Rifle fire, automatic fire and the staccato of machine guns rocked the silence of the night as the onslaught on the Gorgopotamos garrison began in earnest. The attackers at the southern end launched a particularly ferocious assault, starting with a deluge of hand grenades thrown into the pillboxes. The Italian sentries who survived the initial blasts now burst out, desperate to make their escape. 'They just ran away and were shot by the guerrillas,' said one. 'It was just a sort of shambles of noise.'[25]

The assault at the far end seemed to be going like clockwork. The Italian defenders soon gave up the fight and were looking to escape with their lives. 'Nearly an hour after the battle had started, exceptionally loud cheering went up from the south end of the viaduct,' said Myers. 'It was followed almost immediately by a white Very light. The far end was in our hands.'[26]

It was a very different story at the near end, just underneath Myers's lookout position. As the gunfight intensified, one of Zervas's breathless guerrillas ran up to the command post with the terrible news that they were being beaten back. The Italian defenders were too strong. At this critical juncture, Myers showed decisive leadership. He had withheld a small reserve force, to be used in emergency. Now, he sent them into action and they more than proved their mettle. A ferocious shoot-out was followed by sudden and complete silence. It was as if the battle had been switched off. A few seconds later, a second Very light could be seen winking in the darkness. The northern end of the viaduct had also been captured.

Now that the guerrillas were in control, Tom Barnes and his saboteurs could get to work without risk of being fired on from above. They had spent the previous hour slithering their way down into the deep ravine, forcing their mules down treacherous slopes strewn with loose and muddy scree. They eventually reached the bottom, exhausted but unharmed. Now, they had to cross the plank bridge that traversed the torrent, with each man guiding his chosen mule. 'It had to be the right muleteer which led each mule, because mules are mules and they wouldn't go without a rival leader.'[27]

Only once they were all safely across did Barnes look up to the distant command post. As he did so, he saw a flashing torch signalling to him. Then, echoing off the rock walls of the ravine, he heard a shout from Myers. 'Go in Tom! The south end of the bridge is in our hands. Go in!'[28]

Barnes's men now began unpacking the plastic explosives and strapping them to the supporting girders. This took time, but eventually they were all secured. Barnes gave a blast on his whistle, signalling that he was poised to detonate his explosive. He struck the fuse caps, lit them and ran for cover. He and his men had just seconds to take shelter before the explosive charges would blow.

They threw themselves into a ditch just in time. 'Flattened out against the ground, they were shaken by the sudden tremendous blast and by the thousands of pieces of red hot metal flying in all directions.'[29] The cataclysmic explosion was witnessed by Myers, who had inched even closer to the viaduct. He couldn't resist raising his head as a crash of explosive thunder resonated through the deep gorge. 'I saw one of the seventy-foot steel spans lift into the air and − oh what joy! − drop down into the gorge below in a rending crash of breaking and bending steel-work.'

When all the debris had fallen back to earth, Barnes went to admire his handiwork. He was staggered by the extent of the destruction. Two of the vast metal spans had crashed into the gorge and lay tangled beyond all recognition. Where once there had been a viaduct, there was now only stars and sky.

Myers now ran down to the viaduct and walked gingerly along the buckled track until he reached the jagged end. He peered over the edge, curious to see the destruction. 'In front of me I clearly discerned two complete spans which had been dropped into the gorge below.'

Barnes still had a little explosive left so he fixed a second charge to the mangled ruins, in order to cause further damage. 'He blew his whistle again,' said Myers. 'Everyone took cover and a bit more of the bridge came down.' Once this was done, Myers sounded the withdrawal. The exhausted men now faced a fifteen-hour hike back to their hideout. They had suffered no deaths and only one casualty, a Greek fighter wounded by shrapnel. The Italians had fared rather worse. At least thirty had been killed, perhaps more. Myers himself had stumbled over half a dozen corpses.

After a gruelling hike through deep snow, the guerrilla band finally reached their camp, where Uncle Niko was waiting with a hot meal. Myers 'experienced a glow of satisfaction from the realisation that we had achieved our mission'.[30] He thanked all the men, congratulated them and then fell into a deep sleep.

The German high command was furious when it received news of the destruction of the Gorgopotamos viaduct. Sixteen local villagers were arrested at random and shot at the base of the ruined structure. 'It was a terrible, terrible war,' said Woodhouse.

General Alexander Loehr, commander of the Fifth Army Group, ordered the immediate rebuilding of the viaduct. He optimistically informed Berlin that this would take just seven days. In fact it took fully six weeks before the first supply trains could tentatively use the restored viaduct.

The Gorgopotamos sabotage was a triumph, as Chris 'Monty' Woodhouse was quick to recognize. 'It showed for the first time in occupied Europe that guerrillas, with the support of allied officers, could carry out a major tactical operation coordinated with allied strategic plans.'[31] The fact that it coincided with Operation Torch, the Allied invasion of French North Africa, made it an even sweeter act of sabotage.

'It had a great effect on Rommel's supplies,' said Myers, 'because it cut for six valuable weeks all supplies going that way.'[32] In that time, the Afrika Korps was deprived of more than 2,000 trainloads of supplies. By the time the viaduct was finally repaired, the battle for North Africa was fast slipping from Rommel's hands.

The destruction of Gorgopotamos was also a personal triumph for Gubbins, as Joan Bright was quick to point out. She overheard senior army commanders welcoming it as 'an outstanding contribution' to the struggle in North Africa and a near faultless *coup de main* operation 'executed by British officers with the indispensible assistance of Greek guerrillas'.[33]

Eddie Myers's twelve-man team was supposed to be evacuated by submarine just a few days after the attack. But when they finally managed to get a wireless message through to Cairo, they were told to stay in Greece 'with the object of unifying guerrilla activities'. The idea was to form a major guerrilla army that could put relentless pressure on both German and Italian forces in Greece.

Myers worked tirelessly to build his guerrilla force, despite the difficulties caused by intense political rivalry between the different Greek factions. He was soon able to report that he was 'at the head of five thousand armed and disciplined guerrillas' operating against the Italians in western Greece. He was also in contact with another group who were tasked with sabotaging Nazi transport ships heading for North Africa. In a single raid, they managed to sink five heavily laden vessels, 'just one highlight from an underground campaign which has caused the greatest inconvenience to the Axis'.

And so the attacks continued: troop trains derailed, eleven major mines destroyed and Italian outpost garrisons surrounded and liquidated. The German high command was so infuriated by the Italian Army's inability to contain Myers's men that they vowed to send 'two wagon-loads of bloodhounds' from the Russian Front to Greece.

Shortly after the Gorgopotamos viaduct was back in action, Myers's men scored a second triumph when they succeeded in blowing up the Asopos viaduct, the second of the three crucial bridges in the Roumeli Mountains. Churchill grinned broadly when he was shown photos of the wreckage.

Eddie Myers vowed to continue his work, sending a simple wireless message to headquarters. 'Give us the tools and we will do the job.'[34] Colin Gubbins had little doubt he meant it.

14

Man of Steel

CECIL CLARKE WAS having a good war. Three years earlier, he had been struggling to balance the books at his Bedfordshire caravan business. Now, he was one of the country's leading experts in sabotage, responsible for training Colin Gubbins's most intrepid agents. He had developed some of the most effective weapons of the war, notably the grenade that killed Reinhard Heydrich, and his limpet mine was being produced in the tens of thousands. It had been used to blow up everything from factories in the Balkans to transport ships in Greece.

Three weeks before Christmas 1942, Clarke learned that his limpet had played its most spectacular role to date. A team of commandos led by Herbert 'Blondie' Hasler had crept into Bordeaux harbour and slipped limpet mines on to enemy vessels, severely damaging five of them. Operation Frankton, the Cockleshell Raid, was a brilliantly audacious strike at the enemy. Lord Mountbatten said that 'of the many brave and dashing raids carried out by the men of Combined Operations Command, none was more courageous or imaginative than Operation Frankton.'[1] The imaginative element was due, in no small part, to Cecil Clarke.

Mrs Clarke did not share Cecil's enthusiasm for war. While he was blowing craters in the grounds of Brickendonbury Manor, she was struggling to lay her hands on enough food for her three young boys, while simultaneously trying to cope with the running of LoLode. The company now had ten employees who were undertaking orders for the War Office, constructing ambulance trailers and other towed vehicles. Clarke was noticeable only by his absence.

By Christmas of that year, Clarke was growing restless with life at Brickendonbury and was keen to lead a saboteur unit of his own.

He appealed to Colin Gubbins to let him take a freelance band of guerrillas to the Middle East, where he felt sure he could wreak havoc. He was to be disappointed. Gubbins told him it was 'impossible to entertain the suggestion',[2] for he was far too valuable to the home team. Yet he acknowledged his desire for change, allowing him to step aside from his role at Brickendonbury and giving him a temporary posting to Arisaig.

Clarke made his way to the killing school, where he was made Officer in Charge of User Trials. This placed him in charge of fine-tuning all the prototype weaponry that was being tested in the Highlands. His first task was to trial the new generation of limpet mines in the chill waters of Loch nan Ceall. Gubbins knew all about Clarke's hands-on approach to testing weapons – it invariably involved him plunging into the water in his underpants – and offered a piece of friendly advice. 'In view of the cold at this time of year,' he said, 'I suggest you get some of the special Air Force bathing suits which will keep out all the water.'[3]

Clarke had always been a restless individual, distracted by any passing curiosity. He soon requested to be moved again, only this time he asked to be transferred to the Firs, in order to work alongside Millis Jefferis. Stuart Macrae was delighted when he learned that Gubbins had approved the transfer to Whitchurch. 'Like you,' he said to Clarke, 'we have always been irregular and always will be.'[4]

Poor Dorothy was now to see even less of her husband, for the Firs was more than thirty miles from Bedford. Clarke was not inclined to share quarters with the other staff (and they, perhaps, had little desire to share with him). It suited everyone when he rented a cottage in Whitchurch village. He took particular delight in discovering that it was the only one known to be haunted. When his young boys came on a rare visit, he told them that the ghostly apparition of a woman was said to drift through the house at night and that people sleeping in the bedrooms used to 'wake up feeling they'd been throttled'.[5] It was hardly a reassuring image, but Clarke was careful to remind his sons that ghosts didn't exist. When his bottle of Brylcreem inexplicably toppled over, he told young David that he wouldn't believe the house was haunted until the bottle righted itself. It never did.

No sooner was Clarke installed at the Firs than he set to work on a novel little invention called the Aero-Switch. It was designed to be used on German planes while they were on the ground, where they were particularly vulnerable to sabotage. The Aero-Switch was a pressurized explosive charge that, as he explained to Macrae, 'could be inserted into a German bomber by some brave fellow and would explode when the aircraft reached a certain height'. It worked by means of an ingenious metal bellows that expanded with the reduced atmospheric pressure, forcing two wires to connect and detonate the charge, with devastating consequences for the plane.

The explosive itself was housed in a flexible sausage casing and Clarke maintained that although it 'could not be conveniently concealed in the pocket', it could 'without comment be carried in the trousers'. Macrae begged to differ as he watched Clarke parading around the room with a giant sausage in his pants. 'He was wrong about the "without comment",' he said, 'and there was always considerable ribaldry when he demonstrated this method to his pupils.'

The Aero-Switch was an inventive way of reducing the size of the Luftwaffe and the Firs immediately set up a production line. It soon became the weapon of choice for many saboteurs working in occupied territories. German-controlled airbases were often too large to be well guarded, enabling any would-be saboteur to crawl through the perimeter fence under the cover of darkness and plant their weapon on the plane. 'The usual drill was to make a slit in the wing fabric of a German bomber and pop the thing inside so that in due course the wing would be wrecked and the bomber likewise.'

The weapon had not long been in service when Macrae learned from intelligence sources that 'the entire Luftwaffe bombing fleet about to set out for London had been grounded whilst a search was carried out for this sabotage weapon which had already caused them too many casualties.' Macrae proudly passed this information to his wife, who was working at Bletchley Park, 'only to be informed that she knew all about it because she had handled the message'.[6]

While Clarke had been working on the Aero-Switch, Macrae had been busy perfecting his clam, the miniature version of Clarke's limpet. When demonstrated to the Russians, they immediately recognized its potential on the Eastern Front and placed an order for 1 million. Soon after, the Allied armies in the west ordered a further 1½ million. The clam, like the limpet, was another winner for Millis Jefferis's team at the Firs.

Cecil Clarke's move to the Firs left a vacancy for the top job at Brickendonbury Manor. Colin Gubbins had no doubts as to who he wanted as his new commanding officer. George Rheam had first come to his attention a few months earlier, when he had been told of a brilliantly gifted northerner living in a suburban house in High Barnet. He was said to be the country's leading expert in steam turbines, power stations and generators: he was immediately summoned to Baker Street for an interview.

Those who met Rheam rarely forgot the experience, for he was a chilling individual, an unsmiling genius with thatch-coloured hair and penetrating steel eyes that betrayed no hint of his inner thoughts. He spoke sparingly, precisely, as if adjectives and adverbs were a frivolous waste of time. Gubbins was quick to realize that Rheam had a very clear idea of how to destroy the Nazis. His great desire was to turn Occupied Europe into an industrial junkyard and he insisted that 'sabotage, if properly planned and carried out, can reduce a country's war-potential to the point where it becomes impossible to wage war.'[7]

Rheam also knew more than most people about industrial engineering. He had worked for nearly a decade at Metropolitan Vickers, where he displayed more aptitude for interacting with steam turbines than with his colleagues. In 1930 he and Mrs Rheam had moved south so that he could take up his job at the North Metropolitan Power Company's generating station at Southgate, near London. Here, he spent his working day studying the component parts of electricity generators. He was soon the country's leading expert.

In the late 1930s, as Britain drifted towards war, Rheam began to turn his thoughts to the destruction of machinery. One day, he was struck by the exhilarating thought that he could cripple all the most important power stations in Britain with a very small quantity of explosives. Indeed, he reckoned that he could completely paralyse British industry 'for a very long period with less than two tons'.[8]

Colin Gubbins advocated rail sabotage in his controversial 1939 booklet, *Art of Guerrilla Warfare*. 'It is not sufficient to shoot at the train,' he said. 'First derail the train and then shoot the survivors.'

Cecil Clarke demonstrates his 1939 limpet mine: lightweight, versatile, deadly.

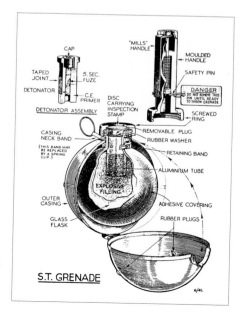

Millis Jefferis's lethal sticky bomb. 'Make one million,' ordered Winston Churchill.

Colin Gubbins, undisputed master of guerrilla warfare. His methods were mistrusted by senior military commanders.

Millis Jefferis, Britain's most brilliant explosives expert and favourite of Churchill.

Joan Bright. By the summer of 1939 she was the lynchpin of the guerrilla headquarters in Caxton Street.

Cecil Clarke, a Bedfordshire caravan engineer, helped to plan many of the war's most audacious sabotage missions.

Stuart Macrae was instrumental in establishing the secret weapons station at the Firs in the autumn of 1940. Witty and charming, he oversaw the production of millions of sabotage weapons.

Cecil Clarke's caravan was an engineering masterpiece and brought him to the attention of the War Office. The family's 1936 Canadian Buick had previously belonged to King Edward VIII.

Eric 'Bill' Sykes and William 'Shanghai Buster' Fairbairn, the world's leading experts in silent killing. They offered their services to the War Office but were turned down, prompting Colin Gubbins to give them immediate employment.

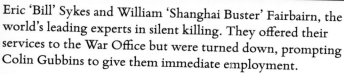

The Fairbairn-Sykes knife was first produced by Wilkinson Sword in 1941. Specially designed for hand-to-hand combat, it was issued to British commandos and their American counterparts.

Arisaig House in the Scottish Highlands. Colin Gubbins's secret killing school, founded in 1940, was run by Eric Sykes and William Fairbairn.

Colin Gubbins's anonymous-looking headquarters in Baker Street was established in summer 1940 and became the hub of his guerrilla empire.

Brickendonbury Manor, an elite school for industrial sabotage. Cecil Clarke and George Rheam ran specialist training courses in killing, destruction and guerrilla warfare.

The Firs, just seven miles from Bletchley Park, was Millis Jefferis's private fiefdom, producing millions of bombs, detonators and booby traps.

Millis Jefferis (*second from right*) at the Firs, with three of his most brilliant members of staff: (*from left to right*) Norman Angier, Stuart Macrae and Ralph Tarrant.

Winston Churchill examining a tommy gun. He was an enthusiastic participant in Millis Jefferis's weapons' demonstrations.

Cecil Clarke's aero-switch. Saboteurs would hide it inside German planes: atmospheric pressure caused it to detonate in mid-air.

Cecil Clarke's largest mechanical beast, the Great Eastern, a bridge-laying machine that used advanced rocket technology to span canals and rivers.

The Garth, Kent. In spring 1940, it became Colin Gubbins's secret guerrilla headquarters, to be used for operations against the anticipated Nazi invasion.

Millis Jefferis's deadly anti-U-boat Hedgehog mortar took two years to develop. It entered the water in a submarine-shaped ellipsis and exploded on impact. The USS *England* sank six Japanese submarines in twelve days, a wartime record for the Hedgehog.

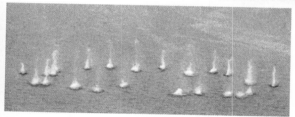

A rare photograph of Millis Jefferis (*centre*) with Churchill and Professor Frederick Lindemann. Jefferis had the prime minister's unwavering support.

Millis Jefferis spent the first year of the war living in a caravan in north London. Stuart Macrae lived in the adjacent caravan.

Millis Jefferis's inventors at the Firs were aided by a team of Welsh women. They were presided over by the formidable Miss 'Fairy' Wond.

Reckless, gifted and driven, Gus March-Phillipps led the piratical raid on Fernando Po in January 1942. The *Duchessa d'Aosta* (*above*) was the target of an audacious 'cutting-out' operation.

The price of sabotage: the St Nazaire raid of March 1942 left 169 British commandos dead and 215 as prisoners of war.

Nigel Tibbits, master of explosives, was among the dead.

Stephen Beattie, captain of *Campbeltown*, a floating bomb used to destroy St Nazaire.

The *Campbeltown* rams St Nazaire dock. Within hours of this photo being taken, the hidden explosives detonated, with catastrophic consequences for the Germans.

Reinhard Heydrich, Hitler's 'Butcher of Prague', was the target of a spectacular assassination. The two assassins (*below*), Josef Gabčik and Jan Kubis, had been trained by Gubbins's team.

The rear wheel of Heydrich's car, where Cecil Clarke's homemade bomb struck its target.

Gorgopotamos viaduct in Greece. Fifty trains a day used it to transport essential weapons to Rommel's forces in North Africa.

The sabotaged viaduct was out of action for six vital weeks between November 1942 and January 1943.

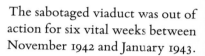

Eddie Myers led the daring operation to destroy it.

Myers's second in command, Chris 'Monty' Woodhouse, led a relentless guerrilla war against the Germans and Italians in Greece.

The Norsk Hydro heavy water plant in Norway. Its destruction by Colin Gubbins's saboteurs in February 1943 deprived Hitler of an atomic bomb.

Norsk Hydro was perched on a bluff of rock. The saboteurs had to scale the rock face in winter darkness. The figures in the bottom of the gorge – including some of the actual saboteurs, re-enacting their mission for a 1948 Norwegian film – give an idea of scale.

Cool-headed Joachim Rønneberg, the twenty-three-year-old leader of the Norwegian saboteurs. This picture was taken in London just prior to the mission and would have been sent to his parents in the event of his death

The Norsk Hydro plant, visible in the centre of the photograph, as seen from the snow-covered Hardanger plateau. The wood cabin in the foreground was the saboteurs' final hideout before their attack.

Even General von Falkenhorst admired the saboteurs' work: 'The most splendid coup I have seen in this war.'

Knut Haukelid crept aboard the *Hydro* and planted a delayed-action bomb. The ship sank, along with Hitler's last supply of heavy water.

Harry Ree started the war a pacifist. A key member of Gubbins's team, he destroyed the Peugeot factory in France.

The Peugeot factory employed 60,000 workers. Seized by the Nazis in 1940, it was crippled by Ree's saboteurs in November 1943.

Railway sabotage was extremely effective. It prevented the mighty 2nd SS Panzer Division, Das Reich, from reaching Normandy in time for the Allied landings.

Tommy Macpherson, an expert in guerrilla warfare. His relentless campaign against Das Reich earned him the praise of General Eisenhower.

Das Reich heads for Normandy. Guerrilla operations turned the division's two-day journey into a seventeen-day nightmare of sabotage and hit-and-run attacks.

Two stills from the post-war film, *School for Danger*, in which Harry Ree
(*on the right in both pictures*) acts out his role as wartime saboteur.

Harry Ree and Jacqueline Nearne are given a detailed briefing about the terrain into which they are to be dropped by parachute.

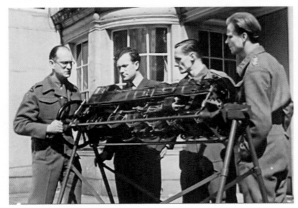

Ree is being taught how best to sabotage a railway engine, prior to the Normandy landings.

By late spring 1944, more than 4,000 tons of sabotage equipment and explosives had been parachuted into France in preparation for the Allied landings in Normandy.

And herein lay his genius. Although he gave the appearance of being narrow-minded and introspective, he was in fact the very opposite. 'A large man with a large mind,' said one, '[and] the inventor of many industrial sabotage techniques.'[9] Gubbins was deeply impressed. 'First class,' he jotted in his notebook. 'A first class officer.'[10]

Now, with Cecil Clarke's permanent departure from Brickendonbury Manor, Rheam was offered the job. He accepted with alacrity and immediately took up his role as commanding officer. The change in regime was instant and total. Clarke had pushed his men hard, but he had done so with a twinkle in his eye. Rheam, by contrast, was never knowingly caught smiling. 'A strong, dour, efficient officer who does not easily brook any outside interference.' Such was the opinion of Colonel Young, one of the junior staff at Brickendonbury. He said that Rheam 'would run most efficiently any post which he undertook', although he added that this would not be done 'through his personal charm'.[11]

Rheam shared one thing in common with the other members of Gubbins's inner circle, 'that rare combination, accurate hands and a highly imaginative brain'. Above all, he seemed to have a far greater understanding of the Nazi mentality than his colleagues and 'knew rather better than most of the rigidities of the systems they were trying to conquer'.[12]

Rheam took up his new post at a time when the number of saboteurs undergoing training at Brickendonbury Manor was on the rise. In the early months there had rarely been more than two dozen students at any given time, but by Christmas 1942, Gubbins was sending more than 150 students a month. This placed strain on the running of Brickendonbury and required the services of a small army of young ladies from the First Aid Nursing Yeomanry.

One of them, Sue Ryder, was quick to note that Rheam did not approve of employing female staff. 'But he had to,' she said, 'because it was laid down by Gubbins.' She went out of her way to avoid the new master, for she found him 'very strict' and rather unpleasant. 'We were all very frightened of him.'

Rheam firmly believed that saboteurs needed to develop an intuitive understanding of the machines they were hoping to blow up. To this end, he ordered the acquisition of industrial plant machinery, sending his staff to scour factories and scrapyards for old turbines, electrical installations and generators. These were all installed in Morgan's Walk, in the lower garden of Brickendonbury Manor, and included 'a two engine Manchester, a Tempest or Typhoon with a Sabre engine and a German JU88'.[13] He also had a Churchill tank parked on the East drive, along with a Great Western Railway locomotive.

Rheam adapted many of Cecil Clarke's ideas, taking his students to transformer stations and teaching them how to locate key parts of plant machinery. Once back at Brickendonbury Manor, in one of his all too rare moments of geniality, he would offer a glass of whisky to any student who could place a detonator on any part of the building, or any item of furniture, timed to set itself off before he could find it. No one ever succeeded. 'He seemed to have a sixth sense,' said one, 'and expected something to be there.'[14]

Colin Gubbins paid frequent visits to Brickendonbury Manor and was impressed by Rheam's thoroughness, noting that his training 'covered the whole field of expertise, from oil wells, arms factories, marshalling yards and shipping, down to tyre-bursters, abrasives and adulteration of lubricants'.

The timing of Rheam's appointment could not have been better, for Gubbins was in the process of planning his most audacious act of industrial sabotage to date. The target was 'of really first-class importance':[15] indeed, there were some who were already arguing that it was the most important target of the war. For the Norsk Hydro plant at Rjukan in Norway was the only one in Europe to produce heavy water, otherwise known as deuterium oxide. This was an essential ingredient in the production of plutonium and therefore in the building of an atomic bomb. If the factory was not destroyed – and soon – Hitler would have enough heavy water to start building a weapon of mass destruction.

Colin Gubbins had foreseen the threat posed by the Norsk Hydro plant ever since General von Falkenhorst's troops had swept into Norway in the spring of 1940. An intelligence report at the time had revealed that Third Reich scientists had requested an immediate increase in production, to 300 pounds a year. In 1942, the output had been increased again, massively, to 10,000 pounds.

That autumn, Professor Lindemann warned Winston Churchill that the Germans had stockpiled one and a half tons of heavy water, most of which was stored at Norsk Hydro. 'When they have five tons,' he said, 'they will be able to start production of a new form of explosive, a thousand times more potent than any in use today.'[16]

The War Cabinet was so alarmed by the prospect of Hitler winning the atomic race that it ordered the destruction of Norsk Hydro to be given 'the highest possible priority'.[17] A two-stage military operation was immediately set in motion. First, a small group of Gubbins's Norwegian guerrillas would be parachuted into the country in order to undertake vital reconnaissance. When this was completed, there would be a full-scale attack by Lord Mountbatten's commandos.

Gubbins's Norwegian saboteurs were initially led by a highly competent Norwegian captain named Martin Linge, who soon knocked his men into shape. His fighting force was given the name Norwegian Independent Company Number One and was placed under the operational direction of John Skinner Wilson, head of Baker Street's Norwegian Section. Gubbins's romantic Highland spirit ran away with him when he described Captain Linge's men. 'The stories of their deeds read like the sagas of old,' he said. 'The ancient Viking spirit had remained alive throughout the centuries of peace.'[18]

Captain Linge's unit rapidly expanded to such an extent that it was given its own headquarters at Gaynes Hall, a classically fronted Georgian mansion in Cambridgeshire. The unit also had its own dedicated endurance centre at Drumintoul, a Victorian shooting lodge in the Scottish Highlands with close links to Arisaig.

The Norwegians selected for the mission against the heavy water plant – Operation Grouse – were successfully dropped into Norway in October 1942. They hid out in the snow-clad wilds of the Hardanger plateau and began laying the groundwork for a commando attack, escaping detection as they lived off the land.

When it came to landing the British commandos – Operation Freshman – the mission turned to disaster. Their two gliders crash-landed, killing fifteen of the men and seriously wounding many of the rest. The survivors were captured within days. The fortunate ones were executed immediately, while the rest were tortured and then killed. Three of the men were taken to a local hospital where a Nazi collaborator devised a particularly gruesome way to dispatch them, injecting air bubbles into their veins.

Operation Freshman proved beyond all doubt that an attack on Norsk Hydro was beyond the scope of the commandos. Yet the need to destroy the heavy water plant was as urgent as ever. Bombing from the air was considered but ruled out. Even if the factory was hit, no bomb was powerful enough to destroy the underground plant room. Indeed the bombs were more likely to kill the Norwegian civilians who worked for Norsk Hydro.

Ultimately, there was only one possible solution and that was to send in a crack team of Norwegian saboteurs, who could make contact with the Grouse team (who were still hiding out in the snow) and launch their attack on Norsk Hydro.

Gubbins remained unconvinced as to the feasibility of such an attack. 'You can't do that, it's too difficult,'[19] was his first reaction when John Skinner Wilson outlined his plans, particularly when he learned that the men were to be landed by parachute. He knew from experience that Norway presented severe difficulties for air operations. 'Possible dropping zones are thickly clustered, precipitous and angry, the broken countryside throws up air-pockets and atmospheric currents.'[20]

Wilson agreed that it was 'a task of some magnitude'.[21] He also knew that parachuting the men into Norway was merely the first of countless difficulties to be overcome. A far greater hurdle was the fact that Norsk Hydro was constructed in the fashion of a medieval fortress, perched atop a 700-foot shaft of vertical rock. Three of its sides were sheer, plunging deep into one of the most spectacular gorges in Norway: 'So deep,' wrote Margaret Jackson, who was involved in the planning, 'that the sun never reached the depths of it.'[22] There was but one point of access: a narrow suspension bridge that was kept under twenty-four-hour armed guard. It was completely inaccessible to a group of saboteurs.

The only other option was to scale the gorge, but even if this was successfully achieved, a forced entry into the plant was almost impossible. The machinery was housed in the bomb-proof basement built of reinforced concrete. The place was also heavily guarded by the Gestapo and the garrison had been greatly strengthened in the wake of the abortive commando operation.

There was good reason to abandon the very idea of such a fool-hardy mission, but Churchill and the War Cabinet were insistent that it be given the highest priority. Gubbins was left with little alternative but to start planning.

The disastrous commando raid had taught him an important lesson: 'it was essential to use only Norwegians. A British person parachuted into Norway, however well he spoke the language, would at once be recognized as a stranger and would arouse intense interest and speculation.'[23] He also felt that British saboteurs were ill-equipped to survive the punishing physical hardships that the Norsk Hydro team would have to endure.

The planning began within hours of Gubbins approving the mission. Joachim Rønneberg was working as an instructor at one of the Scottish physical endurance centres when he was summoned to a meeting with a military adviser named Major Hampton. 'He said he had just got a telegram from London asking if I could take on a job in Norway and if I could pick five of the unit to go with me.'

Twenty-three-year-old Rønneberg accepted immediately. Ever since fleeing from Norway two years earlier, he had been waiting for the moment to strike back at the Nazi occupiers of his country. Now, he had his chance.

Rønneberg was a graduate of Sykes and Fairbairn's training course at Arisaig and it had left a deep impression. Sykes's techniques were so violent that Rønneberg admitted 'it was a bit difficult to sleep' after one of his lectures. He had also been taught how to stab a man to death with the Fairbairn–Sykes knife, 'which was a terrible weapon'. He was told that if you thrust it deep into the chest, it wouldn't stop until it had sliced through the heart and hit the back of the ribcage. He was appalled at the casual way that Sykes and Fairbairn spoke of murder. 'Having been a very, very quiet innocent boy back in Norway, never been in any fight at all, I felt: "What are you doing? And what are they doing to you?"'[24]

Yet his desire to rid Norway of the hated Nazis overrode all other sensibilities. He put more effort into his training than any other student and his physical stamina left a deep impression. One of

Sykes's infamous endurance exercises was a three-mile run from Arisaig to Meoble, a run that included a punishing 1,800-foot climb over the top of Sgean Mor while carrying a full pack. One trainee was struggling up the scree-strewn path when he turned his gaze upwards. He saw 'the incredible sight of a tall young man galloping up the hill like a stag'.[25] This was Joachim Rønneberg, who was so fit that he shaved fully nine minutes off the record time to cover the three miles. He graduated with such good grades that he was offered the job of instructor at the Aviemore training school, established specially for Norwegian guerrillas.

Now, he was asked to select five men to accompany him on an as yet undisclosed mission to Norway. Rønneberg knew exactly which five he wanted and called them to a meeting. 'I have been offered a job,' he said. 'I don't know what it is yet. Do you want to follow?'[26] Their loud cheers were the only answer he needed. He selected the cool-headed Birger Strømsheim as his second-in-command. The others were Knut Haukelid, Fredrik Kayser, Kasper Idland and Hans Storhaug. All six had already undergone punishing physical training. 'We learned to use pistols, knives and poison,' said Knut Haukelid, 'together with all the weapons nature had given us – our fists and feet.' There was one constant refrain: '"Never give a man a chance" were words we were always hearing. If you've got him down, kick him to death.'

Haukelid felt himself an expert after graduating from the course. 'It's incredible what a man can do with a handful of explosive placed at the right place at the right time. He can halt an army or devastate the machinery on which a whole community depends.'[27]

Rønneberg and his team now headed to London where they learned that their goal was the destruction of Norsk Hydro. They were also informed of the disastrous first mission and the fate of the captured commandos. 'They told us everything,' said Rønneberg, 'that those who had survived the crash were shot or experimented on, and that some were thrown into the North Sea. They told us that we would be given poison capsules so that we would not have to suffer the same ordeal.'

There was one thing they were not told, and that was the importance of heavy water. 'No one ever mentioned nuclear weapons,' said Rønneberg. 'I certainly hadn't the faintest idea that Churchill was taking an interest in the raid.'[28]

After the London briefing, the men were driven straight to George Rheam's fiefdom at Brickendonbury Manor, arriving on the morning of Saturday, 12 December. They had precious little time for training: Gubbins hoped to parachute them into Norway before the end of the month.

Colin Gubbins had been able to furnish Rheam with an unusually complete dossier of information about Norsk Hydro and it had come from three impeccable sources. The first of these was Professor Leif Tronstad, a pioneering atomic scientist who had worked at Norsk Hydro during the 1930s and overseen the production of heavy water. A fervent patriot, he had baulked at the Nazi demand to increase the quantities being produced. Instead, he had tried to sabotage the existing stocks by adding drops of cod liver oil. The Germans soon began to suspect him and he had little option but to flee to England in the summer of 1941, delivering to Gubbins a detailed account of the factory's layout.

Gubbins soon found himself with even more up-to-date information. Professor Tronstad's place had been filled by Jomar Brun, another Norwegian patriot who secretly took microphotographs of the plant, concealed them in toothpaste tubes and managed to get them smuggled to London. When Brun came under suspicion, he also fled to England and offered his services to Baker Street.

The most extraordinary coup had come just eight months earlier, when Einar Skinnarland, a twenty-three-year-old engineer at Norsk Hydro, pitched up in London. His story had all the ingredients of a *Boy's Own* adventure. He had told his German employees at the plant that he was in desperate need of a holiday. Granted two weeks' leave, he and five comrades hijacked a 600-ton coastal steamer, *Galtesund*, and ordered its captain at gunpoint to sail for Aberdeen. Once ashore, Skinnarland made his way to London, warned Gubbins of the huge increase in production of heavy water and hand-delivered him the latest plans of the factory, along with all the operational activities.

Gubbins might reasonably have rewarded Skinnarland by giving him a desk job in Baker Street. Instead, he persuaded him to be parachuted back into Norway. He was to return to Norsk Hydro after his *soi-disant* 'holiday', so that he could continue to supply Gubbins with the latest information about the factory, its sentries and its points of access. Skinnarland did exactly that, arriving for work after two weeks' absence and cheerfully informing his colleagues that he had enjoyed a relaxing break.

Rønneberg and his men were put through an intense training programme as soon as they arrived at Brickendonbury Manor. George Rheam had been given the most up-to-date dossier on Norsk Hydro. Now, he used his methodical brain to work out the best plan of attack. He had long believed that a small team of 'thoroughly trained men will always produce better results that a large number of semi-trained', especially on a mission of such complexity.[29] He also knew that there was little option for the saboteurs but to scale the gorge, break into the site, force an entry into the heavy water room and blow up the machinery. All this would have to be done in darkness.

The only sure way to train for such an attack was to build an exact replica of Norsk Hydro's heavy water room, including its plant machinery and elongated metal cylinders. With the help of Jomar Brun and Professor Tronstad – and at great speed – Rheam had one of the outbuildings in the stable yard completely remodelled, so that Rønneberg and his men could familiarize themselves with the machinery and conduct practice attacks in the dark.

The men were also given exact plans of the rest of the factory, down to the very last detail. Professor Tronstad even told them where to find the key to the lavatory, in order that they could lock up one of the plant's Norwegian night guards. 'None of us had been to the plant in our lives,' said Rønneberg, but after the intense training at Brickendonbury Manor, 'we knew the layout of it as well as anyone.'[30]

Much of the training was done in darkness, for nocturnal sabotage was Rheam's particular speciality. A favourite item on the Brickendonbury syllabus was the simulated night attack, 'in which the students were dropped about a mile from their objective; they then had to make their way to the target which was guarded by sentries, gain access to it and place their charges on what they considered was the vital machinery'.[31]

After a few days at Brickendonbury, the firearms instructor handed Rønneberg and his men some new weapons and told them to familiarize themselves with them while he went off to finish his other duties. Rønneberg watched the others 'taking the loading grip and pressing the trigger and everything – "click, click, click" all round the place – and everyone seemed happy'. But when he pulled his trigger, he was in for a surprise. 'It didn't say click – it said "bang!" and there was a big hole in the wall.' Brickendonbury's adjutant burst into the room, demanding to know what was going on. Rønneberg smiled sheepishly and said to him: 'We have new weapons and I have tried mine and it works!'[32]

The time spent at Brickendonbury was physically gruelling, even for men at the peak of their physical fitness. Rheam was not prone to dispense praise, but he told Gubbins he had never met such a professional team. 'This was an excellent party in every way and each member has a thorough knowledge of the target and the methods of dealing with the different sections.' He had found that 'their demolition work was exceedingly good and their weapon training outstanding.' He believed that 'if the conditions are at all possible, they have every chance of carrying out the operation successfully.'[33]

Rønneberg made every effort to have the men kitted out with the best equipment, which was no easy matter in wartime. He was all too aware of the harshness of the Norwegian winter, when temperatures often dipped below minus thirty. He commissioned the bedding manufacturer, Hamptons of Knightsbridge, to make special Arctic sleeping bags, while the men's skis were bought from a specialist Norwegian store in Dumfries. Rønneberg also got water-tight boots and the very best snow goggles. He had previously suffered from snow blindness and knew it was both dangerous and painful. 'It feels,' he said, 'like you have a kilo of sand in your eyes.'

He and Rheam put much care into choosing what guns the team should take. Aware that they would possibly have to fight their way into the plant, and out again, they chose Colt revolvers and tommy guns, 'partly because they used the same ammunition, but also because they were really good stopping weapons'.[34]

George Rheam put much thought into the explosive charges too. After much consultation, he suggested four sets of specially manufactured nine-and-a-half-pound charges, linked with double Cordtex and attached to two-minute delay detonators. The explosives were sausage-shaped and housed in a flexible casing: they were remarkably similar to Cecil Clarke's Aero-Switch and he may even have had a hand in designing them. They were to be strapped to the heavy water canisters on very short fuses. The men would have just two minutes to make their getaway.

The last piece of kit was also the smallest: the death pill gave the men a jolt back into the real world. Knut Haukelid was morbidly fascinated by the pill, which 'was cyanide enclosed in a rubber cover'. The cover enabled it to be kept in the mouth. 'Once bitten through, it would ensure death within three seconds.'

There was only one thing missing from the training. None of the men had yet been told why heavy water was so important to Nazi Germany. One day, Knut Haukelid was chatting with Professor Tronstad when the latter gave him some inkling of the importance of the mission. Heavy water, he was told, 'can be used for some of the dirtiest work that can be imagined. If the Germans can solve the problem, they'll win the war.' Haukelid was still confused until the professor, either by accident or design, 'turned over some papers in the briefcase'. Haukelid only saw them for a few seconds, but realized that his mission 'had to do with splitting the atom'.[35]

Professor Tronstad had something else to say to Haukelid, a message that he wanted transmitted to all the men. 'You must know that the Germans will not take you prisoner,' he said. 'For the sake of those who have gone before you and are now dead, I urge you to make this operation a success. You have no idea how important this mission is, but what you are going to do will live in Norway's history for hundreds of years to come.'[36]

After completing their gruelling training at Brickendonbury Manor, the six men were sent back to their base station in Cambridgeshire. They now had to wait for the necessary conditions for them to be flown to Norway. Haukelid had the feeling 'of being fenced in and protected at every point from the dangers and difficulties of this world, so that we might be used for one single purpose at home in Norway'.

He soon discovered that being 'fenced in' had its advantages. The men were able to enjoy the company of the girls who worked at St Neots. Haukelid dubbed them Gubbins's fannies – he meant FANYs – and assumed they had been hired to entertain him. The girls did little to persuade him otherwise. 'They were always willing to come to Cambridge in the evening for a little party.' One of them would drive the men to a Cambridge pub; the rest would drink champagne 'at the expense of the War Office'. Rønneberg stayed as sober as possible and did his best to persuade everyone to return to their base before matters got out of hand. But Haukelid and the others were in no hurry to go to bed, 'and the girls agreed with us that there was both time and necessity for another bottle'.[37]

The late-night merriment would continue around the piano at Gaynes Hall, although the gaiety was always overlaid with a touch of melancholy on these eve-of-mission soirées. Sue Ryder noted that the favourite songs were 'All Our Tomorrows Will Be Happy Days' and 'Wish Me Luck As You Wave Me Goodbye'. There was always a sense that the men would not be coming back.

Rønneberg's team were due to be parachuted into Norway on 23 January, but the flight had to be aborted due to thick fog. It was deeply disappointing, for the waning moon meant that the next flight wouldn't be for another month.

Rønneberg was increasingly concerned that the men were spending too much time drinking and too little time keeping fit. The others disagreed, although they did accept that jogging across the Cambridgeshire levels was not suitable preparation for the snow-covered peaks of Norway. Rønneberg requested a transfer to Scotland in order to knock his men back into shape. 'The muscles used when running on roads and fields are not the same as marching in broken and hilly countryside,' he explained.[38]

Baker Street answered his call, sending them 'to a solitary place' in the north of Scotland where there were no pubs, no girls and no sunshine.[39] They spent their days training, tracking deer in the relentless rain and waiting for the next moon.

At last, on 16 February 1943, Operation Gunnerside was again given the green light. The men were to be dropped into Norway that very night. Professor Tronstad came to see them off at Tempsford airfield. The rain was tipping down from the sky, soaking the white camouflage suits they were wearing in readiness for the snow on landing.

Pilot Officer John Charrot couldn't believe how much equipment they had: so much that they had to be brought to the airfield in a lorry. He could only wonder what sort of operation they were due to undertake.

The kit was hurled aboard and then the men climbed into the Stirling IV aircraft. The plane's navigator was intending to use dead reckoning navigation to hit landfall after 700 miles crossing the North Sea. A single error in his calculations and Rønneberg and his men would be heading to disaster.

15

In the Bleak Midwinter

A BLIND PARACHUTE DROP into occupied territory was not for the faint-hearted, as Colin Gubbins's team of Norwegian saboteurs had learned from their training sessions. As you were shoved from the plane, your stomach hit your throat and the ground lurched forward at terrifying speed. When the parachute finally opened, it felt like a bullet ripping through your spine.

Joachim Rønneberg and his comrades had trained for this moment at Ringway, near Manchester, where their tutor had led them to a high platform in order to teach them how to land safely. They watched him jump and then heard him scream. 'He broke both his legs,' noted Haukelid without further comment. It was hardly a reassuring sight.

Training was bad enough, but the men were warned that the real jump would be infinitely more frightening. They would be parachuting into pitch darkness, falling through the knife-edge of an Arctic gale so cold it could freeze human skin in seconds. The men's initial goal was scarcely less forbidding than the jump itself. They were heading to the Hardanger plateau, a high-altitude wilderness locked firmly into a thick crust of ice. Here, at the ends of the earth, there was nothing but relentless desolation punctured by the occasional glacier. 'The largest, loneliest and wildest mountain area in northern Europe,' was how Haukelid described it.[1] Nothing but reindeer could survive in this frigid wasteland, for the only winter vegetation was frozen Arctic moss buried deep in the snow.

It was vital that the men should all jump within seconds of each other, for the plane would be flying at a speed of sixty yards per second. A hesitation of just ten seconds would see them landing at least 600 yards from their nearest comrade. If it was snowing hard, they would never find each other.

On this particular night, 16 February, the skies began to clear as the plane approached the Norwegian coastline and the icy expanse of the Hardanger plateau gleamed like a slick of cream in the translucent moonlight. The aim was to drop the men as close as possible to the frozen shores of Bjornesfjord, where there was a remote lakeside hut. The men scanned the bleach-white wilderness far below but could see no recognizable features in the landscape. At one point, the rear gunner commented on the 'pretty fluffy clouds' that they were heading towards at high speed.[2] Fortunately, the pilot realized they were not fluffy clouds but the tops of mountains.

It proved impossible to locate Bjornesfjord from the air, so Joachim Rønneberg ordered a blind drop on to the Hardanger. At exactly two minutes past midnight, he was the first to plunge through the dispatching hatch into the freezing Arctic night, closely followed by his five comrades.

Knut Haukelid glanced upwards as he jumped and 'saw the plane disappearing northwards, returning to England, to rain, to nice hot tea, to a party tomorrow'.[3] He then looked down and got a reality check. The icy plateau stretched to infinity, its treacherous contours blunted by the thick wedge of snow.

The men made a near-perfect landing and the only mishap occurred when one of their twelve supply containers was carried away in a tremendous gust of wind. They chased after it and eventually found it stuck in the fractured surface of a frozen lake. Rønneberg gave a sigh of relief. 'In that package we had rucksacks for half the party, with sleeping bags and weapons and food for the first five days.'[4]

It took almost four hours to gather all their supply containers. Once this was done, the men tried to work out where, exactly, they had landed. They were familiar with the Hardanger, but only in summer, and were completely perplexed as to their location. 'The ground was quite strange to us,' said Haukelid, 'long, low, snow-clad hills.' Rønneberg asked one of the team if he had any idea where they had landed. 'We may be in China for all I know,' was his response.[5]

All six men had been trained in psychological survival. This was one of Arisaig's specialities and a vital tool when bivouacking in one of the world's most extreme terrains. They knew that the very bleakness of the Hardanger offered them their greatest chance of eluding capture. Few German troops dared to patrol this lonely wilderness, where the extreme cold rendered every hour a fight for life. Haukelid had repeatedly been reminded that 'one cannot defy nature, but must adapt and accommodate oneself to her. Nature will not change; it is man who must change if he is to live in conditions where nature is dominant.'[6] Adaptability and confidence were two of the key elements in the psychology of survival.

Nature certainly proved dominant in the bluish-grey hour before dawn. Snow pellets scoured horizontal in the winter gale as the mercury plummeted. The men urgently needed to make contact with the Grouse party who had been living out on the Hardanger for four months.

Rønneberg's team had no wireless transmitter, but they knew that their comrades had based themselves in one of the remote huts on the shores of the frozen Lake Saure. They set off through the heavily falling snow in what they hoped was the right direction. As they did so, Rønneberg cast an anxious glance at the sky. The snow was starting to tip down and threatening to become a white-out.

The men were to have an extraordinary stroke of luck. As they forced a path through the blizzard, they stumbled into a hunters' hut buried waist-deep in snow. The visibility was so poor that they didn't even see it. 'We just walked into it,' admitted Rønneberg. 'We were very, very lucky.'[7]

They smashed open the door with an axe and took shelter, lighting a fire with the stockpile of birch wood. All knew that the hut had almost certainly saved their lives, for the blizzard that now swept across the Hardanger was terrifying in its intensity. 'That night there broke one of the worst storms I have ever experienced in the mountains,' said Haukelid.[8] The Arctic gale screamed for four days, slamming snow against the cabin with such violence that Rønneberg was worried it 'was going to be lifted off the ground'.[9]

At one point the chimney ventilator was snapped by the wind

and Rønneberg had to step outside to fix it. 'I was twice lifted by the storm from the roof and thrown to the other side of the hut.'[10]

Thirty miles distant, the Grouse team were sheltering inside their Arctic refuge. They had a wireless transmitter and were in regular contact with London. They knew that Rønneberg's team had been successfully dropped, but they had no idea how to find them. As the storm continued into its second day – and then a third – they grew seriously concerned.

Rønneberg's men were indeed finding it hard to acclimatize to the dangerously low temperatures. Two of them had developed serious colds and the rest had severe inflammation in their neck glands. The only good news came when they found a discarded fishing logbook which revealed that they were close to the glacier that fed Lake Skrykhen. They had landed eighteen miles off target, but were within striking distance of the Grouse team.

On 22 February the storm finally blew itself out and revealed a spectacular winter's morning. 'The sun rose over the Numedal mountains, first copper-coloured and then golden.' Haukelid looked out on to a winter landscape that was utterly transformed. 'What had been a valley the evening before had now become a high snow-drift.'[11] As he turned his gaze towards the frozen lake, he got the shock of his life. A man was skiing towards them at high speed and clearly making for the hut. If he was German, or even a hated quisling, a Nazi sympathizer, he threatened to jeopardize their entire mission. The men had no option but to seize him.

They waited for him to approach the hut and then grabbed him as he was about to enter. 'Seldom have I seen anyone more terri-fied,' said Haukelid. After a long interrogation, the man – a hunter – confessed to being a quisling. This was followed by a long debate as to what to do with him. 'The boys were now generally in favour of shooting him,' said Haukelid. But Rønneberg felt troubled about killing a fellow Norwegian. In the end, they took him prisoner, tying him to their toboggan and setting off in search of the Grouse team.

As they neared an area known as Kallungsjaa, they got their second shock of the day: a man on skis could be seen making his way up the valley. They flung themselves down into the snow and tried to work out if it was a German soldier. 'He was packed in so many clothes that it was hard to get a proper view of him, while a huge beard made him unrecognisable.'

As Rønneberg studied him through his telescope, he glimpsed another skier, just a few hundred yards behind. He sent Haukelid to go and meet them in the guise of a reindeer hunter. Haukelid skied after them and got within fifteen yards before realizing to his delight that it was Arne Kjelstrup and Claus Helberg, two of the four-strong Grouse team. They were out in search of Rønneberg and his men.

Four months on the Hardanger had taken its toll, as Haukelid was quick to note. Their clothes 'were so ragged and disgusting that the boys looked like the worst tramps imaginable. Behind their beards their faces were wan and thin and their shoulders were bent.'[12]

The two men spilled a terrible story of hardship and deprivation. The Hardanger was indeed a cruel place to live in the depths of winter. They had only survived by eating Arctic moss and, very occasionally, reindeer meat.

Their current base was in a mountain hut at Svensbu, some four hours to the south. The men decided to head there directly, but first Rønneberg wanted to release their prisoner. He made him sign a declaration that he owned a rifle (a crime that carried the death penalty in occupied Norway) and told him that if he ever spoke of his encounter, Rønneberg would betray him to the Nazis. It was a high-risk strategy, but less risky than continuing their mission with a prisoner in tow.

At around four in the afternoon they finally sighted the Svensbu hut, where the other two men from Grouse – Jens Poulsson and Knut Haugland – were hiding out. That evening was one of festivity. The ten men ate reindeer meat accompanied by chocolate and dried fruit contributed by Rønneberg and his men. Then, after catching up on each other's news, they turned their thoughts to Norsk Hydro. In the next forty-eight hours, they were hoping to launch one of the most audacious acts of sabotage ever undertaken in wartime.

Colin Gubbins had received no news of Joachim Rønneberg and his men since the early hours of 17 February, when the plane that had dropped them into Norway returned safely to Tempsford airfield. He had no idea if they had landed without injury and nor did he know if their equipment had survived the drop. It was the same with every operation: months of intense training were followed by days of radio silence.

But on the morning of Wednesday, 24 February, a full week after Rønneberg's team had left England, Gubbins received the message he had longed to hear. It came from Knut Haugland, the radio operator of the Grouse team. 'The party arrived yesterday evening. Everything in order. The spirits are excellent.' He added that they would be 'on the air again after the operation' and signed off, 'heartiest greetings from all'.[13]

Gubbins privately feared that he would never hear from them again. For even if the men succeeded in breaking into Norsk Hydro, there seemed very little hope of them making their escape. They were engaged on a suicide mission that was likely to end with either a bullet in the head or a cyanide capsule in the mouth.

The Germans had dramatically increased security at the plant in the aftermath of the commando disaster. Guards were now posted around the factory and the garrison had been increased to 200 troops. Four anti-aircraft guns had been installed, along with banks of machine guns, and a network of searchlights had been wired around the place and 'could illuminate the whole area and at the same time floodlight the pipeline'.[14] A newly installed tracking station made it impossible for any would-be saboteur to send transmissions while in the vicinity of the plant.

The ten men made their descent from the Hardanger plateau on the day after contacting Gubbins and took shelter in a wood cabin at Fjosbudalen. This was only three miles from Norsk Hydro, but it was perched at the top of an incline that afforded a sweeping view of the surrounding landscape. It was the perfect place to plan the details of their attack.

'We all sat down together and wrote on small scraps of paper all the questions to which we wanted answers,' said Knut Haukelid.[15] One of the Grouse men, Claus Helberg, then arranged a clandestine meeting with Einar Skinnarland, their contact inside the plant.

George Rheam's training had covered every aspect of the attack except one: Rønneberg himself was to decide the best way into the factory, since this would depend on many last-minute variables. One option was to attack from the rear, using the steep slope of rock that linked the stack to the mountainside. But this was quickly ruled out, for the entire area was heavily mined and strategically placed machine-gun posts made it unacceptably exposed.

There was also the narrow suspension bridge, seventy-five feet in length and under constant patrol. To traverse the bridge, the saboteurs would have to shoot all the sentries. This was also ruled out, for the noise of the gunshots was certain to raise the alarm. Within minutes, the entire complex would be swarming with garrison troops working under floodlight.

The only other way into the plant was to descend to the bottom of the deep gorge, cross the river and then scale the other side. The Germans believed that the gorge could not be climbed without specialist mountain equipment but Haukelid was not so sure. He studied the RAF reconnaissance photographs and noticed that there was a segment of the gorge where fir trees grew from the top to the bottom. 'Where trees grow,' he said, 'a man can make his way.'[16]

If the gorge could be scaled, there was a unique weak point in the German defences. A single-track railway line had been hacked into the side of the ravine, hundreds of feet from the bottom. It provided access into the plant, but was only ever used to transport heavy machinery. As far as Rønneberg knew, it was not guarded by the Germans. But it was visible from the suspension bridge and could only be used with extreme caution.

At shortly after 9 a.m. on the day scheduled for the attack, Rønneberg sent Claus Helberg into the gorge on a reconnaissance mission. When he returned five hours later, 'he had a big smile on his face'.[17] He reported that not only was it possible to descend into the gorge, but that there was an ice bridge at the bottom that would enable them to cross the fast-flowing River Maan. The only worrying news was that this was fragile and 'on the point of breaking up'.[18] They would have to hope it would sustain their weight.

The information about the gorge convinced Rønneberg to use it as their point of access. They would attack that very night, descending down to the river and then scaling the other side before entering the plant via the disused railway line. It was a high-risk strategy, but less risky than storming the suspension bridge.

The rest of the day was spent fine-tuning the details of the attack, as well as cleaning weapons and preparing the explosives. The men also settled on passwords to be used in the darkness. The word 'Piccadilly' was to be answered with the words 'Leicester Square'.

They were to split into two groups on arrival at the plant. The first group, led by Rønneberg, would undertake the sabotage. The second, commanded by Haukelid, would provide cover. If Rønneberg's men were sighted, Haukelid's group were to hold off the Germans with their tommy guns for as long as it took to blow up the plant.

After a few last-minute preparations, they set off at eight o'clock in the evening, under the pale light of a half moon. They skied down to the edge of the ravine, where they buried their skis, food and everything else they would need when making their escape. Once this was done, they began the treacherous descent into the depths of the gorge, clutching at trees and spruce branches as they slithered down. The side of the gorge was in places almost sheer, but there were always trees to cling to and a deep cushion of snow. 'We waded and stumbled, leaving most of the work to the law of gravity as we slithered downhill.' At times the snow was up to their armpits, so deep 'that you had to do front crawl to get out'. It enabled them to make the descent without hurting themselves.

When they were halfway down, the ravine twisted slightly, providing them with their first glimpse of the moonlit Norsk Hydro perched atop its stack of rock. To Haukelid's eyes, it looked like 'an eagle's eyrie, high up on the mountainside', sinister and remote. 'It was blowing fairly hard,' he said, 'but nevertheless the hum of the machinery came up to us through the ravine.'[19]

They finally reached the bottom, checked that everyone was unharmed and then crossed the ice bridge unseen by the sentries on the suspension bridge. One by one they ran through the deep shadow towards the sheer rock face that marked the other side of the gorge.

The ascent was far tougher than the descent. They hauled themselves up, clutching at the dangling branches and finding precarious footing on icy ledges of rock. The packs weighed heavy on their backs and they were soon drenched in sweat. Even Haukelid, who was at the peak of his form, confessed that it was 'a wearisome climb'.[20] But the black horizontal line in the rock face above soon sharpened into focus. The men were nearing the ledge that held the single-track railway.

As they climbed on to the ledge, the moon was shrouded in cloud, making their position less exposed. The temperature was on the rise and the thaw that had begun that afternoon was sending down chutes of melting snow from the treetops. They prayed that the ice bridge, upon which their escape depended, would not collapse.

At 11.30 p.m., they reached a snow-covered building some 500 yards from Norsk Hydro. Rønneberg motioned to the men to rest up in the shadows and eat chocolate while they waited for the change of guards on the suspension bridge. As they sat there in the darkness, Rønneberg suddenly appreciated the quality of their training – not just at Brickendonbury but also in the Scottish Highlands. 'When we were sitting there waiting, it was like a short rest on a training exercise in Scotland,' he thought. 'It was the same atmosphere, the same telling of stories and so on, the noise of the factory was so strong we could talk more openly and even laugh.'

Rønneberg felt supremely confident of success, partly 'because everyone seemed tremendously calm'.[21] Indeed they were all so concentrated on the job ahead that they had no thoughts of the danger.

Haukelid looked at his comrades and was struck by how well they were armed: 'five tommy guns, two sniper rifles among nine men, and everyone had a pistol, a knife and hand grenades'.[22]

At precisely 0030 hours, Rønneberg ordered the advance towards the store shed that lay less than a hundred metres from the giant mesh gates. Here, they split into their two prearranged groups. Haukelid made a silent dash towards the gates, clutching his giant bolt-cutters. These snapped easily through the thick chain. As the gate inched open, Haukelid motioned to his covering party to advance inside the plant and on to the upper platform. From here, they could see inside the guard post, lit by a warm glow. The German sentries inside were clearly oblivious to anything untoward taking place. They were equally oblivious to the fact that they would be sprayed with machine-gun fire if they stepped outside.

Rønneberg and his three saboteurs had meanwhile forced a second gate that led down to the lower platform. This provided access to the basement where the plant machinery was housed, along with the high-concentration heavy water cells. 'Everything was still quiet,' he said. 'The black-out of the factory was poor and there was good light from the moon.'[23]

He gave a pre-agreed signal to Haukelid and the covering party now shifted their positions, moving even closer to the hut housing the German guards. Rønneberg's own group split into two pairs, each armed with a complete set of explosives. If one group failed to get inside, it was hoped that the other could complete the task.

As Rønneberg peered through a small window into the dimly lit transformer room, he glimpsed a scientist working on the floor below, 'reading instruments and writing in a log book'.[24] He made his way over to the cellar door that was supposed to have been left unlocked by one of Einar Skinnarland's contacts. It failed to open, for, unbeknown to Rønneberg, the man had fallen ill and been unable to go to work.

He didn't panic. He knew from his Brickendonbury training that there was another means to enter the heavy water plant. A narrow cable shaft led through the bedrock directly into the plant room. He and Fredrik Kayser now clambered up a short ladder and crawled into this shaft, pulling themselves along on hands and knees and trying to avoid snagging their sacks of explosives on 'the mass of pipes and leads'.

When they reached the end of the shaft, Rønneberg slid down into the outer plant room, swiftly followed by Kayser. The two men then approached the high-concentration room in absolute silence and tentatively pushed the door. It was unlocked. Rønneberg knew that his moment had come. He and Kayser burst inside and took the Norwegian guard 'completely by surprise'. Rønneberg later said that the man was 'somewhat frightened, but otherwise quiet and obedient',[25] probably because Kayser was holding a gun to his head.

Rønneberg now unpacked the explosives and began attaching

them to the metal cylinder shafts. He was struck by the accuracy of the models that had been built back in England. The actual machinery was identical and 'the charges that had been made at Station Seventeen' – Brickendonbury Manor – 'fitted like a glove. It was amazing.'[26]

He had already placed half the charges when there was the sound of shattering glass as one of the windows was pushed in. He spun round in alarm, only to see Strømsheim and Kasper Idland climbing down into the room. 'Having failed to find the cable tunnel, they had decided to act on their own initiative.' Their arrival meant that both groups of saboteurs had made it into the factory unseen, a remarkable achievement.

When all the fuses were attached to the charges, Strømsheim checked them twice while Rønneberg coupled them in preparation for detonation. The original plan had been to set the time-delays to two minutes, 'but as everything had gone so well up to now, we did not wish to run the risk of anyone coming in and spoiling our work.'[27] Rønneberg therefore changed the fuses to thirty seconds.

He was just about to light them when the guard, still held at gunpoint, asked if he could fetch his glasses before they were blown up in the explosion. 'They are impossible to get in Norway these days,' he explained.[28] The tension was broken for an instant. They allowed the man to get his glasses and then told him to take cover on the floor above.

Crouched in the snow outside, the covering party was growing increasingly jumpy. Each man was guarding a crucial access point to the factory, with Jens Poulsson and Knut Haukelid hiding behind casks just twenty yards from the German guard hut. 'The factory buildings had seemed large from a distance. Now that we were among them, they seemed gigantic.' The tension was high. 'We waited and waited. We knew that the blowing up party was inside, but we did not know how things were going.'

Jens Poulsson kept his tommy gun trained on the hut. He told Haukelid that 'if the Germans gave the alarm, or showed any signs of realizing what was going on, he would start pumping lead into the hut.'

Haukelid himself had six hand grenades, which he was intending to throw through the windows and door of the hut. 'You must remember to call out Heil Hitler when you open the door and throw the bombs,' whispered Poulsson.

Despite the nerves, Haukelid felt supremely in control. 'We knew that the Germans' lives were now completely in our hands,' he said. 'The thin wall of the wooden hut was no protection against our automatic weapons.'

Three years earlier, while fighting against the German invasion, he had attacked a very similar wooden house occupied by soldiers. 'There were dead Germans hanging out of the window and dead Germans lying inside before we had finished shooting the house to pieces.'[29]

Inside the basement, Rønneberg lit the fuses and then gave a signal to the other three men. Time to get out. All of them rushed outside, using the steel cellar door. They were no further than twenty yards from the building when they heard the muffled thud of an explosion. Knut Haukelid was still crouched behind casks when the detonation occurred. He had been expecting a terrific bang and an erupting ball of fire. Instead, it was 'astonishingly small' and insignificant. It was deeply disappointing.

'Was this what we had come over a thousand miles to do?' he asked himself. 'Certainly the windows were broken and a glimmer of light spread out into the night, but it was not particularly impressive.'[30]

But this is exactly what George Rheam had intended. The explosive charges had been specially designed to wreak maximum damage with minimum risk to the saboteurs. The sausage-shaped charge was a work of genius, for it imploded into the machinery, rather than exploding outwards.

To Poulsson's ears, 'it sounded like two or three cars crashing in Piccadilly Circus.'[31] It was certainly loud enough to attract the attentions of the German guards in the sentry hut. One of them opened the door of the hut, but 'showed no sign of alarm, flashed a torch in the direction of the Norwegian guardhouse and disappeared back into the hut'.

Haukelid and Poulsson breathed a sigh of relief, but they soon discovered it was premature. A second German, unarmed but holding a torch, came out of the hut and walked over to the casks where they were hiding 'and threw the light along the ground'.[32] Poulsson raised his gun and moved his finger on to the trigger. 'Shall I fire?' he whispered.

'No,' said Haukelid. 'He doesn't know what has happened. Leave him as long as possible.'

As the sentry raised the beam of his torch towards the casks, 'once more Jens raised his tommy gun.' But the German suddenly turned and went back into the hut, unaware that he had three tommy guns and four pistols trained on him.

Haukelid knew that Rønneberg and the three other saboteurs must by now be somewhere close to the perimeter fence. His covering party therefore left their positions and made their way over to the fence. As they approached, they saw a figure crouched in the snow. It was Arne Kjelstrup, who called out the agreed password: Piccadilly. Haukelid was anxious not to make any noise and declined to answer. Kjelstrup persisted, whispering Piccadilly for a second time. Haukelid and Poulsson both replied: 'Shut up, for God's sake!' Kjelstrup was indignant. 'What's the good of having passwords if we don't use them?'[33] he said as he rushed over to join the men in their flight.

The ten of them regrouped on the railway track, not quite believing that they had got in and out of the plant without being spotted. Still unnoticed by anyone, they began clambering back down the ravine until they reached the bottom. They managed to cross the ice bridge without mishap and were about to start scaling the other side of the gorge when the first air-raid sirens sounded. 'This was the Germans' signal for general mobilisation in the Rjukan area,' said Haukelid. 'They had at last collected their wits and found out what had happened.'

The men quickened their pace up the snow-clad sides of the ravine, pulling heavily on the branches, until they reached the road. They hid in the snow as several military cars sped past en route to the plant. They then ran across the road, narrowly avoiding being spotted by another car 'that came so close that we had to throw ourselves into the ditch'. They then plunged back into the relative safety of the forest.

It was clear that the hunt was now on. 'On the other side of the valley, away on the railway line, we could see the lights of electric torches moving about. The German guards had discovered the line of our retreat.'[34]

The ten of them collected the skis they had hidden some hours earlier and began climbing rapidly upwards through the forest and on to the mountainside. Within three hours they had reached the bleak expanse of the Hardanger plateau, which afforded some degree of safety. After covering a further seven miles, they took their first break. For Rønneberg, it was a moment to savour.

'It was sunrise, it was a lovely morning, excellent, and we were sitting there knowing that the job was done, nobody had been hurt on either side.' They hadn't even fired their guns. 'And when we were sitting there, we were eating chocolate and raisins and biscuits and nobody said anything at all, they were occupied by their own thoughts.'[35]

They did not rest for long. The sky suddenly darkened, the breeze became a squall and snow began tipping down in earnest. Within a few minutes, they were caught in a ferocious snowstorm and it was a punishing march through the blizzard towards their first goal, the refuge hut on the shores of the frozen Lake Langesjaa. The Arctic tempest drained every last drop of stamina, but it was nevertheless extremely welcome. For they all knew that the Germans would be unable to hunt them down for as long as the snowstorm swept across the wild expanse of the Hardanger. And they also knew that their tracks would soon be obliterated.

Colin Gubbins received news of the successful sabotage within hours. Rønneberg managed to get a wireless message transmitted to London. 'Attacked 0045 on 28.2.43. High concentration plant totally destroyed. All present. No fighting.'[36]

Gubbins was ecstatic. 'Magnificent,' he said to his secretary, Margaret, as she typed up a memo. 'Well planned and beautifully executed.'[37]

News of the success spread rapidly through Baker Street. For months, Gubbins had been facing criticism from Bomber Command, who objected to his constant request for planes. Now, his persistence had been triumphantly vindicated, as Bickham Sweet-Escott was quick to point out. The Norsk Hydro operation 'was the classic proof of our contention that one aircraft which drops an intelligent and well-trained party can do more damage than a whole fleet of bombers'.

Churchill agreed and had but one question for Gubbins: 'What rewards are to be given these heroic men?'[38]

They were all awarded either the Distinguished Service Order, the Military Cross or the Military Medal. Gubbins made sure that the planners were also rewarded, for he knew that without George Rheam's exemplary training 'it is doubtful whether the operation could have taken place at all'.[39]

Over the days that followed, Gubbins received further news about the destruction of Norsk Hydro, including a report from a Norwegian agent working inside the plant. He had arrived less than ten minutes after the explosion and had been witness to the devastating extent of the destruction.

'It was at once evident that the object of the action had been achieved. Each one of the eighteen cells had been blown to pieces and their contents of lye and heavy water had long since run off into the drains.'[40]

It was not just the high-concentration cells that had been knocked out, but also the water tubes feeding the plant. 'The whole room was full of spray,' reported Alf Larsen, the chief engineer, 'which was obviously caused by shrapnel from the explosions having penetrated the water tubes to the plant.'[41]

On 10 March, ten days after the attack, Gubbins received the sweetest news of all. He received a message from another agent at the plant, describing the visit to Norsk Hydro of General von Falkenhorst, the commander of the occupying German forces in Norway.

'At the sight of the ruined plant, he smiled and said: "This is the most splendid coup I have seen in this war."'[42] A consummate professional, he admired the saboteurs' work and conceded that they had pulled off a dazzling act of destruction. Once he had inspected the damage, he ordered the release of all the Norwegian civilians who had been rounded up. He then issued a second order: that all the German sentries on duty that night were to be arrested. Their eventual fate remains unknown, although the senior guard was later said to have been sent to the Eastern Front as punishment.

The saboteurs themselves were to have many extreme adventures as they made their getaway. Rønneberg and most of the men undertook a 400-kilometre endurance trek across the Hardanger plateau towards the border of neutral Sweden. It was 'an awful labour',[43] conceded Rønneberg, and would have been even more stressful if they had known that 2,000 German soldiers were on their trail. All his party eventually made it back to England, where they were handed their various military decorations.

Claus Helberg, one of the Grouse team, stayed behind to help organize resistance to the Nazis. It almost cost him his life. He was surprised by German soldiers while hiding out on the Hardanger and ended up in a marathon ski-chase across the frozen wasteland. He got away after a close-range gunfight, although he broke his arm in the process. He was eventually arrested by the Germans and transported to Oslo, but he jumped off the bus and, after many more scrapes, made it to Sweden.

Knut Haukelid was to provide the Norsk Hydro mission with its triumphant postscript. He had opted to remain in Norway in order to train new recruits to the resistance, but soon found himself with a more urgent role to play. The attack on Norsk Hydro had crippled the heavy water machinery, but the Nazis still had a stockpile of 3,600 gallons. Hitler now ordered that this be transported to Germany, in order that it could be kept secure in specially constructed bunkers in Bavaria until required by the atomic scientists.

Einar Skinnarland was still working at Norsk Hydro and managed to lay his hands on vital intelligence: the heavy water was to be transported to Mel, a little ferry port on nearby Lake Tinnsjo, using the single-track railway line that linked the plant with the port. It was then to be shipped to Hamburg in northern Germany.

Haukelid made it his mission to destroy this remaining heavy water. This was fraught with danger, for the entire Rjukan valley had been placed under SS guard and two aircraft were engaged in round-the-clock patrols of the surrounding mountains. The railway line that linked Norsk Hydro to Lake Tinnsjo was also under heavy guard, since this was the only means by which the Germans could transport their stock to the waiting vessel. The *Hydro* was a train-ferry: the train itself was to be loaded on to the vessel and would continue its journey by rail when it was offloaded at Hamburg. Skinnarland weighed up the options and told Haukelid he believed 'the safest solution to be sinking of the ferry' while it was crossing the lake.[44]

'The enemy was on his toes,' said Haukelid, but they were not as sharp as him. Although the Rjukan area was under constant surveillance, the Germans had neglected the most obvious target. 'By some freak of folly, not a single German guard had been posted on the *Hydro* herself.'

Haukelid decided to exploit this weakness, biding his time until all thirty-nine drums of heavy water had been loaded aboard the ferry. He knew that the ship was due to sail on the following morning, leaving him a unique window of opportunity.

In the early hours of Sunday morning, when the ship's deck was deserted, he clambered aboard with a sack of plastic explosive. 'Almost the entire ship's crew was gathered together below, round a long table, playing poker rather noisily.' In the engine room, the engineer and stoker could be seen hard at work. They were undisturbed by Haukelid.

'I wriggled through a hole in the cabin and crept along the keep, up to the bows.' He laid his charges in the bilges and coupled them to time-delay fuses. 'I reckoned that the charge was big enough to sink the ferry in about four or five minutes.'[45]

The operation took three hours: by 4 a.m., he was finished and left the vessel unseen by anyone. His hope was that the ferry would leave on time and that the time fuses would work. It would be eight hours before he would learn whether or not his mission had been successful.

Others were to have rather more direct experience of Haukelid's sabotage operation. The *Hydro*'s captain, Erling Sørensen, set sail precisely on schedule and by 10.30 a.m. was crossing the deepest part of the lake. Suddenly, quite without warning, there was a huge explosion inside the bowels of the vessel. It blasted such a devastating hole beneath the waterline that the ship was on her side within minutes. Sørensen jumped into the freezing water just as the train containing all the heavy water slid off the ferry and sank into water that was some 400 metres in depth. He swam further away from his ship, to avoid being sucked under, then 'turned around and watched her go down'.[46] Within a matter of seconds, the doomed *Hydro* had disappeared from view, carrying eight people to their deaths. Sørensen himself was fortunate to get plucked from the water.

Haukelid learned of the sinking from Einar Skinnarland, who informed him how the ship had sunk. He was particularly pleased to learn that the railway trucks had fallen irretrievably into the deepest part of Lake Tinnsjø 'having trundled forward, the full length of the deck'.[47]

It was left to Haukelid to write the epitaph on one of the greatest sabotage missions of the Second World War. 'So it was that the manufacture of heavy water ceased in Norway, and so it was that all stocks available to German scientists from that source were lost.' Colin Gubbins had just one thing to add. 'It was a one hundred per cent success.'[48]

16

Enter Uncle Sam

COLIN GUBBINS HAD always been sensitive to criticism from senior officers and he jotted down their more colourful insults in order to recount them to Joan Bright when they met for drinks after work. Millis Jefferis, by contrast, was more of a bulldozer: he had never remotely cared what people thought of him and it was left to Stuart Macrae to shoulder the constant sniping from the army high command. The attitude of the various ministries continued to rankle him throughout the spring of 1943 and he was therefore pleased to notice a subtle change as spring gave way to summer. Senior officials were beginning to court Jefferis and seek his opinion on matters of weaponry. To Macrae's ever observant eyes, it was as if they were trying to make amends.

When the Air Ministry invited the two of them to a bomb-dropping exercise in Wales, officials went overboard in their efforts to please. Macrae expected to be booked into a third-class sleeping carriage for the train journey from London. He was therefore astonished to find that they were given the red carpet treatment on arriving at Paddington Station. 'A reception committee ushered us into a royal train definitely more magnificent than the one in which we had accompanied Winston Churchill to Dover.' He was told that the bar would be kept open all night, that all their expenses had been covered and that they had been assigned first-class sleeping berths.

Macrae awoke at dawn the following morning to find they were already in Fishguard. When he asked how the train had covered the journey so quickly, he was informed that one of the directors of the Great Western Railway had ordered his traffic superintendent to ensure that all trains were 'cleared out of our way on pain of death'. The same superintendent had 'ridden down on the footplate himself to make sure that they were'.[1] After four years of war, Jefferis was at last being treated as one of the most important players in the fight against Nazi Germany.

Macrae hired many more staff that summer as he and Jefferis struggled to cope with the increasing demand for their sabotage weaponry. There were now some 250 people employed full time at the Firs, along with a veritable army of part-time workers, packers and drivers, and the team was producing an eye-stretching amount of weaponry. Six million detonators had rolled off the Firs's production line, along with 4 million anti-personnel switches and almost 3 million L-Delays. This was not all. They were still manufacturing the staples of guerrilla warfare, such as the limpet and clam, along with new weapons like the Puffball, a soft-nosed anti-tank bomb. The Firs now had a global reach, with weapons ending up in places as far afield as Kursk and Bombay.

Jefferis's new recruits rubbed their eyes in disbelief on first being initiated into the Whitchurch country house. It was as if they were being invited to join a parallel world, one that functioned according to its own rules and timetables. The working day often stretched so far into the night that mealtimes became completely inverted. Sleep, when possible, had to be snatched in intensive bursts.

Macrae felt there were distinct advantages to living 'in a closed community', for it enabled the team to work without any distraction. There was 'no wear and tear on the mind and body travelling to work every day', and 'no need to live by the clock'. Everyone could 'just get on with the job'. Yet he conceded that 'it was an odd life', one that was given an extra splash of excitement by the fact that it was entirely forward-thinking.[2] Even the machine tools looked as if they belonged to the future: rotating micrometers, diamond-tipped precision drills, a high-velocity wind tunnel and one of the most powerful centrifuges ever built. 'This was frightening,' confessed one of the early recruits, Edward Daily, when he first saw it in action. 'It was surrounded by a circle of sandbags and things were rotated at enormous speed, often to destruction.'[3] The velocity caused even the thickest steel to fragment into lethal shards.

Jefferis had also built a precision counter-chronoscope that consisted of rows of interlinked valves and dials used to measure the exact speed of a projectile. 'Cables were connected to two cameras at a known distance apart and the time was recorded for a missile to cross the path.'[4] This could then be cross-checked by firing a Winchester rifle across the cameras, with the results logged against Jefferis's algebraic equations. Only if all three readings gave the same calibration would the prototype under test be given the green light. 'We could claim without fear of contradiction,' said Macrae, 'that we had the finest and best equipped armaments development and research station in the country.'[5]

Jefferis was always at his best when confronted with an intellectual jigsaw with no obvious solution. He would stand in front of the giant blackboard that hung in the front office of the Firs, sketching out in coloured chalk the mathematical formulae that would underpin his new weapon. As Macrae watched him at work that summer, toiling through the early hours under the dim light of an electric bulb, it became apparent that he was on the brink of a spectacular breakthrough. For some months, Jefferis had been studying a scientific theory known as the Munroe effect and had reached the conclusion that it could transform the future of weaponry.

More than half a century earlier, an American chemist named Charles Munroe had discovered that it was possible to focus the blast of an explosion if the charge was shaped into a specific form. Traditional shells were pointed like bullets, in the belief that they would more easily puncture armour-plating. But Munroe had discovered that the explosion was infinitely more deadly if the tip of the shell was blunted into an inverted cone. The entire explosive force could be focused backwards into a tiny point. Then, once transformed into a ball of energy, it would shoot itself forward at high velocity with devastating consequences for anything in its path.

Munroe had published his findings in *Popular Science Monthly*, setting out his ground-breaking idea. But no one had truly appreciated the significance of his work until Jefferis began to examine it in detail. 'At this period, practically nothing was known of the mechanism of the hollow charge work.'[6]

He now hoped to put Munroe's theory to practical use. The mathematics was staggeringly complex, yet every equation pointed to the fact that Munroe was right: a hollow cone could indeed be used to focus explosive energy. And Jefferis had a further thought, one that would render the charge even more deadly. If he lined the inside of the cone with metal, the energy of the explosion would instantly melt this metal and transform it into a lethal plug. This could then be discharged with such force that armour-plating would be turned to plasma. Nothing – not even a German tank – could withstand such high-velocity explosive.

Jefferis knew he was on to a breakthrough of great significance. If his idea worked, then the hollow charge could be used to attack not just tanks, but planes and submarines as well. The possibilities were endless.

He was helped in his quest by James Tuck, a thirty-three-year-old physicist with an intense gaze, a neat moustache and a side parting so sharp it was as if someone had drawn a white line across his scalp. Professor Lindemann had poached Tuck from Oxford University and appointed him as his personal assistant, but even Lindemann conceded that Tuck was so smart that his talents would be of greater use at the Firs. Tuck was quick to recognize the theoretical brilliance of Jefferis's work and helped knock the mathematics into shape. But he also knew that the algebra couldn't provide all the solutions. 'The remainder could only be found empirically,' said Macrae, 'so the boys were busy working through the trials programme on the ranges.'[7]

The prototypes tested that summer were slowly transformed into a weapon of spectacular power. Jefferis wanted his hollow charge to be fired from a shoulder gun that could be carried into battle by a single man. In part, this was to lay to rest an image that had haunted him ever since his lightning trip to Norway three years earlier. He had observed British infantry firing their weapons at advancing German tanks and watching in despair as the shells bounced back at them. Now, with his fifteen-kilogram shoulder gun armed with a hollow charge, an infantryman was the equal of an armoured vehicle. When the trigger was pulled, the gun fired a warhead that no conventional tank could withstand.

'Trials with prototype rounds showed that Millis was really onto something,' said Macrae. The first rounds were fired at thick sheets of metal plating installed on the lower lawn at the Firs. 'Remarkable penetration of armour plating was at once achieved. True, the hole would only be a small one, but the blast effect was lethal.'[8] Anyone inside the tank would be torn to shreds by fragments of burning metal.

The tests that followed were undertaken on a tank filled with wooden dummies. The result was devastating for the dummies. They were completely carbonized by the heat of the explosion.

Jefferis's breakthrough was of such importance that news reached the Ordnance Board and the chiefs of staff within days. The top brass demanded an immediate demonstration of the prototype weapon, to be staged at their Small Arms School at Bisley. Macrae watched nervously as the gun was fired, hoping it would blast a hole through the plating. It did indeed create a devastating hole, but not through the metal plate. It misfired backwards, driving a mercifully small plug of metal through the man selected to fire it. He was fortunate not to be killed.

Jefferis rectified the problem and took over the firing. From this point on, the test went like clockwork. 'There was a satisfying bang as the round hit the target and, as was afterwards found, punched a nice hole in it.'[9] All four subsequent shots hit their target and smashed huge holes through steel plate almost five inches thick. Professor Lindemann immediately dictated a memo to Churchill extolling the extraordinary power of the gun. 'German tanks, with two-and-a-half inch armour, should be easy game,' he said.[10]

Jefferis was now told to perfect the weapon. As soon as it was ready for production, the War Office promised to place an order for 1 million, along with 5 million rounds of hollow charge ammunition. They had but one problem: they refused to countenance the idea of the weapon being named the Jefferis Shoulder Gun, claiming that 'no weapon or equipment should be named after its designer'. Lindemann knew that this was due to residual resentment against Jefferis and he took his objections to Churchill. He argued that if weapons couldn't be named after their inventors, then 'it would seem logical to stop the Army talking about Mills grenades, Stokes guns, Hawkins mines, Kerrison predictors, Northover projectors'.[11]

In this particular instance, the War Office bureaucrats got their way. The Jefferis Shoulder Gun was renamed the Projector Infantry Anti-Tank, or PIAT for short.

The very first PIATs were made ready in time for the invasion of Sicily in July 1943. General Andrew McNaughton, commander of the First Canadian Army, witnessed one in action and declared that he had never seen such an effective weapon. 'Really one hundred per cent,' he said.[12]

There was an upsurge in production in the weeks that preceded the invasion of Italy, where the weapon was to prove its devastating power. A BBC war correspondent, Frank Gillard, was recording a news bulletin when he found himself becoming the news rather than reporting on it. He was advancing with a small group of soldiers when they heard four Mark IV German tanks thundering towards them. The tanks were under orders 'to engage these British troops and wipe them out'. As they advanced, 'guns spluttering', Gillard switched on his microphone and then joined his comrades in a ditch. He sensed that the Germans were scenting victory, but added that 'our men were not quite as helpless as the Germans reckoned, for they had a PIAT with them'.

They held fire until the very last moment, waiting until the leading tank was no more than fifty yards away and still pumping out bullets. 'It was kill or be killed,' said Gillard, aware that only one of the outcomes would make it on to the evening news. As the lead vehicle loomed ever nearer, the PIAT proved its worth, scoring a direct hit with its devastating hollow charge.

'The great German tank was knocked out,' Gillard reported, and left as a charred and smoking ruin, its men inside obliterated by shrapnel. 'The other three behind it turned back, obviously in amazement, and made off at top speed.' He contended that an infantryman, equipped with a PIAT, 'seems to have a pretty effective answer to marauding German armour'.[13]

Jefferis had designed the PIAT for regular infantry, but he was quick to realize that it could be adapted for use by Gubbins's saboteurs. 'Once Millis had the hollow charge bit between his teeth, he raced off with it,' said Macrae. He designed a whole range of sabotage weapons that were given the collective name, Beehive. 'The smallest weighed only 6 lbs but would drill a nice hole through two inches of armour plate or a yard of concrete.' A single saboteur could now take on virtually any target, however well protected.

Jefferis next developed a set of larger Beehives that 'would penetrate any concrete pillbox'.[14] This was a crucial development. It had long been recognized that Allied forces would one day have to land on the northern coast of France, defended by a string of fortified bunkers that stretched from Brittany to Dunkirk and beyond. These presented a deadly threat to invading infantry, but Jefferis's invention meant that they would now be equipped with a weapon that could blow a hole through the strongest bunker.

Jefferis's invention had not gone unnoticed in America, whose army was already buying large quantities of sabotage weapons from the Firs. Indeed, it caused something of a stir as its full potential became apparent to a small clique of American scientists. For if the hollow charge could be used to create a concrete-busting explosive, then it could perhaps be adapted to generate the necessary force to trigger a plutonium bomb.

Millis Jefferis was not alone in finding himself courted by America in the summer of 1943. Colin Gubbins was also spending an increasing amount of time consulting with his American allies. His sabotage work had aroused interest in Washington ever since he had been placed in command of the Auxiliary Units back in the summer of 1940. It had left a particularly deep impression on Colonel William Donovan, a much decorated veteran of the First World War who visited Britain twice in that year while working as President Roosevelt's informal emissary to the country. They were visits that were to change his life.

Colonel Donovan had first won his spurs many years earlier while engaged in cross-border gun battles with the Mexican bandit Pancho Villa. His tactics were a mirror to Gubbins's irregular warfare against Michael Collins's Sinn Fein revolutionaries. Indeed Donovan bore many similarities to Gubbins, including irresistible charm, immense force of character and tireless energy. He had a near-legendary status for every American magazine reader, to whom he was known by his nickname, Wild Bill. It had been earned during his dashing exploits in the First World War when he was commander of the famed 'Fighting 69th'.

He had visited Colin Gubbins during his second trip to London and the two of them immediately realized they shared a great deal in common. He leaped at Gubbins's suggestion that they visit the Scottish Highlands together, in order to watch the guerrilla training programme in action. He was so impressed that he decided to establish a similar camp in North America, one that was to be a joint British–American venture. In Baker Street, it was known as Special Training School 103. In America, it was called Camp X.

The location was chosen with care. America was at the time forbidden by the Neutrality Act from being directly involved in the war, making it necessary to situate the camp in Canada, on the wind-blown shores of Lake Ontario. It was easily accessible from New York State, which lay on the other side of the lake, enabling Donovan's first batch of would-be guerrillas easy and surreptitious access to specialist training.

Donovan was quick to recognize Arisaig as the finest guerrilla-training establishment in existence. In the spring of 1942 – having been appointed head of the new Office of Strategic Services (America's answer to Baker Street) – he asked Gubbins if William Fairbairn could be transferred from Arisaig to Camp X. Gubbins signalled his agreement and Fairbairn arrived soon after. He began training the first intake of Wild Bill's guerrillas almost immediately and his silent killing classes caused as much of a sensation among the Americans as they had with the British. Charles Rolo, a young guerrilla volunteer, confessed to never having met anyone quite like Fairbairn. 'Before you have time to blink, his powerful hands have caught you in a mock death grip and you know why Nazi sentries have the "Commando jitters". You know, too, that this Major Fairbairn is a very dangerous customer.'[15]

Only once did Fairbairn find himself outsmarted by one of his students. He goaded a young American trainee named Geoffrey Jones into attacking him with an unsheathed, double-bladed knife. Jones circled Fairbairn for a moment before striking with all the force he could muster. To his horror, he saw he had slashed his tutor down one side of his face, causing blood to spurt from the open wound. 'I thought, Jesus Christ, I've done it now, he's going to kill me'. But Fairbairn declared himself delighted by Jones's skill and beamed broadly as he mopped up the blood. 'Good boy,' he said, 'well done!'[16]

Colin Gubbins had been quick to welcome America's entry into the war. 'The stage was finally set,' he wrote, 'with all the contestants in the ring, in boxing parlance, and the fight to be fought to the bitter end.'[17] He also recognized the potential of American saboteurs, of which there was a potentially inexhaustible supply, and hastily established an office in New York. One of his Baker Street staffers, Bickham Sweet-Escott, was sent to America and was most impressed by what he saw. The offices were on the thirty-fifth and thirty-sixth floors of the Rockefeller Center, where 'fifty or so exquisite Canadian typists made the air hum with activity'.

Sweet-Escott was also able to see Donovan's fledgling organization at work. He felt that the Americans had a great deal to bring to the underhand war against the Nazis, including technical equipment, wireless sets and Americans of Greek, Yugoslav and Romanian descent who were fluent in their native tongues. In short, America offered a rich field for recruitment.

Sweet-Escott had the opportunity to visit Camp X and saw that Fairbairn had stamped his personality on the place. Many of America's military establishments had a 'somewhat happy-go-lucky, lackadaisical atmosphere', with a surprisingly lax approach to discipline. Camp X, by contrast, was ruthlessly efficient. It was 'organized with real Knightsbridge barracks efficiency', and 'there was a great deal of spit and polish, saluting and sharp words of command'. Although Fairbairn had never been a fan of regular warfare, he was a stickler for discipline. His would-be saboteurs graduated from Camp X with a detailed knowledge of explosives, demolition and silent killing, as well as 'a much clearer idea of what secret operations were likely to involve'.

In addition to the New York office, Gubbins also established a liaison bureau in Washington run by Barty Pleydell-Bouverie, whose family seat, Coleshill House, had been the original training centre for the Auxiliary Units. Sweet-Escott visited Barty on several occasions and was impressed to find his offices equipped with 'every conceivable kind of gadget'. It was far more advanced than anything Baker Street had to offer. Barty even had his own 'little machine for squirting iced water into your mouth to quench your thirst or allay your hangover'.[18] Sweet-Escott had never seen anything quite like it.

Wild Bill Donovan established a reciprocal headquarters in London and his team soon came to appreciate Gubbins's brisk, no-nonsense approach to guerrilla warfare. But they found others in Whitehall far less congenial, especially the staff of the Ministry of Information who looked upon the newly arrived Americans with disdain. Malcolm Muggeridge was one of many who refused to take them seriously, saying that they arrived from America looking 'like *jeunes filles en fleur*, straight from finishing school, all fresh and innocent, to start work in our frowsty old intelligence brothel'.[19] The Americans were deeply insulted by such condescending treatment. 'The British kept tactfully reminding us that they had been in the intelligence business since Queen Elizabeth's day,' said one.[20]

The competing interests rapidly descended into a bitter wrangle over which organization – Baker Street or Wild Bill's team – would serve in which geographical area. Early in 1943, Gubbins flew to Algiers in order to clarify matters with both General Eisenhower, Supreme Allied Commander in Europe, and Wild Bill himself. Here, at last, they thrashed out conditions that would apply to all future guerrilla operations. There were still disagreements over sabotage operations in the Balkans, which Donovan was keen to spearhead. When this news reached Churchill, he was adamant that the Americans would not encroach on Gubbins's Balkan fiefdom. He reminded them that Gubbins had established no fewer than eighty guerrilla missions there and that these were working with partisans over an area covering almost 300,000 square miles. Moreover, Baker Street had already delivered 650 tons of explosive and equipment and a further 2,000 tons was on the way. It was unthinkable that such a rich field of operations would be handed over to the Americans.

Other territories were less contentious. Gubbins had always held that any Allied landings in France would need to be preceded by massive acts of sabotage. As the first graduates from Camp X began arriving in Britain, it became clear that they would soon be heading across the English Channel in joint operations with their British allies. Gubbins believed that France was the country in which Nazi Germany would lose the war – both the conventional one and also the unconventional. He also knew that he potentially held the winning hand.

17

Gubbins's Trojan War

S HORTLY AFTER THE news on the evening of 18 July 1943, the
BBC's French service broadcast a curious message to its overseas
listeners, one that had no apparent meaning. '*La guerre de Troie n'aura
pas lieu*,' it said.[1] 'The Trojan War will not take place.'

The message was sent with the blessing of Colin Gubbins and
intended for the ears of just two men. One was an Englishman
hiding out in the Jura Mountains in eastern France. The other was
Rodolphe Peugeot, a member of the illustrious car-making dynasty.

The BBC broadcast hundreds of *messages personnels* to France each
night: they were used by Gubbins's team to transmit information to
the local resistance. Meaningless to all except the addressee, they
provided coded details of forthcoming operations.

The message about the Trojan War was somewhat different. It
was a deeply personal pledge sent from one man to another and was
received by each in very different fashion. For the Englishman, Harry
Ree, it came at the end of a week that had nearly cost him his life.
But for the French recipient, Rodolphe Peugeot, it was to mark
the beginning of a wholly new way of life. A sensational act of
sabotage was in the offing and it was to be spearheaded by these
two individuals.

Harry Ree was one of Gubbins's more unlikely recruits to guerrilla warfare. A conscientious objector, he had signed the peace
pledge at Cambridge University in the autumn of 1939 and joined
the National Fire Service when called up for service. He preferred
to spend his wartime dousing flames rather than shooting Nazis.

But he soon found that deeply held convictions cut two ways. As
much as he was a pacifist, he had a half-Jewish father and was disgusted
by the racist brutality of the Third Reich. He performed a dramatic

volte-face and abandoned his pacifism. 'The concentration camps and the Jewish business convinced me to do everything possible to defeat the whole Nazi thing because of its racial policies.'[2]

Personal enemies can often be deadly ones, and Ree's battle was to become intensely personal. His near-fluency in French gave him swift access to Baker Street and before long he found himself planning an audacious cat-and-mouse game with the Gestapo. And although the Gestapo were adept at such games, they were to find that this one had very different rules. For Harry Ree was determined to play the cat, while they were to be relegated to the role of mouse.

There was only one problem. When Ree was sent to the Scottish Highlands for training, he was found to be clumsy and incompetent. In pistol training he was 'a poor shot'. In explosives he was 'not particularly outstanding'. In signalling 'he has a poor memory and forgets quickly'. Although his 'imperturbable coolness' was not in doubt, he was so cool that he kept nodding off during lectures. 'Rather disappointing,' noted one of his Scottish trainers at the end of his course. 'A very nice fellow,' said another.[3] It was hardly a ringing endorsement.

After scraping through Arisaig, he was transferred to Brickendonbury Manor where George Rheam taught him every conceivable means of blowing up a train. Rheam then moved him on to turbines, compressors, transformers and lathes. He even told him how to fire-bomb a tyre warehouse. Once again, Ree failed to shine.

Gubbins might easily have rejected his services, just as he had rejected so many others. But he was quick to see that Ree had a quality possessed by few other men, one that could only be described as his own personal magic. He had an instinctive ability to empathize with people whose lives, 'at any moment, might be totally and even tragically disrupted'.[4] It was an ability that was to prove of crucial importance. For Gubbins knew that if you can empathize with someone, then you can inspire them. And in wartime, that made Ree a valuable recruit indeed.

There was one last thing for Ree to do before leaving the country and that was to choose his *nom de guerre*. Never short on confidence, he plumped for Caesar. It was an appropriate moniker for someone intending to go on the rampage in the territories of ancient Gaul.

Ree was dropped into France by parachute in the spring of 1943 and initially made his way to a safe address provided by Baker Street. He had left behind a heavily pregnant wife, having been reassured that news of the birth would be transmitted in another of the BBC's coded messages. He was listening to the wireless on 5 May when he heard the phrase: *Clémence ressemble à la grand-mere.* It meant that his beloved Hetty had just given birth to a baby girl.

Ree slowly made his way to Besançon, where he made contact with a member of the resistance. He was still sheltering in the man's house on the night of 15 July when he heard the low rumble of RAF bombers in the sky. Their destination was the nearby village of Sochaux.

Sochaux was no ordinary French village. It was home to the Peugeot car factory, a vast industrial complex that employed no fewer than 60,000 workers. Sprawled over many acres, it functioned like a giant machine, its jib-borers and panel-beaters punching out a ceaseless production of cars and vans. As befitted one of Europe's most sophisticated factories, it even generated its own energy supplies. The rest of France could be shut down – switched off – yet the Peugeot-Sochaux works could continue to function.

At the outbreak of war, the company was still in the capable hands of the Peugeot dynasty, with Robert Peugeot at its head, a gruff old patriarch who had been born before cars were even invented. He was ably assisted by his business-savvy sons, Jean-Pierre and Rodolphe.

The family had tried to keep a firm hand on the steering wheel throughout the early days of war, driving Peugeot safely through the minefield of occupying Nazis. Their disdain for the Vichy regime was matched by a feeling of duty towards their workers. 'A question,' said old Robert, 'of keeping people in employment.'[5] But such a huge complex was far too valuable to the Nazis to remain in the family's hands for long, especially as it lay just forty miles from the frontier of the Third Reich. It was seized by Berlin within weeks of the German occupation and the Peugeot family relegated to factory foremen. Car production was brought to a halt and, in its place, workers spent their days building tanks and aeroplane engines. These were then transported to BMW or Klockner-Humboldt-Denz for the finishing touches.

The Peugeot sons did their best to disrupt production, much to the fury of the new German manager. He complained that six out of every ten vehicles were developing a problem with the clutch. Jean-Pierre Peugeot could offer nothing more than a Gallic shrug: you shouldn't buy a Peugeot if you want a BMW.

In the early months of 1943 the entire complex came under the direction of Ferdinand Porsche, the brilliant inventor of the Volkswagen Beetle and an enthusiastic member of the SS. He was quick to realize the potential for further exploitation of Peugeot-Sochaux. The most skilled workers were now set to work on producing specialist parts for the Focke-Wulf TA154, a prototype twin-engine night-fighter aircraft. More ominously, Herr Porsche ordered them to work on a secret German project with the code-name 1144. This was the infamous V1, a jet-powered missile that Hitler believed capable of winning the war.

Colin Gubbins knew a great deal about Sochaux, for his secretary, Margaret Jackson, had kept him supplied with intelligence from undercover agents. The RAF had also been keeping a close eye on the Peugeot works and ranked it as number three on their list of the industrial targets to be destroyed. Now, as news of increased production reached Whitehall, the army's high command decided it was time to act.

The most sensible course would have been to place the entire operation in Gubbins's hands. Instead, the Sochaux brief was given to the Chief of the Air Staff, Charles Portal, and the head of Bomber Command, Arthur Harris. Portal had already clashed with Gubbins on several occasions and was his antithesis in every respect: a sharp-nosed warmonger with an unswerving belief that might is right. The principal advocate of the indiscriminate aerial bombardment of Germany, his specific recommendation was to carpet-bomb every German city with a population of more than 100,000. 'Cool and detached', is what Gubbins's former secretary, Joan Bright, thought of him. She found his love of hardship somewhat perverse. 'He preferred a bench to a feather bed, a hunk of cheese to a soufflé.'[6]

Portal didn't mince his words when speaking about Gubbins's Baker Street team. 'Your work is a gamble which may give us a valuable dividend or may produce nothing,' he said. 'My bombing offensive is not a gamble. Its dividend is certain. It is a gilt-edged investment.' Irritated by Gubbins's constant demands for more planes, he added: 'I cannot divert aircraft from a certainty to a gamble which may be a gold-mine or may be completely worthless.'[7]

On 15 July Lord Portal and Bomber Harris decided to put their gilt-edged investment to good use. Their intention was to drop so much high explosive on the Sochaux factory that it would cease to function for the rest of the war. No fewer than 165 Halifax bombers set off from their base that evening, preceded by Pathfinders whose task it was to drop incendiary flares around the factory's perimeter as a marker for the bombers.

The raid went like clockwork. The night was clear, there was little enemy flak and the Pathfinder flares were clearly visible to the pilots. As the aerial armada thundered over Sochaux, it dumped vast quantities of explosives on to the industrial complex below. Pilots witnessed the works exploding into a fireball as the bombs hit their target. They returned to their bases with tales of fabulous destruction. Lord Portal's 'gilt-edged investment' had reaped rich dividends and Gubbins had been taught a lesson in destruction. That night, Bomber Harris went to his bed a contented man.

He awoke to news that was rather less edifying. The Pathfinder flares had landed short of the factory, in the residential area of Sochaux, with devastating consequences for the local population. The pilots had dropped no fewer than 700 high-explosive shells on to the villages of Sochaux, Vieux-Charmont, Allenjoie and Nommay.

One hundred and twenty-five civilians were killed instantly and a further 250 gravely injured. The destruction on the ground was catastrophic. More than 100 houses were pulverized and a further 400 seriously damaged. The town hall was flattened, along with the local school, post office and police headquarters. A mere thirty bombs – strays – hit the factory, causing negligible damage. The report handed to Bomber Harris made for unpalatable reading. 'Production [at the factory] was normal immediately after the raid.'[8]

Harry Ree had watched the raid from the garden of his contact in Besançon and was deeply shaken when he learned of the civilian deaths. Now, he decided to act. Aware that Rodolphe Peugeot was a man of high moral principles, he telephoned him, explained who he was and warned that the RAF was certain to bomb the factory again. The only way to prevent more civilian deaths was to sabotage the place from the inside.

Peugeot couldn't quite believe what he was being told. Indeed he suspected the caller was a German provocateur trying to induce him to say something incriminating. But Ree assured Monsieur Peugeot that he could prove he was from London, offering to get any phrase of Peugeot's choosing broadcast on the BBC's *messages personnels*. After much deliberation, Peugeot finally agreed. He said he would trust Ree if he heard the phrase, '*La guerre de Troie n'aura pas lieu*', on the following evening.

The message was duly broadcast and both men heard it. For Ree, it was a call to action. Emboldened, he now paid a visit to Peugeot at his bourgeois residence, 'expensively furnished and hung with tapestries', to discuss the project further. He got straight down to business, picking up from his conversation a couple of days earlier. 'I will tell you quite frankly what the position is,' he said. 'The people in London want the Peugeot factory put out of action. They will bomb you, they say, unless production can be stopped within a short time.' He warned that a second raid was likely to cause yet more casualties. And then he offered an alternative scenario. 'Now if you were to let a few of my men get into the factory one dark night . . .'

Rodolphe Peugeot stopped him in mid-sentence. 'I am to destroy my own factory? My dear man . . .'

Ree nodded. That is exactly what he was suggesting. 'One way or another it will be destroyed,' he said. 'If we do it, there will be few casualties and furthermore we can put the explosive where it will do the greatest harm to production and the least to the fabric of the factory.' Once again he warned that if the RAF returned on a second raid, 'the whole place will be smashed to smithereens.'[9] Rodolphe Peugeot mulled over what Ree had told him and realized he had little choice. He decided to allow saboteurs into his factory.

Once he had made up his mind, his support was wholehearted.

He 'not only gave Henri [Harry] a plan of the factories and details of the machinery halls to be selected as targets for sabotage, but he gave him inside contacts as well'.[10]

Among these contacts was 'a quiet, intelligent man' named Pierre Lucas, the chief electrician at the works, and a few of his comrades.[11] 'We met at a café outside the factory one afternoon,' said Ree. 'They gave me some dungarees and I changed in the lavatory of the café and went with him around the factory.' It was a tense moment. As Lucas led Ree inside the complex, he noticed 'a lot of German security police'.[12]

Only now, as he toured the factory, did Ree appreciate how exemplary had been George Rheam's training at Brickendonbury Manor. He remembered 'with the utmost clarity the many hours he had spent . . . studying the weak spots of presses and lathes'.[13] As he cast his eye over the turbo-compressors, boring machines and turret lathes, he realized that a few pounds of plastic could cripple such machines.

The Peugeot factory was close to the Swiss frontier, as well as the German, and Ree now crossed the border into neutral Switzerland in order to arrange for Baker Street to parachute the necessary explosives into the area. Aware that it would be several months before a mission of this scale and complexity could take place, he requested that the RAF suspend any more bombing raids on the factory. Bomber Harris was extremely reluctant to agree, since he refused to accept that Gubbins's outfit, 'staffed by long-haired civilians, would ever render useful service in para-military operations'.[14]

This, coming less than six months after the Norsk Hydro triumph, left the Baker Street staff speechless. After a stormy meeting with the chiefs of staff, Bomber Harris said he would halt the raids only on the condition that he received regular reports on the plans to disrupt production. This news was transmitted to Ree, who agreed without hesitation. 'It was a wonderful job for an ex-conscientious objector to stop the bombing,' he said.[15]

Pierre Lucas now introduced Ree to André van der Straaten, the foreman of the plant. He was keen to be involved in the forthcoming sabotage. Lucas also persuaded three other workers to take part in the operation, bringing the total number to five. Ree himself was to direct the mission from outside the plant, since everyone agreed that it was far too risky for him to be present on the night of the planned destruction.

Huge quantities of limpet mines and incendiaries had to be parachuted into France and then smuggled inside the factory. Not until the beginning of November – far later than anticipated – was Ree ready to give the green light.

On the evening of 3 November, at the end of the day shift, the saboteurs assembled in the main courtyard at the front of the factory. A few German guards were knocking a football around in the yard and they now shouted across to the would-be saboteurs and asked them to join a France versus Germany match. Fearful of arousing any suspicion, Pierre Lucas and his men reluctantly formed themselves into a team.

André van der Straaten 'took a kick of the ball' and sent it flying across the courtyard.[16] As he did so, a limpet mine fell out of his pocket and clattered to the ground. 'One of the Germans said, helpfully: "*Attention, vous avez laissé tomber quelque chose, monsieur*" – you've dropped something.'

André van der Staten was horrified and 'hastened to pick it up, murmuring something about electric fuses. This was accepted without question and the game continued.'[17]

The football match lasted so long that the attack had to be postponed for the night. Ree rescheduled it for 5 November, Guy Fawkes Night in Britain and a fine date for making loud bangs. This time, the saboteurs avoided contact with the German guards and slipped inside the factory as soon as the workers had left for the night, using their pass-keys to open the door. In the working day, the cavernous machine hall was alive to the sound of clanking, grinding machinery as yet more tank-tracks rolled off the production line. Now, the place was eerily deserted and the fading twilight seeped like dirty water through the grease-smudged glass roof panels.

The saboteurs made their way to the executive floor, where their plastic explosive lay hidden in the cleaning cupboard. There were also boxes of limpet mines in various shapes and sizes, 'so that the bomb could be easily stuck on the sensitive part of a valuable machine'.[18]

The men checked the explosives and then settled in for a long wait. Ree had warned them not to plant their charges until night had fallen. Not until 11 p.m. did they move 'to their prearranged stations in various sections of the factory'.[19] Each saboteur knew his allotted task. One was to blow up the jig-borer, another was to target the gas production plant. The foundry sand dryers and body-work transformers were also on the hit list, along with the biggest lathes and compressors.

The most difficult target was the irreplaceable centrifugal compressor. This was a serious challenge, for the compressor room could only be entered 'under conditions of incredible danger and physical strain, namely crawling up the ducts and into the compressor room'.[20] It was probably André van der Straaten who undertook this task, squeezing himself along the duct and then swinging himself down into the room. This was the very heart of the Peugeot factory and vital to the functioning of the machinery.

In pitch darkness, he groped his hands into the compressor. He then snapped a limpet mine on to the metal. If all went to plan, it would detonate within the hour. He then struggled back down the narrow duct and dropped into the main factory, meeting one of the foremen as he did so. He was 'working with quiet detachment' and the two of them paused for a moment as they listened to two of their comrades who were 'engaged similarly in another sector of the shop floor'.

It took almost an hour to plant all the explosives. Once the last fuses had been activated, the men 'hurried down to a disused side door' which led 'into a deserted yard at the back of the factory'. A second door gave them access to a side alley that ran along the perimeter of the fence. 'They all shook hands and hurried away: they had to get home as quickly as they could, for curfew had started and there would be a terrific turn-out of police and military as the factory went up.'[21]

Colin Gubbins faced an agonizing wait for news. He had staked his reputation on a successful operation and knew that if he could pull off such a massive attack, it would almost certainly guarantee his team a leading role in advance of the planned landings in Normandy.

According to a report by Maurice Buckmaster, head of Baker Street's French Section, the destruction began with a series of muffled bangs. 'At about ten minutes past midnight, the shop-floor of the Peugeot factory was rent by several violent explosions.'[22] The limpets detonated as synchronized, with the noise of the blast being contained by the factory walls. The outdoor explosions were altogether more spectacular, detonating with such force that the inhabitants of Sochaux were rocked from their beds. The concrete transformer houses were split in two by the blasts and one of the heavy outer doors, made of reinforced steel, blown fully eighty feet into the night sky.

The full extent of the destruction would not be known until the morning, but long before daybreak it was clear that Ree's men had caused irreparable damage, for the heat of the explosions had sparked a fire fuelled by a lethal cocktail of oil, petrol and gas.

Ree spent the night in a safe house and awoke with a feeling that life had just taken a turn for the better. Later that morning, he sauntered over to the factory in order to inspect the damage. As he passed one of the transformers, he noted that the 'brick building [was] laid flat and pulverised' while the transformer itself was a mangled ruin. Inside the factory, the destruction was writ large over the smoke-blackened machinery. 'Turbo: huge hole in side. Leaves twisted to blazes. Coussinet [bearing machine] pulverised. 8,000hp motor irreparable.' Most of the targeted machines were contorted beyond recognition.

'I wish you could see the faces of German guards,' he wrote in a gleeful report to Baker Street, 'and compare them with faces of workers, directors and population of Sochaux.'

He gave a full appraisal of the damage, as requested by Bomber Harris. The transformers and turbo-compressors had taken the biggest hit and were so badly damaged that none of them would ever work again. 'A stoppage of five to six months is anticipated.'

Ree appended an addendum to his memo, extending his gratitude to those who had trained him. 'My 17 [Brickendonbury Manor] training is being invaluable in this area. Please thank Rheam and his staff.' He added that 'my Scotland training invaluable for crossing frontier.' In a postscript, written in capital letters, he urged: 'DO YOUR BEST TO KEEP RAF AWAY.'[23]

The Gestapo began their hunt for the perpetrators within hours of the attack. Their first port of call was the Peugeot family, who were subjected to a lengthy interrogation. But they were found to have clean hands and 'there was nothing the Germans could do to incriminate Rodolphe Peugeot'.

The finger of suspicion soon fell on a group of factory workers 'of whom five were missing'.[24] They, along with a rumoured Englishman known only as Henri, were the prime suspects. The Gestapo were highly experienced in rooting out saboteurs, aware that they would be swallowed up by safe houses and then lie low for several weeks. Ree knew this and decided to change the rules of the game. Far from going into hiding, he persuaded his sabo-teurs into undertaking another strike on the following night, when it was least expected. This time, they attacked two new targets, the huge foundry at Sainte-Suzanne and the nearby Marty factory which produced engine parts. He sent a second upbeat message to Baker Street. 'Both transformers pulverised and flying pieces smashed three electric motors, a switchboard and two batteries of accumulators.'[25]

Over the weeks that followed, Ree masterminded a sustained campaign of sabotage, destroying machinery, setting fires and derailing goods trains. On 19 November an auxiliary compressor was delivered to the Peugeot factory to replace the one destroyed in the initial attack. That very evening, as it stood in the front yard, Ree's men scaled the fence and attached a limpet mine, wrecking the machine before it had even been unwrapped.

Ree was by now in real danger, for both the Gestapo and the SS were on his heels. In need of a new safe house, he called at the home of a local schoolmaster, Monsieur Hauger. He soon discovered it was safe no longer. The door was opened by a German officer, who ordered him inside at gunpoint.

Ree had been trained for just such a scenario and that training now proved invaluable. 'Don't be an idiot,' he said to the German in a voice that was intended to display his innocence. 'It's very dangerous to play with firearms like that. For Heaven's sake put it away.'

The man whipped out his card, which revealed him to be a

member of the Sicherheitsdienst, the SS intelligence agency. 'I said, "Oh, I beg your pardon" and put my hands up.'[26]

The German officer informed Ree that Monsieur Hauger had been arrested after having been found hiding explosives. He seemed to swallow Ree's story that he was merely a friend of Monsieur Hauger, but said that he would nevertheless need to be interrogated by the Gestapo. 'Since I knew that they were looking for a certain Henri,' said Ree, 'a tall, fair Englishman in that region, and since I had 50,000 francs on me, I decided not to risk the interrogation.'[27]

Now, his imperturbable coolness once again came into play. He made his way to Monsieur Hauger's drinks cabinet and offered the officer a glass of wine. It was to be a drink to remember. 'I brought the glasses down from the cupboard and as I was walking behind him with the bottle, I hit him on the head with it.'

It should have knocked him unconscious, but he didn't strike with sufficient force. The officer spun round, only mildly concussed, and fired his pistol six times. 'And as he fired I remember thinking, "Good heavens, how extraordinary" – I was by that time hitting him – "they must have been blanks in there" because the pistol was sort of pointing at me.'

When the gun was spent, a brawl ensued, with each man trying to overpower the other. The German repeatedly thwacked Ree on the head with his pistol butt. He then locked his neck 'into one of those bloody grips, a sort of half nelson, and I remember it going through my mind: "If you're ever going to see your daughter, you've got to get out of this one."'

It was now that his Arisaig training proved its worth. Ree had not been the most proficient of students, but he had listened carefully when being taught self-defence. Sykes's technique was designed to cause real pain. Ree flattened his palms and then 'pushed them up into his stomach' and deep into his internal organs. The German 'fell back against the wall' – he was in severe pain – 'and said: *Sortez, sortez.*'

Ree needed no encouragement. He fled by the back door and hurtled across the fields in his boots and raincoat. 'I was getting very wet from the rain and I put my head inside to see if it was going through and it came out covered in blood. And I thought: "God, they weren't blanks."'

He swam across the river and made it to the nearby village where he knocked on the door of a local contact. The man answered in considerable shock, 'seeing this blood-stained, bedraggled figure at the door, on a Sunday afternoon, about six o'clock'.[28] He offered Ree a warm bed and then called a doctor who discovered that Ree had indeed been shot, but only by a single bullet.

Three nights later, Ree was carried across the border into Switzerland and taken to a local hospital, where he was nursed back to health. He continued to pull the strings from his sickbed, sending vital intelligence to his saboteurs and enabling them to pull off a whole new series of spectacular explosions.

Ree was to remain in Switzerland until May, when he eventually set off for England, travelling via Marseille, Pamplona and Gibraltar. Colin Gubbins felt a very personal sense of gratitude, for Ree had seen off not only the Nazis, but Bomber Harris and Lord Portal as well. He recommended that he be 'appointed a Companion in the Distinguished Service Order'.[29]

Back at Brickendonbury Manor, George Rheam had never been known to waste his breath on praise, but even he expressed his admiration for Ree. In goading Rodolphe Peugeot into collaborating with the Allies, he had effectively invented a whole new type of warfare, one that Rheam labelled 'blackmail sabotage'.

'We have not made enough use of managements and owners of installations who, whilst unable to do physical acts of sabotage, can be contacted and from whom technical advice can be obtained which we, in turn, can pass on to saboteurs.'[30]

Winston Churchill was inclined to agree. One factory owner and a few bags of limpets were worth an entire squadron of Bomber Harris's Halifax bombers.

18

Fighting with Hedgehogs

SECRETARY MARGARET JACKSON was able to provide Gubbins with remarkably accurate briefs on the success or failure of the sabotage missions that were by now taking place on a nightly basis. Wireless transmissions were received by the various country sections, where they were collated and forwarded to her. She, in turn, handed them to Gubbins when he arrived for work at Baker Street.

The situation at the Firs was rather different. It was a source of continual frustration to Stuart Macrae not to have any idea as to how and when their weapons had been used. In part, this was because they were too busy to enquire. As summer yielded to autumn that year, 1943, they found themselves working on 'all manner of remarkable projects'. There were 'bombs which jumped about on the ground, bombs which leaped in and out of the sea and rockets which fired bridges over roads'[1] – the latter being the latest invention from the drawing board of Cecil Clarke. Yet news of operations hardly ever reached the sheds and workshops at the far end of the lower lawn.

Macrae tried to keep tabs on successful limpet attacks, but even this proved difficult. Unlike Gubbins, he was not in regular contact with the army high command. As for Jefferis himself, he didn't seem to care. Macrae increasingly found himself in the role of 'a theatrical producer who had found an unwilling star' – Jefferis – 'and forced him to fame'. He felt rather guilty, for 'whereas I had succeeded in making myself happy, it was obvious that I had done the opposite for Millis'.[2] Jefferis wanted nothing more than to be left with his mathematics, his coloured chalks and the occasional tumbler of whisky.

His most complex invention, the anti-U-boat Hedgehog mortar, had started life when the two of them were still working in the War Office back in the early days of war. It had originally been intended as a sabotage weapon to be used in the event of a Nazi invasion of Britain, but had slowly been transformed into an instrument of such complexity that it had required more than two years of fine tuning. The principal difficulty had been to calculate the recoil accurately, essential to the stability of any ship. One newly recruited engineer who found himself travelling in the company of Jefferis said that he 'spent most of one train journey between Bath and London sketching furiously on empty cigarette packets'.[3] As the train pulled into Paddington, Jefferis gave the hint of a smile: the mathematics finally made sense. And by the time the sea trials took place, the Hedgehog was near perfect. The mortars dived downwards in their streamlined casings and then homed in on their underwater foe.

This all took time and it was not until the spring of 1943 that the first Hedgehogs were being installed on Royal Navy vessels. When Commander Reginald Whinney took command of the HMS *Wanderer*, he was told to expect the arrival of a highly secret piece of equipment. 'At more or less the last minute, the bits and pieces for an ahead-throwing anti-submarine mortar codenamed "hedgehog" arrived.'

As Whinney watched it being unpacked on the Devonport quay-side, he was struck by its bizarre shape. 'How does this thing work, sir?' he asked, 'and when are we supposed to use it?' He was met with a shrug. 'You'll get full instructions.'[4]

Whinney glanced over the Hedgehog's twenty-four mortars and was 'mildly suspicious' of this contraption that had been delivered in an unmarked van coming from an anonymous country house in Buckinghamshire. He was not alone in his scepticism. Many Royal Navy captains were 'used to weapons which fired with a resounding bang', as one put it, and were 'not readily impressed with the performance of a contact bomb which exploded only on striking an unseen target'.[5] They preferred to stick with the tried and tested depth charge when attacking U-boats, even though it had a hit rate of less than one in ten. Jefferis's technology was too smart to be believed.

The Americans proved quicker at embracing the Hedgehog,

equipping large numbers of their ships in the final months of 1943. Among them was the USS *England*, which went into service in the Pacific shortly afterwards. She was soon to find herself caught in the opening shots of Operation A-Go, the Japanese quest for the total destruction of the American Pacific fleet in the spring of 1944. It was an operation driven by Admiral Soemu Toyoda, who knew that submarines would play a central role in the battle ahead. Indeed he said that 'the success or failure of Operation A-Go depends on the submarines'. What he didn't know is that he would be pitting his fleet against Jefferis's mathematical genius.

Admiral Toyoda issued his pre-battle orders to Rear-Admiral Naburo Owada on 3 May 1944. Owada was commander of the Japanese submarine force, Squadron Seven, and he was instructed to launch 'a surprise attack against enemy task forces and invasion forces'.[6]

The Americans were quick to intercept the Japanese wireless transmissions: one of the first intercepts revealed that a lone Japanese sub, I-16, was heading towards the Solomon Islands. The I-16 was an enticing prize, one of the largest submarines ever built in Japan. She was almost 350 feet long and heavily armed with eight 21-inch torpedo tubes. She was so big that she could carry a small supplementary sub in her deckhouse. Moreover, she was commanded by the brilliantly gifted Yoshitaka Takeuchi.

American intelligence discovered not only the sub's destination, but also her intended route and speed. This was immediately forwarded to the USS *England*, which set out in hot pursuit.

The *England*'s executive officer, John Williamson, was one of the new breed of navy men: savvy, clean-shaven and passionate about the latest gadgets. With his large ears and goofy smile, he looked like a typical college geek. But he was a geek who was hungry for victory. And in Jefferis's Hedgehog, he smelled triumph. Long before his vessel set sail from San Francisco, he had instigated a series of test firings in the harbour. 'If it hit,' he noted, 'the concentrated power of its thirty-five pounds of TNT was enough to blow a two- or three-foot hole in a submarine's three-quarter-inch rolled-steel hull.' Unlike the depth charge, the Hedgehog only detonated on making contact with the submarine. 'You knew you had scored a hit, and a devastating one.'

Now, as Williamson went in search of the Japanese sub, he felt 'a heady mixture of excitement, eagerness and trepidation appropriate to new boys on the block'.[7] One slip on his part and the *England* herself would come under attack from Commander Takeuchi's torpedoes.

At exactly 1.25 p.m. on 18 May, the *England*'s soundman, Roger Bernhardt, gave a shout from the bridge. 'Echoes sharp and clear, sir!'[8] The echo detection equipment revealed that the submarine was just 1,400 yards away. The chase was now on and the vessel began to shudder as the engines were cranked to full throttle.

Williamson was impressed by Takeuchi's reactions, for he proved a skilled quarry. 'At four hundred yards, the target turned hard left and kicked his screws.' Takeuchi was making his escape, using a procedure known as 'kicking the rudder'. This threw up disturbances in the water, distorting the sonar echoes and making the sub's position impossible to pinpoint with accuracy. But Williamson had made it his business to locate subs, even in turbulent water. He studied the Doppler machine intently as he tried to calculate the exact depth of Commander Takeuchi's sub. At precisely 2.33 p.m., he got a fix. A split-second later, he fired his weapon and the Hedgehogs roared away from the ship and upwards into the clear blue sky, forming themselves into a perfect ellipse and then entering the sea in symmetry, just as Millis Jefferis had intended.

'No one said a word. All eyes were fixed on the water's surface, everyone imagining the huge steel fish below.' Everyone knew that unlike the old depth charge, the Hedgehog would only explode if it hit the sub.

Silence. Tension. And then – '*V-r-r-oom*! We heard it again and again, in rapid-fire succession, four to six hits coming so fast on top of one another as to seem almost simultaneous.' Williamson had just one word in his mind: 'Bull's-eye!'

Deep below the surface, Commander Takeuchi had been engaged in a desperate struggle to evade the *England* when his submarine was hit by six shattering explosions. Jefferis had spent months calculating the mathematical equation that would ensure his Hedgehog would strike with deadly precision. Now, that mathematics reaped dividends. As the I-16's steel hull was punctured by multiple spigots, the rigid hull instantly and violently crumpled in on itself like a tin can crushed by a giant fist. Commander Takeuchi and his crew were engulfed in a catastrophic decompression that sucked in a high-velocity avalanche of water, along with twisted shrapnel from the crippled outer shell. Death was mercifully quick. There was no hope of escape.

There was jubilation aboard the *England* at the sound of the underwater explosions. The crew 'broke out in cheers, everyone jumping and slapping one another on the back like a team that had just won a tournament game'. The cheering continued for fully two minutes, 'and was just beginning to die down when all of a sudden we heard a giant *wham*!' The sea erupted into angry wavelets and the *England* 'shuddered violently and started rocking and reeling'.

Williamson's first thought was that they had been torpedoed. He feared that Commander Takeuchi had somehow detonated his on-board torpedoes as a final, desperate act of revenge. In fact, it was the violent implosion of the submarine that caused the shock-waves. The men on the *England* were nevertheless terrified. The fantail of the ship 'lifted as much as a foot, plopped heavily back in the water, while men throughout the ship were knocked off their feet and deck plates sheared loose in the engine room'. Williamson concluded that the aftershock marked the 'cataclysmic certainty that we had heard the last of the Japanese submarine'. It left the men 'sobered and subdued'. The Hedgehogs had made their job of killing very easy.

The submarine had been sunk at more than 500 feet below the surface and almost twenty minutes were to pass before the first wreckage began to appear. Williamson was staring intently at the sea when he saw some shredded cork insulation pop to the surface. It was followed by deck planking and the remnants of a filing cabinet. Next to float up was a prayer mat decorated with Japanese characters, a lone chopstick and a large rubber container holding a seventy-five-pound bag of rice.

There was increasing excitement on deck as more evidence of their 'kill' started floating to the surface. Everyone was awaiting the inevitable appearance of human remains. Ten minutes passed, then twenty, but they never arrived. John Williamson peered into the water and was quick to see why. 'Soon a dozen or so well-fed-looking sharks were milling around the vicinity.' Commander Takeuchi and his crew had fallen prey to two different enemies, one above water and one below.

A small oil slick soon appeared on the surface, evidence that the Hedgehogs had ruptured the sub's fuel tanks. 'The slick grew steadily in size until profuse amounts of oil were bubbling to the surface, along with more debris.'

All the detritus needed to be collected, for the US Navy would only confirm a 'kill' if there was evidence. One of the *England*'s whaleboats was lowered and a few of the crew began collecting relics of the sub. Williamson was concerned for the men's safety, for 'there were a dozen or more huge sharks swimming excitedly through the floating debris, looking for blood and shredded limbs.'

Over the course of the next twelve days, Williamson achieved a record unbeaten in the history of naval warfare. He and his men sank a further five submarines, all destroyed by Hedgehogs. Each time, the effect was the same: a deep-water vroom, an oil slick on the surface and dozens of marauding sharks. One young mariner aboard the *England* confessed to being upset at the ease with which their Hedgehogs were destroying the subs. Williamson had a ready answer. 'Son,' he said, 'war is killing. The more of the enemy we can kill, and the more of his ships we can sink the sooner it will be over.' He added that 'we are in a war that we must win, for to lose it would be far worse.' It was a sentiment that could have come straight from the mouth of Millis Jefferis.

At the naval headquarters in Japan, Admiral Soemu Toyoda was still unaware of the catastrophe that had befallen Squadron Seven. He was eagerly anticipating the onset of Operation A-Go, aware that his submarines had a unique role to play. At 9 a.m. on 15 June he gave the order for battle, using exactly the same words as Admiral Togo had used to address his fleet on the eve of the famous Battle of Tsushima, thirty-eight years earlier. 'The fate of the empire rests on this one battle. Every man is expected to do his utmost.'[9]

As part of the general deployment, he sent an urgent directive to Admiral Owada: 'Submarine Squadron Seven is to be immediately stationed east of Saipan, to intercept and destroy American carriers and transports, at any cost.' Admiral Owada's reply was succinct. Squadron Seven, he said, 'has no submarines'.[10] Jefferis's Hedgehogs had claimed the lot.

Stuart Macrae was delighted when he was brought the news: indeed, it would remain with him for years. 'The hedgehog was an out and out winner,' he wrote. 'It went into service rather late in the day, but was credited with thirty-seven confirmed submarine killings.'[11] What had begun as a sabotage mortar for use against the Nazis in Kent had been transformed by Jefferis into a devastating weapon of destruction.

19

Operation Gubbins

TRIUMPH AND TRAGEDY marched hand in hand in wartime, or so it seemed to Colin Gubbins. The triumph, when it came, was as unexpected as it was welcome. In the last week of September 1943, Gubbins learned that his boss, Charles Hambro, had resigned. His resignation came after a lengthy wrangle over the running of Baker Street, and there were many who felt it was high time he left. Even one of his supporters referred to him as 'always the gentleman among the professionals'.[1] It was a backhanded compliment and the inference was clear: the professionals, not the gentleman, had been running the show.

There were never any doubts as to his successor. Ever since Gubbins had joined Baker Street in November 1940, he had been the driving force behind its most spectacular missions. He had also displayed a rare gift for hiring brilliant mavericks with unorthodox talents. And he had established a string of secret stations like Brickendonbury Manor and Arisaig, which had become the finest training academies in the world, so good that even the Americans had copied them.

Now, Winston Churchill rewarded Gubbins with the top job: henceforth he was to be known as CD. The C stood for Chief, the D for Destruction. It was a neat little reminder of the early days in Caxton Street, where Gubbins had shared an office with Lawrence Grand of Section D. The new job also came with a new rank. Gubbins was elevated from brigadier to major-general, the first person in the history of the British Army to be so promoted for services to dirty warfare.

Gubbins's first recruit to Caxton Street, Peter Wilkinson, was delighted when he heard the news. When he thought back to the early days, he could scarcely believe their change in fortunes. He and Gubbins had started out with a shared back office in Berkeley Court, furnished with one table and two chairs. Now, less than three years later, Gubbins stood at the head of his own empire with hundreds of office staff and a global reach. 'The Baker Street headquarters had been brought to a hitherto undreamed of level of efficiency,' he said.[2]

Joan Bright was also delighted that Gubbins had at long last been rewarded with the top job. She said that he had transformed Baker Street 'from a community of individual enthusiasts into a military bureaucracy'.[3] It was a formidable fighting force, one that was ready to tackle Hitler head-on.

As the fourth full year of war gave way to the fifth – 1944 – Gubbins began preparing for the battle to come. He first embarked on a whistle-stop tour of his sabotage fiefdom, travelling to the Middle East and North Africa, where he had a meeting with his American counterpart, William 'Wild Bill' Donovan. He visited Italy and reorganized his guerrilla operations in Greece, where Chris 'Monty' Woodhouse and Eddie Myers were still blowing up bridges and barracks. He then headed back to Cairo for a luncheon with Winston Churchill, General Ismay and Fitzroy Maclean (who was leading his guerrilla operations in Yugoslavia). Shortly afterwards, he returned to London in order to overhaul the office in preparation for what he believed would be the final showdown with the Nazis. The chiefs of staff all agreed that his guerrillas would have a potentially vital role to play in the planned invasion of Occupied France.

Aware that even the most sceptical army generals were by now more or less converted to sabotage, Gubbins staged an exhibition of explosive devices, 'on private view in one of the dissecting rooms at the Natural History Museum in South Kensington'.[4] The exhibition displayed the most devious weapons produced by Millis Jefferis's team at the Firs, including scores of booby traps, detonators and limpets. It was an invitation-only show, one that the king himself was delighted to attend. For Gubbins, it was a very personal moment of triumph.

It was quieter than usual in Baker Street on Sunday, 6 February. Gubbins himself was not in the office and weekend duty had been placed in the hands of Alan Ritchie, an air vice-marshal who had only recently joined his staff. Ritchie was busy with paperwork for much of the day, handling wireless telegrams from across the world and placing them in Gubbins's in-tray. One of these telegrams was rather more personal than usual. Ritchie flagged it up for special attention, pushed it close to the top of the pile and then left for the night.

Gubbins arrived early for work the following morning, anxious to read through the backlog of telegrams before secretary Margaret arrived at the office. As he sifted through the pile, he noticed one marked 'deepest sympathy'. Intrigued, he tore it open. As he did so, a chill ran through his veins. It was the one marked up by Alan Ritchie on the previous evening and it informed Gubbins that his elder son, Michael, had been killed in action.

Gubbins was totally unprepared for such devastating news. He had assumed the telegram would be referring to a failed sabotage operation or botched attack. Instead, its terse prose brought news that would mark his life for ever. Stunned, horrified, appalled, he reached for the phone and urgently tried to find out more.

It was some days before the whole terrible story unfolded, one that he eventually confided to Joan Bright. It transpired that young Michael had volunteered to serve in an advance assault group set ashore at Anzio, some thirty miles to the south of Rome. He and his comrade-in-arms, Malcolm Munthe, had been crossing an exposed stretch of no-man's-land when they found themselves under fire. Michael had always been 'eager for excitement', but he now found himself with an overdose of adrenalin. Munthe was hit in the head and chest and collapsed with serious wounds. He was later rescued and nursed back to health. Michael himself was raked with gunfire and killed in an instant. He never stood a chance.

Gubbins had first-hand experience of war. He had seen men maimed, shot and blown apart. But the loss of his own son over-shadowed every other death. One of the ladies working for him recalled him 'walking backwards and forwards murmuring "so useless, so useless"' as he fought back the tears. He tried to explain his grief to Peter Wilkinson, but words failed him. 'A totally useless death,' was all he could muster.

Gubbins would later travel to Italy, where he was comforted by his son's friend, Gerry Holdworth. Holdworth had laid out Michael's kit and clothing on the floor but had the unenviable task of informing Gubbins that 'they never found a trace of Michael'. His corpse was one of thousands that was simply trampled into the winter mud. Holdworth 'was very distressed by Colin's grief, but there was nothing he could do except fetch a carefully hoarded bottle of Black Label whisky which the two men drank together'.[5]

Bereavement takes many forms and Gubbins went through every possible emotion. Michael's death might yet have been the catalyst to bring him and his wife, Nonie, back together. Instead, it did the very opposite, causing a permanent rift. Within months, they would be divorced.

Ultimately, there was only one thing that could make sense of Michael's death, and that was to defeat Hitler at any cost. And that – in the spring of 1944 – was what Gubbins was preparing to do. He began hand-picking a group of young men for what was to be the adventure of their lives. It was an adventure that Gubbins believed could turn the tide of war.

Colin Gubbins had kept a sharp eye on France ever since the attack on the Pessac power station in the spring of 1941. In the intervening time, a growing number of highly trained saboteurs and wireless operators (including thirty-nine women) had been parachuted into the country. By the spring of 1944, he had some 1,200 agents in the field. Their role was to create networks of French resisters (known as 'circuits') that could wreak mayhem in the immediate aftermath of Operation Neptune, the assault phase of the invasion of northern France. It was imperative that Hitler's defensive battalions in Normandy should be deprived of supplies, equipment and reinforcements, and sabotage was a far more effective means of achieving this than aerial bombardment.

Gubbins could count on the support of dozens of circuits working right across France. The one founded by Harry Ree in the Franche-Comté was superbly effective. Operating under the codename Stockbroker, its saboteurs were bold almost to the point of recklessness, causing immense damage to Hitler's war machine. They were well placed to prevent extra supplies of weaponry being delivered to Normandy.

There was the Jockey circuit in Provence; Scientist in Bordeaux; and Armada in north-east France. This latter group had pulled off some spectacular coups, crippling one of the Nazis' principal armaments factories and destroying the canal system that linked the Ruhr with the Mediterranean. They had also assassinated a dozen senior Gestapo officials.

And then there was Pimento, a highly competent circuit working around Montauban in southern France. It was composed of a dedicated group of *cheminots* or railway workers and led by Tony Brooks, a sparky twenty-one-year-old with a cheerful disdain for the Nazis' military might. Brooks was looking forward to future operations with all the zeal of a new-converted missionary. He was particularly pleased when Baker Street managed to deliver him (as requested) a large quantity of ground carborundum. It looked innocuous enough: a thick heavy-duty axle-grease. But Brooks knew that it contained an abrasive so powerful that it would wreck the inner workings of any machine. He was intending to have some fun with his magic grease, for he had found a most enticing target, one that the Germans had foolishly neglected to place under armed guard.

Colin Gubbins's biggest headache was supplying these willing volunteers with enough explosives. Over at the Air Ministry, Charles Portal consistently declined his requests for more planes. This, said Joan Bright, led to 'inter-departmental warfare of exceptional ferocity'. In the end, Winston Churchill swung his weight behind Gubbins and ordered Portal to massively escalate the air support for the French resistance. The weeks that followed saw a five-fold increase in the quantity of weaponry being dropped by parachute. By late spring, when plans for the Allied landings were advancing rapidly, some 4,000 tons of explosives had already been dropped into France, with a great deal more on the way. It was enough to play merry havoc with the occupying German Army.

General Eisenhower's decision to include sabotage and guerrilla warfare in his strategic planning for D-Day now placed Gubbins firmly in the spotlight. 'Transforming vision into reality', was how Joan Bright described his role. He was entrusted with plotting the destruction of targets 'that comprised strategic industries, power stations and rail and canal communications'. If these were hit, and hard, they would seriously hamper the German Army's capacity to defend the Normandy coastline.

Gubbins was given a second role that was to prove of even greater importance. He was to create elite guerrilla teams who were to be parachuted into France at the time of the Normandy landings. Their task was potentially game-changing: 'attacking vulnerable points and connections and preventing the Germans sending reinforcements to the beachheads'.[6] If successful, they could swing the military balance into the Allies' favour.

Gubbins already had a great deal of experience in establishing small teams entrusted with hit-and-run missions. It was exactly what Gus March-Phillipps's force had been created to do three years earlier. Now, this principle was to be replicated on an altogether grander scale. Gubbins was to set up ninety highly trained teams, each comprising three men, who were to be parachuted behind enemy lines. Their mission was so dangerous that it was to require the services of men who were not only uncommonly brave, but who also relished the chance to get their hands dirty.

Among the potential recruits summoned to Baker Street was Tommy Macpherson, a young Scotsman whose family was known to Gubbins. Macpherson was unclear as to why he had been called to this anonymous-looking office block, but was happy enough to chat about his wartime adventures, unaware that he was supplying Gubbins with exactly the information he wanted to hear.

Macpherson had quite a story to tell, for he had seen enough action to put most men off war for life. He had signed up for the Scottish Commandos, taken part in the disastrous attempt to assassinate Rommel and been imprisoned in Italy's notorious Camp 5: 'the camp for bad boys', as he called it. He escaped, was recaptured and then escaped again, this time from a prison camp in Austria. By the time he made it back to his native Scotland, he was already missing the war. 'I was feeling refreshed and ready to re-enter the fray.'[7] This was music to Gubbins's ears. He thanked Macpherson for his time and said he would be contacted in due course.

Macpherson left the Baker Street offices not 'at all certain what the interview was about'.[8]

He was one of a stream of young men who passed through the Baker Street headquarters in the early months of 1944, aware of little more than the fact that they were being vetted for some sort of highly dangerous mission. Gubbins personally conducted the interviews, for he was acutely conscious of the importance of selecting the right men. Joan Bright continued to see him in snatched moments after work and noticed that his grief over young Michael had been transformed into a deep sense of purpose. Each interview he undertook, each new recruitment, 'was a virtuoso performance', she said, in which he was brutally honest about the risks that lay ahead. Few declined the opportunity to serve under him, for he had 'a gift of inspiring confidence and in many cases a loyalty amounting to devotion'. They looked upon him with something akin to hero-worship and he, in return, found it 'gratifying to be accepted by these intelligent and dashing young men, not only as their commanding officer, but as a battle-scarred member of their own tribe'. Yet he found this intense personal leadership 'emotionally exhausting'. Joan, of course, knew why: 'Michael's death had been a tragic reminder of how blindly war destroys its victims.'[9]

The elite teams that Gubbins was recruiting were to consist of 300 men – British, American and French – who would operate in specialist units of three (ideally one from each nationality). The name of these teams, Jedburghs, was chosen at random from a Ministry of Defence codebook. Tommy Macpherson felt it was singularly appropriate, since 'the Borders town of Jedburgh was home to the sorts of rugged scampers I'd like to be sent into battle with.'[10]

Each new recruit was whisked off to Milton Hall, an imposing country house near Peterborough, where they learned of their role as a 'unique fighting force' that would help to determine the outcome of the war. Dropped by plane behind enemy lines, their task was 'to stir up the resistance, harass enemy movements and tie down as many German divisions as possible'.[11] In short, they were to stop Hitler's reserve divisions reaching Normandy.

There was no time for endurance training in Arisaig. Instead, Eric Sykes was brought down to Milton Hall in order to teach them all the usual tricks: the Japanese strangle, the baton cosh and the rock-crusher, as well as how best to dislocate a man's spine. 'The finishing touch is a quick snap upwards and backwards,' he would say.[12] The victim would never walk again.

The Milton Hall course was a distillation of everything that had been learned over the previous four years: silent killing, sharp-shooting and knife-fighting. Once completed, the men were put through George Rheam's intense sabotage programme. They were also trained in the use of limpets, clams and 'a variety of dirty trick gadgets for exploding car tyres, destroying the bearings of tanks, anti-personnel mines of one kind or another, and similar'.[13] At one point a big game hunter from Africa was brought in to show them how to kill farm animals and guard dogs by slicing through the windpipe, 'the head pulled back and the neck bone severed'. Done correctly, it could be achieved 'without a single sound from the beast'.[14]

As the sabotage course reached its conclusion, Macpherson was told that he had passed with flying colours and was being promoted to major in charge of his own three-man team. It was now up to him to pick two other men for his little unit, which was given the codename Quinine.

His first choice was one of the more colourful trainees at Milton Hall. Michel Bourbon, as he was known to his comrades, was actually Prince Michel de Bourbon-Parma and was related to many of the most illustrious dynasties of Europe. He had been taken to America in 1940, when the Nazis overran France, and packed off to school. But Michel was hungry for action and enlisted in the army when he turned sixteen. After a brief induction in America, he was shipped to Britain for more specialist training, first in the Scottish Highlands and then at Milton Hall, where his verve and derring-do made a particularly deep impression on Macpherson. 'Exceptional,' he said. 'A man of great courage and determination, whose unbreakable good humour and genial calm can transform into epic spates of Gallic volatility at any moment.'[15]

Macpherson's second recruit was Arthur Brown, a wireless operator, whose task would be to keep them in touch with London. 'Clearly very able,' noted Macpherson as he observed his skill at signalling. Brown himself was rather surprised to have survived the course, since most of his friends had been rejected. 'Week by week, those who displayed character weaknesses or, in one way or another, showed themselves unlikely to stay the course, were quietly weeded out and sent back to their units.'[16] This was a mission for which only the very finest were selected.

There was one last matter that Macpherson had to attend to before his team was deployed and that was to visit General de Gaulle and pick up his authority to operate in France. It was a formality, but an important one: Macpherson headed to the Hyde Park head-quarters of the French government-in-exile to receive his papers. 'I hear you're going to France,' said de Gaulle as Macpherson was ushered into his presence. 'I won't wish you luck. I disapprove of your mission and that of your colleagues. No one should be going to France without my command.'[17]

Somewhat taken aback by de Gaulle's lack of gratitude for a guerrilla mission that might cost him his life, Macpherson mumbled something about taking orders from his superiors. De Gaulle nodded and reluctantly authorized the paperwork.

On his return to Milton Hall, Macpherson and his two comrades were supplied with their last piece of kit: the cyanide pills that were to be taken in the event of their capture. Prince Michel was told 'to pop the pill in our mouth, hold it in our cheek and if it became necessary, we were to bite down and take a deep breath'. Within a few seconds, it would be 'goodbye Charlie'.[18]

In the days that preceded the Allied landings – in barns, cellars and underground hideouts across France – Gubbins's saboteurs sat huddled next to their clandestine wireless sets listening to the coded *messages personnels* transmitted by the BBC. These would tell them exactly when to go into action.

For many, the signal came in the early hours of 6 June, when the first Operation Overlord vessels were already crossing the English Channel. Gubbins himself spent that night in his office in a state of nervous excitement, aware that the ultimate showdown was entering its definitive stage. 'On the house opposite my window, the wind-cowl on the chimney was flying round at fantastic speed. The invasion had already been postponed twenty-four hours owing to the weather but now the incredible armada was on its way, come hell or high water.'[19] It was the make or break moment: Gubbins had staked everything on his saboteurs being able to stage hundreds of devastating hit-and-run operations.

It was an equally nerve-racking time for the men and women on the ground in France. At last, after months of preparation, the destruction could begin. Under the cover of darkness, teams crept out into the blustery night, their knapsacks filled with explosives. Bridges were blown, vital junctions destroyed and all the roads leading to Normandy scattered with tyre-busters. The railways were hit particularly hard, with the system cut in almost 1,000 places. Gubbins would later learn that this was more than the British and American air forces had achieved over the previous two months.

Every devious device invented by Millis Jefferis's team at the Firs was put into action as a systematic campaign of destruction got under way. Limpets, clams and L-Delays were all used to target installations of vital importance to Hitler's army. But this was merely the opening overture. As a weak dawn broke through the sky on 6 June – a squally day in northern France – and the greatest amphibious force in history began landing on the beaches, the German divisions stationed inland were to find that it would be a day of many unwelcome surprises.

Field Marshal Erwin Rommel was in overall command of the defences of France's northern coastline. He had long argued of the importance of throwing every possible resource against the anticipated Allied landings. Indeed he believed it a strategic imperative to prevent the Allies from establishing a bridgehead in Normandy. To do this would require troops that were stationed across France.

One of his most formidable fighting forces was the 2nd SS Panzer Division Das Reich, commanded by General Heinz Bernard Lammerding. The Das Reich was stationed at the town of Montauban, just north of Toulouse, having been moved there six weeks earlier on the grounds that it would be conveniently placed to intervene on both the southern and northern coasts of France, the two possible areas where the Allies might land. Feared as much as it was respected, this crack division was one of the great SS forces of the Third Reich.

It had fought with distinction (and horrific brutality) in the mighty battles of the Eastern Front and its commander, General Lammerding, had proved particularly ruthless, liquidating entire villages whose inhabitants stood in his way. It represented one-tenth of the entire German armoured strength in the west and had the potential to push the Allies back into the sea. Not only did it have more than 200 heavy tanks and assault guns, but its recruits were inspired by its illustrious military record. General Lammerding himself had already won two Iron Crosses. If he could kick the Allies from the Normandy beaches, he would surely win a third.

Moving such a huge division was a logistical nightmare. Heavy tanks could not travel by road over long distances: they were slow, guzzled fuel and their tracks ripped up the tarmac surfaces and rendered them impassable. They needed to be transported to Normandy on flatcars – transporters – that had been specially designed to sit low on the track in order that the tanks could pass through the numerous tunnels of the Massif Central.

The importance of these flatcars had not gone unnoticed by young Tony Brooks and his network of saboteurs in the Pimento circuit. For weeks, he had been waiting to use his pots of carborundum, the sticky axle grease laced with abrasive. Now, in the hours before the Allied landings, his time had finally come. Tipped the wink by Baker Street, his team – which included two young sisters, one sixteen, the other fourteen – launched their highly idiosyncratic war of sabotage against the Das Reich division. Brooks had located every tank transporter in the Montauban region. Now, under the mantle of darkness, his fellow saboteurs siphoned off the axle oil, replaced it with carborundum and then vanished into the night.

Amid the spectacular explosions that took place on that night in June, Brooks's contribution seemed too small to be significant. But he knew differently. His sticky paste was to give General Heinz Lammerding a surprise he would never forget. And it was not the only surprise being prepared for the general.

Tommy Macpherson and his two comrades were handed their orders on 5 June, just a few hours before the Allied landings. Each Jedburgh team had been assigned its own geographical area in which to operate, and his was to be in the Massif Central, just to the north of Montauban. His three-strong group was dropped by plane and met by a 'reception committee', a local partisan group, who could help them identify the most important targets for destruction.

Macpherson was the first to jump from the Halifax, closely followed by Michel Bourbon and Arthur Brown. The plane's pilot had correctly identified the landing ground and the men landed 'smack-bang among our host', illuminated by the light of a gleaming moon. As Macpherson unstrapped his parachute, he overheard one of the partisans calling to his leader: 'Chef, chef, there's a French officer and he's brought his wife.' Macpherson smiled to himself. 'I was wearing my Cameron Highlander's uniform, with a battledress top and kilt, and over that my jumping smock.' The young lad saw the kilt, mistook it for a dress and thought Macpherson was a woman.

Macpherson's first impression of the local resistance was positive. Their leader, Bernard Cournil, was 'a splendid, large, jovial fellow of great courage and initiative'. It was he who had organized the dropping zone and he, too, who had brought four ox-drawn carts to help transport the nine metal containers of explosives that had also been parachuted from the plane. They were to be hidden in woodland owned by a taciturn and toothless peasant named Monsieur Puech, 'as strong as one of his own bulls and enormously reliable to his friends'.[20]

After a few hours' rest, Macpherson and his two comrades were introduced to the other members of the resistance. They were disappointed to find that the group consisted of 'a dozen rugged, ill-armed men with no contacts of any sort'.[21] This was not a force equipped to fight the Nazis and Macpherson immediately realized that if he was to wreak carnage, it would be entirely down to his own initiative. 'Unless things changed radically,' he said, 'we weren't going to be causing the Germans any discomfort at all.'

Over a cup of acorn coffee, he quizzed Bernard Cournil about strategically important railway lines in the vicinity. Cournil said the one most used by the German Army was the Aurillac to Maurs branch line, just seven miles away. Macpherson decided to blow one of the bridges as a warm-up exercise, killing any German guards if necessary. 'We certainly had the means to do so,' he said. 'In the containers that had dropped with us there were Sten guns, rifles, ammunition, a bazooka, a small two-inch mortar with ammunition and a couple of smoke bombs, a crate of grenades and, finally, the Army's favourite light machine gun, a Bren gun.'

Heavily equipped with explosives, his team crept to the bridge, reconnoitred it and laid their charges. They blew with a tremendous bang and had a dramatic effect on the Frenchmen, just as Macpherson had anticipated. 'From that moment on, they were enthusiastic participants, eager to strike a blow against the Germans at every opportunity.'[22]

They were soon to find themselves with a far more spectacular target. Macpherson and his team were taking shelter in a farmyard when two members of the local resistance pitched up on a motorbike. Breathless with excitement, they brought news that a huge, heavily armoured panzer division was grinding its way northwards along the *route nationale*. It made for an unforgettable sight: some 1,400 tanks and armoured cars churning the highway into a thick cloak of dust. The air was filled with the roar of engines, the stench of diesel and the metallic crunch of tank tracks on tarmac. The infantry was following in the wake of the vehicles: 15,000 men dragging their military hardware northwards along the D940.

If Field Marshal Rommel had got his way, General Lammerding's division would have reached Normandy within hours of the Allied landings. But the German high command was in such a state of confusion – and its communications system so crippled by sabotage – that fully twenty-eight hours passed before the general received his orders to head for Normandy. The delay was regrettable but not disastrous. The Das Reich division operated like a well-oiled machine, driven with ruthless determination by its much decorated commander. It could still reach northern France in time to avert a catastrophe.

General Lammerding's senior staff officer, Albert Stuckler, immediately swung into action, issuing an order that all tanks and heavy guns were to be transported to Normandy by rail transporter. It was an order that could not be fulfilled. He was brought the unwelcome news that every single transporter had inexplicably seized up. Their axles were locked and their wheels refused to budge. It was as if they had been fused by rust. Tony Brooks's pots of carborundum had worked their lethal magic, just as he had hoped, and Obersturmbannführer Albert Stuckler had the unenviable task of informing General Lammerding that the entire armoured column of the SS Das Reich would have to grind its way northwards by road. It was a disastrous and wholly unexpected setback.

It was 450 miles to the north coast, a journey that was likely to take a minimum of seventy-two hours. General Lammerding's map revealed but one route to take as he prepared to thrust his panzer division northwards. The *route nationale* struck like an arrow through central France, spearing its way through the towns of Brive, Limoges and Poitiers. The road crossed a landscape of loosely folded fields, scooped valleys and dramatic escarpments, crossing bridges and viaducts that ought to have interested General Lammerding, an engineer by profession. They also ought to have interested him as an army commander, for such countryside was a guerrilla's dream.

News of Tommy Macpherson's presence in the area soon reached local resistance leaders, one of whom approached him and asked for help in staging a rapid frontal attack on the Das Reich column of vehicles. Macpherson refused point-blank. 'It is the absolute antithesis of guerrilla warfare to group people together,' he told the man, 'because the moment they're grouped together, they're easy meat for regular forces to mop up.' He added that attacking the bridges and viaducts of the *route nationale* was likely to prove more effective – and less costly in human lives – than targeting Hitler's most battle-hardened troops.

The French leader went away in a fury, hurling accusations at Macpherson and saying that the British 'weren't pulling their weight'.[23] He decided to press ahead with his attack without Macpherson's support, leading his men into action at the little village of Bretenoux. They paid a high price for their valour. Eighteen of the French fighters were killed in a shoot-out with the crack troops of Das Reich.

Macpherson's training at Milton Hall had taught him that guerrilla warfare was about hitting hard and running fast. Now, as dusk fell over the Massif Central, he planned a textbook sabotage operation that he intended to put into action with immediate effect: 'a whole series of daring ambushes to slow down the Germans'. His priority was not to attack the convoy, nor even to engage it, but to slow it to a snail's pace. 'Lots of small operations, hit over a wide area of ground.' He had his own mantra, one he transmitted to his French comrades-in-arms. 'Don't get caught. Get away. Be a will-of-the-wisp.'[24]

General Lammerding knew that his division was at its most vulnerable while on the move and had therefore taken the decision to bring it to a standstill each evening. On this particular night, the tanks and armoured carriers were parked in makeshift camps and placed under heavy guard. Then, after a snatched supper, the Germans bedded down. They were oblivious to the fact that they were being spied on by Tommy Macpherson.

'I was able to move through the thick screen of trees and bushes that flanked the road.' He was pleased to note that 'as well as trucks and partly armoured half-track trucks, there were tanks and armoured cars stretching out as far as we could see down the road.'

In the low moonlight, Macpherson reconnoitred the road ahead in order to work out the best places to ambush the column. The division had halted in three separate encampments and there was a considerable distance between each. Macpherson decided that striking in these gaps would cause maximum chaos and confusion. He and his team spent the rest of the night preparing a series of surprises for General Lammerding.

As the sun rose on the following morning, the air was filled with the 'almighty noise of every engine in the column starting up'.[25] One by one the vehicles swung on to the route nationale as they continued their journey northwards. It was not long before they were brought to a halt at the first of Macpherson's roadblocks. Two felled trees lay across the road and blocked the convoy's passage, bringing every tank to a standstill. The lead vehicle – an armoured car – was followed by a half-track containing half a dozen troops. The men got out and 'walked up to the barrier, scratched their heads and talked to the armoured car chaps'. The driver then tried to use his vehicle to push the trees out of the way, but Macpherson's men had brought down two of the biggest trees and the armoured car didn't have the necessary power.

There was then a wait of several hours as a much heavier vehicle was summoned from the rear of the convoy. This was a powerful tank support vehicle that was equipped with a bulldozer and scoop. It succeeded in clearing the trees, but only with great difficulty and the whole operation took more than three hours. As the troops made their way back to their vehicles, one of Macpherson's men, who had been watching the entire debacle from the wooded roadside, opened fire with his Sten gun. The Germans dived for cover and then prepared to return fire, but they could not work out where the bullets were coming from. Macpherson's man was able 'to skip into cover, disappear down the hill and get away safely'.[26] Macpherson's first surprise had delayed the Germans by more than four hours.

His next trap concealed a nasty sting. A few kilometres further along the road, his men had felled two more trees, once again blocking the convoy's passage, 'only this time I put our only two anti-tank mines underneath them, well-camouflaged with dust and gravel'. When the convoy was forced to stop for a second time, the troops were so worried about being ambushed again that they remained in their vehicles until the entire roadside had been swept by infantry brought up from the rear. 'All this took a nice lot of time,' noted Macpherson. Only once they had given the all-clear could the tank support vehicle be brought into action and shift the trees. As it began to push the heavy tree trunks from the road, there was a blinding flash and devastating blast as the anti-tank mine exploded underneath the vehicle's tracks, 'causing it to slew across the road and rendering the road completely impassable'.[27] Macpherson felt a satisfying sense of glee. 'It meant a very long delay while they sent for another heavy vehicle.'[28]

And so his devious game continued for the rest of the day: trees felled, booby traps hidden in the branches and the occasional burst of Sten gunfire to hinder the Germans yet further. After just two days on the road, General Lammerding was in a state of despair. Even the Eastern Front hadn't been this bad. His panzer division had set off from Montauban in an orderly column. Now, after repeated ambushes and breakdowns, it had covered less than fifty miles and was dispersed across three French *départements*. The true picture was even bleaker. After consulting with his regimental commanders, he learned that six out of every ten tanks had broken down due to driving on tarmac. The half-track vehicles had fared a little better, but at least a third of them had become unserviceable. In a progress report, Lammerding said that the tanks alone would require four days for repairs, assuming that spare parts were forthcoming. But this seemed increasingly unlikely, for he had been brought intelligence that widespread sabotage to the railway system had cut all the main lines. In a note of rage, he said that 'terrorists' – his word for the resistance – had achieved 'the complete crippling of rail movement'.[29]

Das Reich continued to lurch its way northwards at an agonizingly slow pace, hindered by ambushes, blown bridges and an almost total lack of spare parts. It eventually staggered into the town of Tulle, at which point it was beyond the reach of Tommy Macpherson and his area of operations. He and his men had done all they could to slow its progress. Now, the work was passed to a new group of guerrillas, who scored the singular coup of kidnapping one of General Lammerding's senior officers, Major Helmut Kämpfe. He was never seen again.

Das Reich had a reputation for ruthlessness and it now revealed this as it passed through the village of Oradour. In retaliation for the capture of Major Kämpfe – and a blaze of partisan activity around the town of Tulle – 624 inhabitants of Oradour were slaughtered in cold blood.

Macpherson remained coolly detached from such reprisals, aware that they were part of the price of war. 'We were there for a major objective of helping win a singularly bloody war,' he said. 'If we could expedite the end of the war by making the landings more successful, then we were saving more casualties than we could possibly have caused.'[30]

Das Reich's journey to Normandy should have taken no more than seventy-two hours. Instead, it took seventeen days for the main body to arrive, and it was even longer before the last of the vehicles reached the battlefield. By the time General Lammerding's men and tanks were ready for action, it was too late. The Allied beachhead was secure.

As the Allied armies began the long thrust eastwards towards the frontiers of the Third Reich, even Gubbins accepted that the time for sabotage and guerrilla warfare was almost at an end. He had always hoped that France would prove his finest hour. This had indeed proved to be the case.

'A spectacular success', was Joan Bright's assessment of Gubbins's Jedburgh teams: they had pulled off audacious acts of sabotage across the length and breadth of France. Gubbins himself was quietly satisfied. 'We are in good heart,' he admitted in a memo to an absent Peter Wilkinson. He added that he no longer had 'to cheat and crawl' – his expression for dealing with Whitehall officials – and had been at the receiving end of 'the highest unsolicited testimonies'.[31] These had come from General Eisenhower, the chiefs of staff and even General Montgomery, who had mistrusted guerrilla warfare ever since Gubbins's men had sabotaged one of his lectures back in the summer of 1940.

It was to take many weeks for a full assessment of the contribution that the Jedburgh teams had brought to the Allied landings, but when it came, it vindicated Gubbins's belief that carefully planned sabotage could cripple a modern army. General Eisenhower's staff at the Supreme Headquarters of the Allied Expeditionary Force said that the Jedburghs had 'succeeded in imposing more or less serious delays on all the divisions moved to Normandy'. This had prevented Hitler from striking back in the crucial opening hours of Operation Overlord.

Eisenhower's staff singled out the work of Tommy Macpherson and his comrades-in-arms for particular praise. The most 'outstanding example was the delay to 2nd SS Panzer Division', they said, and added that such operations had 'made a substantial contribution to the victory of the Allied Expeditionary Force'. General Eisenhower added a very personal endorsement, agreeing that the work carried out under Gubbins's leadership played 'a very considerable part in our complete and final victory'.

Others were swift to add their praise. Lord Mountbatten had worked closely with Gubbins ever since the triumphant raid on St Nazaire. Now, as he read the official report on the Jedburghs' triumph, he expressed his wholehearted agreement with its conclusions. He said it was 'one of the most thrilling accounts of operations in this war and must make you and your whole organisation feel very proud'.

Hugh Dalton, the first ministerial head of Baker Street, laid all his praise at Gubbins's feet. In a private letter, he wrote that 'the growth of this great instrument of yours, from my small beginnings, reflects very great credit on you who planned its growth and triumph.' Even King George VI wrote to Gubbins to express 'his hearty congratulations'. It was a job well done.

Gubbins was anxious to share the praise, aware that his wartime successes would not have been possible without his inner circle of experts: Millis Jefferis, Cecil Clarke, Eric Sykes, William Fairbairn and George Rheam. He was also quick to point out the real heroes were the men and women who had dared to operate behind enemy lines. Their work had been 'one long continuous struggle, with torture and unbelievable suffering and death waiting round every corner and at every moment'. Yet for all the risks, he had never been short of volunteers, fearless heroes who 'dedicated themselves to a cause they knew to be higher than self'. They had risked their own lives in order to save those of others.

The final word went to Edward Grigg, Minister Resident in the Middle East. He met some of those who had taken part in Gubbins's sabotage missions and could scarcely believe the eye-stretching stories that spilled from their lips. They were more exhilarating than any novel, more colourful than any film. 'I trust the epic for which they were responsible will be written and published as soon as possible,' said Grigg. 'They have worked and dared with such amazing secrecy that few at home have the remotest inkling of their existence, far less of their achievements.'

He felt sure that their spectacular acts of destruction would one day go down in history 'as proof that the spirit of Elizabethan times is still alive in all its brilliant daring'. But until that happened, he could only be grateful to have had the honour of paying tribute to 'a most Gallant Company of Gentleman Adventurers'.[32]

Epilogue

MILLIS JEFFERIS'S TEAM at the Firs continued to work a sixteen-hour day right through to the armistice on 8 May 1945: in the months that followed the Normandy landings there had still been the need for mortars, detonators and booby trap devices. Not until Jefferis received confirmation that the war in Europe was finally over was everyone permitted to lay down their tools.

Stuart Macrae felt sure that after five long years of intense work, the team would celebrate with equal intensity, yet even he was surprised by the scale of the revelries. 'Everybody went mad,' he said as he watched all 250 staff head straight to the bar. He assumed that Jefferis would play no part in the celebrations – wrongly, as it transpired. It was Jefferis who set the tone for the antics that were to follow. 'Millis, having stoked up nicely in the bar, collected a Sherman tank from the ranges and contrived to get it into our front drive.' Then, cranking up the engine – and with him at the controls – he slammed it into a constant spin, with spectacular results. As it whizzed round and round at increasing speed, it flung all the gravel outwards in an arc of flying stones. He then hit and burst the water mains, putting it completely out of action. Macrae was relieved when Jefferis 'got tired before knocking down any walls and decided to go home without the tank'.

But the tank's role in the festivities was not over yet. Macrae's wife, Mary, had been busily sluicing her way through the bar, along with one of the Firs's old hands, Brian Passmore. When they spied the tank outside, they 'thought it would be a good idea if they went off for a ride in this machine, although Brian had no idea how to drive it'. Off they went, clattering down the main street in Whitchurch towards the village of Oving, accompanied by a boisterous crowd of revellers until – as Macrae put it – 'they came over all religious and decided to go to church to give thanks.' Macrae only learned what happened next when he received a frantic phone call from an Oving local who reported seeing a large tank charging towards the main door of the church, where its passage was blocked by the low lintel. The revellers, Macrae was told, were 'having trouble to get the tank to go inside'.[1] But the church's woes were not yet over. One of the Firs's senior staff, Norman Angier, fired off a powerful rocket that he had brought with him and managed to score a direct hit on the crypt. 'Oh what fun,' noted a sardonic Macrae in his diary.[2]

The revelry continued until the early hours. Explosives were detonated and spigot mortars fired into the skies above Whitchurch. On that joyful armistice night, many people up and down the country watched fireworks' displays. But the villagers of Whitchurch were treated to a spectacle they would never forget. It was as if the sky itself were exploding.

Everyone awoke the next morning with sore heads, only to discover that Jefferis had reinstated the sixteen-hour day. The war in the Far East was far from over and the Americans were placing orders on a scale that outmatched even Baker Street. Yet even with the new workload, there was a sense that the end was finally in sight. Macrae and his team felt 'like people who had been pushing a bus up an incline for a long while and now saw it disappearing over the top'.[3]

The Firs was to have one final role to play and it was a spectacular one. The Americans had been deeply impressed by Millis Jefferis's hollow-shaped charge and were keen to develop it further. Jefferis himself could not be spared for a lengthy trip to America, so in early 1944 he had sent his young protégé, James Tuck. Tuck was immediately taken to Los Alamos to work on America's nuclear programme.

It soon became apparent that he had brought a solution to a hitherto intractable problem. The Americans were unable to produce enough uranium to make two atomic bombs in the short time available, obliging them to use plutonium for their second nuclear warhead. But this required a wholly different method to detonate it: indeed, it needed a massive force to trigger the violent implosion of the bomb's two masses. Millis Jefferis's hollow charge was now fine-tuned by the brilliant young Tuck and incorporated into the triggering device for the Nagasaki bomb. It was an extraordinary postscript to the work of the Firs.

On 16 August 1945, the morning after VJ Day, 'everything went flat as a pancake'. After five years of working with relentless energy, Macrae said that 'the spirit had suddenly gone out of us and there was no incentive to go on.'[4] It was as if they had been working on adrenalin for the last five years, and that the adrenalin had abruptly ceased to flow.

The sense of gloom only increased when Macrae picked up alarming rumours that the Firs might not survive the post-war era. These rumours were fuelled by the news that Millis Jefferis had been offered the job of Chief Engineer to the Indian Army, a post he promptly accepted. At Churchill's insistence, Jefferis was also made a Knight Commander of the British Empire and promoted to acting major-general.

With Jefferis's departure from the Firs, Stuart Macrae was placed in temporary charge of the place and 'fought like a wild cat to save it', aware that many of his old enemies were plotting to have it closed down. He felt sure that Winston Churchill would have guaranteed its future, if only he had won the 1945 general election. But he had lost and with his defeat went any long-term hope of saving the facility. 'It was now more than ever evident that the plan was to wipe MD1 off the earth as completely as possible,' said Macrae. In October – less than eight weeks after VJ Day – a Whitehall bureaucrat bluntly informed him that 'the plant must go, the equipment must go and the staff must go'.

A swansong party was held in the second week of November and the staff celebrated until dawn, aware that they were fast approaching the end of an era. A few of the more fortunate members of staff were to find themselves transferred to other military departments. The rest were allowed to remain on short-term contracts until the spring of 1946, when they were all fired. 'This left the way clear for the Ministry of Works to tear down all the factory equipment, load it together with most of the machinery into trucks and take it to Wescott' – a government research establishment – 'where it was thrown on the rubbish dumps.'

Macrae surveyed the wreckage in a state of blank incomprehension. 'The Americans envied us and freely admitted that they could not rival us here. We had the materials, the men, the equipment and the know-how.' They also had a glittering track record. Professor Lindemann had tried to keep a tally of the numbers of weapons produced by the Firs during the long years of war. The exact total was impossible to compute, but it included at least 3½ million anti-personnel mines, 1½ million sticky bombs, 1 million puff-balls and 2 million anti-aircraft fragmentation bombs, not to mention the many millions of innovative booby traps, specialist explosives and complex fuses. This had all been done on an annual budget of £40,000 and by a staff of just 250 people. It was an astonishing achievement.

But Macrae had always known that the success of the Firs was also its greatest weakness: other ministries had wanted the place shut down ever since the spring of 1940. Now the war was over, they saw their chance for revenge. 'It was totally destroyed through jealousy,' he said.

Macrae had been the first person to visit the Firs; it was appropriate that he was the last one to leave, packing his bags in the autumn of 1946. Before he left, Winston Churchill had requested that he collect one example of every weapon produced by the team. These were to be saved for the nation and given to the Imperial War Museum where they could be put on special display. Churchill was anxious that the efforts of Jefferis's workforce should have some sort of public recognition.

Macrae set to the task with as much enthusiasm as he could muster, handing over limpets, sticky bombs and any number of booby traps. But it was all to no avail. None of them went on display, and nor was there to be any mention of MD1 in the museum's exhibits about the war.

'We created an establishment which contributed more to the war effort than any other weapons design department,' said Macrae. But it was an establishment so ungentlemanly in its outlook that it was to be for ever erased from history.[5]

Colin Gubbins faced a similar problem at the war's end. As an increasing number of countries fell under Allied control in the early months of 1945, so the area in which his saboteurs could operate became correspondingly restricted. Some of his more audacious Jedburgh teams were transferred from France to South-East Asia, along with a small army of saboteurs from the Balkans. Here in the sweltering tropics, amid mango swamps and malarial marshland, their training at Arisaig and Brickendonbury proved its worth. Joan Bright was to hear many stories of their derring-do and concluded that they were 'as outstandingly successful in jungle warfare as they had been with the European Resistance'.[6]

By the time Japan surrendered in the summer of 1945, Gubbins was in command of a slick, well-oiled machine. Baker Street's success was no longer in question: one expert contended that it had proved a great deal more efficacious than Bomber Command, especially in France. For four years, Arthur Harris and Charles Portal had sent wave after wave of bombers across the English Channel and had made 'much larger holes in the ground [than Baker Street] and damaged a great deal more inessential property'. Gubbins's saboteurs, by contrast, had crippled ninety Nazi-run factories – factories essential to Hitler's war machine – and put them completely out of action 'with a total load of explosives that was less than that carried by one light bomber'.[7] And that, of course, had been just one small part of their work.

In spite of the successes, Peter Wilkinson overheard rumours that the new government was planning budget cuts and dismissals: he felt sure that Baker Street's days were numbered. In the post-war world 'there were few peaks left to conquer' – indeed there was none – and when Wilkinson paid a visit to Gubbins, he found him 'depressed and preoccupied with the search for tasks which would hold the organisation together in the post-war years'.[8]

It was to prove a forlorn search. Even Winston Churchill had privately accepted there was no longer any place for an organization dedicated to sabotage and guerrilla warfare. When the ministerial head of Baker Street, Lord 'Top' Selborne, had asked for support in safeguarding its future, he received a most disappointing reply. 'My dear Top,' wrote Churchill, 'the part which your naughty deeds in war play, in peace cannot at all be considered.'[9]

Selborne reminded Churchill that Gubbins had created 'a highly specialised weapon which will be required by His Majesty's Government whenever we are threatened'. But he knew, deep down, that Gubbins and his inner circle would be 'put to sleep' – a sleep 'from which they will never wake up'.[10]

Gubbins clung to the hope that he could preserve 'a skeleton headquarters in some dark corner of Whitehall'.[11] It was not to be. The Labour victory in the 1945 election sealed the fate of Baker Street, just as it had sealed the fate of the Firs. The new Foreign Secretary, Ernest Bevin, wrote a stiffly formal letter to Gubbins on behalf of the government expressing his 'high appreciation of your distinguished service'.[12]

His words signalled the death warrant for Baker Street: it was to be abolished with the same secrecy as it had originally been established. On 15 January 1946, five months to the day after the Japanese surrender, Gubbins's outfit was dissolved at the stroke of a pen. The staff was to be dismissed, the buildings returned to civilian use. No one would ever know of the extraordinary missions that had been orchestrated from Number 64 Baker Street.

It was a curiously bland end to the most swashbuckling organization ever to be sponsored by a British government. Ernest Bevin's letter of valediction made no mention of the audacious undercover operations, the daring acts of destruction, the demolition of bridges and railways. There was no mention of the 7,500 successful air sorties that had seen hundreds of brave men and women parachuted into occupied lands. Nor was there any mention of the fact that guerrilla movements in Greece and the Balkans, led by men like Eddie Myers and Chris 'Monty' Woodhouse, had tied down fifty enemy divisions in the most critical phase of the war. But perhaps the most striking omission in Bevin's letter was that there was no mention of Gubbins's inner circle of brilliant, devious and wildly creative experts, without whom there would have been no guerrilla warfare.

The closure of Baker Street spelled doom for all its offshoot stations up and down the country. Arisaig House in the Scottish Highlands was returned to its owners, who dismantled the firing ranges and 'killing rooms' in the cellars and restored the place to something resembling a family home. Brickendonbury Manor – Station 17 – was to have an even less glamorous post-war role. Over the previous five years it had played host to some of the most daring gentlemen adventurers of the Second World War. Now, it was acquired by the Highways Department of the local county council. One of their first acts was to slick the damaged walls with government-issued mustard-brown paint.

One by one, the requisitioned properties were returned to their rightful owners, often in a sorry state of disrepair. Their plaster was chipped, their furniture broken and their once immaculate croquet lawns pitted with craters. The wartime story of these houses was to remain an absolute secret. No one was ever to know of the ungentle-manly antics that had been taught behind closed doors.

And what of the gentlemen themselves? What of Gubbins's elite circle of mavericks who had worked so assiduously during the long years of war? A Special Confidential Report produced shortly before the armistice acknowledged Eric Sykes as the consummate master of silent killing. 'Few equals and no superior,' was the verdict. But Sykes was also to be one of the war's final casualties. Four days after the armistice with Germany was signed, on 12 May, he died of a heart attack 'caused by overwork, anxiety and standing about in snow, rain and mud'. He had told a female friend that 'he didn't want recognition' and nor did he want medals or honours. All he wanted – all he had ever wanted – was to preserve the lives of as many of Gubbins's saboteurs as possible. His death was a sad end to a brilliant, complex individual who, in the words of his unnamed lady friend, was 'the kindest, straightest man I have ever known'.[13]

Sykes's partner-in-crime, William Fairbairn, fared rather better. His genius in knife-fighting and the martial arts was recognized by the American government, which honoured him with the Legion of Merit for his work at Camp X. 'Outstanding ability',[14] was the verdict of William 'Wild Bill' Donovan, who knew that Fairbairn's training had saved the lives of hundreds of American servicemen. Fairbairn had a curriculum vitae unlike any other and it was to stand him in good stead in the post-war world. He spent time training Singapore's anti-riot squad before moving to Cyprus, where he taught SWAT teams in counter-insurgency tactics.

Millis Jefferis headed to India at the end of 1945 in order to take up his post as Chief Engineer to the Indian Army. He found it a strange experience to be in the regular army, where rules and regulations were there to be obeyed. In a letter to Professor Lindemann, he spoke of his hankering for the old days. 'I expect I shall find my way back to unorthodoxy again.'[15]

In those post-war years, he was to find himself granted an honour that was both unsolicited and surprising. The Royal Commission on Awards to Inventors offered him a six-figure sum in recognition of his pioneering wartime inventions. Jefferis was gratified but turned it down. 'His Edwardian principals of right and wrong were very strong,' said his son John.[16] He did not believe he should profit from having helped to defeat Hitler.

When he died in September 1963, his obituary in *The Times* betrayed little about his wartime work, describing him as 'a backroom boy' who had somehow earned himself a KBE.[17] It was left to Macrae to produce a more compelling portrait of the complex and idiosyncratic Jefferis. He could be irritable, moody and introverted, as Macrae knew only too well, but he was also intensely loyal and – whisky in hand at the end of a sixteen-hour working day – a most genial companion-in-arms.

George Rheam had been the last member to join Gubbins's inner circle but he had swiftly made himself indispensible, displaying his mastery of the sabotage brief when planning the Norsk Hydro mission. He found it hard to return to civilian life after the exhilaration of the war. In the immediate aftermath of the conflict, he wrote a secret report on the decisive role that sabotage had played in the Allied victory. He was looking forward to the next war with a glint of malice and hoped that sabotage would this time begin at the very outbreak of hostilities. If so, he intended to play a leading role, aware that 'it will have an immediate and decisive influence on the course of events.'[18]

Cecil Clarke's war came to an end with the closure of the Firs. His last invention was a monstrous steel bridge-laying contraption whose name, Great Eastern, was a doff-of-the-cap towards Isambard Kingdom Brunel. It was a beast of a machine, equipped with a massive girder ramp that enabled tanks to cross the canals and rivers of Holland, whose bridges had been destroyed by the Nazis. In building such a monster, Cecil Clarke's war had turned full circle. He had first come to the notice of Winston Churchill on account of his vast digging machine. Now, his final project was even more lavish in scale.

The first ten Great Easterns had been shipped to the Continent in the dying months of 1944, but they came too late in the day. Clarke was furious that they had not been more useful and told his son of his 'private disgust and disappointment' that the Germans had surrendered before his machine could prove its worth.[19] It was as if Hitler had personally insulted him.

Clarke returned to LoLode in November 1945 and continued to build state-of-the-art trailers and caravans. He spent his leisure hours designing labour-saving domestic contraptions that proved rather less efficient than the weapons he had built during the war. His daughter-in-law Ann was on hand to see the test drive of his homespun pressure cooker. 'It exploded,' she said, 'and bits of chicken had to be picked out of the kitchen ceiling.'[20] Indeed everything that Cecil touched in that post-war period seemed to explode, even his jars of homemade tomato soup. They blew up in the larder, splattering everything with fermented juice.

Clarke's wartime work had seen him devise some fiendishly powerful weapons. But the mass destruction caused by the bombs dropped at Hiroshima and Nagasaki so appalled him that he became an enthusiastic member of the Campaign for Nuclear Disarmament and continued to lobby against nuclear weapons until his death in 1961. In common with many of Gubbins's men, he was a gentle individual who turned his talents to destruction only because Hitler had forced his hand.

Gubbins had been aided throughout the long years of war by two formidable ladies, Joan Bright and Margaret Jackson. Joan's wartime had been rather more extraordinary than most. She had always aspired to be at the vanguard of a feminist revolution and so it proved to be. After leaving Gubbins's service, she was hired to run the Secret Intelligence Centre of the Cabinet War Rooms, with custody over all the greatest wartime secrets. Later, she was given a new role as personal assistant to General Hastings 'Pug' Ismay, with near constant access to Churchill. Indeed, she travelled with Churchill to the Yalta summit, meeting with Stalin and Roosevelt, as well as accompanying him to the summits at Teheran and Potsdam.

Joan briefly dated Ian Fleming – 'a ruthless man'[21] – and was rumoured to have been Fleming's model for Miss Moneypenny, James Bond's secretary. She later married Colonel Philip Astley, a specialist in political warfare, who had previously been married to Madeleine Carroll, the world's highest-paid actress at the time. Many years after the war, in collaboration with Peter Wilkinson, Joan wrote a book about Colin Gubbins's outstanding role as maestro of sabotage and guerrilla warfare. She lived until the ripe age of ninety-eight, dying in 2009.

Margaret Jackson also had a distinguished post-war career. She first joined the Allied Commission for Austria, taking all the notes at the quadripartite meetings. Later, she worked for the Organisation of European Economic Cooperation, which implemented the Marshall Plan for the reconstruction of a continent shattered by war. Margaret had once jested that her ardent desire in life was to make men fall in love with her, yet she remained single until her death in 2013, aged ninety-six.

Colin Gubbins kept in regular touch with both Margaret and Joan: they remained bright links to a war that had cost him his marriage and his elder son. The armistice brought a further blow, leaving him without gainful employment. His first post-war job was with a rubber company, but he found it deeply uninspiring and soon quit. He was next offered a job in a textile firm run by his old Baker Street friend, Edward Beddington-Behrens, in whose Regent's Park mansion he had first interviewed recruits to the fledgling MI(R). But after the excitement of blowing up the Nazi war machine, selling carpets seemed dreadfully dull and humdrum.

There were the occasional bright moments. He was to find himself much decorated for his wartime work and even gained the grudging appreciation of General de Gaulle. The French general invested him with the Légion d'Honneur at a colourful military ceremony at Les Invalides, the first of a string of awards that Gubbins would receive from the grateful leaders of countries in which his saboteurs had operated.

In London, he devoted much of his time to establishing the Special

Forces Club, whose purpose was to foster the comradeship of the saboteurs and guerrillas who had survived the war. Here, he continued to meet with both Joan Bright and Margaret Jackson in order to reminisce about the old times. The club exists to this day, housed in an anonymous red brick Edwardian mansion in one of the quieter streets behind London's Sloane Square. If you succeed in getting inside – and make your way to the bar – you'll likely as not find a handful of nonagenarian ladies, still formidable in spite of their vast age, who will spill you stories of the days when dashing young Colin was at the helm.

Gubbins hoped his greatest legacy would be the devotion to expertise: he wanted British Special Forces to be the best in the world. Yet his most enduring triumph was not to be found in Britain, nor even in Europe, but across the ocean in North America. He had travelled to Washington shortly before the war's end and been astonished by the 'lavish scale' of Wild Bill Donovan's guerrilla headquarters. He realized that the Office of Strategic Services was establishing itself as a 'serious institution' – one that intended to play a vital role in shaping the post-war world.[22]

He found it a humbling experience. Donovan's organization had been born out of the trip that the two of them had taken to the Scottish Highlands in 1940. Now, with President Truman in office, it was to be expanded, modified and given a permanent role in both America and the world. Today's CIA, as it became known, has a pedigree of which few are aware: it is the direct descendant of a tiny and secret organization that began life in a smoke-filled room in Caxton Street, St James's. It was here, back in the spring of 1939, that a giddy young secretary named Joan Bright first learned that the world was a more complex and far less gentlemanly place than she had ever imagined.

Gubbins had divorced Nonie in 1944: in 1950 he married his new love, a Norwegian widow named Anne Elise. Ever gracious, Nonie asked to meet his new bride and expressed her approval. She confessed that she'd never really understood Colin's 'blythe spirit', as she put it.[23] He was too energetic, too charismatic, too relentlessly dynamic for a wallflower like her.

In the summer of 1975 Gubbins and Anne Elise decided to move to Harris, in the Outer Hebrides. This was where Gubbins felt truly at home, amid the limpid sea lochs and windblown headlands. Here, just sixty miles from Arisaig, was a place to reflect on everything that had passed.

The two of them were settled in by Christmas and were looking forward to their new life in the Highlands. But it was to be rudely cut short. After less than six weeks, Gubbins collapsed and died of a heart attack. He was seventy-nine.

His funeral eulogy was given by Peter Wilkinson, appropriately enough, since he had been Gubbins's first recruit to Caxton Street. 'Whatever Colin Gubbins was called on to do in his long life,' he said, 'he not only did it extremely well, but he contrived in the process to make life extraordinarily rewarding and agreeable for anyone who had the good fortune to be with him.'

Gubbins had fought a good war. And so had those who had fought it with him.

Acknowledgements

This book has brought out a destructive tendency in me that I never knew existed. For some years now, I've crossed Chelsea Bridge each morning as I make my way to the London Library, pausing for a moment to gaze at the eddying river, the seabirds and the exposed mudflats of the Thames foreshore. But ever since embarking on *The Ministry of Ungentlemanly Warfare*, I've found myself examining instead the bridge's vast iron girders and working out where I would plant my explosives if I were attempting to blow it up.

Sabotage is by its very nature a subversive business: after two years spent researching this book, I can understand why Colin Gubbins and Millis Jefferis were so careful to ensure that information about irregular warfare was kept under wraps. It was essential that documents, diagrams and technical drawings did not fall into the wrong hands.

Their caution made researching the book a tricky business, for information is not readily forthcoming. Even Gubbins's handbook, *The Art of Guerrilla Warfare*, is extremely hard to find in its original form.

I owe a debt of gratitude to descendants of the principal characters in the book – the saboteurs, guerrillas and creative architects of destruction – who have preserved a wealth of material in lofts and wardrobes.

John Jefferis (Millis's son) was not only generous with his time, but also made available to me his family's extensive archival material. Without these letters, diary extracts and anecdotes, my account of life at the Firs would have been much the poorer. Other members of the extended Jefferis family also gave their help and agreed to be interviewed.

Thank you to Ann Clarke, daughter-in-law of Cecil Clarke, for generously welcoming me into her Plymouth home and allowing me access to her impressive family archive. 'I've got a spare bedroom full of Cecil's letters and papers,' she told me when I first contacted her in the autumn of 2014. This was no exaggeration: she had boxes of documents, diagrams and photographs, including letters from Winston Churchill himself. Thank you also to the Reverend David Clarke, Cecil's son, for regaling me with colourful family stories.

I am grateful to John Macrae, son of Stuart Macrae, for allowing me to quote extracts from his father's informative and highly entertaining book, *Winston Churchill's Toyshop*. Thank you also to Amberley Publishing, who have republished this book.

Thank you to Tony and Peter Goodeve, sons of Charles Goodeve, for providing a great deal of background information about their father's ground-breaking inventions. Goodeve's extraordinary wartime work is much in need of a full-length study.

I owe gratitude to Gordon Rogers, who has spent half a lifetime gathering information on the Firs. Not only did he provide me with photocopied documents from various archives, but he also provided me with contact details for experts in the field of Second World War sabotage. Mr Rogers gives regular talks about the work of Millis Jefferis and the team at the Firs; more details can be found on his website: www.gordonrogers.co.uk.

Much of this book has been researched in specialist archives. Thank you to the staff of the Churchill Archives Centre at Churchill College, Cambridge, which houses all of the surviving archive of the Firs, along with much other material that proved of use, particularly for the chapter on Colin Gubbins's Norwegian campaign.

Sincere thanks to the ever-helpful staff at the archive of the Imperial War Museum who helped me locate a great deal of hitherto unknown material. I spent many fruitful hours in the museum's archives during the autumn and winter of 2014, when the museum was closed to the public for its extensive renovation. The constant crashes and bangs caused by workmen demolishing walls provided a fitting soundtrack to my sabotage researches.

I would particularly like to thank Jane Fish, senior curator of the IWM film archive, for allowing me to view the transcripts of Carlton

Television's series *Churchill's Secret Army*, broadcast in 2000. Carlton's in-depth interviews with saboteurs such as Tommy Macpherson – and secretaries such as Margaret Jackson – proved invaluable. Sadly, many of these interviews never made it into the final documentary.

Thank you to the staff at the National Archives, where so many surviving documents relating to individual guerrilla operations are now safely housed. Some of the files – notably those concerning Operation Josephine B, Operation Gunnerside and Operation Anthropoid – contain a wealth of information.

I am grateful to John Andrews of the Special Forces Club for his help in putting me in touch with various survivors of the grand old days, notably Kay O'Shanohun,

Thank you to the staff of the British Library, with particular mention to Steven Dryden of the sound team, who kindly commissioned (at my request) a digital copy of an inaccessible master-tape interview with Colin Gubbins and others.

Thank you also to the staff at the Liddell Hart Centre for Military Archives in King's College, London; to Laura Dimmock-Jones of the Royal United Services Institute for finding a very rare account of Colin Gubbins's guerrilla operations in Norway, 1940; and to Lydia Saul, Keeper of Social History, Cecil Higgins Museum, Bedford.

I would also like to thank Bernard O'Connor for his help, as well as Bill Tibbits, whose grandfather lost his life in the raid on St Nazaire.

A warm thank you, as ever, to the staff of the London Library, where so much of this book was written. A handful of library regulars – writer friends – generously offered their time in order to read the book and make much needed suggestions. I am particularly grateful (in alphabetical order) to Peter Ettegui, John McNally, Rick Stroud and Rupert Walters.

Thank you to my wonderful agent, Georgia Garrett at Rogers, Coleridge and White, and also to Emma Patterson, for seeing the project through from half-baked idea to completed book. Thanks also to RCW's foreign sales team for their usual sterling work.

Roland Philipps, my editor at John Murray, was instrumental in launching my writing career some two decades ago when he published *Nathaniel's Nutmeg*. Separated by force of circumstance, but never out of touch, we are once again under the same publishing roof. I am delighted that Roland was so quick to see the potential of the book; grateful, too, that he has proved such a capable, generous and experienced editor.

I would also like to take this opportunity thank the rest of the John Murray team who work so tirelessly behind the scenes: Becky Walsh, Yassine Belkacemi, Rosie Gailer, Ross Fraser and Ben Gutcher. Also, to Juliet Brightmore for help with the plate sections and to Morag Lyall for her eagle-eyed copy-editing.

Thank you equally to my film and television agent, Rob Kraitt of Casarotto Ramsey and Associates, and to other players in the screen world who have provided much encouragement and support: Tom Mangan and Kit Golden in New York; Shawn Slovo and David Freeman in London.

Lastly, the warmest of thanks (as ever) to the home team: my girls – Madeleine, Héloïse and Aurélia – who have grown up in an environment where creativity always goes hand in hand with angst. It remains to be seen whether the creative urge will rub off on them.

As ever, my most sincere thanks and gratitude go to Alexandra, who has always been ready to break off her own creative endeavours in order to indulge mine. Her support, encouragement and advice are deeply appreciated.

Illustration Credits

Akg-images: 14 below. Alamy: 10 above left/Pictorial Press Ltd. Bundesarchiv, Bild: 1011-065-2302-31/Koch: 9 above right. Courtesy of Ann Clarke: 1 below left, 2 below left, 3 above, 6 below right. © Crown Copyright/OGL v3.0: 7 centre left, 8 below right, 9 centre right, 10 centre left and centre right, 11 centre left. Getty Images: 12 above/Keystone. Greek Railways: 11 above. Greynurse at the English Language Wikipedia/licensed under the Creative Commons Attribution-Share Alike 3.0: 3 below right. © Andrew Hackney: 4 below. Courtesy of the family of Knut Haukelid/*Skis Against the Atom*, 1954, by Knut Haukelid: 12 below left (still from *The Fight for the Atomic Bomb* 1948, Hero-Film/Le Trident), 13 above left and below right. Hodder & Stoughton Publishers: 4 centre. Courtesy of John Jefferis: 7 below right, 8 above right and centre left. Keystone-France/Gamma-Keystone via Getty Images: 10 below. Courtesy of John Macrae and Amberley Publishers *Winston Churchill's Toyshop* 2012, by Stuart Macrae: 1 below right, 2 above right and below right, 5 below, 6 centre and below left. © The National Archives, London: 8 below left, 14 above left. © National Museums Scotland: 15 above right. Courtesy of the Norwegian Resistance Museum: 13 below left. Private collections: 2 centre right, 3 below right, 4 above left, 7 above left, 13 above right, 14 centre. Courtesy of the family of Joachim Rønneberg: 12 below right. *School for Danger* 1947, produced for the Central Office of Information by the RAF Film Unit: 16 above and centre. Courtesy of the Special Forces Club: 2 above left, 3 below left, 16 below. Tabor of Aylesbury: 5 above (postcard *The Firs, Whitechurch, Aylesbury*). © Andrew Tibbits: 9 centre left. TopFoto: 1 above/Roger-Viollet, 6 above left, 7 centre right, 9 below. Courtesy of Philip Vickers/*Das Reich* Battleground

Europe 2000, Leo Cooper, Pen & Sword Books Ltd: 15 below. ©
C. M. Woodhouse *Something Ventured*, Granada Publishing 1982: 11
below right.

Every reasonable effort has been made to trace copyright holders, but
if there are any errors or omissions, John Murray will be pleased to
insert the appropriate acknowledgement in any subsequent printings
or editions.

Notes and Sources

Abbreviations

CC: Churchill Archives Centre, Cambridge
CP: Cherwell Papers, Nuffield College, University of Oxford
IWM: Imperial War Museum archives
LH: Liddell Hart Centre for Military Archives, Kings College, London
NA: National Archives
RUSI: Royal United Services Institute

Prologue

1. Joan Bright Astley, *The Inner Circle: A View of War at the Top*, Hutchinson, 1971, p.31.
2. IWM: Documents 16248: Private Papers of Professor D. Dilks.
3. Astley, *Inner Circle*, p.31.
4. IWM: Documents 16248.
5. Astley, *Inner Circle*, p.31.
6. Stuart Macrae, *Winston Churchill's Toyshop*, Roundwood Press, 1971, p.8. My account of the work of Millis Jefferis and Stuart Macrae at Portland Place and the Firs is derived from two principal sources, Macrae's book and the extensive archive of the Firs's work now housed in the Churchill Archives Centre in Cambridge under the general shelfmark MCRA 1-6. There is also impressive documentation of the Firs's work in the Cherwell archive, Nuffield College, University of Oxford. This has proved most useful in assessing the work of the Firs.

Chapter 1: The Third Man

1. *Caravan and Trailer*, April 1937, p.269.
2. BBC *People's War* interview with John Vandepeer Clarke, www.bbc.co.uk/history/ww2peopleswar/stories/34/a5961134.shtml
3. Stephen Bunker, *The Spy Capital of Britain: Bedfordshire's Secret War*, Bedford Chronicles Press, 2007, p.14.
4. Bernard O'Connor, *Nobby Clarke: Churchill's Backroom Boy*, Lulu Press, 2007, p.5.
5. *Caravan and Trailer*, June 1937, p.443.
6. Macrae, *Toyshop*, p.7.
7. Ibid., pp.1–6.
8. Ibid., p.6.
9. 'Memel in the Reich', *The Times*, 23 March 1939.
10. Keith Feiling, *The Life of Neville Chamberlain*, Macmillan, 1946, p.404.
11. Macrae, *Toyshop*, pp.8, 9.
12. BBC *People's War* interview with John Vandepeer Clarke, www.bbc.co.uk/history/ww2peopleswar/stories/34/a5961134.shtml
13. Macrae, *Toyshop*, pp.10, 11. See also 'Limpet Bomb', *The Times*, 17 November 1953.
14. Astley, *Inner Circle*, p.34.
15. Joan Bright Astley and Peter Wilkinson, *Gubbins and SOE*, Pen & Sword, 1993, p.35.
16. IWM: Documents 16248.
17. Astley, *Inner Circle*, pp.32, 33.
18. Ibid., p.34.
19. Peter Colley in Astley and Wilkinson, *Gubbins*, p.28.
20. Astley, *Inner Circle*, p.34.
21. Astley and Wilkinson, *Gubbins*, pp.7, 9.
22. IWM: Documents 12618.
23. Peter Colley in Astley and Wilkinson, *Gubbins*, p.28.
24. Astley and Wilkinson, *Gubbins*, p.18.
25. Ibid., pp.26, 34.
26. IWM: Documents 18587: Interview with Sir Peter Wilkinson.
27. Astley and Wilkinson, *Gubbins*, p.35.
28. IWM: Documents 12618.
29. Astley, *Inner Circle*, p.34.

Chapter 2: Thinking Dirty

1. 'The Sword', *The Times*, 22 March 1937.
2. 'The Sword', *The Times*, 29 March 1937.
3. 'Use of Force', *The Times*, 27 May 1937.
4. 'Use of Force', *The Times*, 10 June 1937.
5. http://www.theyworkforyou.com/debate/?id=1940-05-08a.1326.1
6. Astley, *Inner Circle*, p.34.
7. John Jefferis, *The Life and Times of Millis Jefferis*, privately published memoir, n.d.
8. Astley, *Inner Circle*, p.34.
9. *Royal Engineers Journal*, vol. 77, December 1963.
10. Jefferis, *Jefferis*, pp.39, 123.
11. Macrae, *Toyshop*, pp.16, 12, 33.
12. Astley, *Inner Circle*, p.36.
13. Macrae, *Toyshop*, pp.33, 19, 59.
14. Bickham Sweet-Escott, *Baker Street Irregular*, Methuen, 1965, p.24.
15. Macrae, *Toyshop*, p.13.
16. Astley, *Inner Circle*, p.36.
17. Peter Wilkinson, *Foreign Fields*, I.B. Taurus, 1997, p.62.
18. Vera Long in IWM: Documents 16248.
19. James Darton in ibid.
20. Vera Long in ibid.
21. Astley and Wilkinson, *Gubbins*, p.28.
22. Astley, *Inner Circle*, p.37.
23. Ibid., p.39.
24. Wilkinson, *Foreign Fields*, p.68.
25. Astley, *Inner Circle*, p.39.
26. Ibid., p.41.
27. Wilkinson, *Foreign Fields*, pp.85, 86.
28. Stephen Dorril, *MI6*, Fourth Estate, 2000, p.250. For more detail on the possible identity of Professor Sandwich, including interviews with survivors, see Brian Johnson, *The Secret War*, BBC Books, 1979, chapter 6.

Chapter 3: Making Bangs for Churchill

1. The king's speech is cited in *Historic Royal Speeches and Writings* (online): www.royal.gov.uk/pdf/georgevi.pdf

2. Ann Hagan interview with John Clarke for Bedford Museum.
3. Astley, *Inner Circle*, p.39.
4. Macrae, *Toyshop*, p.27.
5. Astley, *Inner Circle*, p.40.
6. Ibid.
7. Sweet-Escott, *Baker Street Irregular*, p.17.
8. Astley, *Inner Circle*, p.40.
9. Macrae, *Toyshop*, pp.17, 178, 18, 26.
10. Ibid., *Topshop*, p.59.
11. A.J.P. Taylor, *English History*, Clarendon Press, 1965, p.444.
12. Macrae, *Toyshop*, p.61.
13. Late 1930s advert cited on http://www.gracesguide.co.uk/Boon_and_Porter
14. Macrae, *Toyshop*, pp.29, 23.
15. Ibid., p.11.
16. Sweet-Escott, *Baker Street Irregular*, p.31.
17. Macrae, *Toyshop*, pp.21, 178, 22.
18. Ibid., p.20.
19. Ibid., p.25.
20. Ibid., p.31.
21. Winston Churchill, *The Second World War*, Cassell, 1948–54 (6 vols.), vol. 2, p.321.
22. NA: WO32/5184 and WO32/5185.
23. Macrae, *Toyshop*, p.32.
24. Churchill, *Second World War*, vol. 1, p.456.
25. Macrae, *Toyshop*, p.31.
26. Hastings Ismay, *The Memoirs of General the Lord Ismay*, Heinemann, 1960, p.172.
27. Macrae, *Toyshop*, pp.31, 33, 35.
28. Ibid., p.45.
29. Ibid., p.35.
30. Churchill, *Second World War*, vol. 1, p.574.
31. Churchill, *Second World War*, vol. 2, p.36.
32. Macrae, *Toyshop*, p.51.
33. Churchill, *Second World War*, vol. 2, p.583.

Chapter 4: Sweet Fanny Adams

1. Astley and Wilkinson, *Gubbins*, p.47.
2. Ibid.

3. Kim Philby, *My Silent War*, MacGibbon & Kee, 1968, chapter 1.
4. Astley and Wilkinson, *Gubbins*, p.49.
5. Wilkinson, *Foreign Fields*, p.87.
6. IWM: Documents 14093, John McCaffery, 'No Pipes or Drums' (manuscript).
7. *Pittsburgh Press*, 19 September 1939, p.8.
8. Ernest Turner, *The Phoney War on the Home Front*, Michael Joseph, 1961, chapter 12.
9. www.warsailors.com/homefleet/shipsp.html
10. Nicholas Rankin, *Ian Fleming's Commandos*, Faber & Faber, 2011, pp.69, 70.
11. Astley, *Inner Circle*, p.43.
12. NA: HS 8/263.
13. Astley, *Inner Circle*, p.44.
14. NA: HS 8/263.
15. RUSI: Anon., 'An Interlude in the Campaign in Norway', *Journal of the United Service Institution of India, 1941*.
16. Ibid., p.27.
17. NA: WO 168/103.
18. Macrae, *Toyshop*, p.65.
19. NA: HS 8/263.
20. Macrae, *Toyshop*, p.66.
21. NA: CAB 65/7/1.
22. Jefferis, *Jefferis*, p.66
23. NA: CAB 65/7/1.
24. Ibid.
25. E.H. Stevens, *The Trial of Nikolaus von Falkenhorst*, William Hodge, 1949, p.xxix.
26. François Kersaudy, *Norway 1940*, HarperCollins, 1990, p.45.
27. Astley and Wilkinson, *Gubbins*, p.52.
28. Ibid.
29. Colin Gubbins, *The Art of Guerrilla Warfare*, Ministry of Information, 1939.
30. Anon., 'Interlude', p.30.
31. Rankin, *Commandos*, p.71.
32. Gubbins, *Art of Guerrilla Warfare*.
33. NA: WO 168/103.
34. Ibid.
35. Anon., 'Interlude', p.30.
36. NA: WO 168/103.
37. Captain William Fell, CC: Fell 2/3.

38. Astley, *Inner Circle*, p.44.
39. Astley and Wilkinson, *Gubbins*, pp.68, 67.
40. Anon., 'Interlude', p.34.
41. IWM: Documents 12618.
42. Colin Gubbins, Introduction to Knut Haukelid, *Skis Against the Atom*, North American Heritage Press, 1989.

Chapter 5: The Wild Guerrillas of Kent

1. Cecil Clarke, *The Development of Weapon Potential*, Clarke Family Papers.
2. *The Times*, 9 September 1939.
3. NA: AVIA 11/2.
4. NA: PREM 3/320/1.
5. NA: AVIA 11/2.
6. Astley, *Inner Circle*, p.45.
7. Astley and Wilkinson, *Gubbins*, p.46.
8. Comer Clarke, *England Under Hitler*, New English Library, 1972, pp.104–6 (a copy of this scarce book is available at the IWM).
9. Ibid.
10. David Lampe, *The Last Ditch*, Cassell, 1968, p.65. See also Sweet-Escott, *Baker Street Irregular*, p.38.
11. Clarke, *England*, pp.104–6.
12. Astley and Wilkinson, *Gubbins*, p.69.
13. Clarke, *England*, pp.104–6.
14. Gubbins in Leo McKinstry, *Operation Sealion*, John Murray, 2014, pp.263–4.
15. Astley and Wilkinson, *Gubbins*, p.69.
16. IWM: Documents 16248.
17. Lampe, *Last Ditch*, p.80.
18. Donald Hamilton-Hill, *SOE Assignment*, William Kimber, 1973, p.13.
19. Astley and Wilkinson, *Gubbins*, p.69.
20. Lampe, *Last Ditch*, p.82.
21. Astley, *Inner Circle*, p.76.
22. Clarke, *England*, pp.104–7.
23. Lampe, *Last Ditch*, p.91.
24. IWM: Documents 12618.
25. Clarke, *England*, pp.104–7.
26. Peter Fleming, *Invasion 1940*, Rupert Hart-Davis, 1957, p.70.

27. McKinstry, *Sealion*, p.18.
28. William Shirer, *The Rise and Fall of the Third Reich*, Secker & Warburg, 1961, p.782, citing army directive from Von Brauchitsch.
29. Hamilton-Hill, *SOE*, p.13.
30. Lampe, *Last Ditch*, pp.84–5.
31. McKinstry, *Sealion*, p.267.
32. Lampe, *Last Ditch*, p.102.
33. Sweet-Escott, *Baker Street Irregular*, p.36.
34. Macrae, *Toyshop*, pp.76, 124, 98, 125-6, 131.
35. Lampe, *Last Ditch*, p.103.
36. IWM: Documents 12618.
37. Henry Hall interview in McKinstry, *Sealion*, p.272.
38. Lampe, *Last Ditch*, p.98.
39. Wilkinson, *Foreign Fields*, p.102.
40. IWM: Documents 12618.
41. Churchill, *Second World War*, vol. 2, pp.584, 231.
42. Erich Raeder, *Grand Admiral*, Da Capo Press, 2000, p.324.
43. Astley and Wilkinson, *Gubbins*, p.74.

Chapter 6: The Enemy Within

1. Macrae, *Toyshop*, pp.61, 82.
2. CC: MCRA 2/2.
3. Gerald Pawle, *The Secret War*, Harrap, 1956, p.125.
4. Barnaby Blacker, *The Adventures and Inventions of Stewart Blacker: Soldier, Aviator, Weapons Inventor*, Pen & Sword, 2006, p.vii.
5. Macrae, *Toyshop*, p.79.
6. Jefferis, *Jefferis*, unpaginated.
7. Pawle, *Secret*, p.27.
8. Macrae, *Toyshop*, pp.85–6.
9. Ibid., p.96.
10. This and previous, Churchill, *Second World War*, vol. 2, p.294.
11. Macrae, *Toyshop*, p.179.
12. Ibid., pp.108, 87, 88.
13. CC: MCRA 4/1.
14. Macrae, *Toyshop*, pp.114, 99.
15. NA: CAB 121.
16. Hugh Dalton, *Fateful Years*, Frederick Muller, 1957, pp.366–7.
17. David Stafford, *Secret Agent*, BBC Books, 2000, p.12.

18. Brendan Bracken, in Mark Seaman (ed.), *Special Operations Executive: A New Instrument of War*, Routledge, 2005, p.62.
19. Dalton, *Fateful Years*, pp.367, 366.
20. Astley and Wilkinson, *Gubbins*, p.112.
21. Obituary, *The Times*, 13 August 1966.
22. Sweet-Escott, *Baker Street Irregular*, p.56.
23. Ibid., p.44.
24. Astley and Wilkinson, *Gubbins*, p.79.
25. Ibid., p.76.
26. Wilkinson, *Foreign Fields*, p.107.
27. Ewan Butler, *Amateur Agent*, Harrap, 1963, p.75.
28. Peter Wilkinson, in Russell Miller, *Behind the Lines*, Secker & Warburg, 2002, p.3.
29. Astley and Wilkinson, *Gubbins*, p.81.
30. Sweet-Escott, *Baker Street Irregular*, p.27.
31. Ibid., p.28.
32. Carlton TV interview with Margaret Jackson, IWM: Documents 23245.
33. Ibid.
34. 'Margaret's Secret War', *For a Change*, vol. 19, no. 4, August 2006.
35. Leo Marks, *Between Silk and Cyanide: A Codebreaker's War*, HarperCollins, 1999, p.346.
36. IWM: Documents 23245.
37. IWM: Documents 12618.
38. IWM: Documents 16248.
39. IWM: Documents 23245.
40. John Connell, *The House by Herod's Gate*, Sampson Low, Marston, 1947, p.19.
41. Sue Ryder interview, IWM: Documents 10057.
42. Astley and Wilkinson, *Gubbins*, p.96.
43. IWM: Documents 23245.
44. Philby, *Silent*, p.54.
45. IWM: Documents 23245.
46. Sweet-Escott, *Baker Street Irregular*, p.57.
47. IWM: Documents 23245.

Chapter 7: The First Big Bang

1. Macrae, *Toyshop*, pp.93–4.
2. Interview with Mrs Ann Clarke, 17 December 2014.

3. Des Turner, *Station 12: Aston House, SOE's Secret Centre*, History Press, 2006, p.184.

4. NA: HS 8/371.

5. Macrae, *Toyshop*, p.195.

6. Philby, *Silent*, p.49.

7. Peter Kemp, *No Colours or Crest*, Cassell, 1958, p.38.

8. Philby, *Silent*, p.8.

9. Macrae, *Toyshop*, p.195.

10. youtube.com/watch?v=-UlmaSMg104

11. Eveleigh Earle Denis 'Dumbo' Newman, interview, IWM 27463.

12. IWM: Documents 14093.

13. Sweet-Escott, *Baker Street Irregular*, pp.57, 53.

14. Brian Lett, *Ian Fleming and SOE's Operation Postmaster*, Pen & Sword, 2012.

15. Sweet-Escott, *Baker Street Irregular*, p.21.

16. M.R.D. Foot, *SOE in France*, Routledge, 2004, pp.153, 141.

17. NA: HS 6/347.

18. IWM: Interview 9421.

19. NA: HS 6/347.

20. www.bbc.co.uk/history/ww2peopleswar/stories/51/a5961251.shtml

21. *The Times*, 10 May 1941.

22. NA: HS 6/347.

23. Ibid.

24. Henri Noguères en collaboration avec M. Degliame-Fouché et J.L. Vigier, *Histoire de la Résistance en France de 1940 à 1945*, Robert Laffont, 1981.

25. NA: HS 6/347.

26. Foot, *SOE in France*, p.144.

27. NA: HS 6/347.

28. IWM: Documents 12618.

29. NA: HS 6/347 and HS 6/345.

Chapter 8: Killing School

1. Churchill, *Second World War*, vol. 4, p.536.

2. Macrae, *Toyshop*, pp.115, 114, 111, 99, 97, 110, 182.

3. CC: MCRA 4/1.

4. Pawle, *Secret*, p.8.

5. CC: GOEV 3/3.

6. Pawle, *Secret*, p.126.

7. Ibid., p.130.

8. Macrae, *Toyshop*, p.164.

9. Pawle, *Secret*, p.131.

10. Ibid., p.128.

11. Ibid., pp.134–5.

12. Ibid., p.130.

13. IWM: Documents 12618.

14. Sweet-Escott, *Baker Street Irregular*, p.63.

15. Kemp, *Colours*, p.23.

16. Sweet-Escott, *Baker Street Irregular*, p.37.

17. Roderick Bailey, *Forgotten Voices of the Secret War*, Ebury Press, 2008, p.49.

18. George Langelaan, *Knights of the Floating Silk*, Hutchinson, 1959, p.65.

19. Charles J. Rolo, *Major W.E. Fairbairn*, NA: HS 9/495/7.

20. Langelaan, *Knights*, p.65.

21. NA: HS 9/495/7.

22. Ibid.

23. Langelaan, *Knights*, p.65.

24. Peter Kemp in Tom Keene, *The Lost Band of Brothers*, History Press, 2015, p.32.

25. James Owen, *Commando*, Little, Brown, 2012, p.24.

26. Stafford, *Secret Agent*, p.27.

27. William Pilkington audio interview, IWM: 16854.

28. Bailey, *Forgotten*, p.45.

29. NA: HS 9/495/7.

30. Langelaan, *Knights*, p.67.

31. William Pilkington interview, IWM: 16854.

32. William Pilkingon audio interviews, ibid. and IWM: 18478.

33. Kemp, *Colours*, p.44.

34. Churchill, *Second World War*, vol. 2, p.217.

35. Marcus Binney, *Secret War Heroes: The Men of Special Operations Executive*, Hodder & Stoughton, 2005, pp.121–2.

36. Keene, *Lost*, p.54.

37. John Geoffrey Appleyard, *Geoffrey*, Blandford Press, 1945, p.44.

38. Lett, *Fleming*, chapter 7.

39. Suzanne Lassen, *Anders Lassen VC*, Frederick Muller, 1965, p.26.

Chapter 9: Gubbins's Pirates

1. *The Times*, 9 August 1941.
2. Keene, *Lost*, p.61.
3. Mike Langley, *Anders Lassen*, New English Library, 1988, p.87.
4. NA: HS 7/221.
5. Langley, *Lassen*, p.61.
6. Appleyard, *Geoffrey*, p.84.
7. Sir Richard Francis Burton, *Wanderings in West Africa*, Tinsley Brothers, 1863, vol. 2, p.295.
8. NA: HS 3/86.
9. Keene, *Lost*, p.84.
10. Colin Gubbins, *The Partisan Leaders' Handbook*, Ministry of Information, 1939.
11. Binney, *Secret*, p.127.
12. Keene, *Lost*, pp. 94–9.
13. Ibid., p.100.
14. NA: ADM 199/395.
15. NA: HS 3/87.
16. Appleyard, *Geoffrey*, p.72.
17. NA: HS 3/91.
18. Langley, *Lassen*, p.84.
19. Binney, *Secret*, pp.134–5.
20. Ibid., p.139.
21. NA: HS 3/91.
22. Keene, *Lost*, p.108.
23. Tim Moreman, *The British Commandos 1940–46*, Osprey Publishing, 2006, p.54.
24. NA: HS 3/91.
25. Ibid.
26. NA: HS 3/91.
27. Appleyard, *Geoffrey*, p.75.
28. NA: HS 3/91.
29. Ibid.
30. Binney, *Secret*, p.140ff.
31. Ibid., pp.140–1.
32. NA: HS 3/91.
33. Henrietta March-Phillipps, BBC interview in Keene, *Lost*, p.114.
34. NA: HS 3/91.

35. Henrietta March-Phillipps, BBC interview in Keene, *Lost*, p.114.
36. Binney, *Secret*, p.149.
37. NA: HS 3/87.
38. Binney, *Secret*, pp.147–8.
39. Ibid., p.147.
40. NA: ADM 116/5736.

Chapter 10: A Deadly Bang

1. IWM: Documents 12618.
2. Churchill, *Second World War*, vol. 4, p.98.
3. NA: DEFE 2/130.
4. Ibid.
5. Lucas Phillips, *The Greatest Raid of All*, Heinemann, 1958, p.23.
6. Astley and Wilkinson, *Gubbins*, p.98.
7. Phillips, *Greatest*, p.29.
8. IWM: Documents 12618.
9. Macrae, *Toyshop*, p.148.
10. Phillips, *Greatest*, p.92.
11. Ibid., p.55.
12. Ibid., p.58.
13. Macrae, *Toyshop*, p.155.
14. Corran Purdon, 'List the Bugle', in James Dorrian, *Storming St Nazaire*, Leo Cooper, 1998.
15. NA: HS 9/495/7.
16. Dorrian, *St Nazaire*, p.26.
17. Phillips, *Greatest*, pp.92–3.
18. Dorrian, *St Nazaire*, p.69.
19. Phillips, *Greatest*, p.83.
20. Ibid., p.109.
21. Ibid., p.127.
22. Dorrian, *St Nazaire*, p.126.
23. Phillips, *Greatest*, p.138.
24. Dorrian, *St Nazaire*, pp.134–6.
25. Ibid., p.137.
26. Phillips, *Greatest*, p.142.
27. Ibid., p.155.
28. Ibid., p.158.

29. Ibid., p.254.
30. Ibid., p.xvii.
31. Gubbins, *Art of Guerrilla Warfare*.

Chapter 11: Masters of Sabotage

1. Jefferis, *Jefferis*, unpaginated.
2. Macrae, *Toyshop*, pp.115, 112, 206, 183, 154, 101.
3. CP: Lord Cherwell letter to Churchill, 27 November 1942.
4. Gordon Rogers, *From Bangs to Black Holes*, pp.121–2.
5. Sweet-Escott, *Baker Street Irregular*, pp.101–2.
6. Astley and Wilkinson, *Gubbins*, p.93.
7. Ibid., p.115.
8. IWM: Documents 23245.
9. Dalton, *Fateful Years*, p.384.
10. Astley and Wilkinson, *Gubbins*, p.100.
11. Sir David Dilks (ed.), *The Diaries of Sir Alexander Cadogan, 1938–1945*, Cassell, 1971, p.437.
12. Astley and Wilkinson, *Gubbins*, p.112.
13. Dalton, *Fateful Years*, p.369.
14. Astley and Wilkinson, *Gubbins*, p.113.
15. Ben Pimlott (ed.), *The Second World War Diary of Hugh Dalton*, Jonathan Cape, 1986, p.128.
16. Sweet-Escott, *Baker Street Irregular*, p.125.
17. Astley and Wilkinson, *Gubbins*, p.102.
18. IWM: Documents 12618.
19. Astley and Wilkinson, *Gubbins*, p.116.
20. IWM: Documents 12618.
21. Astley and Wilkinson, *Gubbins*, p.28.
22. Letter to Joan Bright Astley in *Gubbins*, p.245.
23. IWM: Documents 23245.
24. Astley and Wilkinson, *Gubbins*, p.243.
25. Ibid., p.144.
26. S.G. Brandon and M. Elliot-Bateman (eds.), *The Fourth Dimension of Warfare*, Manchester University Press, 1970, p.104.
27. IWM: Documents 29955.
28. IWM: Documents 29955 (interview with Daphne Maynard).
29. Van Maurik in IWM: Documents 12618.
30. Margaret Jackson, IWM: Documents 23245.

Chapter 12: Czech-Mate

1. IWM: Documents 23245.
2. Astley and Wilkinson, *Gubbins*, p.83.
3. Frantisek Moravec, *Master of Spies: The Memoirs of General Frantisek Moravec*, Bodley Head, 1975, p.160.
4. Callum MacDonald, *The Killing of Obergruppenführer Reinhard Heydrich*, Macmillan, 1989, p.51.
5. Astley and Wilkinson, *Gubbins*, p.107.
6. Moravec, *Master*, p.211.
7. Leslie Horvitz and Christopher Catherwood, *Encyclopedia of War Crimes and Genocide*, Facts on File, 2006, p.200.
8. Mario Dederichs, *The Face of Evil*, Greenhill Books, 2006, p.92.
9. Astley and Wilkinson, *Gubbins*, p.107.
10. Moravec, *Master*, p.211.
11. Astley and Wilkinson, *Gubbins*, p.107.
12. Moravec, *Master*, p.209.
13. Astley and Wilkinson, *Gubbins*, p.107.
14. NA: HS 4/39.
15. MacDonald, *Killing*, p.116.
16. NA: HS 4/39.
17. Moravec, *Master*, p.215.
18. Ibid., p.212.
19. NA: HS 4/39.
20. Moravec, *Master*, p.212.
21. MacDonald, *Killing*, pp.100–102.
22. Moravec, *Master*, p.213.
23. Wilkinson, *Foreign Fields*, p.125.
24. Turner, *Aston*, p.110.
25. MacDonald, *Killing*, p.124.
26. Robert Harris and Jeremy Paxman, *A Higher Form of Killing*, Random House, 1982, p.94.
27. IWM: Documents 27463.
28. Cecil Clarke Family Papers.
29. Wilkinson, *Foreign Fields*, pp.125–6.
30. NA: HS 4/39.
31. Sue Ryder, *Child of My Love*, HarperCollins, 1986, p.78.
32. NA: HS 4/39.
33. IWM: Documents 80013010.

34. Moravec, *Master*, p.216.
35. MacDonald, *Killing*, p.172.
36. Moravec, *Master*, p.217.
37. NA: HS 4/39.
38. MacDonald, *Killing*, p.182.
39. Moravec, *Master*, p.210.

Chapter 13: Sabotage in the Mountains

1. Colin Gubbins, Introduction to Haukelid, *Skis*, p.2.
2. Sweet-Escott, *Baker Street Irregular*, p.64.
3. Stafford, *Secret*, p.89.
4. Gubbins, *Art of Guerrilla Warfare*.
5. C.M. Woodhouse, *Something Ventured*, Granada, 1982, p.21.
6. Obituary, *Guardian*, 20 February 2001.
7. Obituary, *The Times*, 10 December 1997.
8. E.C.W. Myers, *Greek Entanglement*, Alan Sutton Publishing, 1985, pp.14, 66.
9. Woodhouse, *Ventured*, p.25.
10. Myers, *Greek*, pp.27, 33.
11. Woodhouse, *Ventured*, p.32.
12. Stafford, *Secret*, p.95.
13. Woodhouse, *Ventured*, p.35.
14. Gubbins, *Art of Guerrilla Warfare*.
15. Woodhouse, *Ventured*, pp.39–41.
16. Myers, *Greek*, p.69.
17. Woodhouse, *Ventured*, p.42.
18. Myers, *Greek*, p.72.
19. Woodhouse, *Ventured*, p.43.
20. Myers, *Greek*, p.72.
21. CC: Macrae papers, MCRA 3/3.
22. Myers, *Greek*, pp.60, 74, 78.
23. Woodhouse, *Ventured*, p.48.
24. Myers, *Greek*, p.78.
25. Stafford, *Secret*, p.101.
26. Myers, *Greek*, p.80.
27. Stafford, *Secret*, p.101.
28. Myers, *Greek*, p.80.
29. M.B. McGlynn, *Special Service in Greece*, War History Branch, Department of Internal Affairs, New Zealand, 1953, p.13.

30. Myers, *Greek*, pp.81, 85.
31. C.M. Woodhouse, *The Struggle for Greece*, Rupert Hart-Davis, 1976, p.26.
32. Bailey, *Forgotten*, p.131.
33. Astley and Wilkinson, *Gubbins*, p.137.
34. NA: HS 5/346.

Chapter 14: Man of Steel

1. Ewen Southby-Tailyour, *Blondie: A Life of Lieutenant-Colonel H.G. Hasler*, Leo Cooper, 1998, p.123.
2. Letter from Gubbins to Clarke: Cecil Clarke Family Papers.
3. Cecil Clarke Family Papers.
4. Ibid.
5. Interview with Rev. David Clarke, 9 February 2015.
6. Macrae, *Toyshop*, pp.155–6.
7. NA: HS 8/415.
8. Ibid.
9. M.R.D. Foot, *Special Operations Executive*, Pimlico, 1999, p.90.
10. NA: HS 9/1250/7.
11. Ibid.
12. Foot, *Special*, p.90.
13. IWM: audio interview, 10057.
14. Bernard O'Connor, *Churchill's School for Saboteurs, Station 17*, Amberley Publishing, 2013, p.59.
15. IWM: Documents 12618.
16. Professor Lindemann in Ray Mears, *The Real Heroes of Telemark*, Hodder & Stoughton, 2003, p.80.
17. Stafford, *Secret*, p.105.
18. IWM: Documents 12618.
19. IWM: Documents 16489.
20. Gubbins, Introduction to Haukelid, *Skis*, p.6.
21. IWM: Documents 16489.
22. IWM: Documents 23245.
23. Gubbins, Introduction to Haukelid, *Skis*, p.4.
24. Bailey, *Forgotten*, pp.136, 48.
25. Hamilton-Hill, *SOE*, p.24.
26. Bailey, *Forgotten*, p.137.
27. Haukelid, *Skis*, p.43.

28. Mears, *Telemark*, p.117.
29. NA: HS 8/370.
30. Mears, *Telemark*, p.118.
31. NA: HS 8/370.
32. Bailey, *Forgotten*, p.138.
33. NA: HS 52/185.
34. Mears, *Telemark*, p.121.
35. Haukelid, *Skis*, pp.74–5.
36. Mears, *Telemark*, p.123.
37. Haukelid, *Skis*, pp.76–7.
38. NA: HS 52/185.
39. Haukelid, *Skis*, p.78.

Chapter 15: In the Bleak Midwinter

1. Haukelid, *Skis*, pp.46, 82.
2. J. Charrot, *Memoirs*, cited in O'Connor, *School*, p.215.
3. Haukelid, *Skis*, p.82.
4. Bailey, *Forgotten*, p.139.
5. Haukelid, *Skis*, p.83.
6. Ibid., p.162.
7. Mears, *Telemark*, p.140.
8. Haukelid, *Skis*, p.84.
9. Mears, *Telemark*, p.141.
10. IWM: Carlton TV interview, 23257.
11. Haukelid, *Skis*, p.87.
12. Ibid., pp.84–7.
13. Mears, *Telemark*, p.148.
14. Haukelid, *Skis*, p.100.
15. Ibid., p.97.
16. Ibid., p.12.
17. Mears, *Telemark*, p.154.
18. NA: HS 52/186.
19. Haukelid, *Skis*, p.108.
20. Ibid., pp.107, 100, 105.
21. Stafford, *Secret*, p.118.
22. Haukelid, *Skis*, p.109.
23. NA: HS 52/186.
24. IWM: Carlton TV interview, 23257.

25. NA: HS 52/186.
26. IWM: Carlton TV interview, 23257.
27. NA: HS 52/186.
28. Mears, *Telemark*, p.161.
29. Haukelid, *Skis*, pp. 112–13.
30. Ibid., p.112.
31. Ibid., p.113.
32. Mears, *Telemark*, p.163.
33. NA: HS 52/186.
34. Haukelid, *Skis*, pp.113–14.
35. IWM: Carlton TV interview, 23257.
36. Stafford, *Secret*, p.122.
37. NA: HS 52/186.
38. Mears, *Telemark*, p.206.
39. Sweet-Escott, *Baker Street Irregular*, p.114.
40. NA: HS 52/186.
41. Mears, *Telemark*, p.169.
42. NA: HS 52/185.
43. Mears, *Telemark*, p.180.
44. NA: HS 2/173.
45. NA: HS 52/189.
46. Mears, *Telemark*, p.224.
47. NA: HS 52/189.
48. Ibid.

Chapter 16: Enter Uncle Sam

1. Macrae, *Toyshop*, p.209.
2. Ibid., p.206.
3. Edward Daily, *My Time at The Firs*: www.whitchurch.org/assets/other/my-time-at-the-firs-2
4. Ibid.
5. Macrae, *Toyshop*, p.114.
6. Jefferis, *Jefferis*, unpaginated.
7. Macrae, *Toyshop*, p.189.
8. Ibid., p.189.
9. Ibid.
10. CP: Professor Lindeman letter to Winston Churchill, 27 February 1942.

11. Ibid.
12. Ibid.
13. CP: BBC broadcast transcript, 6 February 1944.
14. Macrae, *Toyshop*, p.192.
15. Charles Rolo, NA: HS 9/495/7.
16. IWM: Documents 16248.
17. Miller, *Behind the Lines*, p.62.
18. Sweet-Escott, *Baker Street Irregular*, pp.131, 143, 133.
19. Nelson Lankford, *The Last American Aristocrat*, Little, Brown, 1996, p.136.
20. Henry Hyde in Max Hastings, *Das Reich*, Michael Joseph, 1981.

Chapter 17: Gubbins's Trojan War

1. Foot, *SOE in France*, p.256. The exact content of the message is disputed, with several variants. Maurice Buckmaster claims it was the message cited above.
2. Bailey, *Forgotten*, p.30.
3. NA: HS 9/1204/3.
4. Stephen Hawes and Ralph White, *Resistance in Europe*, Viking, 1975, p.25.
5. François Marcot, 'La direction de Peugeot sous l'Occupation: pétainisme, réticence, opposition et résistance', in *Le Mouvement Social* (no. 189), Éditions de l'Atelier, 1999, p.28.
6. Astley, *Inner Circle*, p.129.
7. Foot, *SOE in France*, p.15.
8. Chris Everitt and Martin Middlebrook, *The Bomber Command War Diaries*, Pen & Sword, 2014, entry for 15–16 July 1943.
9. Maurice Buckmaster, *They Fought Alone*, Odhams Press, 1968, pp.55–6.
10. E.H. Cookridge, *They Came from the Sky*, Heinemann, 1965, p.46.
11. NA: HS 9/1240/3.
12. Harry Ree, 'Experiences of an SOE Agent in France' in Brandon and Elliot-Bateman, *Fourth Dimension*, p.121.
13. NA: HS 9/1240/3 and Buckmaster, *Alone*, p.156.
14. Cookridge, *Sky*, p.7.
15. Binney, *Secret*, p.204.
16. Hawes and White, *Resistance*, p.44.
17. NA: HS 9/1240/3.
18. Hawes and White, *Resistance*, p.44.

19. Buckmaster, *Alone*, p.157.
20. NA: HS 9/1240/3.
21. Buckmaster, *Alone*, pp.157–8.
22. Ibid., p.158.
23. NA: HS 9/1240/3.
24. Buckmaster, *Alone*, p.158.
25. NA: HS 9/1204/3.
26. Bailey, *Forgotten*, p.189.
27. NA: HS 9/1204/3.
28. Bailey, *Forgotten,* pp.189–90.
29. NA: HS 9/1240/3.
30. NA: HS 8/370.

Chapter 18: Fighting with Hedgehogs

1. Pawle, *Secret*, p.130.
2. Macrae, *Toyshop*, p.137.
3. Pawle, *Secret*, p.131.
4. David Owen, *Anti-Submarine Warfare*, Seaforth Publishing, 2007, p.145.
5. Pawle, *Secret*, p.138.
6. John A. Williamson, *Antisubmarine Warrior in the Pacific*, University of Alabama Press, 2005, pp.145, 110.
7. Ibid., p.82.
8. The account of this attack is drawn from ibid., chapter 9. See also http://www.ussengland.org for diaries, logbooks and interviews with survivors.
9. S.E. Morison, *History of United States Naval Operations in World War II*, vol. 8, *New Guinea and the Marianas*, Little, Brown, 1948, p.231.
10. Williamson, *Antisubmarine*, p.145.
11. Macrae, *Toyshop*, p.194.

Chapter 19: Operation Gubbins

1. Charles Hambro, *Dictionary of National Biography*, Oxford University Press, 2009.
2. Wilkinson, *Foreign Fields*, p.213.
3. Astley and Wilkinson, *Gubbins*, p.192.

4. Ibid.

5. Ibid., pp.168–9, 189.

6. Ibid., pp.176, 193, 173.

7. Tommy Macpherson with Richard Bath, *Behind Enemy Lines*, Mainstream Publishing, 2010, p.117.

8. Macpherson Carlton TV interview, IWM: 23256.

9. Astley and Wilkinson, *Gubbins*, pp.175, 155.

10. Macpherson, *Enemy*, p.119.

11. IWM: Documents 12674.

12. Denis Rigden (ed.), *SOE Syllabus*, PRO, 2001, p.367.

13. O.A. Brown, IWM: Documents 12674.

14. Harry Verlander, *My War in SOE*, Independent Books, 2010, p.55.

15. Macpherson, *Enemy*, p.123. Bourbon's story is also told in Robert Hall, 'Allied "Bandits" Behind Enemy Lines', 5 June 2006: http://news.bbc.co.uk/1/hi/uk/8085383.stm

16. IWM: Documents 12674.

17. Macpherson, *Enemy*, p.125.

18. http://news.bbc.co.uk/1/hi/uk/8085383.stm

19. IWM: Documents 12618.

20. Macpherson, *Enemy*, pp.130–31.

21. IWM: Documents 12674.

22. Macpherson, *Enemy*, pp.132–3.

23. Miller, *Behind*, p.152.

24. Macpherson Carlton TV interview, IWM: 23256.

25. Macpherson, *Enemy*, p.139.

26. Miller, *Behind*, p.153.

27. Macpherson, *Enemy*, p.139.

28. Miller, *Behind*, p.153.

29. Lammerding report to General Commander, 58th Panzer Corps, in Hastings, *Das Reich*, p.145.

30. Macpherson Carlton TV interview, IWM: 23256.

31. Astley and Wilkinson, *Gubbins*, pp.193–4.

32. IWM: Documents 12618, SHAEF report into Special Operations Executive's work, June 1944. Eisenhower's report, Special Operations Executive's work, June 1944; Lord Mountbatten, personal letter to Colin Gubbins; Hugh Dalton, personal letter to Colin Gubbins; King George VI, letter to Colin Gubbins; note by Colin Gubbins; Edward Grigg, Minister Resident in the Middle East, personal letter.

Epilogue

1. Macrae, *Toyshop*, p.210.
2. CC: Macrae diary, MCRA 4.
3. Macrae, *Toyshop*, p.211.
4. Ibid., p.212.
5. Ibid.
6. Astley and Wilkinson, *Gubbins*, p.224.
7. Brandon and Elliot-Bateman, *Fourth Dimension*, p.45.
8. Wilkinson, *Foreign Fields*, p.213.
9. Astley and Wilkinson, *Gubbins*, p.217.
10. Lord Selborne, personal letter, in ibid., pp.232–3.
11. Wilkinson, *Foreign Fields*, p.213.
12. Astley and Wilkinson, *Gubbins*, p.235.
13. Eric Sykes's SOE file, NA: HS 9/1434.
14. William Donovan's assessment in Fairbairn's SOE file, NA: HS 9/495/7.
15. CP: Jefferis to Lord Lindemann, 1945, K165/3.
16. Interview with John Jefferis, 5 December 2014.
17. *The Times*, 7 September 1963.
18. George Rheam's 'Report on Sabotage', NA: HS 8/3705.
19. Bedford Museum unpublished interview with John Vandepeer Clarke, 23 April 2004.
20. Interview with Mrs Ann Clarke, 17 December 2014.
21. Obituary of Joan Bright Astley, *Independent*, 28 January 2009.
22. Astley and Wilkinson, *Gubbins*, p.213.
23. Ibid., p.243.

Bibliography

Primary Sources

Cecil Vandepeer Clarke Family Papers
Cherwell Papers, Nuffield College, University of Oxford
Churchill Archives Centre, Cambridge
Imperial War Museum, London
Liddell Hart Centre for Military Archives, Kings College, London
Millis Jefferis Family Papers
National Archives, Kew, London
Royal United Services Institute

Secondary Sources

Allen, Stuart, *Commando Country*, NMS Enterprises, 2007
Anon., 'An Interlude in the Campaign in Norway', *Journal of the United Service Institution of India*, 1941
Appleyard, John Geoffrey, *Geoffrey*, Blandford Press, 1946
Ash, Bernard, *Norway 1940*, Cassell, 1964
Astley, Joan Bright, *The Inner Circle: A View of War at the Top*, Hutchinson, 1971
—— and Wilkinson, Peter, *Gubbins and SOE*, Pen & Sword, 1993
Bailey, Roderick, *Forgotten Voices of the Secret War*, Ebury Press, 2008
Beevor, J.G., *SOE: Recollections and Reflections*, Bodley Head, 1981
Binney, Marcus, *Secret War Heroes: The Men of Special Operations Executive*, Hodder & Stoughton, 2005
Blacker, Barnaby, *The Adventures and Inventions of Stewart Blacker: Soldier, Aviator, Weapons Inventor*, Pen & Sword, 2006
Brandon, S.G. and Elliot-Bateman, M. (eds.), *The Fourth Dimension of Warfare*, Manchester University Press, 1970

Buckmaster, Maurice, *They Fought Alone*, Odhams Press, 1968

Bunker, Stephen, *The Spy Capital of Britain: Bedfordshire's Secret War*, Bedford Chronicle Press, 2007

Burton, Sir Richard Francis, *Wanderings in West Africa*, Tinsley Brothers, 1863

Butler, Ewan, *Amateur Agent*, Harrap, 1963

Churchill, Winston, *The Second World War*, 6 vols., Cassell, 1948–54

Clarke, Comer, *England Under Hitler*, New English Library, 1972

Connell, John, *The House by Herod's Gate*, Sampson Low, Marston, 1947

Cookridge, E.H., *They Came from the Sky*, Heinemann, 1965

Cunningham, Cyril, *Beaulieu: The Finishing School for Secret Agents*, Leo Cooper, 1998

Dalton, Hugh, *Fateful Years*, Frederick Muller, 1957

Dalzel-Job, Patrick, *From Arctic Snow to Dust of Normandy*, Sutton Publishing, 2001

Dear, Ian, *Sabotage and Subversion*, Cassell, 1996

Dederichs, Mario, *The Face of Evil*, Greenhill Books, 2006

Delaforce, Patrick, *Churchill's Secret Weapons*, Robert Hale, 1998

Derry, T.K., *The Campaign in Norway*, Imperial War Museum, 1995

Dilks, David (ed,), *The Diaries of Sir Alexander Cadogan 1938–1945*, Cassell, 1971

Dorrian, James, *Storming St Nazaire: The Gripping Story of the Dock-Busting Raid*, Leo Cooper, 1998

Dorril, Stephen, *MI6*, Fourth Estate, 2000

Edgerton, David, *Britain's War Machine*, Allen Lane, 2011

Everitt, Chris and Middlebrook, Martin, *The Bomber Command War Diaries*, Pen & Sword, 2014

Fairbairn, W.E., *All-In Fighting*, Faber & Faber, 1942

Feiling, Keith, *The Life of Neville Chamberlain*, Macmillan, 1946

Fleming, Peter, *Invasion 1940*, Rupert Hart-Davis, 1957

Foot, M.R.D., *Special Operations Executive*, Pimlico, 1999

——, *SOE in France*, Routledge, 2004

Gubbins, Colin, *The Art of Guerrilla Warfare*, Ministry of Information, 1939

——, *The Partisan Leaders' Handbook*, Ministry of Information, 1939

Hamilton-Hill, Donald, *SOE Assignment*, William Kimber, 1973

Harris, Robert and Paxman, Jeremy, *A Higher Form of Killing*, Random House, 1982

Harrison, David, *Para-Military Training in Scotland*, Land, Sea and Islands Visitor Centre, 2001

Hastings, Max, *Das Reich*, Michael Joseph, 1981

Haukelid, Knut, *Skis Against the Atom*, North American Heritage Press, 1989

Hawes, Stephen and White, Ralph, *Resistance in Europe*, Viking, 1975

Horvitz, Leslie and Catherwood, Christopher, *Encyclopedia of War Crimes and Genocide*, Facts on File, 2006

Ismay, Hastings, *The Memoirs of General the Lord Ismay*, Heinemann, 1960

Jefferis, John, *The Life and Times of Millis Jefferis* (privately published memoir)

Jefferis, Millis, *How to Use High Explosives*, Ministry of Information, 1939

Johnson, Brian, *The Secret War*, BBC Books, 1979

Keene, Tom, *The Lost Band of Brothers*, History Press, 2015

Kemp, Peter, *No Colours or Crest*, Cassell, 1958

Kersaudy, François, *Norway 1940*, HarperCollins, 1990

Lampe, David, *The Last Ditch*, Cassell, 1968

Langelaan, George, *Knights of the Floating Silk*, Hutchinson, 1959

Langley, Mike, *Anders Lassen*, New English Library, 1988

Lankford, Nelson, *The Last American Aristocrat*, Little, Brown, 1996

Lassen, Suzanne, *Anders Lassen VC*, Frederick Muller, 1965

Lett, Brian, *Ian Fleming and SOE's Operation Postmaster*, Pen & Sword, 2012

MacDonald, Callum, *The Killing of SS Obergruppenführer Reinhard Heydrich*, Macmillan, 1989

McGlynn, M.B., *Special Service in Greece*, War History Branch, Department of Internal Affairs, New Zealand, 1953

Mackenzie, William, *The Secret History of SOE*, St Ermin's Press, 2000

McKinstry, Leo, *Operation Sealion*, John Murray, 2014

Macpherson, Tommy with Bath, Richard, *Behind Enemy Lines*, Mainstream Publishing, 2010

Macrae, Stuart, *Winston Churchill's Toyshop*, Roundwood Press, 1971

Marcot, François, 'La direction de Peugeot sous l'Occupation: pétainisme, réticence, opposition et résistance', *Le Mouvement Social*, no. 189, Éditions de l'Atelier, 1999

Marks, Leo, *Between Silk and Cyanide: A Codebreaker's War*, HarperCollins, 1999

Mears, Ray, *The Real Heroes of Telemark*, Hodder & Stoughton, 2003

Miller, Russell, *Behind the Lines*, Secker & Warburg, 2002

Moravec, Frantisek, *Master of Spies: The Memoirs of General Frantisek Moravec*, Bodley Head, 1975

Moreman, Tim, *The British Commandos 1940–46*, Osprey Publishing, 2006

Morison, S.E., *History of United States Naval Operations in World War II*, 15 vols., Little, Brown, 1947–62

Myers, E.C.W., *Greek Entanglement*, Alan Sutton Publishing, 1985

Noguères, Henri, Degliame-Fouché, M. and Vigier, J.L., *Histoire de la Résistance en France de 1940 à 1945*, Robert Laffont, 1981

O'Connor, Bernard, *'Nobby' Clarke: Churchill's Backroom Boy*, lulu.com, 2010

——, *Churchill's School for Saboteurs, Station 17*, Amberley Publishing, 2013

Owen, David, *Anti-Submarine Warfare*, Seaforth Publishing, 2007

Owen, James, *Commando*, Little, Brown, 2012

Pawle, Gerald, *The Secret War*, Harrap, 1956

Philby, Kim, *My Silent War*, MacGibbon & Kee, 1968

Phillips, Lucas, *The Greatest Raid of All*, Heinemann, 1958

Pimlott, Ben (ed.), *The Second World War Diary of Hugh Dalton*, Jonathan Cape, 1986

Powell, Michael and Pressburger, Emeric, with Christie, Ian (ed.), *The Life and Death of Colonel Blimp*, Faber & Faber, 1994

Raeder, Erich, *Grand Admiral*, Da Capo Press, 2000

Rankin, Nicholas, *Ian Fleming's Commandos*, Faber & Faber, 2011

Richardson, F.D., 'Charles Frederick Goodeve', *Biographical Memoirs of the Fellows of the Royal Society*, vol. 27, 1981

Rigden, Denis, *SOE Syllabus: Lessons in Ungentlemanly Warfare*, Public Record Office, 2001

Rogers, Gordon, *From Bangs to Black Holes*, MyBookLive.com, 2014

Ryder, Sue, *Child of My Love*, HarperCollins, 1986

Schellenberg, Walter, *Invasion 1940*, St Ermin's Press, 2000

Schenk, Peter, *Invasion of England*, Conway Maritime Press, 1990

Seaman, Mark (ed.), *Special Operations Executive: A New Instrument of War*, Routledge, 2005

Shirer, William, *Rise and Fall of the Third Reich*, Secker & Warburg, 1961

Smith, Michael, 'Margaret's Secret War', *For a Change*, vol. 19, 2006

Southby-Tailyour, Ewen, *Blondie: A Life of Lieutenant-Colonel H.G. Hasler*, Leo Cooper, 1998

Stafford, David, *Secret Agent: The True Story of the Special Operations Executive*, BBC Books, 2000

Stevens, E.H., *The Trial of Nikolaus von Falkenhorst*, William Hodge, 1949

Sweet-Escott, Bickham, *Baker Street Irregular*, Methuen, 1965

Sykes, E.A. and Fairbairn, W.E., *Shooting to Live with the One-Hand Gun*, Oliver & Boyd, 1942

Taylor, A.J.P., *English History*, Oxford University Press, 1965

Terrell, Edward, *Admiralty Brief*, Harrap, 1958

Turner, Des, *Station 12: Aston House, SOE's Secret Centre*, History Press, 2006

Turner, Ernest, *The Phoney War on the Home Front*, Michael Joseph, 1961

Verlander, Harry, *My War in SOE*, Independent Press, 2010

Warwicker, John, *Churchill's Underground Army*, Pen & Sword, 2008

Wheatley, Ronald, *Operation Sealion*, Clarendon Press, 1958

Wilkinson, Peter, *Foreign Fields: The Story of an SOE Operative*, I.B. Tauris, 1997

Williamson, John A., *Antisubmarine Warrior in the Pacific*, University of Alabama Press, 2005

Woodhouse C.M., *The Struggle for Greece*, Rupert Hart-Davis, MacGibbon, 1976

——, *Something Ventured*, Granada, 1982

Index

About the Author

GILES MILTON is a writer and journalist. He has contributed articles to most of the British national newspapers as well as many foreign publications, and specializes in narrative history. In the course of his researches, he has traveled extensively in Europe, North Africa, the Middle East, and the Americas. He has written several books of nonfiction, including the bestselling *Nathaniel's Nutmeg,* and has been translated into twenty languages worldwide. He is the author of the novel *Edward Trencom's Nose.*